WITHDRAWN

S0-BLV-258

Comparative Ethnic Studies Collections
Ethnic Studies Library
30 Stephens Hall #2360
University of California
Berkeley, CA 94720-2360

O ANS'D

Asian American Studies Library
101 Wheeler Hall
University of California
Berkeley, CA 94720

Comparative Ethnic Studies Collections
Ethnic Studies Library
30 Stephens Hall #2360
University of California
Berkeley, CA 94720-2360

Comparative Ethnic Studies Collections
Ethnic Studies Library
30 Stephens Hall #2360
University of California
Berkeley, CA 94720-2360

A SAND-LOT MEETING IN SAN FRANCISCO

Comparative Ethnic Studies Collections
Ethnic Studies Library
30 Stephens Hall #2360
University of California
Berkeley, CA 94720-2360

A HISTORY OF THE LABOR MOVEMENT IN CALIFORNIA

BY

IRA B. CROSS

PROFESSOR OF ECONOMICS ON THE FLOOD FOUNDATION
IN THE UNIVERSITY OF CALIFORNIA

UNIVERSITY OF CALIFORNIA PRESS
BERKELEY, LOS ANGELES, LONDON
1935

Asian American Studies Library
142 Dwinelle Hall
University of California
Berkeley, CA   94720

HD8083
.C2
C7
1974
cop.2

CES
8402

Comparative Ethnic Studies Collections
Ethnic Studies Library
30 Stephens Hall #2360
University of California
Berkeley, CA 94720-2360

UNIVERSITY OF CALIFORNIA PUBLICATIONS IN ECONOMICS
VOLUME 14

COPYRIGHT, 1935
BY THE
REGENTS OF THE UNIVERSITY OF CALIFORNIA

UNIVERSITY OF CALIFORNIA PRESS
BERKELEY, CALIFORNIA

UNIVERSITY OF CALIFORNIA PRESS, LTD.
LONDON, ENGLAND

CALIFORNIA LIBRARY REPRINT SERIES EDITION, 1974
ISBN 0-520-02646-2
LIBRARY OF CONGRESS CATALOG CARD NUMBER 73-93026

PRINTED IN THE UNITED STATES OF AMERICA

Affectionately Dedicated to

JOHN R. COMMONS

Inspiring Teacher and Friend

CONTENTS

LIST OF ILLUSTRATIONS

LIST OF ILLUSTRATIONS—*(Continued)*

PREFACE

IN THE FOLLOWING PAGES I have presented a history of the labor movement in California in some detail down to 1901. Only a few of the more noteworthy events since that date have been mentioned, because my specific purpose has been to provide the historical background necessary for an understanding of the present position of the labor movement in the State. By 1901 the labor movement in California had really got under way. City, county, district, and state labor organizations had been formed and policies had been adopted which have since remained in effect with no changes worth noting. After 1901 the movement spread rapidly throughout California. An attempt to do full justice to the efforts of those persons in each community who have been moved by a sincere desire to improve the lot of the working class, would require the writing of many volumes. Only a few have found mention here.

Labor leaders of past and present have been most helpful in enabling me to piece together the threads of the narrative. The valuable collections of material in the public libraries of Los Angeles, San Francisco, and Sacramento, in the libraries of Stanford University and the University of California, in the Bancroft Library, the Sutro Library, and the State Library at Sacramento, have been generously placed at my disposal. I have greatly profited from the suggestions of two of my colleagues, Dr. Felix Flügel and Dr. Charles A. Gulick, Jr., who read the original manuscript. Grateful acknowledgment is made to the San Francisco *Call-Bulletin* for portraits of Andrew Furuseth and Walter Macarthur, and to the San Francisco *Chronicle* for portraits of P. H. McCarthy and O. A. Tveitmoe. Financial aid has been received from the Carnegie Institution and from the University of California.

IRA B. CROSS.

Berkeley, California,
November 10, 1934.

[xi]

Chapter I

THE MISSION ERA

FOR THREE HUNDRED YEARS preceding 1822, California was a dependency of Spain, but the least known and least esteemed of that monarchy's New World possessions. Not until the latter part of the eighteenth century, when both Russia and England were suspected of having designs on certain parts of California, did Spain make any attempt to establish governmental authority in this far distant province.[1]* In this belated action, Spain resorted to the agency it had so successfully employed in subjugating the inhabitants of Mexico and South America—namely, the Roman Catholic Church and its missionary fathers. The Church gladly agreed to send missionaries to California to establish places of worship among the Indians and to teach them the rudiments of civilization. The Government promised to furnish military protection and the funds necessary for spreading the influence of the Church among the natives. Ostensibly, the end sought was the spiritual and material advancement of the native population, and such was, indeed, the ideal which inspired the zealous and courageous friars. The Government, however, never lost sight of "an ever-present idea of advantage to the State."[2] The saving of souls was but a means to an end: the goal was the establishment of Spanish civil authority.

In the last quarter of the eighteenth century, eighteen missions were founded at advantageous and strategic points. In subsequent years three more were established.[3] For more than half a century (1776–1835) the life of the inhabitants of California centered around these outposts of Christianity, and in the mission system we encounter the first labor problem in California.[4]

In spreading the word of God among the Indians the Spanish

---

* Notes indicated by superior figures will be found at back of book. Only occasional footnotes are appended in the following pages. The original manuscript, containing source references to all statements made herein, has been deposited in the Library of the University of California, Berkeley, where it may be consulted by persons interested in pursuing the subject farther.

padres first established themselves in the south and gradually worked their way north, displaying judgment and foresight in the selection of sites for their mission buildings. After deciding upon a site, with the aid of the soldiers who usually accompanied them they erected a few rough huts.[5] Then by various devices they attracted the attention and aroused the curiosity of the ignorant natives who gathered to see the strange things that were taking place. Through friendliness and good will, small gifts, and acts of kindness, the friars induced the Indians to help them construct the mission buildings. As they labored side by side, the priests told the story of the Virgin Mary and the Christ child.

When the confidence of the natives had been secured, the padres persuaded them to take up their abode within the mission enclosure. Conversion and baptism followed. Little by little the friars extended their influence among the neighboring tribes. The converted Indians, or neophytes as they were called, carried the strangely interesting faith to their former companions; new converts were made and baptized; and in a surprisingly short time the mission was established in its work of redemption. Thus thousands were taught the story of eternal salvation and subsequently were baptized into the Church.[6] These results were not always obtained, however, with the whole-hearted coöperation of the natives. Not infrequently they rebelled against the missionaries, and soldiers were dispatched into the surrounding country to bring the unwilling ones back to the mission for religious instruction.

These California Indians for whose salvation the padres lived, worked, and prayed, were not to be compared in habits and characteristics with the "noble redskin" of the Atlantic Coast and the plains of the Middle West. One author has described them as being

almost as degraded as any human beings on the face of the earth. [They were] stupid and brutish, [and in general] resembled mere omnivorous animals without any government or laws. . . . The characteristics which most forcibly struck all writers on the California aborigines were their laziness and uncleanliness. . . . They had no ambition of any kind and seemed to take a lively interest in nothing; all their operations, both of their bodies and minds, appeared to be carried on with mechanical, lifeless, careless indifference. Hunger alone compelled them to make some exertion in search of food, but they labored no further than was necessary to secure a supply of anything that would sustain life, without much reference to its quality.[7]

It was from such discouragingly unsatisfactory human material that the padres were expected to fashion loyal subjects for the King and Queen of Spain.

To convert the Indians to a belief in the Catholic faith was not, however, the sole object of the missionary fathers. They also hoped to teach them the arts of peace and civilization. It was primarily for the latter reason that all neophytes lived in or near the mission where they could be under the constant surveillance and guidance of the priests.[8] The men and boys were taught the care of fields, gardens, and orchards, the herding of sheep and cattle, and the use of bench and forge. They erected buildings, tanned leather, and made soap, shoes, harness, crude farming-tools, and many other articles for use about the mission and in the fields. The women and girls were taught weaving, spinning, sewing, cooking, and other household duties. They were also employed occasionally in "harvesting and cleaning the grain, in cutting grapes, in cleaning wool . . . and sometimes in bringing clay for the manufacture of tiles" and adobe brick.[9] They also carried stone and brick, and in other ways helped with the construction of buildings. Since very few of the padres had been trained in the trades, the government sent capable artisans from Mexico to serve as instructors for the neophytes under the general supervision of the padres.[10] Some of the convicts who were sent into California were also used as artisan instructors, often with satisfactory results.[11]

Virtually all the manual labor in and about the mission was carried on by the neophytes, the padres busying themselves chiefly with supervision and religious instruction. There has been some discussion concerning the length of the working day. It seems to have lasted from sunrise to sunset with an hour's rest at noon. In the morning the neophytes assembled to hear mass, after which a breakfast of boiled corn or barley was served. They then separated into gangs, and went to their tasks, some to work in the fields and vineyards, others to herd sheep and cattle, still others to labor about the mission. At noon, a meal of gruel with meat and vegetables was served. Shortly before sundown a supper of boiled corn or barley, preceded by devotional services, brought the day to a close.[12] But although the workday was thus nominally from sunrise to sunset, the hours of actual labor were considerably less;[13] for

racist

it must be remembered that the Indians were inherently slow of thought and action, unaccustomed to toil, and unwilling to work long hours. As wages, the males received, in addition to mainten- ance, a blanket or two and a shirt; the women and girls were given cloth from which to make petticoats, and occasionally a few cheap and gaudy trinkets.[14] It was this poorly paid labor of the neo- phytes, however, that enabled the missions to accumulate great wealth, represented by large herds and flocks, crops of various grains, and stores of simple manufactures. Duflot de Mofras esti- mated that in 1834 the missions possessed a total of 424,000 horned cattle, 62,500 horses, and 321,500 sheep, pigs, and goats, and that they raised annually a total of 70,000 hectares of wheat, corn, bar- ley, and beans.[15]

The picture of these ignorant natives working under the direc- tion of the padres, busy with the daily tasks of mission life, may appear idyllic to some; in reality, its shadows were long and deep. To these children of Nature, whose ancestors for centuries had been undisciplined, Christianity and civilization came as virtual en- slavement. After the Indians had acknowledged faith and had been baptized into the Church, the friars looked on them as part and parcel of the mission's property. From that time until death or their escape from the mission, they worked, ate, slept, and prayed as they were ordered. They had less freedom than the serfs under feudalism. Obedience and discipline were rigorously en- forced by the use of the lash, the stocks, the irons, and by even more severe means of punishment. It was asserted that force was neces- sary in order to secure respect and to compel the Indians to per- form the tasks assigned to them. Undoubtedly the padres sincerely believed that it was better to be a "converted soul in chains than a free heathen." Statements concerning the treatment of the neo- phytes are many and conflicting. Some chroniclers of the period, especially those in any way influenced by their connection with the Church, emphasize that "towards the converts and actually do- mesticated servants, they [the padres] always showed such an af- fectionate kindness as a father pays to the youngest and most help- less of his family."[16] Other observers of the time insisted that the lot of the christianized Indians was no better than that of slaves or serfs.[17]

In one respect, at least, the condition of the neophytes was greatly improved by the coming of the missionaries: they were better fed, better clothed, and better housed than they had been in their native state. But it must not be overlooked that they had formerly obtained the simplest necessaries of life without any great amount of effort. They had tilled no fields, and had possessed no herds of cattle or flocks of sheep. But they had not been required to work daily for others, to live constantly under supervision, to go

OREGON

LOCATION OF THE MISSIONS OF CALIFORNIA

through the (to them) meaningless routine of religious worship, or to endure punishments imposed for even trivial offenses. Many of the Indians, resenting the mission life, returned to their former haunts and habits, and armed expeditions sent after these runaways often met with determined resistance. Many of the neophytes, however, were satisfied with their condition and willingly remained attached to the mission, comfortably assured of food, shelter, and clothing.

The problem, thus early encountered, of maintaining a labor supply, was to persist for nearly a century. Indeed, not until many years after the gold rush was an adequate supply of satisfactory labor available to the local industries, insignificant in extent though they were. There was a definite reason for the scarcity of labor during the mission era. During that era the territory had few inhabitants other than priests and Indians, because only a small number of Spaniards had seen fit to settle in California, and because Spain objected to the presence of foreigners in its colonies.[18] Humboldt estimated that in 1801 there were but 1,300 whites in California;[19] although Bancroft states that in 1800 there were at least 1,800.[20] A large number of these early residents were deserting or shipwrecked sailors. Even after 1822, when California had come under the sovereignty of Mexico, the hostility to foreign settlers persisted. California was not opened up to unrestricted settlement until the late forties. It is not strange, therefore, that by 1830 the white population had increased to only a bare 4,000.[21]

The scarcity of white inhabitants made it difficult to obtain laborers other than Indians. In the latter part of the eighteenth century the Spanish government enlisted men as sailors, and paid them to go as laborers to California where they received about $10 per month and food. However, both on the ranches and in the primitive industries (whether or not they were connected with the missions), most of the work was done by Indian labor. When neophyte Indians were hired they were obtained from the missions, to whom their wages were paid; but if the Indians were "gentiles" (unchristianized) they were usually obtained through the chief of the tribe.[22] The wages of the neophytes varied greatly, at times amounting to $4 per month and maintenance. The wages of the unchristianized Indians were usually food and shelter and whatever else their employers saw fit to give them, which frequently was nothing at all. During the middle years of the mission period (1810–1820) it was said that a "large number of the settlers were content to be idle, giving the Indians one-third or one-half of the crop for tilling their lands, and living on what remained."[23] Markoff is quoted as having said that in 1835 the Indians were satisfied to receive a fathom of black, red, and white glass beads for a season's work.[24] With the gradual increase in white population, Mexicans and Spaniards were employed on the ranches to perform the more skilled tasks as overseers and foremen. They received from $3 to $10 per month and board. The Indians continued to be employed as unskilled laborers; domestic servants were almost exclusively Indian girls and women. At the presidios (military posts) prisoners and military deserters were put to work as laborers, but when they could not be had in sufficient numbers gentile and neophyte Indians were employed.

It was not uncommon in the later years of the period under discussion for ranchers to live "in feudal style, each having his band of Indian retainers, subject to his authority."[25] These Indian laborers on the large privately owned ranches were nominally free in legal status, but in reality they were as near serfdom as the mission neophytes, although in a somewhat different manner : they could not leave their employer if they were in debt to him. This regulation aided greatly in the establishment of a most iniquitous system of peonage. Nor could the Indian laborers move from place to place without first having obtained a properly signed discharge from their last employer showing that they were not in debt to him.[26] Although a penalty of $5 was imposed on any master who refused to give a written statement of discharge to those who were entitled to it, and on any person who accepted a servant (except a day laborer) without one, there was no law to prevent an employer from keeping his laborers continually in debt to him.

The Spanish government had from the first planned to secularize the missions as soon as the Indian population should be sufficiently prepared for the establishment of civil authority. This policy of secularization was gradually carried out by means of a series of laws enacted from 1813 to 1822. From 1822, the year in which California became a Mexican province, until 1834, Mexico carried the task to completion. The padres were thus shorn of all temporal power, their buildings and lands were sold, and the mission system was abolished.

With secularization came the legal emancipation of the neophytes; but the change proved most unfortunate in not a few respects. Many of the Indians continued to suffer the lot of serfs, being treated as such by ranchers and others who had work to be done. Moreover, they refused to work either under the padres or for them, insisting that they had been freed from all connection with the missions. The greater number of them wandered off and returned to their old ways of living.[27] Frequently they took with them the horses, cattle, and sheep of the missions, and in other ways helped themselves freely to the padres' wealth and stores. Protest and supplication by the mission fathers were in vain. Their sixty years of patient effort and sacrifice in christianizing and in teaching the Indians the more rudimentary of the useful arts were as so much wasted labor.

Slavery in the Mexican province of California was formally abolished on September 25, 1829; but, as has been noted, the abuses that existed in connection with the employment of the Indians continued for many years thereafter. On October 23, 1829, the Mexican governor of California issued an order which aided somewhat in abolishing one of the more objectionable practices.

It had been the custom under various pretexts, but especially in military expeditions against the unchristianized or gentile Indians, to seize their children and hold them, nominally as pupils of Christian manners, but really as domestic servants and slaves; and there were large numbers of these scattered about from place to place.[28]

The governor ordered these children released and restored to their parents, or, if the latter could not be located, they were to be placed in the nearest mission. The enslavement of the Indians, adult as well as children, did not cease with the proclamation of 1829 or with the secularization of the missions, for, as Captain John Sutter stated, "It was common for both Indians and Hispano-Californians to seize Indian women and girls and sell them."[29] Another early pioneer, John Chamberlain, asserted that "while he was living at the Sacramento in 1844–1846 it was the custom of Sutter himself to buy and sell Indian girls and boys."[30]

WHITE LABOR BEFORE THE GOLD RUSH

During the years just preceding the gold rush, the wages of white agricultural laborers were comparatively low, owing to the large supply of Indian laborers. White farm hands received from $3 to $10 per month, and overseers about $16 per month. Yet the wages of other white workers in and about the settlements were comparatively high. One observer commented as follows: "Labor is also high; common hands $1.50 per day, mechanics $2.00 to $3.00, millwrights $4.00; so that although we pay high for clothing and all that we want for use, yet we get high prices for labor. . . ."[31]

The first labor legislation enacted in California was an ordinance adopted by the city fathers of San Francisco in 1847, and directed against desertion by sailors. For many years before the discovery of gold, San Francisco was a port of little importance. Vessels trading along the coast occasionally entered the harbor in search of hides and tallow, which were then the staple commodities of trade. It was not unusual, even in those days, for sailors to desert as soon as their ships dropped anchor in San Francisco Bay. As the city increased in population[32] and the attractions of the port became greater, desertions were so frequent that the local authorities decided that steps should be taken to protect the interests of the shipowners. It was felt that, if this were not done, the vessels would not stop at San Francisco, and thus would reduce what little trade the city then had. An ordinance was accordingly drafted and passed on September 16, 1847, imposing a sentence of six months' imprisonment at hard labor on any deserter who should be captured and convicted. A reward of $50 was offered for every deserter apprehended and turned over to the proper authorities.[33] A number of deserters were arrested and imprisoned; but the ordinance was only in effect a short time. Its provisions were virtually nullified by the changed conditions which followed the discovery of gold in 1848.[34]

On February 2, 1848, California, by the terms of the Treaty of Guadalupe Hidalgo, was ceded to the United States by Mexico. Gold had already been discovered in its river beds, and within a few months, its entire political, social, and industrial life was to be changed through the arrival of thousands in search of golden treasure.

CHAPTER II

GOLD, 1848–1850

GOLD IN PAYING QUANTITIES was discovered in northern California in January, 1848, by men employed in the construction of a sawmill at a place known as Coloma, on the American River. The news soon reached San Francisco, but it did not arouse any great amount of interest. A few of the more venturesome spirits went into the gold fields to try their luck, but the many were skeptical of the value of the deposits. Presently, however, stories concerning their richness, authenticated by bags of gold dust, began to reach San Francisco, and by the following May and June the inhabitants had become greatly excited over the prospects of immediate and easily gotten wealth. Stores and offices were closed, houses were boarded up, and farms and crops were abandoned, as their owners rushed pell-mell into the New Eldorado. The whole country resounded with the cry of "Gold, GOLD, G-O-L-D!"

No field of activity was free from the effects of the excitement.[1] "Real estate and all other property, except mining tools and provisions, fell to extremely low figures; and great sacrifices were made ... to procure means to reach the mines."[2] Mechanics, laborers, professional men, abandoned their tasks to become gold hunters. It was impossible to procure labor at any price. Offers of $10 per day interested no one.[3] The news of the remarkable discovery was carried by sailing vessels to the Hawaiian Islands, whence it spread to all countries bordering on the Pacific Ocean. As early as October, immigrants from Oregon, South America, and the islands of the Pacific began to pour into California through the Golden Gate.

Under these circumstances, it is no wonder that desertion among both soldiers and sailors became the rule rather than the exception. Entire companies of militia threw down their arms and rushed into the up-river country. It was virtually impossible for a captain to retain his crew.[4] Indeed, frequently captain *and* crew stripped the vessel of its provisions and journeyed off together in search of gold. Captains who were anxious to put to sea raised the wages of their men and hurriedly set sail,[5] while others, more resourceful, turned their crews over to the United States authorities to be held as prisoners until the day of departure. Hundreds of abandoned vessels lay in the harbor, at the mercy of wind and waves. Some were filled with cargoes, the unloading of which was not profitable because of the high charges demanded for labor, lighterage, and warehouse privileges. Scores of vessels rotted and finally sank; others were purchased by enterprising speculators, anchored along the waterfront, dismantled, and fitted up as saloons, restaurants, and gambling houses.

For about ten years following the discovery of gold, the desertion of sailors was a matter of concern to persons interested in the commerce of the growing city. Shipowners and captains often found it impossible to obtain or keep a crew. Vessels could not sail without seamen, and it was not unusual for their masters to resort to the most brutal measures in order to gather a sufficient number of men to enable them to leave the harbor. Shanghaiing was openly practiced, and was tacitly sanctioned by the civic authorities. The latter consistently refused to interfere with the water-front boarding-house keepers who acted as agents through whom crews were usually recruited. Scores of men were drugged, taken on board the vessels, and forced into service at sea. This was the fate, not only of thousands of sailors, but also of innumerable clerks, bookkeepers, miners, and others, men who knew nothing whatever about the work or life of a seaman. Lack of knowledge and training were no excuse. Kicks and belaying pins supplied the needed information. Irons and a fare of bread and water broke the spirit of the more rebellious. It is impossible to describe adequately the brutal treatment dealt out to sailors in those early days. Books and papers of the times make frequent mention of the extremely revolting practices and inhuman conditions which existed.[6] Years were to elapse before the lot of the sailors was to be improved, and then only through their unionization.[7]

The story of the discovery of gold spread in a remarkably short time throughout the eastern states. There was scarcely a community in which preparations were not made by many for the long journey to the western coast. Thousands of restless young men, fresh from the Mexican War, eager and straining for excitement, found in California the outlet for their energies. By land and sea they came—across the plains in wagons and on horseback, and by sea in vessels of all sorts and descriptions. Argonauts of every nationality and of every clime mingled together in the mad rush for gold.[8] It is estimated that 77,000 persons entered California in 1849, and 82,000 in 1850.[9]

The embryo miner, upon arriving in California, purchased his outfit at exorbitant prices[10] and made his way with all possible haste to the gold regions. It required no skill or ability to stand in water or to squat along the shore and pan sand for flakes of gold. A day or two of practice, and the inexperienced farm hand or office clerk was as expert as the oldest miner. Earnings varied greatly, averaging from $10 to $30 per day, although as high as $500 per day was not unusual. A few fortunes were made, but by far the greater number of the gold seekers returned home poorer than when they had set out.[11] Bancroft estimates that in 1852, the most prosperous year for the individual miner, the average annual wage was not over $600, or at the rate of about $2 per day. If proper deductions are made for the more fortunate individuals and for the miners who employed labor, $1 would more nearly approximate the average daily wage.[12]

The miners moved restlessly from place to place as placers were worked out or as rumor beckoned. In the earliest days of the gold era, it was "every man for himself." Very little capital was required, only enough to purchase the necessary outfit and supplies. The placers were there to be worked; the miner was independent and foot-loose. Consequently, the mining population was continually shifting from one region to another; cities were made and unmade in a night; nothing was stable but the desire to possess the golden metal.[13]

In time, however, the situation changed. Hydraulic mining, with its costly flumes and canals, was introduced, and quartz mining, with its expensive shafts, stamp mills, and smelters, followed. The corporation with accumulated capital and hired laborers superseded the individual miner with his crude methods. In the days of '48 and '49, however, the employer as such was virtually unknown. Some of the ranchers of the State took their Indian servants into the diggings, and sometimes miners hired Indians to work for them.[14] Occasionally one finds mention of Southerners who brought slaves with them, but these were the exception rather than the rule.[15] Those who gained riches did so truly "by the sweat of their brows." Every man was a laborer, whether or not he had previously been a teacher, lawyer, farmer, mechanic, preacher, or sailor. Physical labor was honorable. Class lines and class distinctions were forgotten, and a universal spirit of rough democracy prevailed. This whole-hearted democratic spirit of the mining days permeated virtually every phase of early Californian life. Anyone who wishes to understand or to interpret the character, the institutions, and the life of the people of northern California, up to within recent years, must necessarily take note of this enduring frontier influence.

Seldom, even under gold's magic scepter, has any community changed so rapidly from a sleepy trading-post to an active, bustling, prosperous, commercial center as did San Francisco. From San Francisco went all routes to the mines, and to it returned the results of the miners' labors. As the hordes of immigrants began to enter the Golden Gate, its merchants prepared to reap a golden harvest from the sale of outfits and supplies. Stores, hotels, and houses were hurriedly built; wagons piled high with merchandise were sent out, headed for the up-river country; on all sides the greatest energy and enterprise were displayed. Many of the newcomers, after trying their luck, and learning from hard experience that placer mining was not their forte, drifted back to San Francisco, eager to work at anything in order to get money for their passage "back home." In the city, as in the mining districts, men from all walks of life labored at the most disagreeable and menial tasks. Typical of the situation was the building of a brick warehouse in San Francisco in 1849, on which thirty "carpenters" were employed, of whom three were preachers, two were lawyers, three were physicians, six were bookkeepers, two were blacksmiths, and one was a shoemaker.[16] Employment was plentiful, and at the unusually high wages prevailing, ranging from $8 to $20 per day, no man was ashamed to engage in physical labor.[17] It is surprising to note, also, that, in spite of the great influx of laborers, these exorbitant wages were maintained through the first few years of the gold era.[18] Explanation may perhaps be found in part in the fact that the early immigrants were men of the frontier. They brooked no interference with things which they considered theirs by right of possession, and among these the most important was a "job." Records of the period show that force and intimidation were not uncommonly employed to maintain high wages and to control the job.[19]

Prices and rents fluctuated greatly, but for the most part remained exceptionally high.[20] Variations in prices were caused primarily by the fact that the eastern shippers had scanty information concerning the needs of the people of California, either in respect of articles or of quantities. The orders of the San Francisco merchants reached them through the mail, which came by the roundabout and slow route across the Isthmus of Panama. Because of this lack of rapid communication between California and the eastern markets, goods of all kinds, useful and much that was not useful, were shipped to California in great quantities, and the market was thus kept in a state of confusion. At times of overabundance, even the necessaries of life were sacrificed at astonishingly low figures, and a few days later a dearth of the same commodities sent prices soaring to dizzy heights. Vegetables and farm products were always in demand. So many farms and gardens had been abandoned in the mad desire of their owners to dig for gold, that those who remained at home to cultivate the soil not uncommonly reaped a much larger reward than did their neighbors who had gone into the placers.

As far as can be ascertained, the first demand by a group of California workers for higher wages was made by the carpenters and joiners of San Francisco in the winter of 1849. The prevailing rate was $12 per day; on November 10 they asked that it be raised to $16. This was refused, and a strike resulted. On November 18 the issue was compromised, the employers agreeing to pay $13 per day until December 7, after which they were to pay $14.[21] About the same time (November 14, 1849) the carpenters and joiners of Sacramento made a similar demand. With the hope that the employers might more readily grant the higher rate, the workers proposed that an agreement be drawn up in which they would pledge themselves to work for no person other than a boss carpenter for less than $20 per day. The employers refused to accede to their demand and a strike followed.[22]

Investigation has not disclosed the existence of any formal organization among the workers of California prior to 1850. In that year "The San Francisco Typographical Society"[23] was formed, a notice of its meetings appearing in the local papers as early as June 24, 1850.[24] This, the first trade union on the Pacific Coast,[25] grew out of a demand of the printers for piece wages instead of day wages. They had been receiving from $50 to $75 per week, but asked that they be paid at the rate of $2 per 1,000 ems. This rate was granted by the newspaper proprietors and was maintained until June, 1852, when it was reduced to $1.50 per 1,000 ems.[26]

In July, 1850, the teamsters of San Francisco organized an association for the twofold purpose of regulating their charges and protecting themselves against the competition of the Australian teamsters; the Australians had entered the local field with stronger and better horses, and were beginning to control an increasing share of the drayage business. The call for the meeting of the teamsters contains the following statement of one of the objects for which organization was to be effected: "... and if necessary, nominate a candidate for one of the vacancies in the Council, so that we may have at least one representative who will be in favor of protecting the laboring citizens."[27] The meeting was held, the Teamsters' Association was organized, and a schedule of charges was adopted. Before adjournment, the association nominated James Grant as its candidate for the City Council. An objection, however, was raised to his nomination, and "fifty-three and many others, embracing a majority of the teamsters in the city," nominated William Ledley as the rival candidate. Grant, who was also the regular Democratic nominee, was elected by a large majority. Thus even at that early date the workers of the State combined trade unionism and politics, a policy which they have since pursued with varying success. One interesting result, apparently of activity by the Teamsters' Association, was the enactment of an ordinance in San Francisco on August 5, 1850, prohibiting aliens from engaging in draying, in driving hackney coaches, and in rowing boats for the conveyance of passengers.

From notices appearing in the newspapers of the day, it seems probable that there was some sort of organization among the boatmen of San Francisco. They participated in the Admission Day parade of 1850, and frequently inserted accounts of their meetings in the daily papers. It has been impossible to uncover any definite data on their association.[28]

In the year 1850, two strikes of minor importance occurred in San Francisco.[29] In August, the sailors attempted unsuccessfully to resist a reduction in wages. Many of the miners had drifted back to San Francisco, disheartened, penniless, and eager to work on board the vessels in return for their passage home. The captains took advantage of the opportunity to get cheap labor and to force down the wages of the sailors.[30] The second strike occurred in October when the musicians refused to take part in the celebration of the admission of California to the Union unless paid an increased wage for the occasion. They had been receiving $18 and $20 for men and leaders, respectively, and demanded a wage of $26 and $32, respectively. The committee on arrangements refused to grant the increase, and the exercises were carried on without their presence. In Sacramento in September, 1850, the bricklayers won a strike for an increase in wages from $12 per day to $14.

An agitation beginning in the period under discussion but becoming more prominent in subsequent years was popularly known as "the anti-foreigner movement."[31] From all corners of the globe thousands of fortune-seekers had come to California, and it was but natural that questions should arise concerning the rights of foreigners in the placer regions. It has been estimated that by the summer of 1849 there were at least 20,000 men at work in the diggings, and that of this number only one-fourth were Americans.[32] As months passed, the proportions changed, and with the change came open opposition to the foreigners. Among the first to enter the mining districts had been many who had served in the Mexican War. Naturally they did not take kindly to the presence of Spaniards and Mexicans in the mining camps. These dark-skinned men appear to have been as peaceful and as law-abiding as any other group. Many of them had had experience in the mines of Mexico. They were skilled miners, and therefore able to locate the more valuable claims and to work them to better advantage; frequently they succeeded where others failed, which of course further aroused the antagonism of the white-skinned groups. As the latter increased in number, they began forcibly to eject the dark-skinned foreigners from the more desirable claims. On numerous occasions they met with armed resistance; blood flowed freely; and lives were sacrificed on the altar of jealousy and greed.[33] In the northern camps, where the foreigners[34] were in a minority, they were forced to give way to their aggressors, but in the southern camps they held their ground in a most determined manner.

On April 13, 1850, in recognition of the intense agitation, the State legislature passed a law requiring all miners who were not native born citizens of the United States (California Indians excepted) or who had not become citizens under the terms of the Treaty of Guadalupe Hidalgo, to pay a tax of $20 per month for the privilege of working in the mines.[35] Great difficulty was had, and much fraud practiced, in collecting the tax. The dark-skinned foreigners tried to retain what was theirs by Federal law and international treaties, but the whites were determined to obtain for themselves all the golden wealth of California. Frenchmen, Spaniards, Mexicans, Peruvians, Chileans, and others were driven from the mines, often at the point of revolvers and shotguns.[36] Anarchy reigned in many camps. Finally, the foreigners were compelled to abandon their claims. Many moved to the cities or to the southern districts, where, in the mines of the San Joaquin Valley, strength of numbers gave them greater power of resistance. Thousands left the State and returned to their native lands rather than submit to indignities and persecution.[37] Many became robbers and bandits, and in the next few years California reaped its reward in a series of daring holdups, murders, and robberies.

The obnoxious law was repealed on March 14, 1851.[38] Then the succeeding legislature reënacted the measure, but lowered the tax to $3 per month.[39] In 1853 the rate was increased to $4 per month,[40] and in 1855 to $6 per month, with provision for an automatic increase of $2 per month for each year thereafter.[41] On April 19, 1856, the legislature again set the rate at $4 per month.[42] Although later amended at different times, the law remained virtually unchanged until 1870, when it was declared unconstitutional.

The persecution of the dark-skinned foreigners was not restricted to the mining districts, but early became pronounced in San Francisco. An organization known as "The Hounds" was formed among the rougher elements of that city in the summer of 1849. The objects of the association were supposedly mutual assistance to its members in time of sickness and distress and protection in time of danger, but its real purpose was to shield its members from arrest and prosecution. Its attacks were directed chiefly against the Chileans and other South Americans, who were beaten and maltreated in a most shameful manner, and whose tents and shacks were robbed and burned. The gang was finally disrupted through the united effort of public-spirited citizens, and its leaders were severely punished.

In the mining districts the opposition of the whites was at first directed chiefly against the Spanish-Americans, but it was later turned against the Chinese, who early began to enter the placer regions in ever increasing numbers. It has been estimated that there were 54 Chinese in California in 1848, 791 in 1849, 4,018 in 1850, 7,370 in 1851, and 25,116 in 1852.[43] At first, like men of other nationalities, they engaged in mining. Their methods, however, were cruder and yielded a smaller return, but their plane of living was far below that of the others, so that earnings of a dollar or two per day were more than sufficient to satisfy their needs. So carefully and slowly did they labor that scarcely a flake of gold remained after they had finished working a claim. As their number increased, opposition to their presence became more pronounced. It was in these early days that the foundations were laid for the anti-Chinese agitation of later years, which played such an important part in the history of the State. Driven from the mines and thus practically forced into the cities, many Mongolians entered into competition with the whites as gardeners, domestics, laundrymen, and day laborers. They also found employment in the manufacture of cigars, boots, shoes, woolen goods, and clothing. Thousands of their countrymen came from across the Pacific to join their ranks. Such was the genesis in California of one of the most difficult racial and economic problems that has ever harassed the people of any state.

CHAPTER III

A PERIOD OF BEGINNINGS, 1851–1859

SCARCELY ANY OF THE THOUSANDS of gold seekers who came to California in the pioneer days had any intention of remaining permanently. "Most of the population felt themselves pilgrims in the land, temporary residents, enduring merrily severe privations for the sake of a future of plenty and enjoyment in a distant home."[1] All were determined to make their fortunes as easily and as quickly as possible, it mattered not by what means. Friends in the East were too ignorant of conditions to ask embarrassing questions of the triumphantly returning argonaut. California was a land of unknown resources and possibilities. Its newly acquired population was composed almost entirely of daring and reckless spirits who had journeyed westward with but one desire—gold! With absolutely no restraining influences at hand, what better setting could be had for the creation of a society grounded chiefly, if not entirely, on gambling and speculation? The very gifts of Nature—the evenness of climate, the broad expanse of the valley floors rich in fertility, the long sweep of the distant mountains, the "bigness" of everything—encouraged the spirit of chance, of playing close to the edge in all life's activities, whether commercial, industrial, or social. Californians eagerly assumed business and financial risks that would have startled their eastern townsmen. Fortunes were made and lost on the slightest turn of the wheel of chance. Extreme recklessness marked even the most ordinary business transactions.

Under such circumstances it is not strange that as early as the autumn months of 1850 California had a serious business depression. Several misadventures aided in bringing it about. The disastrous fires in San Francisco in 1849 and 1850 ruined many of her merchants and seriously diminished commercial transactions. The fire of December 14, 1849, caused a loss of approximately $1,000,000, while those of May 4 and June 14, 1850, destroyed property valued at from $3,000,000 to $4,000,000. The light rainfall in the winter of 1849 had not provided water enough for a satisfactory operation of the placers. Eastern firms glutted the market with goods, and this meant subsequent losses for the local merchants. In the fall of 1850, three banks in Sacramento and the pioneer banking firm of San Francisco closed their doors.[2] Wages and prices declined somewhat, but real estate values decreased greatly.[3]

Nevertheless, the speculative spirit was not easily curbed. A few months of cautious buying and selling, and business conditions again became unsettled. Each bit of encouraging news from the mines brought fresh shipments to California; the market became overstocked, prices declined, and eastern firms refused to grant further credit to the California merchants. There were other untoward events: the fires of May and June, 1851, which caused a loss of approximately $10,000,000;[4] the dry winter season of 1850; and a reign of crime, which called forth a Vigilance Committee—all combined further to hinder the return of normal conditions. It was not until the fall of 1852 that the situation improved and merchants once more looked hopefully toward the future.

Little of importance occurred in the field of Labor during the first two years (1851–1852) of this period. As might be expected, there was widespread unemployment. An advertisement for a bookkeeper in San Francisco brought two hundred applicants.[5] The construction of wharves and piers, running far out into San Francisco Bay, meant unemployment to hundreds of lightermen and boatmen. The situation, however, was somewhat relieved by the building activity which followed the fires of 1851. One newspaper commented at length upon the fact that for a time the sawmills ran day and night in order to supply the demand for lumber.[6]

There were few strikes in San Francisco in these two years (1851–1852). In May, 1851, the stevedores and the longshoremen struck for $6 per day,[7] and the printers successfully opposed a reduction in wages. In 1852, a quarrel among the printers disrupted their organization, and no meetings were held by their union during the greater part of that year. In May, 1852, the coal heavers struck unsuccessfully against a reduction in wages from $100 to $60 per month. The musicians failed in their demand for $50 each for playing at the Fourth of July celebration. The unions of the teamsters and the boatmen met frequently; in January, 1852, the former petitioned the Board of Supervisors for a reduction in the annual license tax, but the request was not granted.[8] Unions were organized, among the bricklayers in February, 1852, and among the bakers two months later. The bakers had been compelled, according to the custom of the trade, to work Saturday nights and Sundays. Well attended meetings were held on April 18 and 25, 1852, at which a union was organized and resolutions adopted demanding the abolition of the objectionable Saturday night and Sunday work. After some agitation, an ordinance, approved by a majority of the master bakers, was passed by the Board of Supervisors, forbidding the sale and vending of bakers' goods on Sunday.[9]

Outside of San Francisco[10] the only organization of workingmen concerning which any data appear available is that of the printers of Sacramento, which was formed some time before March, 1852.[11]

In spite of the more settled business conditions, there was much destitution throughout the State and especially in San Francisco throughout the winter of 1852. One of the city newspapers commented on the situation as follows:

We have had among us a large class of unfortunates during the winter. The streets of San Francisco have supplied a living to hundreds, either by acts of charity, the giving of alms at the street door, or by the tolerance of a class whose wants have driven them into every conceivable method of wringing a dime from the passer-by. . . . There has never been so deplorable an exhibition of mendicancy in our streets as may be witnessed daily at this time, . . . hundreds of destitute men and scores of women and children besieging the pockets of society in public and private, indoors and out. Troops of girls perambulate the streets day and night with hand organs, tambourines, and essays at vocal music. . . . Little girls . . . are to be found in front of the city saloons at all hours of the day, going through their graceless performances.[12]

The heavy rainfall of the winter season, however, provided an abundance of water in the placers, so that with the coming of spring, 1853, thousands of the unemployed left for the interior to try their luck in the diggings. Apparently their emigration did not reduce in any noticeable degree the amount of idleness in San Francisco, for in May another newspaper said, "There are more idle men in San Francisco now than in any other city in the Union, and the number is reduced to one-half of what it was two months ago."[13] Many who were able to pay or to work for their passage on board the sailing vessels returned to their homes in the Atlantic states; several thousand left for Australia, where, it was rumored, mines of great richness had been discovered; others went into agriculture, which was just beginning to develop on an extensive scale.[14] Stories to the effect that the golden era of California was passing were carried to all parts of the globe and greatly reduced the immigration into the State. It has been estimated that the number of persons arriving in 1853 was smaller by at least 20,000 than the number arriving in any of the preceding four years.

But the depression passed, confidence was restored, business ventures prospered, and capital found remunerative investment, not only in quartz mining, but also in various industries which were becoming established in the city beside the Golden Gate. At that time San Francisco supported

half a dozen important foundries, machine and boiler works, employing several hundred men; four saw mills, besides sash, blind, and box factories; eleven flouring mills with a capacity of 1,100 barrels daily; a steam cracker factory; a large sugar refinery; a dozen and a half breweries, besides distilleries, soda and syrup works; billiard table manufactories; a beginning in furniture making; and a host of establishments concerned in supplying necessities and luxuries for mining, field, and home life, a large proportion of an artistic stamp.[15]

During the summer months of 1853, employment, especially in the building trades, was plentiful. Approximately six hundred brick and stone structures were erected, representing an investment of about $2,000,000. The improved business conditions were also reflected in the increased assessed valuation of personal and real property in San Francisco, which increased from $18,500,000 in 1852–1853 to $28,900,000 in 1853–1854.

Coincident with returning prosperity came the organization of workers into trade unions, followed by demands for higher wages[16] and demands, on the part of some unions, for shorter hours. Organization was especially rampant among the workingmen of San Francisco in the months of July and August, 1853, when unions were formed among the carpenters, plasterers, painters, tinners, shipwrights and caulkers, longshoremen, steamship and steamboat firemen and coal passers, blacksmiths, and riggers and stevedores. A union had been organized among the tailors in February. The teamsters, printers, and bricklayers reorganized their unions in the same year.[17] In Sacramento unions were formed among the hodcarriers and the bricklayers.

In all trades, either before or after these associations came into existence, strikes were declared by the workers, and more often than not their demands were won.[18] Business was active, labor was in demand, and the workingmen were determined to share in the prosperity of the community. Strikes were not limited to San Francisco, but also occurred among the workers of Sacramento,[19] Marysville,[20] and Stockton.[21] Frequently, and especially in San Francisco, the strikes were accompanied by rioting and violence. The strikers, armed with clubs and stones, threatened or drove away those who had refused to strike or who had taken their places. A few arrests were made, and some of the offenders were punished, but in spite of the demands of the public press that order be preserved, no determined effort was made to that end.[22]

The trouble between the printers and the *Alta California*, which had been festering for some time, finally came to a head in October, 1853. This influential San Francisco newspaper had steadfastly opposed the Typographical Society, asserting that it did so only because the printers' organization insisted upon maintaining a rate of wages that had governed the craft in the flush years of California. In August, 1851, the proprietors of the *Alta California* called a meeting of the publishers of San Francisco in the hope that united action might be obtained in reducing wages, but the plan "was frustrated through the failure of one of the prominent establishments to abide by the understanding then made."[23] In the summer of 1852, a second conference was called for the same purpose, and probably because the "movement was unexpected and found the [printers'] society somewhat disorganized," the publishers on June 30 succeeded in establishing the rate of $1.50 per 1,000 ems. This did not end the controversy, however, for the printers through their association at once adopted regulations governing their work which were objectionable to the employers and vigorously opposed by them.

No further trouble occurred in the society [the typographical union] until the fall of 1852, when a violent split was made in its councils by the rash and reckless conduct of some of its more prominent members. . . . Suffice it to remark that personal interests, intermingled with bitter sectional prejudices and animosities, prevailed to the bad extremity of the dissolution of the society. It had increased from a membership of barely eight at its organization, to the number of 147 at the time of its precipitated dissolution.[24]

On May 22, 1853, the printers reorganized as the San Francisco Typographical Union, with H. C. Williston as president. The *Alta California* persisted in its opposition, and in the fall of 1853 discharged all union employees, replacing them with men who were brought out from eastern offices. The San Francisco Typographical Union refused to "rat" the *Alta California* office, whereupon the loyal union men formed a new society, the Eureka Typographical Union, with James Risk as president.[25] For some months thereafter the new organization waged a bitter but unsuccessful fight against its opponent. The union remained active, however, and in December, 1854, received the first national charter granted to any group of organized workers on the Pacific Coast. Henceforth it was known as Eureka Typographical Society, No. 21.[26] It continued until 1858, when it was forced to disband because of the determined attacks of the employers, who were insistent upon effecting a wage reduction.

The prosperity of 1853 had inspired overconfidence. Office buildings, stores, and houses were erected for which there were no tenants;[27] employment was difficult to obtain; great quantities of supplies of every sort had been imported for which there were no buyers; the merchants had misjudged the needs of the community. An additional reason for the unsettled condition of business during the next few years was the insufficient rainfall of 1854 and 1855. Without water the placers could not be worked to the best advantage, and from 1853 to 1855 the production of gold decreased by about $10,000,000. Many of the miners who had previously paid cash for their supplies, were forced to ask for credit, thus greatly increasing the outstanding accounts of the merchants. In 1854, there were seventy-four insolvencies, in one of which the liabilities exceeded $800,000. Real estate values and rents decreased by 20 per cent to 50 per cent. In February, 1855, the business and financial structure of the State collapsed as a result of the forced suspension of the San Francisco banking firms of Adams & Company, Page, Bacon & Company, Robinson & Company, Burgoyne & Company, Argenti & Company, Palmer, Cook & Company, and Wright's Miners' Exchange Bank. The banking houses of George W. Plume, of Marysville, and of Hamlet Davis, of Nevada City, also closed their doors.[28] Many business firms and express companies also succumbed in the panic which followed. Before the year ended, 197 insolvencies had been recorded, with liabilities totaling $8,377,827.[29] The seriousness of the situation cannot be fully appreciated unless it is remembered that at the time San Francisco was a relatively small town with a population of only about 40,000.

Business in California was slow in recovering from the crash of 1854–1855. It was not until the autumn months of 1858 that signs of returning confidence and normality were in evidence. An important reason for this delay (and incidentally for the crash itself) was the state-wide industrial revolution which took place during these years. Mining methods were undergoing transformation.[30] The placers had given way to the quartz mines; the man with the pan and shovel had been replaced by the employer with large capital and hired laborers. Many who had been engaged in mining on a small scale drifted into agriculture, which seemed to offer more certain returns and a more settled life. Agriculture thus expanded rapidly, and within a comparatively short time California was producing not only sufficient foodstuffs for her own needs, but also a surplus which was exported to eastern sections of the United States and to other countries. Concurrently her imports decreased at an astonishing rate because much of the goods shipped into the State in earlier years had consisted of grains and other foodstuffs. The decrease, however, was not so great as it should have been under the circumstances.[31] The *Evening Bulletin* of March 27, 1856, pointedly remarked: "The truth is that, with very few exceptions, we are overstocked with merchandise. It is rare indeed of late years that we are not overstocked." "The shipping entering the harbor fell from 407,000 tons in 1853, not counting the coasters and steamers which carried but little freight, to 197,000 tons in 1857."[32] This significant decrease eliminated the need for many brokers, merchants, teamsters, longshoremen, boatmen, and unskilled laborers. Thousands were without employment, and many were penniless.

The return to normal business was further hindered by the dry winter of 1856, by a reign of crime and terror which brought forth a second Vigilance Committee, and by the decisions of the State Supreme Court, which declared that the State debt of nearly

$4,000,000, as well as certain financial obligations of the city of San Francisco, had been illegally incurred. In 1855, the ranks of the unemployed were somewhat reduced by the departure of about 5,000 men for the Kern River district where a rich gold strike was reported. There was further relief in the spring and summer of 1858 through the exodus of more than 18,000 men who rushed into the Fraser River territory in British Columbia, lured by tales of golden riches along the banks of that stream. It is said that some of the mining counties lost more than one-third of their population because of the intense excitement which prevailed.[33]

Although the effects of the panic of 1854–1855 lasted until the latter part of 1858 and the merchants of California lost heavily, the panic proved a godsend in disguise. The reckless speculations of the days of '49 and '50 were replaced by saner, safer practices, which resulted in the creation of a much more satisfactory and stable condition in the local business world.

In the depression of 1854–1857, wages and prices declined to the lowest levels ever reached in California up to that time. The San Francisco *Morning Call*, on December 24, 1857, complained that "each succeeding year brings with it a reduction in the rate of wages, and if the declension is not soon arrested, we shall have labor in California depressed even lower than in the over-crowded communities of the Eastern States."[34]

In these years a majority of the unions which had been formed in the prosperous days of 1853 quietly disbanded. But also in these years a few new unions were organized. Notices of the Laborers' Union Association, the Granite Cutters' Association, the Sailmakers' Union, and the Cartmen's Association are found for the first time in the San Francisco newspapers in February and March, 1854. In 1856 the musicians and the watermen[35] formed protective unions, and in 1857 organization was effected among the ship and steamboat joiners, the painters, and the hatters. In the parades of 1857, the newspapers reported the following trades as being represented by their respective unions: coopers, boatmen, draymen and teamsters, riggers and stevedores, watermen, ship and steamboat joiners, and printers.[36]

Several inconsequential and for the most part unsuccessful strikes occurred in the period 1854–1857, the issue being always a demand for an increase in wages or opposition to a decrease.[37] In 1857, an agitation was begun against the sale of convict-labor goods, it being asserted that they competed with the products of free labor.[38] Protesting articles were written for the press and pamphlets were printed and distributed, but no results were obtained at the time.

As 1858 came to a close, business and industry began slowly to show signs of recovery from the long period of stagnation, but it was not until the Comstock lode was opened in 1859–1860 that there was any great activity displayed by the merchants and employers of the State. Wages and prices rose gradually, but not to their earlier levels; real estate values increased slightly, and in all branches of trade a healthier and more prosperous condition was in evidence. The exodus of gold seekers to the Fraser River region was so great in the spring and summer of 1858 that fears were expressed for the possible effect upon business. The *Alta California* of March 24, 1860, however, recorded:

Although the mining trade lessened, the coast trade increased, and a demand arose for many articles of foreign and domestic produce, as well as local tonnage, in both steam and sail vessels. The agricultural districts, receiving fair prices for their produce, were large in their orders and prompt in their payments, and thus our city business received some compensation for the temporary loss of the mining trade.

The decreased labor supply made it possible for those who had remained in San Francisco to demand and obtain higher wages. In June, the masons received an increase from $5 to $7 per day, and the hodcarriers $4 per day, while the carpenters demanded $6 per day. Wage increases were also requested by the firemen and sailors on ocean vessels,[39] the deckhands on river boats, the draymen,[40] the laborers in the bread and cracker factories, the sawmill and planing mill employees,[41] the sugar refinery workers, the tinsmiths,[42] and the laundresses and domestic servants. Wages in the mines were also increased by 25 to 50 per cent. The *Morning Call* of June 22, 1858, commented that "there are few if any branches of labor that have not felt the effects of the Fraser River excitement, and as a general thing the wages of the workingmen of this city have advanced from ten to twenty-five per cent."[43]

Very few trade unions were organized in San Francisco in the closing years of the decade. Occasional notices are found of the meetings of the Riggers' and Stevedores' Association, the Draymen's, Teamsters' and Watermen's Union, the Caulkers' Association, the Bricklayers' and Laborers' Union, and the Cigar Makers' Association. On August 14, 1859, about seventy-five printers met and reorganized their association. On August 28 they elected officers and adopted a scale of wages.[44] During the subsequent decade this union played a prominent part in all matters affecting the interests of Organized Labor in San Francisco. The printers of Sacramento also reorganized their union on September 10, 1859, their association thenceforth being known as Typographical Union, No. 46.

The period 1851–1859 was one of "beginnings." In it many movements were originated that came to occupy prominent places in the later history of Labor in California. Virtually all trades were organized at one time or another in the decade, although, with the possible exception of the printers and the riggers and stevedores, the associations were of a temporary, ephemeral sort and survived for only a few months, or at best a year. In 1854 the printers received the first national charter granted to a union of California workingmen,[45] and the fact that no other organization, except that of the printers of Sacramento, applied for or received a national charter in the next ten years, is evidence of the instability and local limitations of the California labor movement during this period. The first steps were also taken toward the enactment of labor legislation, a mechanics' lien law having been passed by the State legislature in 1850,[46] and a law establishing a ten-hour day in 1853.[47] The employment of children also attracted the attention of the public, but nothing was done at that time to safeguard their interests.[48] The campaign against the competition of convict labor and of Chinese labor was begun in this decade. It may also be of interest to note that, beginning in 1853, efforts were made by employers, individually and through associations, to induce the immigration of laborers from eastern states so as to lower the wages of the workers, a practice which persisted down to the opening years of the twentieth century.[49]

CHAPTER IV

PROSPERITY, 1860–1869

THE DECADE OF THE SIXTIES was an era of prosperity in California, characterized by the extensive development of mining, agriculture, and manufacturing. Capital was plentiful and was eagerly invested. Labor was thoroughly organized and was uniformly successful in enforcing its demands for shorter hours and higher wages. The prosperous condition which prevailed during the period formed a striking contrast to the destitution and business uncertainty which marked the subsequent decade. From 1860 to 1870 the population of the State increased from 380,000 to 560,200, and that of San Francisco from 56,802 to 149,473.

During the sixties the mines of the State annually yielded millions of dollars in dividends. That fact, coupled with the growing popularity of the stock company, inevitably encouraged widespread speculation in mining stocks, many of which were the issues of "wildcat" companies of a most disgraceful sort.[1] In May, 1864, stock prices began to decline and in a few months "they depreciated, with slight exceptions, more than one-half, some of them falling several hundred per cent," with a consequent loss of millions of dollars.[2] In general, however, the business and industrial interests of California were so prosperous that they were not noticeably affected by this temporary depression in the stock market, and only a few bankruptcies occurred.

The drought of 1862–1864 aided greatly in bringing about a much more intensive cultivation of the soil and the development of horticulture and viticulture. Earlier, the lands in the central and southern sections had been held in huge tracts, and utilized almost exclusively for grain and for cattle-grazing. Because of the drought, wheat could not be raised. Thousands of cattle died of thirst and hunger on the ranges. Many large landholders hastened to subdivide their holdings, and to dispose of them in smaller acreages. With the smaller ranch came the more intensive cultivation of the soil, the development of numerous irrigation projects, and the planting of large areas to grapes, orchards, and berries.

Notable progress was also recorded in growth of manufactures. The Civil War, by cutting off commerce between California and the eastern states, forced the people of the State to a greater dependence upon their own resources. Many new industries were started, and these gave employment to thousands of workers. Californians refused to accept or use the "greenback" currency. Instead, they maintained a specie basis for their financial transactions, thereby providing a more stable foundation for industrial and business activities. Eastern capitalists, as well as those of Europe, were not slow to recognize the possibilities of the situation, and they freely invested in California enterprises. The *Evening Bulletin* of October 4, 1864, in commenting upon the industrial situation in the State, said:

The late Mechanics' Institute Fair revealed the interesting fact that there are in San Francisco thirty or forty prosperous manufacturing establishments in some of the most important branches, not to speak of many minor ones requiring but little capital. The woolen and sugar mills, two of each, employing many hundreds of men and turning out several millions worth of goods per annum; the glass factory, the wire rope, paper, cordage, powder, tobacco, tin, and hardware manufacturing concerns, and the great foundries, made displays which surprised the most intelligent and hopeful friends of California, and which must afford great encouragement to those who contemplate adding to the list of local manufactures. Since the Fair, there is less question than before as to the profitableness of such ventures, and we may look to see their number considerably increased in another year.

This decade is also important because it marks the completion of the Central Pacific railroad and the establishment of rail connection with the eastern states. Large numbers of men were employed on this and other projects. In San Francisco, many buildings were erected,[3] wharves were built, the harbor was dredged, and a streetcar service was installed. The Washoe mining excitement and the subsequent uncovering of fabulous riches in the hills of Nevada brought great prosperity to the iron trades in San Francisco. "Quartz mills were ordered by the wholesale; the demand for mining machinery was unprecedented, and the local requirements increased to a great extent." Foundries and machine shops ran night and day to supply the demand.[4] Although the mining excitement was soon over, business conditions remained satisfactory until the close of the sixties.

In the first years of the decade, a few unions were formed, others were reorganized, and a small number of strikes were declared,[5] but for the most part the labor situation remained fairly quiet.

The agitation against convict labor, which had been started in 1857, assumed more definite shape in July, 1861. The coopers of San Francisco, asserting that their trade had been seriously injured because of the competition of convict-made goods,[6] assembled on the sixteenth of that month and, after organizing a protective association, adopted the following resolutions:

In view of the disgraceful action of our state authorities in bringing their criminals into competition with us, thereby trying to deprive us of our means of support, as well as to insult and degrade the trade to which we belong; and

Whereas, we are compelled to organize for the protection of ourselves and families and the honor of our present trade:

Resolved: That we resort to all legal means in our power to prevent the authorities from carrying out their designs for the enrichment of heartless capitalists and our degradation and ruin; and we pledge ourselves to maintain this organization and to leave nothing untried to effect our objects, viz., the prevention of convict labor in opposition to industrious mechanics.[7]

On August 1, 1861, a well attended mass meeting of workingmen was held at Mechanics' Hall and an association, the Mechanics' League, was formed for the purpose of carrying on the fight against the abuses of convict labor. The Mechanics' League held a few meetings in August, and in September joined with the Anti-Coolie Association in pledging candidates for the legislature to enact laws to protect the workers against convict and Chinese labor. Contrary to expectations, however, the league, instead of controlling the politicians, was controlled by them, and when, following the election of 1861, the politicians had no further use for it, it quietly passed out of existence, having accomplished nothing toward obtaining the objects for which it had been organized.

Beginning in 1863, the workingmen of San Francisco organized a number of trade unions. They had two motives: (1) to take advantage of the prosperous conditions existing in industry, and (2) to counteract the effects of a rise in prices. In that year associations existed among the machinists, bakers,[8] blacksmiths, bricklayers, cracker bakers, boot- and shoemakers, riggers and stevedores, plumbers, grooms, house painters, plasterers, printers, boilermakers, tailors, shipwrights, cigarmakers, stonecutters, ironmolders, upholsterers, waiters, patternmakers, grainers, and coopers. As one result of all this activity an agitation was begun which resulted in the formation of the first labor council in California, namely, "The San Francisco Trades' Union." As early as 1859 a central labor body had been proposed by the Cigar Makers' Association, following a suggestion contained in an editorial in the *Morning Call* of October 28, 1859. It was thought that a federation of the local unions would aid the Cigar Makers' Association in its campaign against the employment of Chinese labor in the cigar trade.

The San Francisco Trades' Union of 1863 grew immediately out of a strike called in June, 1863, by the tailors' union, for an increase in wages. After the strike had continued for some weeks and appeared to be lost, the tailors organized a "Tailors' Joint Stock Association," capitalized at $50,000, with the intention of establishing a coöperative tailor shop. Several of the local unions had contributed funds and had given their moral support to the strikers. The tailors, however, had come to the conclusion that the local workers could expect to gain nothing from their employers except through unity of action, and, in association with the upholsterers, they issued the following appeal on September 12, 1863:

> To Mechanics' Societies of San Francisco: A movement has been initiated for the purpose of uniting the Mechanics' Societies of this city. We hold that labor, the chief source of wealth, can receive its merits only by the united and earnest efforts of its devotees. The power and benefits of union and united action are well understood. For the furtherance of this object so generally conceded to be of the greatest importance, we recommend that the various Mechanics' Societies elect delegates to meet at Minerva Hall, corner Kearney and California Streets, on THURSDAY EVENING, Sept. 24, at 8 o'clock.
>
> By order of   THE TAILORS' AND UPHOLSTERERS' SOCIETIES.

The riggers and stevedores, plasterers, shipwrights, tailors, stonecutters, and upholsterers sent delegates, and after some discussion the following resolution was adopted and ordered published:

> Resolved, That it is the opinion of the delegates present that the interests of the Mechanics' Societies of this city will be materially enhanced by a Union of all the Trade Associations of this city, which union will have for its objects the giving of moral and material aid in times of distress to the industrial associations.

A committee was appointed to issue a call for a second meeting to be held on October 3. Three additional unions, namely, of the printers, the ironmolders, and the bricklayers, were represented at the second gathering. After the selection of William D. Delaney as secretary pro tem., a committee was appointed to draft a constitution and by-laws. At a meeting held a week later, delegates from the machinists' union were admitted. On October 26, the following officers were elected: president, John M. McCreary; vice-president, William C. Cummings; recording secretary, W. D. Delaney; corresponding secretary, Daniel Lore; financial secretary, J. F. Gormley.[9] In the early days of December a committee composed of Kenaday, Brady, and Gormley was appointed to visit the trade unions and urge them to become members of the central body. The committee was fairly successful in its mission and in January, 1864, fifteen local unions, representing from 2,000 to 3,000 workers, were associated with the Trades' Union.[10]

At no time during its short existence does the San Francisco Trades' Union appear to have had the ardent "work together" spirit necessary to the welfare of a central labor organization. It aided several unions in their demands for higher wages and shorter hours; it petitioned the legislature against the repeal of the Specific Contract Law[11]—a law which had helped to keep the business transactions of California on a gold basis during the Civil War; it agitated for the enactment of a more satisfactory mechanics' lien law;[12] and during the closing months of its existence, it took part in a determined but unsuccessful demand for a State law establishing an eight-hour day. Nevertheless, it had but little influence upon the condition of the workers of California. It continued to meet monthly until the spring of 1866, and then quietly disbanded as a result of petty internal dissensions which had arisen in connection with the agitation for the eight-hour day.[13]

The San Francisco Trades' Union was formed at a time of great activity among the workers of the eastern states.[14] John R. Commons and John B. Andrews say:

The immediate cause of the organization of wage labor [in the eastern states] was the rise of prices and cost of living, which began with the disappearance of gold and the appearance of greenbacks in 1862.... The effect of paper currency was first seriously noticed toward the end of 1862; but the great stimulus to business and the enlistment of wage earners in the army brought about such an increase of employment that the need of organization was not felt. The situation was different in 1863, and the failure of wages to rise with prices provoked the sporadic organization of local unions.[15]

California had refused to accept the greenbacks and remained upon a gold basis; hence the disturbing influence of paper money was not experienced by its citizens. Prices, however, advanced somewhat, because the Civil War decreased the supply of eastern goods in California and increased the eastern demand for some of the State's products.

Commons and Andrews also state that

soon these local unions came together in city central bodies. . . . The first one was organized at Rochester, N. Y., in March, 1863, and thirty of them were organized before the end of 1865. Their object was almost solely that which at the present day would be known as the boycott, although occasionally they made appeals for financial help for striking unions.[16]

In California the labor movement was not far behind that of the eastern communities, especially in the matter of organizing a central body, although the purpose of organization appears to have been somewhat different. The boycott as a trade-union weapon was not much used by the workers of California until some years later, although in the sixties it was occasionally resorted to in the agitation against the Chinese—not by the unions, however, but by various anti-coolie associations. Nor did the San Francisco Trades' Union appeal for money to help striking unions. Its most important work arose in connection with the campaign for the enactment of a State eight-hour day law.

As a result of the increased cost of living, and perhaps partly because of the prevalence of strikes in the eastern states—for the desire to strike is strangely contagious—the workingmen of San Francisco were very active from 1863 to 1865 in demanding higher wages, shorter hours, and more satisfactory working conditions. The *Evening Bulletin* of November 4, 1863, said:

Of late there seems to be a general disposition on the part of operatives in the different branches of trade to "strike" . . . demanding a considerable increase of wages.

Two days later it added, editorially:

Striking for higher wages is now the rage among the working people of San Francisco. There are few employers that have not felt the upward pressure within three months, and probably some branches of business that heretofore proved fairly profitable are now pursued at a loss on account of increased expense for labor.

Virtually all the strikes ended successfully for the workers.

Among the more important contests between employer and employee[17] were those of the tailors in June, 1863, for an increase in wages; of the hotel and restaurant waiters in September and October, 1863, for increased wages;[18] of the bakers in October, 1863, for a twelve-hour day, no Sunday work, and increased wages; and of the grooms or hostlers employed in the livery stables and horse-car barns of the city in December, 1863, and January, 1864, for increased wages, shorter hours, and a change in working rules.[19]

In April, 1864, the ironmolders' union demanded a minimum wage of $4 for a ten-hour day, and $4.50 a day for those who had been receiving $4. The employers refused the demands, whereupon the molders struck, taking care to notify all fellow-craftsmen in California and elsewhere not to interfere with the strike, and at the same time threatening violence to any persons who should attempt to take their places. A few days later the molders were joined by the Journeymen Boilermakers' Protective Union, whose members, then receiving from $4 to $4.50 per day, struck for an increase of 50 cents. The contest was bitterly waged for some months. The workers undoubtedly would have been defeated had they not most skilfully checkmated the plans of their employers. Just after the strike had been declared, the latter had formed an Employers' Association —the second defense association of employers to be organized on the Pacific Coast, the first having been that of the restaurant proprietors, organized in 1861. It was publicly stated that the members of the Employers' Association had "entered into a combination" according to the terms of which the first one who acceded "to the workmen's demands" should forfeit $1,000. The Employers' Association telegraphed to New York, Boston, Providence, and Portland, Maine, and succeeded in hiring a number of molders and boilermakers, agreeing to advance them the cost of passage to San Francisco and to pay higher wages than were then prevailing in the eastern states. The strike breakers, however, were met at the Isthmus of Panama by representatives of the San Francisco Trades' Union, the molders, and the boilermakers, who explained the circumstances of the controversy. Upon reaching San Francisco the imported men refused to go to work, and instead applied for union membership. The employers acknowledged defeat and granted the demands of the strikers. In the ensuing months, however, the former retaliated by gradually discharging those workers who had been most active in the strike.

In October, 1864, the steamship firemen struck against a reduction in wages. Strike breakers were employed and several serious clashes occurred. A number of the strike breakers were injured, and some of the strikers were arrested and subsequently convicted of assault and battery. A unique strike occurred in the same month among the Italian fishermen of San Francisco. For years they had sold the greater part of their catch to Chinese peddlers, who hawked the fish from house to house. The imposition of a city license of $25 per quarter had driven the Chinese out of the business and had forced the Italians to sell only to white fish-dealers. The latter then combined to lower the prices which they paid for the fish, whereupon the fishermen struck. A union was organized and a coöperative fish-market was established which was successfully operated for a number of years.

The early-closing movement, which was to reappear frequently in subsequent years, began in 1863. In November of that year a number of clerks in the dry-goods stores of San Francisco organized and were successful in inducing their employers to close at 8 P.M. during the winter and spring months. In February, 1869, the clerks asked that the stores close at 7 P.M., except on Saturdays. A large number of the merchants granted the request; the few who did not were vigorously boycotted by the Clerks' Association.

Notices of the meetings of the unions of the following crafts appeared in the papers of San Francisco in 1864: gas fitters, carpenters, brass finishers, ironmolders, boilermakers, journeymen shipwrights, painters, lathers, ship and steamboat joiners, carriage painters, journeymen barbers and hairdressers, bakers, brick-masons, grainers, machinists, plasterers, plumbers, riggers and stevedores, stonecutters, tailors, upholsterers, printers, and steamship firemen.

The Eight-Hour Day

The shorter workday[20] did not become an issue of any consequence in California until 1865. As already noted, the ten-hour day
had been legally established in 1853, but the passage of the law had
caused no comment either among the workers or by the press.

In the eastern states the shorter workday had been an issue from
the early years of the nineteenth century, the demand for eight
hours being but a later phase of that agitation. The movement for
the shorter day is said to have been started about 1842, when the
carpenters and caulkers of the Charlestown Navy Yard obtained
a limitation of eight hours for "old work."[21] But the agitation progressed slowly, and it was not until the early sixties that it enlisted
any considerable following. Since the labor movement of San Francisco had always been more or less closely in touch with developments in the eastern states, it is not surprising that, beginning with
1865, there arose an insistent demand for the eight-hour day among
the laborers of the western city. From that time until 1870 it remained the most important and popular labor issue with them.

The agitation in California owed its origin chiefly to the efforts
of Alexander M. Kenaday,[22] a printer, who had been elected president of the San Francisco Trades' Union in 1865.[23] Kenaday had
taken an active part in the organization of the union in 1863 and
had served as its secretary. He had been a close observer of the
labor movement in the eastern states and had been much impressed
with the influence of Fincher's *Trade Review*, a Philadelphia labor
paper, which carried at the head of its editorial column the slogan,
"Eight Hours a Day." In April, 1865, he attempted to follow its
example by establishing a weekly San Francisco labor paper, *The
Journal of Trades and Workingmen*, but he was forced to abandon
it after struggling through five issues.

In his inaugural address as the newly elected president of the
Trades' Union, Kenaday said:

Another subject of momentous importance, I desire to call to the serious
and enlightened consideration of the Delegates, a question that is being seriously agitated in the Trades Unions of the East, and one which of itself
should unite every class of laboring men, is the passage of a law constituting
eight hours a legal day's work. . . . This reform, gentlemen, is one of the most

important within the scope of your duties, and care should be taken not to endanger its ultimate accomplishment by hasty, indiscreet, and unwise agitation.

The subject was made a special order of business for the December meeting of the Trades' Union, and was discussed at great length. Four thousand copies of Kenaday's address were published and distributed. On December 12, 1865, an advertisement appeared in the *Morning Call,* announcing a mass meeting to be held by all workingmen interested in the eight-hour day. Some carpenters had read Kenaday's address and had called the meeting for the purpose of getting the movement under way.

A large gathering assembled, and J. M. McCreary, former president of the Trades' Union, presided. At Kenaday's suggestion a committee was appointed to draft resolutions calling for the eight-hour day, and these resolutions as drafted by Kenaday were adopted unanimously. The resolutions also called upon the Trades' Union to prepare a suitable petition to be presented to the legislature at its approaching session. At the meeting of the Trades' Union on December 15, the petition, prepared by Kenaday, was adopted. A committee, composed of Kenaday, McMillan, and Loane, was appointed to arrange for a second mass meeting to discuss and ratify the action of the Trades' Union. The meeting was held on December 22. Kenaday was appointed to bring the matter to the attention of the San Francisco legislative delegation and to urge the enactment of the proposed measure; and for the next three months he spent all his time and paid his own expenses in furthering the campaign before the legislature.

A petition, 22 feet long, containing 11,000 names, was presented to the legislature on February 13, 1866, asking that an eight-hour day law be adopted.[24] Mass meetings were held in San Francisco, Sacramento, and Marysville; a number of articles favoring the measure appeared in the press of the State; and great enthusiasm was aroused among the workers.

The bill, championed by Assemblyman J. W. Wilcox, was passed by the Assembly on February 2, 1866, by a vote of 64 to 6. Unsuccessful attempts were made to amend it by requiring that wages should be paid in gold and silver unless otherwise specified, by having it apply only to incorporated cities, and by adding that all contracts between employers and employees should be by the hour instead of by the day.[25]

In the meantime, there had arisen among the workers of San Francisco a dissension caused partly by the jealousy of certain

ALEXANDER McCONNELL KENADAY

labor leaders who felt piqued by Kenaday's prominence, and partly by political matters. Kenaday was a Democrat and was opposed to "doing politics" within the unions; his antagonists were Republicans with political aspirations and were seeking to use the unions for their political advancement. Strenuous opposition had also arisen among the employers. The *Evening Bulletin* vigorously attacked the bill in its editorial columns. The Typographical Union, when less than one-tenth of its members were present (and for the most part the latter were employees of the *Evening Bulletin*), voted to withdraw its delegates from the Trades' Union. As Kenaday was one of the delegates, it was thought that this action would force him to abandon his campaign for the measure. Needless to say, it did not.

The bill was finally presented to the Senate. On February 6, it was referred to a select committee for consideration. Strong opposition, especially on the part of the employing foundrymen, developed at the hearings before the committee, and the bill was reported back to the Senate with the amendment that it should not take effect until New York and Massachusetts should have adopted similar statutes. It was then passed by a vote of 23 to 5 [26] and returned to the Assembly. The latter by a vote of 56 to 7, however, refused to accept the Senate's amendment, and a joint committee on free conference was appointed to arrange a compromise. After some discussion a majority report was brought in, framed in accordance with a suggestion from Kenaday, recommending that the Senate recede from its amendment and that an additional section be added which should provide that the act should take effect and be in force from and after January 1, 1867.[27] On March 20 the suggested changes were rejected by the Senate by a vote of 15 to 17. A motion to adhere to the original amendment was then made, and the vote stood 16 to 16. On a recount the final vote was recorded as 19 noes and 18 ayes,[28] and the first efforts of the workers of California to secure an eight-hour law had been defeated. Kenaday did not give up the struggle until after he had discussed the situation with Assemblyman Wilcox and other supporters of the measure and had been assured by them that there was absolutely no hope of its being revived at that session of the legislature. Later he forwarded a copy of the petition of the Trades' Union to the California representatives in Congress in the hope that its presentation before that body would aid in the campaign for the enactment of a Federal eight-hour law.[29]

Several San Francisco trades had already established the eight-hour day. The shipbuilding trades were the first to introduce it, both in the eastern states and in California. The caulkers obtained the eight-hour day in December, 1865, the ship joiners and ship-wrights in January, 1866,[30] and the ship painters in March, 1866.

If a law establishing the eight-hour day could not be obtained from the legislature, the unions felt that they could and would get it by other means. A few of them resorted to strikes as a method of bringing about the desired end.[31] The most common practice, however, was for a union to meet and adopt resolutions fixing a certain date after which its members would work but eight hours per day. The employers, thus notified, were prepared to enter into future contracts on that basis. On November 1, 1866, the Bricklayers' Protective Union fixed February 1, 1867, as the date upon which it would adopt the eight-hour day. This date was also decided upon by the Laborers' Protective Benevolent Association (hod-carriers). The Operative Stone Masons' Union chose March 1, 1867; the stonecutters, in April, 1867, chose May 1; the Metal Roofers' Association in April chose June 10, and the plumbers and gas fitters somewhat later chose July 1. The lathers began working eight hours on May 6, 1867, and the boilermakers on August 10, 1867. As the year progressed an increasingly large number of trades obtained the shorter day, and as early as June 2, 1867, the *Morning Call* noted that "despite the existence of Eight-Hour Laws in other communities, the fact exists that the eight-hour system is more in vogue in this city than in any other part of the world, although there are no laws to enforce it."

Although the eight-hour agitation had been started partly because of the interest aroused among some carpenters by the published inaugural address of A. M. Kenaday, the carpenters did not make any united effort to obtain the shorter workday until January, 1867. But from that time until the close of the decade they were the leaders in the movement. On the evening of January 28, 1867, a large mass meeting of the craft was held in Temperance Legion Hall "for the purpose of making arrangements for the general adoption of the eight-hour system." Henry S. Loane, a local labor leader, prominent among the water-front unions, and Assemblyman Wilcox, familiarly known as "The Mariposa Black-

smith" and "The Workingman's Friend," were present and urged
the men to organize in order to get the shorter workday. The leader
who arose to conduct the agitation was A. M. Winn,[32] popularly
known as "General" Winn because he had previously been a briga-

A. M. WINN

dier general in the state militia of California. Winn, in his younger
days, had been a carpenter, and later a building contractor and
real estate dealer. He had retained a kindly interest in the welfare
of men who worked at his former trade, and he threw himself into
the campaign for the eight-hour day with an unselfishness and devotion that has seldom been equaled in the history of Labor in
California.

General Winn proposed that the assembled workers organize as "The Eight-Hour League, No. 1," but after some discussion it was voted to limit the membership to carpenters only, and to call the association "The House Carpenters' Eight-Hour League, No. 1."[33] B. C. Donnellan and Frank D. Morrell were chosen president and secretary, respectively. At a subsequent meeting a committee was appointed to select a date for the inauguration of the eight-hour day in the craft, and on March 11, 1867, a resolution was unanimously adopted specifying June 3.[34] Carpenters' Eight-Hour League, No. 2, was formed a month later among the carpenters of the Fourth District of San Francisco. The movement spread rapidly to other trades, and in May eight-hour leagues were organized among the gas fitters, the iron pipe workers, and the plumbers. Leagues were also formed among the workingmen of Oakland and Sacramento.

As June 3 approached, elaborate preparations were made by the house carpenters to celebrate the inauguration of the eight-hour day. A great procession was planned, to be participated in by only those crafts which had declared for, or were then working, eight hours a day. On June 3 more than 2,000 men marched through the streets of San Francisco, carrying flags and banners, accompanied by bands, military companies, and floats of various descriptions. The *Morning Call* of June 4 reported that Market Street was crowded with people "until that capacious avenue was so completely gorged that a passage along the sidewalks became a matter of almost impossibility." Position in line was determined according to the dates upon which the unions had adopted the eight-hour day. The ship and steamboat joiners led the procession, followed by the plasterers, bricklayers, Laborers' Protective Benevolent Association, stonecutters, lathers, riggers, gas fitters,[35] house carpenters, and house painters. After the procession had disbanded in Union Square, speeches to the assembled marchers were made by a Dr. Rowell, who was an anti-Chinese orator, C. C. Hickey, a stonecutter, and John Wilcox, the "Mariposa Blacksmith." The *Evening Bulletin*, commenting upon the demonstration, said that it

reflected great credit upon the workingmen of this city. The arrangements were carried out with a promptitude and regularity that is seldom witnessed in so great an undertaking; the procession was orderly and well conducted, and not a drunken man was seen in the ranks; in fact, a more respectably appearing body of men has seldom been seen in this city. There was nothing incendiary in the character of their speeches; no threats were indulged in, nor any efforts made to intimidate those who disagreed with them, but they evidenced a determination to achieve success by proper and legitimate means.

The shorter workday for the carpenters was thus introduced in a most favorable manner. Feeling that some of their fellow-craftsmen might be displaced by the new time schedule, the carpenters established a Committee of Relief to serve as both a relief committee and an employment bureau.

The proprietors of the planing mills held out for some time against the demands of their men, but finally were forced to capitulate. In order to guarantee "eight-hour material" to the workers in the building trades, the carpenters on August 3, 1867, organized a House Carpenters' Eight-Hour Protective Union and established a coöperative planing mill, which was successfully operated for several years.[36]

To further the interests of the eight-hour agitation and at the same time to prevent discrimination against men who had taken an active part in the movement, a secret, state-wide organization, the Industrial League, was formed in January, 1867.[37] All branches of the association in the northern part of the State were grouped into Industrial League, No. 1, while those in San Francisco and to the south were grouped into Industrial League, No. 2.[38] The objects of the association were veiled in secrecy. Passwords and signs were used and all the calls for meetings were signed with stars. Soon the newspapers began to comment upon this "powerful secret organization, ramifying through all the state,"[39] and to express fears that perhaps there was to be "another Know Nothing raid."[40] In a communication signed "Industrial League," presumably an official statement, the objects of the organization were set forth as follows:

The League was formed to unite the industrial classes into one body, extending throughout the Pacific Coast, having its divisions in the different cities and towns. Many joining are not represented by delegates but represent themselves in its councils. Its objects are not only to secure the passage and maintenance of the eight-hour law, but other reforms needed by the industrial classes, to elevate their condition, morally, socially, pecuniarily, to establish libraries, and procure suitable places for the mechanic and citizen to pass his leisure under the control of mechanics. Every branch of mechanical pursuit in San Francisco is represented in Division 2.[41]

These, without doubt, were the aims of the league, and it sought to obtain them primarily by political means.

In February, 1867, the Industrial League issued a call for a convention of workingmen to be held in San Francisco on March 29, for the purpose of "devising some plan for the promotion of the general welfare of the workingmen of San Francisco."[42] One hundred and forty delegates, representing about thirty trade unions and anti-coolie associations, were present at the first meeting. The objects of the association were stated to be the petitioning for an "eight-hour day, a practicable mechanics' lien law, opposition to Chinese immigration, and the founding of co-operative stores and manufactures."[43]

J. J. Ayers was elected president of the convention, and a Mr. Dickson, secretary. A committee, consisting of A. M. Kenaday, H. S. Loane, A. T. Enos, A. M. Gray, and J. W. Wilkerson, was appointed to draft resolutions and to present them at the next meeting. The composition of the committee courted trouble, for Loane and Kenaday had been at loggerheads since January, 1866, over matters that had arisen in connection with the agitation for the eight-hour law. At the next meeting of the convention, a majority report was presented containing the following preamble:

Whereas: After the lapse of more than a quarter of a century of passive indifference to their own rights and interests, the mechanics and workingmen of the United States have awakened to the necessity of uniting together for the enforcement of their own rights and the advancement of their own interests: and being convinced by sad experience that the professional office seekers of all parties have no interest or sympathy with the cause of the workingmen except to get their votes, they in self defense have been forced into the necessity of assuming control of their own affairs, and of relying upon themselves for success. For this purpose they have already organized associations in almost every branch of labor and have united the associations into state organizations, with a view of holding state and national conventions of workingmen in order to present their claims for reform to the public at large, and thus invest the cause of labor with a national importance: and inasmuch as the workingmen of this State are suffering under the same grievances and disabilities which our brethren of the Atlantic and Western States are seeking to remove, it becomes our duty in furtherance of our interests, to do all in our power to unite the workingmen of California in the bonds of fraternity so as to concentrate their influence and direct it in such manner as to insure a compliance with our just demands.

The resolutions which followed called for the enactment of a law for an eight-hour day, the passage of a more satisfactory mechanics' lien law, the prohibition of Chinese immigration, and the abolition of convict labor.

Kenaday introduced a minority report. This called for a state convention and the inclusion of the Settlers' and Miners' Association in the organization; asked for the appointment of a State Central Directory, embracing representatives from the Chamber of Commerce, the Mechanics' Institute, the Miners' Association, and the State Settlers' League; recommended that each trade association send a delegate to the Chicago convention of the National Labor Union; and concluded by demanding "the entire independence of this Convention from the Industrial League or any other secret organization."[44] After a long and acrimonious debate, the majority report was adopted.

At the adjourned meeting of the convention held on April 9, the Bricklayers' Protective Association withdrew its delegates. Accusations and personalities were again indulged in by Loane and Kenaday. Some time before the calling of the convention, Kenaday had been appointed state organizer in California for the National Labor Union, and had also been made one of its vice-presidents. Unable to overcome the manifest opposition, he decided to call a rival state convention of labor and reform associations for the purpose of carrying out the ideals of the National Labor Union, and did so on April 30, 1867. At the next meeting of the Workingmen's Convention he was expelled and labeled "an enemy of Labor." On June 22 Kenaday withdrew his call for a National Labor Union convention, and announced that "the necessity no longer existed for an independent State Convention of workingmen," because the desired ends had been secured by other means.[45]

Frequent meetings of the Workingmen's Convention were held in the next few months, and as time passed they grew more and more tempestuous. The question of Chinese immigration became increasingly prominent in all discussions, and caused the withdrawal of some of the unions; also the political machinations of the leaders were increasingly evident. The latter were eager to control the organization so as to use it to their advantage in the approaching election. The convention finally agreed that a Workingmen's ticket should be placed in the field in order to ensure the election of only those delegates to the county, Congressional, and State conventions, who were pledged to nominate candidates favorable to the demands of the workers. A list of delegates was selected by a committee, but when it was brought before the convention a bitter debate ensued. The *Morning Call* asserted that the convention had been sold out to the "Gorham ring" (Union Republicans), and described a scene on the convention floor as follows:

A member rises and says: "This is too nice a thing. I thought this was a Workingmen's Convention. I find that there are brokers, politicians, and Custom House officials being placed in nomination and endorsed."[46]

Protests were made that the nominees were not workingmen, and that the list of delegates was being "crammed down the throats" of the laboring class.[47] In the primary election which followed, the Workingmen's ticket was credited with victory, but the actual victors were the Gorham-Union Republican nominees.

On June 27 the Workingmen's Convention was called together to discuss an accusation that Assemblyman Wilcox, its candidate for the Congressional nomination, had "sold out." After much wrangling, the convention adjourned without having disposed of the matter. On July 11 it again assembled. The meeting was controlled by the Democrats, and amidst great uproar and confusion they expelled the president, J. J. Ayers, and voted to support the Democratic state ticket.

The Workingmen's Convention, the first assembly of the working class of California, had been called in the hope that something might be accomplished for the workers by means of non-partisan politics. Its failure was characteristic of many similar attempts subsequently made to unite politics and trade unionism in California. It was the means, however, of bringing the demands of the workers prominently before the people of the State, and in the subsequent Republican and Democratic conventions platforms were adopted pledging the enactment of the desired legislation. It was instrumental also in directing attention to the advisability of a closer unity among the labor organizations of the State, especially among those of San Francisco, and before many months passed this ideal was achieved.

In order to "protect Labor's interests" and to ensure that candidates favorable to its demands would be chosen at the polls, the workingmen of San Francisco in August, 1867, organized a Mechanics' Eight-Hour League. The league questioned candidates concerning their attitude toward the eight-hour day, the mechanics' lien law, and other matters, and instructed the workers to vote for only those whose answers were satisfactory. A majority of the legislators subsequently elected were thus pledged to vote for measures in which the workers were vitally interested.[48] The *Dispatch* of September 6, 1867, characterized the outcome as a victory for the workingmen "such as is unprecedented in political annals of this or any other state."

In the summer and fall months of 1867, a determined effort was made by employers along the water front to abolish the eight-hour day of the ship carpenters, ship joiners, shipwrights, and caulkers. On July 8 the Pacific Mail Steamship Company discharged all its employees who had been working eight hours per day, and a few days later the California, Oregon, and Mexican Steamship Company did likewise. On July 22 the *Alta California*, which had steadfastly opposed the eight-hour movement, said:

A large number of mechanics are employed in the city who labor ten hours and they are represented to be excellent workmen. . . . It would appear that the difficulty is not so great as anticipated in finding hands who are willing to adhere to the old system of ten hours.

This certainly seemed to be the attitude of a number of employers, who had formed a Ten-Hour Association on July 8. The association adopted resolutions pledging its members

to use all just and honorable measures to prevent the eight-hour labor system being adopted in this city as a day's work, knowing as we do that it is incompatible with the best interests and growth of the city. . . . We furthermore agree to employ no mechanics to work for less than ten hours as a day's work, or pro rata for the hour's work, and it is mutually agreed and understood that we will encourage all journeymen mechanics, who are willing to work at the above rates, and most decidedly discourage all those who are opposed to this system. By so doing we believe that we are working for the best interests of the journeymen mechanics themselves as well as for the best interests of the city and the state at large.[49]

The association then proceeded to form a "Ten-Hour League Society" for the purpose of uniting all mechanics

willing to work at the old rates, neither unjust to the laborers nor ruinous to the capital and enterprise of the city and state, together with all Master Builders and Master Workmen and Capitalists injured by the Eight-Hour rule.[50]

The society failed to arouse any interest among either employers or employees and soon disbanded.

The steamship companies, however, were determined to abolish the eight-hour day, and accordingly advertised in the eastern states for men to work nine hours for $5.50 per day. In order to counteract the results of these advertisements, the shipwrights met on August 27, 1867, and authorized the expenditure of about $400 for the purpose of denying the reports of the steamship companies. They also asked for a conference with other water-front unions; and delegates were subsequently appointed by the ship joiners, boilermakers, and ship caulkers. W. D. Delaney, a prominent member of the shipwrights' union, who had been authorized by his organization to call the conference, also sent a note to the House Carpenters' Eight-Hour League, No. 1, which appointed a delegation and also called a conference of representatives of the different eight-hour leagues for October 10. The necessity of united action on the part of the workers was apparent, inasmuch as a few days after the publication of the call for the conference twenty-three ship carpenters and nineteen caulkers, who had been imported by the steamship companies, arrived to replace the eight-hour men.

At the meeting on October 10, 1867, delegates were present from the shipwrights, ship joiners, ship caulkers, ship painters, house carpenters, stonecutters, plasterers, plumbers and gas fitters, house painters, and bricklayers, the twenty-four delegates representing approximately 2,120 trade unionists.[51] A. M. Winn was elected chairman of the conference, with W. D. Delaney, secretary. A committee was appointed to look into the difficulty which had arisen between the unions and the steamship companies and to attempt its solution. Apparently the trouble was adjusted, and the men returned to work on the eight-hour basis; but the employers later repudiated the terms of the settlement, and it was only by taking a cut in wages that the men were able to retain the shorter workday.

The opposition of the employers strongly impressed upon the trade unionists the necessity of organizing a labor federation, and when another conference was held, on November 6, 1867, such an organization was proposed by General Winn.[52] In fact, he had come to the meeting prepared with a constitution and by-laws, and these, when presented, were unanimously adopted. The name of the new federation was "The Mechanics' State Council." The following officers were elected: president, A. M. Winn; vice-presidents, H. S. Loane and C. C. Terrill; treasurer, A. M. Gray; secretary, W. D. Delaney.[53]

The time proved favorable for the formation of such a body. Within less than two weeks after the meeting of November 6, 1867, the Mechanics' State Council had a membership of 15 unions, representing about 4,000 workers. By June, 1868, this number had increased to 21 unions with about 6,000 members, and in 1870, at the height of its popularity, the council was composed of delegates from 23 unions, with about 11,000 members. The council did not limit its field of activities to San Francisco, but by means of "corresponding delegates"[54] and at times by personal representation, kept in touch with unions in Oakland, San Jose, Vallejo, and Sacramento. The influence of the council also spread to far-away Los Angeles, as is shown by an advertisement appearing in the *Weekly Los Angeles Republican* of July 18, 1868, notifying the employers of that city that for the

Carpenters, Bricklayers, Stone Masons, Plasterers and Painters of the Mechanics' League of Los Angeles ... eight hours of labor will constitute a legal day's work without reduction from present rates for all of the above mentioned trades ... from and after the 10th day of August, A.D. 1868.

During the concluding years of the decade, the Mechanics' State Council was active in all matters concerning the welfare of the workers. Through this agency they set forth their demands, enforced trades rules, and obtained remedial legislation. The *Dispatch* of May 22, 1868, declared:

The Council of this State is no doubt the best organized and most efficient body of representative mechanics in the United States. There was wisdom in its origin; the energy of its members has made a proud movement on the Pacific Coast, and their names will be found in an honorable page in the progressive history of the world.

How ungrateful is posterity! It is doubtful if there is any person now connected with the labor movement of California who has ever heard of the men active in the Mechanics' State Council or of any of the things accomplished by them or by the council itself.

The decline of the organization dates from August, 1870, when politicians tried to use its influence in organizing and supporting a Labor Party in the San Francisco municipal elections. Dissension at once arose within its ranks, and a few months of wrangling brought to an end its existence as a united and effective body. For several years thereafter it met only at the call of the president, usually once or twice a year, and finally disbanded at the time of the Kearney agitation of the later seventies.

The Mechanics' State Council was a non-political organization. Its leaders steadfastly held that politics and trade unionism could not satisfactorily be combined without the absorption and disruption of the latter. Indeed, it was because of this attitude that the council at first refused to affiliate with the National Labor Union, although it later joined that organization and was represented at the latter's national conventions in 1869, 1870, and 1871.[55] It always opposed active participation in politics by its constituent associations, yet did not hesitate to question candidates for office concerning their attitude on labor measures and to advise the workers to vote for only those who were favorable to the interests of Labor.

The primary object sought in organizing the Mechanics' State Council was to retain the eight-hour day, and in that cause it did its most effective work. It engaged actively in the formation of eight-hour leagues, and was so successful that in February, 1868, General Winn could announce that there were fifty eight-hour leagues in California, and that only one-half of them were in San Francisco. As the legislative session of 1867–1868 approached, the council appointed a committee to draft an acceptable bill for an eight-hour day, and a mechanics' lien bill, with the intention of having them presented to the legislature. The former was introduced in the Assembly by J. J. O'Malley and in the Senate by E. W. Roberts. Assemblyman Matthew Canavan looked after the interests of the mechanics' lien measure. Loane and Terrill were sent to Sacramento as agents of the council to lobby for the bills, and they met with but little opposition. Both measures were passed by the legislature and signed by the governor. A third measure, designed "to protect the wages of labor," was also enacted at that session through the efforts of Assemblyman T. E. Farish.[56]

In order to celebrate fittingly the passage of the eight-hour law, the trade unionists of San Francisco held a torchlight procession on the evening of February 22, 1868. They were joined by a delegation from Oakland composed of about 450 men from the Oakland House Carpenters' Eight-Hour League, No. 1, the plasterers, the bricklayers, and their apprentices. Position in line was determined by the dates on which the associations had obtained the shorter workday. The order of the procession was as follows: ship caulkers (December, 1865); shipwrights (December, 1865); ship joiners (January, 1866); ship painters (March, 1866); plasterers (August, 1866); bricklayers (February, 1867); Laborers' Protective Benevolent Association (February, 1867); stone masons (March, 1867); stonecutters and marble polishers (May, 1867); lathers (May, 1867); riggers (June, 1867); House Carpenters' Eight-Hour Leagues, No. 1 and No. 2, of San Francisco (June, 1867); wood turners (June, 1867); metal roofers (June, 1867); house painters (June, 1867); plumbers and gas fitters (July, 1867); and the machinists, ironworkers, brass finishers, and their apprentices, not then working eight hours.[57]

Shortly after its organization, the Mechanics' State Council established a Mechanics' Labor Exchange as an employment bureau for eight-hour men, and maintained it successfully for several years. In October, 1868, the Board of Supervisors of San Francisco voted for the use of the Labor Exchange an appropriation of $250 per month for one year, a similar amount having been given previously to the California Labor and Employment Exchange, an employers' labor bureau. The members of the council also proposed to erect a Mechanics' Hall or labor temple, and steps were taken to launch the venture, but the proposal was later abandoned when it was found impossible to secure the coöperation of a sufficient number of unions.

The Mechanics' State Council was successful in obtaining the passage of a city ordinance by the Board of Supervisors of San Francisco, establishing eight hours as the legal workday for all city employees. The ordinance also required "that all contracts for work given out by the Board [of Supervisors] should specify that employes shall labor only eight hours for a day's work."[58] For some time thereafter the council was active in having the law enforced.

The influence of the Mechanics' State Council was also felt in the national agitation for the eight-hour day. Petitions were circulated throughout the State, calling upon Congress to enact a Federal eight-hour law. Legislators at Sacramento were urged "not to vote for any person for Senator of the United States unless he was in favor of a National Eight-Hour Law," with the result, as the president of the council declared, that "our friend Eugene Casserly was elected."[59] In August, 1869, General Winn went to the Atlantic states, where for several months he assisted in the campaign for a Federal eight-hour law. While he was in Washington he presented to each Congressman a copy of the resolutions which had been adopted by the Mechanics' State Council, demanding that Congress "pass an eight-hour law that will positively require that the public works shall be done at eight hours for a day's work, making it a penal offence for its [the United States'] officers and contractors to evade its provisions."[60] His character and ability were recognized by the labor leaders of the eastern states, who later elected him chairman of the National Eight-Hour Executive Committee, composed of the presidents of state and national mechanics' organizations. This committee was not successful in its efforts to amend the Federal law.[61]

Shortly after the State eight-hour law had gone into effect, the laborers on public work demanded its enforcement. The bricklayers and hodcarriers employed in the erection of the Capitol building at Sacramento were the first to declare a strike for that purpose, and they were successful. A few days later the street workers in San Francisco struck for the shorter day on public work. The contractors refused to grant it, whereupon there followed "a display of clubs and threats of violence" by the workers directed against those who had taken their places.[62] An organization was effected among the strikers and an appeal for aid was made to the Mechanics' State Council. As has already been noted, the Board of Supervisors of San Francisco had passed on December 3, 1867, an ordinance declaring:

Eight hours' labor shall be the legal day's work for all mechanics and laborers in our employ, or that may be employed by persons doing work for the
city and county of San Francisco under direction or control of this Board,
and a stipulation to that effect shall be made a part of all contracts hereafter
let by this Board or any committee thereof.

The Mechanics' State Council insisted that the ordinance be enforced, and finally brought the matter to the attention of the City
Attorney; but the latter said, "The city is not a party to the contracts made by the Superintendent of Streets,"[63] and held that the
city therefore could not force contractors on public work to accept
the eight-hour day. Later, however, the Superintendent of Streets
stipulated in each contract for street improvements that contractors would not receive compensation for the work done if more
than eight hours a day were required of their employees. One of
the contracting firms, Drew & Carroll, sued for a writ of mandamus
to restrain the Superintendent of Streets from inserting such a
clause in the city contracts. Although the lower courts upheld the
practice, the State Supreme Court reversed the decision and ordered that the mandate be issued.[64] The court directed attention to
the fact that section 1 of the law enacted by the legislature in 1868
stated that eight hours was to be the legal workday "unless otherwise expressly stipulated between the parties concerned, and that
consequently it permitted a workday of more than eight hours
when such an agreement had been entered into by the employer
and his employes." This defect in the law was partly remedied in
1870 by an amendment which declared that no work on State buildings should be done under contract.[65]

In 1869 and 1870 a most determined effort was made by the employers of San Francisco to force their workingmen to return to
the ten-hour day. Some firms imported laborers to replace the
eight-hour workers. The advertisements and circulars of the California Labor and Employment Exchange, a bureau supported by
employers and organized chiefly for the purpose of obtaining cheap
labor, attracted a large number of immigrants to California.

The conclusion of the Civil War, together with an industrial depression, caused widespread unemployment in the eastern states,
and as a result many workers made their way to the Pacific Coast.
The completion of the Central Pacific railroad in 1869 threw out
of employment several thousand laborers, and they too drifted into

the San Francisco Bay region. The new rail connection made possible a greatly increased immigration from beyond the Rocky Mountains. The eight-hour day could not withstand the effects of such an overstocked labor market. The ardent activity of capable leaders, the holding of mass meetings, and the distribution of pledges among the workers could not offset the presence of men who wanted work and who were willing to work ten hours per day.[66] In the greater number of trades ten hours again became the normal workday, although in a few the workers maintained the eight-hour day until some years later.[67]

In August, 1870, the Mechanics' State Council, recognizing the difficulty of maintaining the eight-hour day in a single community, had adopted resolutions favoring a nation-wide demand for the introduction of the eight-hour day on a definite date; and the National Labor Congress, which was to meet in Cincinnati on August 15, 1870, was accordingly memorialized to name it. In June, 1872, under the direction of the untiring General Winn, the remnants of the Mechanics' State Council again attempted to revive the demand for the eight-hour day by organizing an "Eight-Hour League." By-laws and constitution were adopted, a pledge for members was formulated,[68] and several unions signified their approval of the plan, but nothing further resulted. Still undaunted and with faith in the efficacy of a national movement, General Winn again called the council together in August, 1875, and appealed to the Industrial Congress, which was to meet at Indianapolis in 1875, "to declare the Fourth of July, 1876, as the day for the national commencement of the eight-hour system of labor."[69] The convention of the Industrial Congress set the date as requested, but no effort was made to carry out the plan, either in the East or in California.

In the history of the eight-hour movement in California, the two men to whom most credit is due are A. M. Kenaday and A. M. Winn. Kenaday originated the movement for the shorter day, and Winn led it to temporary success. These two leaders gave freely of their time, energy, and funds, and labored unceasingly for the betterment of the conditions of the workers, the former because he was of the working class and was imbued with its ideals, the latter because he was an unselfish and interested friend of humanity.

Kenaday had suggested the eight-hour day and had taken a very prominent part in the early stages of the agitation, drafting resolutions, calling meetings, and lobbying for the first eight-hour bill before the legislature. Jealous and less capable leaders attacked him, and finally succeeded in putting him in a very unfavorable light before the workingmen of the State. He then severed his connection with the labor movement and devoted himself to furthering the interests of the Mexican War Veterans' Association, in the organization of which he had been instrumental.

General Winn was the head and heart of the Mechanics' State Council. It had been formed primarily at his suggestion, he had drafted its constitution and by-laws, and he served almost continuously as its president. The success of the eight-hour movement, as well as that of the working-class agitation in California in the later sixties and early seventies was more largely the result of his efforts than of those of any other man or group of men. He was genial, whole-souled, and sympathetic, comparatively wealthy, a fluent speaker, and an able organizer and executive. In 1867–1868 he was active in organizing eight-hour leagues and trade unions, and at his own expense journeyed to Sacramento and later to Washington to lobby for the enactment of eight-hour legislation. In January, 1873, he began the publication of a weekly labor journal, *The Shop and Senate,* which was also the organ of the Ecumenic Order of United Mechanics. It lacked support, however, and was discontinued in March, 1874. His labors on behalf of the working class have never been fully appreciated, either by the workers themselves or by their leaders. Today his name, as well as that of Kenaday, is unknown to the rank and file of Organized Labor in California.

Several strikes were declared in the closing years of the decade, but only a few are especially worth noting.[70] In the latter part of June, 1867, about 3,500 Chinese employed by the Central Pacific railroad on construction work near Cisco, struck for the twelve-hour day and $40 per month, an increase of $10. The company refused to grant their demands and threatened to import white laborers from the eastern states, whereupon the Chinese capitulated and returned to work. In February, 1867, the white boot- and shoemakers of San Francisco struck against a reduction in wages caused chiefly by the competition of Chinese laborers.[71] Violence and arrests followed in quick succession. The strike was lost and the Chinese continued at work, although it was necessary to give them police protection. In April, 1869, about five hundred boot- and shoemakers struck for an increase in wages. They had been receiving from $20 to $28 per week. A lodge of the Knights of St. Crispin, a national organization of the members of that craft, had been formed in San Francisco some months earlier, and this strike was the first to be conducted under its direction. The strikers were defeated. During the next two or three years the Crispins were active in opposing the employment of Chinese in the boot and shoe industry.[72] At that time (1869), there were six boot and shoe factories in San Francisco, employing about six hundred men and women, of whom the greater number were members of the Crispin lodges. The boot and shoe manufacturers had had a serious struggle for existence because of the competition of eastern factories and the high rates of wages demanded by the California workers. Chinese laborers had early been employed in the trade, and as years passed and as new demands were made upon the employers by the white workers, the Orientals were hired in increasing numbers. Opposition to their employment naturally became more bitter and determined.

The boot and shoe manufacturers of California also had to contend against the establishment of small, coöperative shops by groups of skilled workers.[73] The work was so subdivided that the industry lent itself readily to the coöperative plan, and at different times in the later sixties and early seventies coöperative shops were started with lively interest by the workers, only to succumb after a short existence because of dissension within the organizations or because of a slight depression in business. The employers could not guard against the formation of such companies; they could not know at what moment their most skilled workmen would leave their employ and engage in business for themselves. Under such circumstances it was not possible for them to undertake large contracts, or to build extensive factories and equip them with up-to-date machinery, or to buy supplies in large quantities. Employment of Chinese seemed the only solution to the problem. The Orientals were reliable, docile, and conscientious laborers, and although ac-

knowledged to be slower workers than the whites, they were not
given to striking or to the formation of coöperative enterprises.
They were also willing to accept lower wages and less satisfactory
conditions of employment. Before the close of the sixties the agitation against them had grown to threatening proportions, and in
the later seventies it came to a most startling climax.[74]

Notices of closed-shop agreements and strikes for the closed shop
first appear in the San Francisco press in the sixties. In December,
1863, the Journeymen Painters' Union obtained a closed-shop
agreement from their employers, and in March, 1864, struck because of its violation.[75] In October, 1867, the Metal Roofers' Protective Union,[76] and in December, 1867, the Plasterers' Union publicly announced that their members would not be permitted to
work with non-union men. In May, 1868, a strike was called by the
plasterers for the purpose of enforcing the closed shop. Similar
working rules were adopted by the carpenters' eight-hour leagues
of San Francisco and Oakland and by a number of other unions in
1868, and strikes were frequently called and members were expelled because of a violation of that principle.

The earliest occurrence of the use of a walking delegate in San
Francisco is found late in the sixties; it was the duty of the secretary of the Carpenters' Eight-Hour League to go about the city and
inspect each job in order to make sure that only union men of that
craft were being employed. In this decade, also, the first labor
papers appear. Reference has already been made to Kenaday's
Journal of Trades and Workingmen, and to Winn's *Shop and
Senate.* In January, 1867, W. F. Russell began the publication of
The Industrial Magazine in the interests of the working class. It
was a substantial journal of customary magazine shape and size,
but was mild in tone, colorless in content, and made no appeal to
the workers. It was abandoned after the appearance of the third
monthly issue.[77]

The period from 1860 to 1870 was remarkable in many ways. It
was one of the most prosperous decades in the history of California.
Industry was much more settled and less speculative than it had
been in preceding years, owing chiefly to the establishment of tele-
graphic connection with the eastern states. Workers were in
great demand, labor difficulties were relatively unimportant, and

wages for the most part were fairly high, although not so high as in the years immediately following the discovery of gold or in the later fifties. Virtually all trades were organized, city and state central bodies were formed, and connections were made with the national labor movement.[78] The first material progress in the enactment of labor legislation was shown by the adoption of an eight-hour law and a more satisfactory mechanics' lien law. The eight-hour day was in general effect during the latter part of the decade, although it was subsequently replaced by the ten-hour day. The agitation against the Chinese became intensified, and, for the first time in the history of the State, the two chief political parties pledged themselves to enact legislation which would protect Californians from Mongolian competition.

CHAPTER V

DEPRESSION, 1870–1877

WITH THE DEVELOPMENT of industrial, agricultural, and commercial interests following the inrush of gold seekers, the citizens of California began to look with eager expectancy and hope to the day when a group of daring men, possessed of courageous faith in the future, would lay the rails that would join the West with the plains of the Mississippi Valley. The completion of a transcontinental railroad would ensure cheaper and quicker transportation of goods and products, shorten the long, tedious, and dangerous journey across the plains or by sea and the Isthmus of Panama, and provide better military protection for the western coast. General Fremont, it may be recalled, is quoted as having declared, as the agent of the Federal government, that his expedition to California in 1845–1846 was for the purpose of finding the "shortest route for a future railroad to the Pacific, and especially to the neighborhood of San Francisco Bay."[1]

Seldom has the accomplishment of any single undertaking so generally concerned the people of all sections of the United States as did the construction of the Central Pacific and Union Pacific railroads. California, as well as the cities and counties through which the rails of the Central Pacific were to be laid, contributed lavishly. Bonds were purchased, taxes were levied, and lands were freely given to encourage and assist the project.

As the day of its completion approached, that part of the State through which the railroad passed was filled with an eagerness of expectancy such as California had never before experienced. Men in all branches of business awaited with lively interest the driving of the last spike. New industries were established, extensive improvements were undertaken, and a new era of unbounded prosperity appeared to be dawning for California. Land values especially were greatly inflated. Large tracts of farm land were bought and subdivided in the expectation that sales could easily be made at greatly increased prices to the immigrants who would undoubtedly arrive in the near future. For miles in every direction around San Francisco Bay, the land was laid off in lots and town sites. Speculators doubled, trebled, and quadrupled the past growth of the city in their calculations, and then discounted the result, confident that there would still remain a margin.[2]

In May, 1869, the task was completed by the junction of the two railroads at Promontory Point, Utah. The great day had arrived; but the results were far different from those that had been visioned. As early as 1868 a steady stream of immigrants from the eastern communities had begun to flow into California, far surpassing in volume that of any year since the halcyon days of the fifties. Many of the newcomers had been attracted by the highly colored accounts of prosperity and plenty which had been broadcast by the California Labor and Employment Exchange and by the Immigrant Aid Association with a view to obtaining an oversupply of laborers so that the wages of labor might be reduced and the eight-hour day eliminated. In 1868–1869, the actual gain in California's population was more than 50,000. Many arrived penniless, and the small local industries could not absorb the increased labor supply. Unlike the pioneers, these immigrants could not go into placer mining, because the placers had for the most part been worked out. Relatively few knew anything about California farming methods, which differed greatly from those of eastern communities. They lacked money with which to buy land. The city seemed to be their only salvation, and into San Francisco they flocked in ever increasing numbers. The seriousness of the situation was increased by the discharge of thousands of unskilled laborers who had been employed on the construction of the Central Pacific railroad;[3] these also, for the most part, drifted back to San Francisco. The regulations of trade unions and of eight-hour leagues could not withstand the pressure of unemployment; high wages and the shorter workday were perforce temporarily relinquished.

The completion of the transcontinental railroad likewise resulted disastrously, at least for the time being, for persons who had invested their capital in the industrial and mercantile enterprises of California. After the discovery of gold, all commerce entering the State had come to San Francisco by water, and all exports also had passed through the hands of her merchants; trade and profits were theirs without exertion or effort. It could not well have been otherwise. "Nevada, Oregon, Washington Territory, Idaho, Montana, and Utah all bowed down to San Francisco as the great center of Commerce." The completion of the railroad, however, wrought a revolution. Almost before its construction had begun, the merchants and manufacturers of Chicago realized the vast possibilities that would be open to them, and with customary energy and foresight they planned to make the most of the situation. As the Union Pacific railroad was pushed farther and farther into the West, their agents followed in its wake, winning trade and customers. When "the junction was made at Promontory Point . . . Chicago was there represented by her agents, while San Francisco, down by the sea, was reading accounts of the event."[4] In a short time many inland merchants were ordering their goods from eastern houses, instead of from San Francisco firms. The eastern manufacturers and wholesalers, moreover, were not content with the trade of Idaho, Montana, Utah, and Nevada. The *Evening Bulletin* of April 6, 1870, protested:

The merchants of Chicago and other Atlantic cities acted as though new gold mines of fabulous wealth had been opened up to them on this coast by the laying of the iron tracks across the continent, and as if the people were actually starving for supplies. Hence drummers were sent on by scores and hundreds, soliciting orders from a pair of shoe-strings to a well stocked variety store. They canvassed the coast thoroughly, not forgetting the smallest retail establishment, even accosting private individuals at the mines, on the farms, in the workshops, and on the street; and as a reward for their perseverance, for the unusual inducements offered, and also for the sake of the novelty of the transaction, they secured a considerable number of orders, and subsequently forwarded a large quantity of goods in response to such orders and for speculative account.

California markets, which were already well stocked, became oversupplied with goods, and business stagnation resulted. Locally the high rates of wages and the high cost of raw materials made impossible any effort at successful competition. California merchants temporarily lost control of their markets.

Several other factors conspired to bring about a period of business uncertainty and depression.[5] The yield of the gold mines had declined steadily after 1865. A deficiency in the rainfall of 1869–1871 materially affected the agricultural interests, especially in the southern counties, and diminished the demand for farm laborers.[6] The value of both urban and rural land depreciated greatly,[7] exports decreased rapidly, money became tight, and prices fell.

Samuel Bowles, writing in the Springfield (Mass.) *Republican* under date of February 12, 1870, summarized the situation in the following words:

> The year (1869–70) has indeed been a hard one with them [the people of California]. All of the great interests of the State are depressed. Several thousand laborers are reported idle in San Francisco alone, and 50,000 to 100,000 in the State. Her great machine shops are nearly all still; building has ceased; real estate and rents are falling; the eight-hour leagues have crumbled to ash; and the manufacturers are either closing their shops altogether, or are successfully forcing their workmen to accept lower wages.... To some extent the whole civilized world is sharing her experience of business depression and trial; but in the main, this is her own special affliction. It is the revolutionary stage in her social and business life, the struggle into conformity with the modes and morals and money of the nation of which she forms a part. For twenty years she has been living, as it were, apart, isolated, and building up a magnificent provincialism. Her nature was original, her resources original, and her modes of doing business took on original laws as all her life took on original habits. Speculation was the groundwork of all her wealth and all her growth; uncertainty and irregularity were the laws of her prosperity. High prices and vast profits, a grand and reckless way of business and of life pervaded all her society and her movements.... At first the people seemed stunned with the revelation and the revolution. They cursed the railroad, they cursed the Bank of California, and they cursed the Chinese, one and all, as parents of their disappointment.

California was undergoing a rapid transition in her commercial and industrial life; business uncertainty, unemployment, and destitution accompanied it. The *Evening Bulletin* of January 12, 1870, said:

> The particular point we have in view is the lamentable lack of employment for laborers, which is so crying an evil of the day.... There are those who estimate the proportion of laborers in California who are out of work, to the rest of the population, as high as twenty per cent, or one-fifth of the entire mass of inhabitants. We think this too high an estimate. It may be true of our large cities, and of some portions of our mining districts this winter, but not of the entire population of the state.[8]

Even the State legislature realized that the situation had become critical and that some effort should be made to assist the unemployed. Many relief measures were introduced, but only a few were passed.[9] One of the more important bills adopted authorized the supervisors of San Francisco to expend not more than $50,000 in grading and otherwise improving Yerba Buena park.[10] On March 22, 1870, when the work was to be started, there was a stampede of more than 1,000 men seeking employment. Only 115 were hired. This naturally created much dissatisfaction among those who could not share in the work. The crowd, clamoring for jobs, increased each day, and before the close of the week more than 2,000 men gathered daily at the park. At first, when they were told that nothing could be done for them, they marched to the mayor's office, only to hear the same statement repeated. There were several of these demonstrations, and some well attended mass meetings; and finally, at a mass meeting held on March 31, 1870, the men, under the leadership of J. J. Goodman, Michael Foley, and Ed Champion, formed the San Francisco Workingmen's Society for the announced purpose of self-aid. The organization survived for about a month, but accomplished nothing except the publication of resolutions and the calling of mass meetings.

In the early months of this period of stagnation, in fact down to the close of March, 1870, scant mention had been made of the presence of the Chinese. Toward the close of April, however, the agitation of the unemployed took on a strongly anti-Chinese aspect. This was caused in part by an announcement of the Southern Pacific railroad that it intended to use Chinese labor on its projected construction work, and in part by the arrival of 1,300 Chinese at a time when economic conditions were most unsatisfactory. Committees of the unemployed went from shop to shop, demanding the discharge of the Orientals, but without effect. Boycotts were levied on firms which employed Chinese in any capacity. The agitation was subsequently taken up by the Knights of St. Crispin[11] and the Mechanics' State Council. It was pushed vigorously during July, August, and September, 1870, but without material results.[12]

Because of the exceptionally dry winter season, which seriously interfered with agricultural and mining operations, the depression continued through the greater part of 1871.[13] The annual output of the mines declined to $20,000,000, considerably less than for any previous year. Conditions were somewhat relieved, however, by a noticeable decrease in the number of people entering the State and a decided increase in the number departing. Many, thoroughly discouraged with the state of affairs in California, returned to eastern communities. Rebuilding operations following disastrous fires in Chicago and Virginia City, Nevada, drew away some of the unemployed workers. An abundant rainfall in the winter and spring of 1871–1872 and a revival in the prices of mining stocks aided in bringing about a brief period of business activity. The tone of the press of the time was exceedingly hopeful. The people of California looked forward expectantly to a return of prosperity.[14]

Their hopes, however, were not to be realized. Business was still being conducted on too speculative a basis, although not to the same degree as formerly. Speculation in mining stocks was especially prevalent. Millions of dollars had been sunk in the securities of the Crown Point and Belcher mines on the Comstock lode, and in those of the Raymond and Ely mines at Pioche, Nevada. These mines had given promise of unparalleled ore yield. The extent of the speculation is shown by the fact that from January to May, 1872, the total value of silver-mining stocks for sale in the San Francisco market had increased from $17,000,000 to $81,000,000.[15] Accompanying this marked inflation of values was the recapitalization of many of the mining companies and the floating of additional amounts of securities. The *Evening Bulletin* of May 3, 1872, published a list of eleven mining corporations with a total of 85,440 shares representing a par value of $19,598,000, which was to be increased to 547,610 shares representing a par value of $74,000,000. The excitement in the local stock market was without precedent. Prices reached dizzy heights. "Yet it is noteworthy that only four of the one hundred and fifty claims offered to the public through the Stock Boards" were paying dividends at the time.[16] Such a state of affairs could not long continue, and on May 8, 1872, the market broke. In one week security values declined more than $48,834,000, and before three weeks had passed the shrinkage amounted to more than $61,000,000.[17] Millionaires were unmade in a day; business was at a standstill; thousands of men were unemployed. As the months passed, the tone of the business world gradually improved. By August, business was again fairly active, although the results of the depression persisted until 1874.

From 1870 to 1872, trade unions played an unimportant part in the affairs of the local industrial world.[18] A large number of labor organizations had been disrupted because of the pressure of the unemployed and because of attacks upon the eight-hour day by employers. The organizations which survived were chiefly interested in the agitation against the Chinese. The San Francisco newspapers reported seventeen unions present at an anti-Chinese mass meeting, held on the evening of July 8, 1870, which had been called by the Knights of St. Crispin. Further evidence of their activity in this respect will be presented in Chapter VI.

As already noted, dissension arose within the ranks of the Mechanics' State Council in 1870; its decline may be said to date from that year. Its members made several ineffectual attempts to revive the eight-hour day. Thereafter it met only once or twice a year until 1878, when it finally passed out of existence.

Although Kenaday in 1867 had not been able to organize a branch of the National Labor Union in California, in 1871 success attended the efforts of W. D. Delaney, who had gone to the national convention of that organization in 1870 as a delegate from the Mechanics' State Council. It appears that at least fourteen locals of the National Labor Union were formed in California, since mention is found of Local No. 14, organized January 20, 1872, although it is doubtful if there were fourteen locals in existence at any one time. All the local branches were short-lived; they held meetings for the discussion of public questions, but took no action. In September, 1871, the various locals united to send a petition to the State legislature and to the President and Senate of the United States, praying for relief from the encroachments of the Chinese. In January, 1872, the organization held a state convention in San Francisco, adopted a platform, and announced that it intended to enter the political arena as a representative of the working class.[19] The results, however, were dissension and subsequent disruption because of attempts by politicians to control the organization. Its end was hastened by the fact that the national organization passed out of existence in the same year as a consequence of its having entered politics in association with the Patrons of Husbandry.[20]

From 1871 to 1872 several labor papers were started in San Francisco. On July 24, 1871, C. C. Merrill began the publication of

The Daily Plebeian, a five-column paper which sold for only 10 cents per week. At the same time, *The Industrial Reformer* was being issued by the Industrial Reformers, an anti-Chinese association. Both papers survived for a short time only. In 1871–1872, *The South San Francisco Enterprise* was issued as a workingman's paper. In 1872 it merged with *The Coöperator,* but was forced to suspend after a brief existence. In the latter part of 1869, *The Workingmen's Journal,* a weekly publication, had entered the field as a champion of the rights of Labor. It later became *The People's Journal,* and, in 1871, *The Evening Journal.* After these changes it was not, strictly speaking, a labor paper, although it was strongly pro-labor in its views. It ceased publication after a brief struggle.

Comparatively few strikes occurred in San Francisco from 1870 to 1872, owing undoubtedly to the lack of employment.[21] Reductions in wages were made in virtually all crafts. In February, 1870, a serious state-wide strike occurred among the printers. In the fall of 1869 their employers had complained that "the recent opening of the overland railroad brings the offices of this city into direct competition with those of the East, where work can be done at much lower wages." They therefore asked their employees to consent to a reduction in wages, the proposed scale being 50 cents per 1,000 ems for day work and 60 cents per 1,000 ems for night work, with $24 per week for compositors hired by the day. Under the existing scale, the printers had been receiving from $40 to $54 per week, but under the proposed schedule it was estimated that they could earn but from $25 to $35 per week. A strike resulted. The employers made preparations to import compositors from the eastern cities, whereupon the printers acknowledged defeat and returned to work. Similar reductions were made at Marysville, Sacramento, Stockton, and Virginia City, Nevada. Some months later, a secret organization was formed among the printers. As a result of the activity of its members in the councils of the Typographical Union, the latter on August 1 demanded the restoration of the former wage scale. Strange to say, this demand was granted by a majority of the newspapers; but not by the *Evening Bulletin* and the *Morning Call,* both of San Francisco. A strike against these two lasted several weeks, but the printers were again defeated, and returned to work at the reduced rates. The failure of the San Francisco strike caused reductions to be made elsewhere, and subsequently brought about the dissolution of some of the typographical unions in the State.[22]

A serious strike occurred among the Amador County miners in June and July, 1871. In July, 1870, the miners had organized a Laborers' Association to protect "white labor, to maintain its dignity, to secure a fair compensation therefor, and to discourage the competition of inferior races."[23] Its members were mostly Austrians and Italians, with a few Irishmen who naturally assumed the rôle of leadership. In June, 1871, the organization, with a membership of 500 men, struck for a ten-hour day and the following schedule of wages: first hands and engineers, not less than $3 per day; second hands, not less than $2.50 per day. The miners threatened violence to persons who should attempt to take their places. Pumps were stopped and the mines flooded, entailing a loss of from $125,000 to $200,000. The situation became so serious that the governor visited the scene of conflict, and subsequently called out the State militia.[24] A few miners went to work under the protection of the soldiers. After being out for a month and a half, the strikers obtained a compromise agreement which gave to all underground workers $2.50 to $3 per day, although the men employed above ground were to be paid as formerly.

During the years 1873 and 1874 the commercial and industrial life of California was active in spite of a serious depression in the eastern states. California, consistently refusing to accept the greenbacks, had remained on a gold basis. This, together with its virtual isolation from the rest of the nation and its almost complete independence of eastern markets for the sale of its products, kept it free from the immediate consequences of the panic of 1873.[25] Market conditions, however, were slightly unsettled, because of the business uncertainty prevailing throughout the nation. For the most part, both Labor and Capital in California found remunerative employment. Large crops were ensured by an abundant rainfall. Several unimportant strikes occurred, but in general the local labor situation was very quiet.[26]

Toward the close of 1874, mining stocks fluctuated widely and in October of that year they depreciated more than $20,000,000 within a few days. The market steadied itself for several months, but with the continued decline in ore production and in dividends, another severe panic in mining stocks occurred in January and February, 1875.[27] The decline in stock values of two mines, the Mexican and the Ophir, amounted to about $24,000,000. Many speculators were ruined. The stock market failed to recover as quickly as in former years, and it seemed that California was destined to suffer another period of financial embarrassment. An insufficient and unseasonable rainfall, together with an unusually cold winter and frequent frosts, seriously damaged the crops and caused considerable loss to the farmers.

In August, 1875, another mining-stock panic occurred. In three weeks (August 5 to August 26) the values of securities listed on the San Francisco exchanges declined more than $60,000,000. The Bank of California, in San Francisco, a bank which had dominated the financial world of the Pacific Coast, closed its doors on August 26; and its failure was at once followed by the temporary suspension of two other banks and by the closing of the stock exchanges.[28] The crisis had been precipitated by the savings banks, which had permitted a large share of their ready funds to pass into the hands of a group of speculators who intended to purchase the capital stock of the Spring Valley Water Company. It was planned to sell that company to the City of San Francisco at an estimated profit of approximately $8,000,000. Six weeks later fire destroyed a large part of Virginia City, Nevada, causing a loss of more than $5,000,000, the greater part of which fell upon residents of San Francisco.[29]

The serious situation was aggravated by the unceasing stream of immigration into California. Eastern communities were still suffering from the depression of 1873; and many Kansas and Nebraska farmers had been ruined by the grasshopper plague. Reports of fairly prosperous conditions in California had turned the attention of the people to the land beyond the Sierra. In the period 1873–1875, a larger number of immigrants (154,300) arrived from the East than had come in the eleven years prior to 1867.[30] At least 25 per cent of the newcomers were factory hands, incompetent for work in orchards, fields, and lumber camps.[31] Whatever their vocation, they tended to gravitate to the city. When the harvesting season closed, farm hands were discharged, and they also drifted to San Francisco, either to search for work or to spend their summer's earnings. During the winter months, widespread destitution prevailed among the city's poor, and thousands were supported by charity.[32] Complete stagnation of business was temporarily postponed by a slight revival in financial circles. On October 2, 1875, the Bank of California reopened its doors. Two days later the Bank of Nevada was established. The local stock exchanges resumed operations on October 5. With the onset of a very wet winter, the hopes of the business leaders were buoyed up by prospects of an abundant yield from both agriculture and mining.

Notwithstanding a steady decline in the value of real estate[33] and the occurrence of several stock flurries, 1876 proved a fairly prosperous year in California, especially for the farmers, who harvested a record wheat crop. Labor on the farms and in the mines was in fair demand during the summer and early fall months.

No important developments took place in trade union circles in San Francisco in the years 1874–1876.[34] On September 4, 1876, the first California council of the Sovereigns of Industry was established in San Francisco. It was a national labor body similar to the National Labor Union. A few months later a second council was organized in the same city; in January, 1877, one was formed in Oakland. At no time did the Sovereigns attain a position of any importance among the workers of the Pacific Coast. The prevailing uncertainty of employment discouraged widespread interest in trade union affairs.

As the rainy season of 1876–1877 ended, unmistakable signs of an approaching business crisis were clearly evident. The rainfall had been the lightest in twenty-five years—considerably less than one-half the normal amount.[35] The drought was felt most severely by the agriculturist in the San Joaquin Valley and in the southern counties, where up to that time irrigation had been little developed. The yield of the placer mines was greatly decreased by the dry season. The decision of the Texas and Pacific railroad not to extend its line west of the Rocky Mountains affected adversely the financial interests of the State, especially those of the southern counties. The Centennial Exposition at Philadelphia in the preceding year had diverted a large number of tourists from California, thus greatly diminishing the income of many Californians. Real estate values continued to decline.

The crisis was not reached, however, until January, 1877, when announcement was made that the Consolidated Virginia Mines of the Comstock lode would not pay the customary monthly dividend of $1,000,000.[36] For some months the prices of mining stocks had been declining, but it was the passing of the monthly dividend by the Consolidated Virginia that created a panic on the local stock exchanges; the value of the Consolidated Virginia securities alone declined from $80,000,000 to $10,000,000. In "three months there had been a shrinkage of $140,000,000 in the market value of the two leading mines, nearly all of whose shares were owned in San Francisco." Two years earlier, advantage had been taken of some discoveries on the Comstock to boom stock prices; great excitement had prevailed; people in all walks of life had purchased shares in the various mining ventures. When the crash came, thousands lost the sums, large or small, which they had invested in the hope of receiving huge returns.[37] The depreciation represented a loss amounting to $1,000 for every white adult in San Francisco.[38] Although "a large majority had never owned any of these shares, all were affected indirectly, if not directly, by the decline." Business houses failed, banks and mines closed, agriculture suffered for want of rain and capital, and California faced its most serious industrial and financial depression up to that time.

Thousands of men tramped the city streets and the country roads in search of work. The number of unemployed customarily found in San Francisco during the winter months was greatly increased by the many thousands who could find no jobs in the mines or forests or on the farms.[39]

At times the crowds that gathered at places of possible employment were so great that the police had to be called to clear the thoroughfare. From all parts of the State came complaints of an increasing number of tramps, who, as one paper said, were "a specimen of humanity . . . new to the Pacific Coast."[40]

As the months passed, the outlook became more hopeless; destitution and misery increased on all sides. More than 4,000 applications for relief were made at the office of the San Francisco Benevolent Association in April, May, and June, 1877. In July the society issued a statement saying that the calls for aid were more numerous than at any time since its organization in 1865.[41]

The attitude of the unemployed became one of increasing discontent accompanied by surly threats of violence. Crimes of all kinds increased in number. Crowds of desperate men gathered on the street corners, on empty lots, and elsewhere, eager for excitement and willing to follow blindly and to the end any leader who might promise relief. All that was needed to unleash the pent-up wrath of the mob was a palpable excuse and a leader whom it might follow; both were not long in appearing. The leader was an uneducated Irish drayman, Dennis Kearney; the excuse was the Chinese. Kearney, through his radical utterances and threats to stop at nothing, completely captured the imagination of the unemployed and won their support. The Chinese, the workers protested, had brought low wages, unemployment, and hunger to the white laborers of California. Against them the fury of the mob was relentlessly directed. Mass meetings, processions, riots, violence, and bloodshed followed in quick succession; thousands of men throughout the State organized to follow Kearney. Shouting the slogan, "The Chinese must go," they made preparations to drive the Mongolians from the Pacific Coast.

CHAPTER VI

THE CHINESE IN CALIFORNIA

No other issue has played so prominent a part in the crowded history of the California labor movement as has Oriental immigration. From the earliest years agitation directed against the immigrants from the Far East has been almost incessant, and frequently violent. At first it was the Chinese against whom anti-coolie clubs, ordinances, laws, the boycott, and other forms of attack were used in rapid succession. When Congress finally excluded the Chinese, the farmers and employers of California found satisfactory substitutes in the Japanese. In time, however, the organized and unorganized white workers just as relentlessly opposed Japanese immigration. In later years, objections have been raised to the Hindus, Koreans, and Filipinos, but this latest phase of the agitation has never assumed proportions of any consequence because these people have never been present in large enough numbers to constitute a serious menace.

The subject of the Chinese in California merits a much more extended treatment than is accorded to it here; but other writers have so fully and ably discussed its various phases that the following brief sketch of the agitation against the Mongolians is restricted to the pertinent effects of that agitation upon the labor movement of the State.[1]

Chinese immigration dates properly from the discovery of gold in California. A few Chinese had arrived earlier, but the news of untold riches along the river bottoms and in the mountains of California soon reached China and brought more than 10,000 of her inhabitants to the United States before 1852. In 1852, 20,026 arrived; in 1853 the number decreased to 4,270, but in 1854 it rose to 16,084. From that date until and including 1868 (the year the Burlingame treaty was signed by the United States and China), the number of Chinese immigrants totaled 65,763.[2]

As has been noted in preceding pages, the Chinese first went into the placer mines, where they worked the poorer, and frequently the abandoned, claims. Their earnings varied greatly, but were usually below those of miners of other nationalities because of the slowness with which they worked and the crudeness of the methods which they employed. They early aroused the antagonism of the whites, not because of their numbers, but because of the anti-for-eigner feeling then existing in the mining regions. Frequently they were prevented from working in or near the mining camps of the whites, and at times they were forcibly, even brutally, driven from their claims. Their habits of living and working, as well as their physical appearance and dress, marked them as objects of attack. The fact that they were without political influence also tended to encourage the abuses to which they were subjected. Driven from the mines because of the opposition of the whites and because of the exaction of the oppressive foreign miner's tax, many of them drifted into farming and gardening, others engaged in the laundry business, while still others obtained employment as unskilled labor-ers, domestics, and cooks. A scarcity of labor had previously existed in all these occupations, and the entrance of the Chinese greatly assisted in meeting the demands of the times.

As years passed, however, and as their numbers increased, they were not content to remain in the menial and unskilled occupa-tions, but moved gradually into the skilled trades.[3] This naturally brought them actively in competition with white labor in an in-creasingly large number of occupations. In 1869 Henry George thus described the situation:

In the construction of the San Jose Railroad in 1860, it was discovered that they were cheap and effective road builders; the Mission and Pioneer Woolen Mills found that they made first class operatives, and now they are rapidly ob-taining employment wherever patient manual labor, without any great amount of brain work, is requisite. Large numbers are engaged as servants in families, hotels, etc., taking the places of girls in chamber work and cooking, in which they become very expert.... In fact, the Chinese are rapidly monopolizing employment in all the lighter branches of industry allotted to women, such as running sewing machines, making paper boxes and bags, binding shoes, label-ling and packing medicines, etc.... They are not only used in grading rail-roads and in opening roads, cutting wood, picking fruit, tending stock, weav-ing cloth, and running sewing machines, but are acting as firemen upon steam-ers, running stationary engines, painting carriages, upholstering furniture, making boots, shoes, clothing, cigars, tin, and wooden ware.

Stand, say at Clay and Sansome Streets, San Francisco, about six in the afternoon, and you will see long lines of Chinamen coming from American workshops. Pass up Jackson, Pacific, or Dupont Street, into their quarter, and you may see them at work on their own account. Besides the stall where the Chinese butcher carves his varnished hog, or makes mince meat of stewed fowl, you will see Chinamen running sewing machines, rolling cigars, working up tin with the latest Yankee appliances. In front of the store window, in which great clumsy paper clogs and glistering anklets are displayed, and through which you may watch the bookkeeper casting up his accounts on an abacus, and entering them with a brush from right to left in his ledger, the Chinese cobbler sits half-soleing and "heel tapping" "Melican" boots. Underneath the Buddhist Temple a disciple of Confucius mends the time pieces of the American Watch Company and repairs Waltham watches. In the Mail Steamship Company's office, a Chinese clerk will answer your questions in the best of English. And in one of the principal drug-stores of Sacramento, a Chinaman will put up a prescription for you, or if your tastes run in that way, in a saloon nearby a Chinaman will concoct a mint-julep or whiskey cocktail; while wherever you go, in hotel or boarding house, it is more than probable that hands better used to the chop stick than the fork prepared the food you eat, let it be called by what high sounding French phrase it may.[4]

There was scarcely a trade in which they did not engage.

They were to be found in lumber, paper, and powder mills, tanneries, rope-walks, lead-works, tin-shops, and factories for jute, oakum, sack, bag, bleaching, soap, and candles. Some were employed as cabinet-makers and carvers, others as brick-makers, ... and in condensing salt from the sea. At Isleton ... they worked in a beet root sugar refinery. At Marysville, a number of broom and sack makers employed them. ... They also assisted in making curled hair and coir for upholsterers.[5]

They were employed in the manufacture of slop clothing, boots, shoes, slippers, underwear, and overalls. It is not surprising, therefore, that opposition on the part of the Californians developed at an early date.

It was alleged that Chinese competition reduced wages, and thus, by lowering the plane of living, hindered the immigration of workingmen from the eastern states. It was also protested that they were filthy and loathsome in their habits and ways of living, and vile in their customs; that they spread the use of opium, the evils of gambling, and the practice and diseases of prostitution; and that socially they were in every way undesirable as workers and as residents of the country. They did not and would not assimilate.[6] They worked and lived apart, were secretive in their actions, and

ultra-conservative in their point of view. Consequently, they remained a distinct group, completely cut off from the life of other
races about them. They were looked upon as "coolies," as slaves of
the Six Companies[7] or of some Chinese "boss" upon whom they
were dependent either wholly or in part.

Their friends, and these were few, stoutly declared that opposition to the Chinese was based solely on race prejudice and unsound
arguments. Their supporters made the following assertions: The
Chinese supplied the need for a vast number of unskilled and
easily managed laborers to build roads, canals, levees, and railways, to develop the resources of the State, and to plant, care for,
and harvest the grain and fruit crops of the large ranches. Without their assistance that work could not be satisfactorily done.
In the cities they worked only at those trades and occupations
which were objectionable and repugnant to white laborers, and
consequently their employment had no effect upon the wages or
working conditions of the latter.[8]

It was not long before the antagonism of the whites took form
in various legislative enactments, working-class agitations, and the
formation of anti-coolie clubs. Many writers allege that there was
no prejudice or hostility to the Chinese in the early days, that they
"were welcomed as a unique addition to the society and a valuable
ally in the development of the material resources of their new
home." This is true, but misleading. The Chinese were warmly ap-
plauded when they appeared in gorgeous and grotesque costumes
in public processions in San Francisco in 1850 and 1852. Throughout the State, however, and especially in the mines, the people were
bitterly hostile. Even a hasty perusal of the press of the time will
disclose this attitude. It was plainly in evidence as early as 1852,
when a bill was introduced into the State legislature proposing to
make enforceable all contracts for labor made in a foreign country;[9] the intent was to permit contracts to be drawn for ten years
or less and for any amount greater than $50 per year. By that
means, it was hoped, there would be obtained a sufficient supply
of labor, especially Chinese, with which to develop the resources of
the State. The bill was passed by the Assembly, but action in the
Senate was postponed indefinitely.[10] The measure had been vigorously opposed by the people, who held mass meetings and adopted

resolutions demanding its defeat.[11] The alarming influx of Chinese immigrants in that year (1852) had brought home to the people the necessity of restrictive legislation.[12] From that date until the abrogation of the Burlingame treaty in 1880 and the subsequent enactment of Federal Chinese exclusion acts, the people attempted by various means to prohibit their immigration.

The opposition first bore fruit in the passage of a law imposing the foreign miner's tax by means of which the Americans hoped to drive the Mongolians and other foreigners from the mines. This tax, and the results of its enforcement have already been described (pp. 17–18). On April 28, 1860, the State legislature imposed an occupational tax of $4 per month on all Chinese fishermen.[13] This statute was repealed on April 4, 1864.[14] On May 13, 1854, the legislature petitioned Congress to permit California to levy a head tax on all Asiatic immigrants, to be paid by the owners of the vessels in which they were brought into the country.[15] By an act of April 28, 1855, a tax of $50 per person was placed on all immigrants entering by way of water who could not become citizens of the United States, the tax to be paid by the owner, master, or consignee of the vessel.[16] In 1857, however, the State Supreme Court declared that law to be unconstitutional.[17] On April 26, 1858, another act was passed, prohibiting the Chinese from entering the State or from landing at any port thereof, unless driven ashore by stress of weather or by unavoidable accident.[18] On April 26, 1862, the so-called "Police Tax" law was passed, whereby all Mongolians eighteen or more years of age, unless they had already paid the foreign miner's tax, and unless they were engaged in the production of sugar, rice, coffee, or tea, were required to pay a monthly capitation tax of $2.50.[19] The State Supreme Court declared these two statutes also to be unconstitutional.[20]

Greater success attended the efforts of the people to exclude the testimony of Chinese in the courts, either for or against white persons. A statute adopted on April 16, 1850, excluded the testimony of Negroes and Indians.[21] In 1854 the State Supreme Court interpreted its provisions as also excluding the testimony of the Chinese.[22] The law of March 16, 1863, removed the ban from the Negroes,[23] but it was retained for the Chinese and the Indians until 1872.[24]

In the cities the opposition to the Chinese did not become organized until 1859. Before that date, the Chinese had been drifting gradually into the cigarmaking trade. Sooner or later, of course, the antagonism of the white workers was bound to be aroused. A protective association composed of white proprietors and their journeymen had been in existence for some time, but it had been formed solely for trade purposes. When, in September, 1859, it was discovered that several of the employers were hiring Chinese cigarmakers, they were expelled by the association and a boycott was levied on their products.[25] The campaign against the employment of Chinese cigarmakers continued for some weeks, and finally culminated in a rousing mass meeting held on the evening of November 1, 1859, at which the People's Protective Union was launched. The objects of the organization were declared to be as follows:

We, the undersigned citizens of California, in answer to the appeal for protection of a body of citizens representing the cigar manufacturing business, recognizing the justice of the claim of Free Labor when protected in all its actual rights from ruinous competition with the systematized and enslaved Chinese labor that is now encroaching and forcing itself into our general industrial pursuits, tending to destroy the true basis of our country's prosperity, and to bring want and suffering into the homes of our people; solemnly impressed with the gravity of the subject and its consequences, and feeling it to be the first duty of all good citizens to exercise their power for general safety in this cause, do in all sincerity, as expressive of our firm convictions and as evidence of our irrevocable determination,

RESOLVE, That the security and prosperity of our industrial classes is first in importance, and ever should be the constant care of all good citizens.

That competition between enslaved labor of Coolies and that of our own people in our own fields of industry will prove destructive to the general welfare, and retard the advancement of civilization and the manifest destiny of our country, and that as this people are wanting in the natural status of essential qualities for voice in forming our laws, they are socially, morally, and politically detrimental and inimical to the healthy tone of our body politic.

That we shall ever combat and resist, with all the legitimate means, the introduction of Chinese into pursuits of our people; that we will condemn, discountenance, and view as enemies of our general interest, all persons who shall employ, encourage, or assist the Chinese to engage in any of those occupations, as attempting, either through design, cupidity or ignorance, to inflict a deadly injury on our dearest rights.

That it is ever the effect of a prosperous condition of our industrial classes to increase the general welfare of our country, and that all theories as to cheap labor through an unassimilative and enslaved human element, are false in experience, conflicting with the true sources of our country's greatness, and but the special and fallacious pleading of selfishness and anti-republicanism.

That we do now and will ever stand ready to co-operate with all persons who seek to maintain the rights of free labor, and that we will by counsel and means, and in all legitimate and constitutional rights, encourage and aid them in procuring legitimate measures (or others) to free our state from the evils or the cooly system, in which good work, we earnestly ask the support of our fellow citizens.

Lastly, that to maintain the foregoing, we pledge our sacred honors as true citizens and our good faith as servants of God.[26]

On November 17, 1859, the People's Protective Union adopted the following resolution, which marks the beginning of the practice of publicly boycotting Chinese-made goods:

RESOLVED, That every member of the People's Protective Union will hereafter wherever he finds Chinese employed, refuse to patronize such employers; and further that the People's Protective Union recommends every friend of white labor throughout the State to pursue a similar course.[27]

Other meetings were subsequently held, several employers were induced to discharge their Chinese help, and the political conventions which met in San Francisco were prevailed upon to adopt anti-Chinese resolutions, but otherwise the People's Protective Union failed to accomplish anything of note. By 1862 the employment of the Chinese in the cigarmaking trade had become an accepted practice. Four years later, approximately 1,800 of the 2,000 persons thus employed were Chinese. By 1870 the number of Chinese cigarmakers had increased to 2,800. Later many of them set up in business for themselves; as early as 1866 it was said that they comprised at least one-half of the total number of proprietors of cigar factories in San Francisco.[28]

Opposition to the Mongolians steadily mounted. It was further intensified in February, 1867, by a riot directed against their employment in grading a certain piece of property in San Francisco.[29] The arrest, conviction, and sentencing of eleven men to eighteen months' imprisonment for participation in that disturbance aroused the white workers to a high pitch of excitement. The local press vigorously protested against the heavy penalty meted out to the rioters. On the evening of February 20, 1867, a mass meeting was held and an organization formed, one person being selected from each ward to establish anti-coolie clubs in San Francisco. The association voted to oppose any office seeker who would not ally himself with the anti-coolie forces, and pledged its members to cease giving custom to any employer of Chinese labor. A still larger mass meeting followed on March 6, as a result of the activity of the ward organizers. Speeches were made, anti-Chinese resolutions were adopted, and a formal organization with constitution and by-laws was effected under the name of "The Pacific Coast Anti-Coolie Association." Within a comparatively short time, branches were established in each of the twelve wards of the city as well as in other parts of the State. Many of the delegates to the Workingmen's Convention, which met in San Francisco on March 29, 1867,[30] were members of these anti-coolie clubs, and the convention voiced their unalterable opposition to the immigration of the Mongolians.

On May 13, 1867, a state convention of anti-Chinese clubs was held in San Francisco. Delegates were present from Butte, Lake, Placer, and San Francisco counties. The customary fiery speeches were made and the customary resolutions were adopted, but otherwise nothing was accomplished.

In 1868, China and the United States formally ratified the terms of the Burlingame treaty in spite of the bitter opposition of the citizens of California. The treaties of 1844 and 1858 had opened some of the Chinese ports to American merchants and had secured for them certain privileges of trade and commerce; the Chinese government had also agreed to accord protection to the property and lives of American citizens. Neither treaty, however, contained any provision relating to the rights and privileges of Chinese citizens residing in or trading with the United States. Consequently, when the Burlingame treaty was drafted, China insisted upon and obtained for her citizens "the same privileges, immunities, and exemptions in respect to travel or residence as may be . . . enjoyed by the citizens or subjects of the most favored nation." The right of citizens of the United States in China, or of those of China in the United States, to become naturalized, was not granted by the treaty. Scarcely a year passed following its ratification before efforts, unsuccessful at the time, were made in Congress to limit the privileges which it conferred upon the Chinese.[31] As was to be expected, the Californians were incensed at the action of the Federal government in agreeing to the terms of a document which gave them no protection against the Chinese menace. Throughout the next twelve years they carried on an unceasing and vigorous campaign for abrogation.

In spite of the fact that virtually all State legislation directed against the Mongolians had been declared unconstitutional, the California legislature continued its search for some means of freeing the people from the abuses arising out of the presence of the Chinese. On March 18, 1870, it imposed a penalty of not less than $1,000 on any person who should bring an Asiatic into the State without first presenting evidence of his good character.[32] This act, although intended to prohibit the importation of lewd women, was declared unconstitutional by the Federal courts after it had been sustained by the State courts.[33] In 1872 and again in 1874 the legislature petitioned the California delegation at Washington to have the Burlingame treaty amended in order that the State might be permitted to enact laws designed to bring relief from the results of Chinese immigration. On April 31, 1876, and on March 25, 1878, the legislature passed laws forbidding the employment of Mongolians in the construction of certain irrigation and reclamation projects.[34] On April 3, 1876, it empowered the Board of Supervisors of San Francisco to expend a sum of money, not to exceed $5,000, to send a delegation to Washington for the purpose of securing the abrogation of the Burlingame treaty.[35] On the same day, the State Senate appointed an investigating commission empowered to make recommendations concerning the best methods of solving the Chinese question. The report of the commission, published in 1878, strongly recommended complete exclusion.[36]

In San Francisco, several unique ordinances were passed in an effort to cope with this increasingly serious problem. One of them prohibited any person from walking on the sidewalks while carrying baskets suspended from a pole resting across the shoulders.[37] This measure was directed solely, of course, against the Chinese, for they alone delivered vegetables, laundry, and merchandise in the manner described. The State Supreme Court, in an oral decision by Judge McKinstry, upheld the ordinance on the ground that it attempted to remove a practice which was a nuisance and an obstruction dangerous to public safety.[38] Another ordinance was known as the "Cubic Air" ordinance. The Chinese customarily slept "sardine-like" in crowded, filthy quarters. In order to prevent such unhealthful crowding the Board of Supervisors on July 25, 1870, issued an order forbidding any person to hire or let rooms for sleeping purposes in which there was less than 500 cubic feet of air per person. Both lodger and landlord were to be punished for its violation. In September, 1873, however, the County Court declared the ordinance void.[39] In 1876 the State legislature enacted practically the same measure, by requiring 500 cubic feet of air per person for sleeping quarters. For the violation of this act landlords were to be fined not less than $50 nor more than $500, or to be subject to both fine and imprisonment, while lodgers were to be fined not less than $10 nor more than $50, or to be subject to both fine and imprisonment.[40]

On May 26, 1873, two other anti-Chinese measures were brought before the San Francisco Board of Supervisors. They were known as the "Queue" and the "Laundry" ordinances. Many of the Chinese, when arrested by the San Francisco police and found guilty by the local courts, had refused to pay their fines, preferring instead to serve their sentences in the county jail. This proved costly to the community. After some discussion an ordinance was adopted requiring the sheriff to cut to the length of one inch the hair of all persons committed to his care. To a white person the regulation meant merely a free haircut, but to a Chinese it meant the loss of his queue, and consequent disgrace in the eyes of his countrymen. The "Laundry" ordinance, which was an amendment to a previous order, decreed that the keeper of a laundry, if using one horse for delivery purposes, should pay a tax of $2 per quarter; if using two horses, $4 per quarter; and if using more than two horses, $15 per quarter; but if no horses were used, he was required to pay a tax of $15 per quarter. Here again was an ordinance directed solely against the Chinese.[41] These two measures were passed by the supervisors, but were vetoed by the mayor. An attempt was made to pass them over his veto, but a sufficient number of votes could be obtained for the "Laundry" ordinance only. The following year it was declared unconstitutional by the County Court, in the case of *People v. Soon Kung.* Nevertheless, the supervisors on March 13, 1876, again passed the same type of "Laundry" ordinance, and on

May 2, 1876, it was declared unreasonable, oppressive, and void by the District Court.

Numerous arrests followed the enactment and enforcement of the State "Cubic Air" law, and because of the crowded conditions of the city jail, arising from the refusal of the Chinese to pay their fines, the Board of Supervisors of San Francisco again passed the "Queue" ordinance. It was signed by the mayor on June 14, 1876. The Chinese contested the ordinance in the courts, and on July 7, 1879, it was declared unconstitutional on the ground that it was special legislation.[42]

In 1869, the presence in San Francisco of thousands of Chinese, many of them recently discharged by the Central Pacific railroad,[43] coupled with the conditions resulting from the business depression, aroused the antagonism of the unemployed. The opposition, fostered and encouraged by members of the Knights of St. Crispin (boot- and shoemakers), who had suffered severely from the competition of the Chinese, found its culminating expression in a large parade and mass meeting on the evening of July 8, 1870. The usual speeches were made and resolutions adopted calling for the exclusion of the Chinese. A second meeting, held on July 15, was attended by more than 10,000 persons. After much discussion, an association known as "The Anti-Chinese Convention of the State of California" was organized by representatives of the trade unions and anti-coolie clubs who were present.[44] A number of subsequent meetings were held at which plans were formulated for a vigorous campaign against the Chinese. At a meeting on the night of August 10, 1870, a very bitter argument arose over the advisability of using the convention as a nucleus of a new political party which should be of and for the workingmen of California. The debate continued through several sessions. Finally, on August 24, it was decided by a vote of 30 to 23 to call a state convention in May, 1871, for the purpose of nominating a state ticket. Representatives of thirteen associations at once withdrew, but their withdrawal did not prevent the nomination of a complete ticket for the ensuing city election (1870). Without exception, the candidates were selected from those who had already been announced by the Taxpayers', Republican, and Democratic parties; and, if one can believe the newspapers of the time, the selections were made with very little judgment, or none at all. Though about three-fourths of the candidates whose names appeared upon the convention's ticket were elected, the results were not looked upon as constituting a victory for the convention or for the workingmen of the city.

About the same time, a vigorous anti-Chinese association, the Industrial Reformers, became active. It was formed on February 22, 1870,[45] and within a year was said to have enrolled about 10,000 members.[46] Its objects were to obtain the abrogation of the Burlingame treaty and "totally to exclude the Chinese from all branches of the trades by refusing to patronize those who employ them."[47] The association was non-partisan, but hoped to attain its ends through the assistance of the dominant political parties. With this in view, it held a state convention in February, 1871, which decided to send a committee of conference to the Democratic and Republican state conventions in an effort to have both those parties insert an anti-Chinese plank in their platforms. In this the association was successful, although no direct results followed.

In 1872 the anti-coolie clubs subsided, only to be revived in 1873. This revival, as well as the agitation in the succeeding years, reflected a changed attitude of the employers toward the Chinese. Prior to 1873 the fight had been waged, for the most part, by the workingmen. The disastrous consequences of Chinese competition had fallen upon them. Through strikes, boycotts, legislation, and various other measures, they had attempted to better their condition, and had met with little or no success. But, as the years passed, the employers also began to feel the effects of Chinese competition. As long as the Chinese were willing to work under the conditions and for the wages set by the white employers who had taught them their respective trades, the employers were satisfied. But when the Chinese began to establish their own shops, to hire their countrymen, and to enter into direct competition with their former employers and instructors, it was a different story. To attempt to meet their prices was useless. As one newspaper said:

A Chinese manufacturer has many advantages over an American in the employment of Chinese labor. In the first place, they employ for at least half the wages, and then they get twice the amount of work out of them. Hence, they can at any time undersell the American proprietor. In fact, in the boot and shoe trade, the white manufacturers are obliged to purchase the cheap grade of boots and shoes from the Chinese manufacturers. So that the nemesis of cheap labor is now affecting the white employer as well as the white mechanic and laborer.[48]

Another source of irritation for the white employers was that the Chinese learned to use the strike as a means of exacting higher wages and improved conditions of employment. Thus threatened, Capital began in the seventies to ally itself with Labor in the struggle against the Chinese. Thenceforth, real progress began to be made in the contest to exclude the Chinese from the United States.

On March 11, 1873, the Workingmen's Alliance of the Pacific Coast, a local organization with a high-sounding name, was formed at Sacramento. It accomplished nothing, and passed quickly from the field. A few months later the People's Protective Alliance was organized in San Francisco for the purpose of uniting into one central body all the anti-coolie associations of the State. Within a short time it had established branches in Alameda, Sacramento, San Francisco, and San Jose; also in Oregon. Under its guidance a state convention was held in San Francisco in November, 1873, with no important result. The People's Protective Alliance, together with the local branch of the National Labor Union, took an active part in obtaining signatures to a huge anti-Chinese petition, which was forwarded to Congress and to the President of the United States.

The agitation continued unchecked during the next few years. Mass meetings and conventions were held; speeches were made and resolutions were adopted; societies and associations were organized and dissolved in such rapid succession that many pages would be required even to enumerate them; pamphlets and circulars by the thousands were printed and distributed—all without any noticeable effect upon the immigration of the Chinese, who poured into the country in greater numbers than before. In 1876, at the very time when economic and financial conditions in California were at their worst, more than 22,000 entered the United States.[49] Thousands of white laborers were out of work and had been unemployed for months. They could see but one cause of their condition: the competition of Chinese labor. With that thought uppermost in their minds, and led by Dennis Kearney, their discontent broke forth in a short reign of violence and anarchy, from the effects of which the State did not quickly recover.

In the United States, Chinese immigration concerned chiefly the State and people of California. They had tried by various means to cope with the problem, but after 1868 their efforts were set at naught by the terms of the Burlingame treaty. Clearly, the solution must come through further Federal action. Unceasing propaganda ultimately had its effect. In 1876 both of the national political parties inserted anti-Chinese planks in their platforms; in the same year Congress appointed a commission to investigate conditions in California; in 1877 the commission submitted a voluminous report recommending that immediate action be taken to restrict Chinese immigration;[50] and in 1879 a bill was passed by both houses of Congress, limiting the number of Chinese immigrants to fifteen per vessel. Although this was only a short step toward total prohibition, it was warmly approved by citizens of the Pacific Coast. Great pressure was brought to bear upon President Hayes to sign the bill,[51] but on March 1, 1879, he sent a vigorous message to Congress vetoing the measure as a partial abrogation of the Burlingame treaty. The citizens of California were enraged at the action of the President and denounced it in no uncertain terms. On September 3, 1879, a state-wide vote on the advisability of complete exclusion recorded the almost unanimously favorable decision of 154,638 citizens for exclusion and 883 against it.

The Federal government, apparently realizing that it could no longer withstand the popular demand, appointed a commission to visit China for the purpose of drafting a new treaty. The outcome was the treaty of November 17, 1880 (proclaimed on October 5, 1881), in which, among other things, it was provided that the United States should have the power to regulate, limit, or suspend, but not absolutely to prohibit, the immigration or residence of Chinese laborers.[52] The immediate effect was a greatly increased number of immigrants from China. In the next two years, 1881–1882, more than 51,400 Chinese entered the United States, fearful lest the gates should be forever closed to them. On May 6, 1882, by an act of Congress, immigration from China was formally suspended for a period of ten years,[53] and on May 5, 1892, the period of exclusion was extended for another ten years.[54] The treaty itself was amended on March 17, 1894 (proclaimed on December 8, 1894), and gave to the United States increased powers to control Chinese immigration.[55] On April 29, 1902, Congress extended indefinitely all laws relating to Chinese exclusion.[56] The campaign against Chinese immigration had finally been won.

CHAPTER VII

"THE CHINESE MUST GO"[1]

ONE OF THE MOST INTERESTING PHASES of the history of the
labor movement in California is the sand-lot agitation
against the Chinese, which began in 1877. Led by a drayman, Dennis Kearney, who was a modern Jack Cade of violent and
intemperate utterances but at heart a coward, the laborers of the
State in a comparatively short time formed a political party,
elected mayors, assemblymen, and senators, took an active and
prominent part in the drafting and adoption of a new State Constitution, frightened employers into granting their demands, and,
last but not least, forced the Federal government to negotiate a
new treaty with China and to enact a Chinese exclusion law.

For some years conditions in California had so shaped themselves that a violent demonstration by the workers was virtually
inevitable. Yet it is doubtful whether the subsequent developments
would have assumed such alarming proportions and destructive
temper had not certain events in the eastern states given the needed
impetus just at the critical moment. News of the great railroad
strike of 1877 and of the labor riots in Pittsburgh[2] aroused a lively
interest among the workers of California. Since meetings had been
held elsewhere for the purpose of adopting resolutions supporting
the cause of the strikers, it was proposed by some of the labor leaders that a similar gathering be held in San Francisco. At that time
there was no central city or state labor council in California; the
Mechanics' State Council had degenerated into a mere "resoluting"
body, meeting but once or twice a year at the call of its president;
the Knights of Labor had not yet appeared on the Pacific Coast; the
only persons in a position to make the necessary arrangements were
the local officers of the Workingmen's Party of the United States,
two sections of which had been organized in San Francisco, and one
in Sacramento. This organization had absorbed many of the members of the Marxian International Workingmen's Association after

the latter had disbanded at Philadelphia in 1876.[3] Several branches of the International Workingmen's Association had been organized among the French, German, and English residents of San Francisco. With the passing of the parent body, the local associations had affiliated with the Workingmen's Party of the United States; and it was the local central committee of the latter that called a mass meeting on the sand-lots in front of the City Hall[4] for the evening of July 23, 1877.[5]

The attitude of the unemployed of California toward the constituted authorities, and especially toward Capital, was none too cordial. The masses seemed ready, and only awaiting an excuse, to let loose their discontent and pillage the city. To many readers this statement may seem an exaggeration, yet a careful perusal of the current press, and interviews with many persons who were either interested spectators or active participants in the agitation, justify the conclusion. The bitterness of the laborers had been further increased by the announcement of a reduction in the wages of railway employees. This reduction was subsequently rescinded, however, because of the hostile demonstration which it called forth.

On the day of the meeting called by the Workingmen's Party of the United States, several men were arrested for parading the streets with banners advertising its time and place. This show of authority by the police led to the circulation of a rumor that a riot was being planned by the mob with the object of burning the docks of the Pacific Mail Steamship Company and then pillaging Chinatown.[6] The alarmed public officials held "the entire police force,—regulars, specials, and substitutes,—in readiness to act in any emergency. The militia was also given orders"[7] to hold itself ready to move at a moment's notice. It was only after solemnly promising that no threats of violence or incendiary language would be indulged in that the leaders of the Workingmen's Party of the United States were allowed to go on with the meeting.

At least eight thousand persons assembled on the sand-lots that evening. The gathering was quiet, orderly, and good natured. The only serious disturbance was caused by an intoxicated man, who without provocation fired three shots into the crowd from a near-by window. He was at once arrested and hurried away before the crowd could lay hands on him.[8]

The meeting was addressed by James d'Arcy, organizer of the Workingmen's Party of the United States, Dr. J. H. Swain, Mrs. Laura Hendricks, and others. Their remarks dealt solely with the Labor question and with the eastern railway strike; no mention was made of the Chinese. Resolutions were adopted, expressing sympathy for the strikers, attacking the evils of watered stock, opposing the granting of franchises and land and money subsidies to private parties, deprecating the encroachment of Capital on the rights and privileges of the people, and demanding immediate action by the State and Federal governments to bring about the desired reforms.

Before the meeting was over, an anti-coolie club with band and transparencies pushed its way into the crowd and insisted that the speakers say something about the Chinese. A declaration that the audience had assembled for another purpose was met with cheers and jeers. A gang of hoodlums had gathered on the outskirts of the crowd, intent upon creating a disturbance; and shortly after nine o'clock one of them knocked down a passing Chinese. He was arrested but was rescued by his companions. Someone shouted, "On to Chinatown," and upon this suggestion a hooting, excited crowd rushed up a near-by street and demolished a Chinese laundry with a fusillade of rocks and brickbats. Dispersed by the police, the mob again assembled farther up the street and wrecked another Chinese laundry. A liquor store was looted, after which the hoodlums continued their depredations. At one place an overturned lamp set fire to the building. When the firemen appeared, the mob cut the hose and otherwise interfered with the work of extinguishing the flames. Before the night was over a score of Chinese laundries had been wrecked, a plumbing shop, which had been mistaken for a Chinese laundry, had been demolished, and the Chinese Methodist Mission had been stoned. San Francisco had never had such a serious disturbance. The police, after strenuous effort, dispersed the mob, but not before it had destroyed property valued at about $20,000.

The city was tense with excitement. The hoodlums and the unemployed had gathered confidence from the night's escapades, and it was difficult to surmise to what lengths they would go. The merchants and propertied classes, becoming apprehensive of probable results, called a meeting of the "law and order" citizens the next day and organized a Committee of Safety, with W. T. Coleman, a leading merchant, at its head. Coleman was well fitted for the position because he had been chairman of the Vigilance Committee of 1856. He at once issued a call for volunteers, and thousands responded.[9] Many, it is said, were hoodlums who joined in the hope of being able to riot and pillage under the cloak of the organization. In response to an appeal for funds, more than $58,000 was subscribed. Committees gathered up the available arms and ammunition in the gunshops of the city. Within forty-eight hours after the first night of rioting, the United States authorities had agreed to supply rifles, carbines, and ammunition to the Committee of Safety; the gunboats "Pensacola," "Lackawanna," and "Monterey" had been ordered to give all possible assistance in protecting the city from the mob, and San Francisco had ready an organized force of 252 policemen, 1,200 militiamen, and about 4,000 members of the Committee of Safety, in addition to Federal troops at the Presidio and sailors and marines on gunboats lying off shore.[10]

The Committee of Safety thought it inadvisable to equip its members with firearms, so an uncommon and effective substitute was adopted. Six thousand hickory pick-handles, to be attached to the wrist with a leather thong, were purchased and distributed among the volunteers. The men were divided into companies, drilled, and assigned to duty in localities where it was thought that rioting might occur.

The outlook in Oakland also appeared threatening, and similar preparations were made by citizens of that community. Funds were collected, and about a thousand men were enlisted in a "pick-handle brigade."

On the next evening, a thousand hoodlums and unemployed gathered in front of the United States Mint in San Francisco. The police attempted to disperse the crowd, but did not succeed until a part of it had marched up Mission Street threatening to burn the Mission Woolen Mills, which had regularly employed a large number of Chinese laborers. The factory was strongly guarded, however, by the militia, so that the crowd was forced to content itself with demolishing some Chinese laundries near by.

On the third evening (July 25), after a day of unrest and excitement, the rumor was again spread that the Pacific Mail docks were to be burned. A large detachment of police and "pick-handle men" was sent to protect them. When the mob arrived and discovered that it had been outwitted it set fire to a neighboring lumber yard, and then gathered on a near-by hill from which it showered rocks upon those who fought the flames. It also cut the hose and in other ways interfered with the efforts of the men who sought to extinguish the blaze. The mob was charged repeatedly by police and "pick-handle men," and shots were exchanged, but it was only after a most persistent attack upon the rioters that they were scattered. Four men were killed, fourteen were wounded, and $80,000 worth of property was destroyed. Smaller riots and fires occurred in other parts of the city, but they were quickly brought under control by the authorities.

An anti-Chinese mass meeting on the sand-lots had been announced for that evening. About six hundred persons were present and were addressed by N. P. Brock, Daniel Spelman, and Dr. C. W. Moore. Brock, in a speech that was extremely inflammatory, said that he favored exterminating the employers of the Chinese and blowing up the vessels of the Pacific Mail Steamship Company. He also expressed a willingness to lead his audience to Chinatown. Another evening of rioting followed; several Chinese laundries were demolished before the police succeeded in dispersing the crowd.

The public authorities had given orders to "shoot down any person caught in the act of demolishing property or interfering to prevent the extinguishment of fires."[11] It was undoubtedly this early expressed determination to quell the disturbance that made possible the effective handling of the situation.

The Committee of Safety through its "pick-handle brigade" so thoroughly broke the reign of hoodlumism that on July 28 the governor of the State telegraphed to the Secretary of the Navy that the danger had passed, and thanked him for assistance given. The "pick-handle brigade" quietly disbanded, and the money not expended was returned to the subscribers in pro rata amounts.[12]

At first, frightened by the outbreak, many employers hastened to discharge their Chinese laborers and hire white men, but within a short time they discharged the white workingmen and again hired the Chinese.

The feeling of unrest and discontent persisted among the workers. The methods used by the Committee of Safety to quell the disturbance had seemingly increased the bitterness of the situation, for the unemployed now felt that they were opposed by a united propertied class. The strong class feeling thus produced soon showed itself in various ways and on many occasions.

Among the members of the "pick-handle brigade" was an Irish drayman, Dennis Kearney. He has been described as "below medium height, compactly built, with a broad head, slight moustache, quick but lowering blue eyes, and of nervous temperament."[13] Born in 1847 in the County of Cork, Ireland, he sailed the seas for some years and then settled in California in 1868. He was temperate in his habits, and was reputed to be a radical opponent of drink and tobacco. Crude in his ideas, and with little schooling, he had gathered considerable information from newspapers, public meetings, political clubs, and similar sources. He had regularly attended the Sunday meetings of the Lyceum for Self-Culture, and had taken part in the open discussions of that organization, although its members considered him a persistent buffoon inflated with an exaggerated idea of his own importance, and greeted with laughter and derision his appearance on the floor. His remarks were always directed against the shiftlessness and extravagance of the working class, and in favor of employers and the Chinese. He was never too modest to refrain from referring to his own prosperous condition, which he asserted was the result of close application to business.

Kearney aspired to enter politics. He was discerning enough to realize that under the prevailing conditions a Labor Party would have far better chances to succeed than any other, so he made application for admission into the Workingmen's Party of the United States, an organization that was beginning to enlist the support of workingmen, not only in San Francisco, but also throughout the country. Its leaders in San Francisco, aware of Kearney's contempt for the working class, rejected his application. He then declared that he would form a party of his own, and in August, 1877, he called together a few followers and organized the Workingmen's Trade and Labor Union of San Francisco, with J. G. Day as president, J. J. Hickey as treasurer, and himself as secretary.[14] Kearney knew that in order to gain the support of the workers he would have to reverse his position on the Labor question. Accordingly, at the meeting at which the new party was organized, he made a speech which the press characterized as "forcible in lan-

DENNIS KEARNEY

guage and rather incendiary in sentiment." He was quoted as saying that "all other parties are breeders of thieving broadcloth and enemies of the workingmen."[15]

The Workingmen's Trade and Labor Union of San Francisco held but one subsequent meeting, at which the executive committee was authorized to nominate a ticket. The committee merely made a selection from among the names of candidates announced by the other parties. In the ensuing election the organization was not heard of; it printed and distributed no tickets, and cast no votes.[16] It was only a "piece party." There were no less than fifteen such groups concerned in the San Francisco elections of that year, and all had been formed solely for the purpose of extracting contributions from candidates for office.[17] The Workingmen's Trade and Labor Union is said to have collected from $600 to $1,000 from various candidates, but none of this money found its way into the hands of the party's treasurer.[18] A quarrel between Day, Hickey, and Kearney over the division of the spoils disrupted the organization, which was the first to be formed by Kearney for the purpose of furthering his political aspirations.

The Workingmen's Party of the United States nominated a ticket, but cast only a few votes at the election. It continued to hold Sunday meetings on the sand-lots, at which its speakers discussed Socialism, Labor, and allied topics.

Kearney, from his brief experience in politics, realized that a splendid opportunity awaited someone to become the recognized leader of the unemployed and discontented masses. His attitude and public utterances became more violent and intemperate, and in a short time he found himself at the head of a considerable following. His coarse vituperation and radical statements pleased the mob, which by its hearty applause urged him on to more inflammatory and violent utterances. He associated himself with J. G. Day and H. L. Knight, and with them held his first meeting on the sand-lots on September 16, 1877.[19] His audience was small, not more than 200 persons being present. Kearney declared that the unemployed were willing to take the places of the Chinese, and if necessary at Chinese wages. Resolutions were adopted demanding that soup kitchens be established and that the city supply work to the unemployed. At a meeting of the unemployed, held in a hall on September 21, he predicted that within a year San Francisco would have at least 20,000 laborers armed and organized to demand and to take what they desired, regardless of the police, the militia, and the Committee of Safety. He said that "a little judicious hanging would be the best course to pursue with the capitalists," and that "a few fires would clear the atmosphere."[20] Two days later Kearney and his lieutenants held their second meeting on the sand-lots, which was attended by at least 700 people who were eager to hear and see the new savior of the oppressed classes. Kearney did not disappoint them; he again indulged in frenzied declarations, asserting among other things that San Francisco would meet the fate of Moscow unless the Chinese were driven from California and the misery of the workers alleviated. The cry, "The Chinese must go," became the rallying slogan for the masses, and was echoed and reëchoed in ever increasing volume, from one end of the State to the other.

Kearney, considering the time propitious for the organization of another political party, called a meeting for October 5, 1877. About 150 persons were present, and these took part in the formation of the Workingmen's Party of California. Kearney was chosen president, J. G. Day, vice-president, and H. L. Knight, secretary.[21] The meeting adopted as the platform of the new party the following set of principles, which had been drawn up by H. L. Knight:

The object of this Association is to unite all poor and working men and their friends into one political party, for the purpose of defending themselves against the dangerous encroachments of capital on the happiness of our people and the liberties of our country.

We propose to wrest the government from the hands of the rich and place it in those of the people, where it properly belongs.

We propose to rid the country of cheap Chinese labor as soon as possible, and by all the means in our power, because it tends still more to degrade labor and aggrandize capital.

We propose to destroy land monopoly in our state by such laws as will make it impossible.

We propose to destroy the great money power of the rich by a system of taxation that will make great wealth impossible in the future.

We propose to provide decently for the poor and unfortunate, the weak, the helpless, and especially the young, because the country is rich enough to do so, and religion, humanity, and patriotism demand that we should do so.

We propose to elect none but competent workingmen and their friends to any office whatever. The rich have ruled us until they have ruined us. We will now take our own affairs in our own hands. The republic must and shall be preserved, and only workingmen will do it. Our shoddy aristocrats want an emperor and a standing army to shoot down the people.

For these purposes, we propose to organize ourselves into the Workingmen's Party of California, and to pledge and enroll therein all who are willing to join us in accomplishing these ends.

When we have 10,000 members, we shall have the sympathy and support of 20,000 other workingmen.

The party will then wait upon all who employ Chinese and ask for their discharge, and it will mark as public enemies those who refuse to comply with their request.

This party will exhaust all peaceable means of attaining its ends, but it will not be denied justice when it has the power to enforce it. It will encourage no riot or outrage, but it will not volunteer to repress, or put down, or arrest, or prosecute the hungry and impatient who manifest their hatred of the Chinamen by a crusade against "John" or those who employ him. Let those who raise the storm by their selfishness, suppress it themselves. If they dare raise the devil, let them meet him face to face. We will not help them.[22]

The socialistic Workingmen's Party of the United States continued to hold weekly meetings on the sand-lots, but owing to the counter-attraction of Kearney, Knight, and Day, it ceased to attract a crowd as formerly. Several serious clashes occurred between the two organizations, the Kearney crowd being the aggressors and attempting to disrupt the meetings of its rivals. Overtures were finally made to some of the leaders of the socialistic group, and they subsequently united with the Kearney-Day-Knight party, thereby increasing the strength and popularity of the new organization. Among the men thus drawn away from the Workingmen's Party of the United States was Thomas H. Bates, an Irish painter, who for some years had been active in the cause of Labor

Following the formation of the Workingmen's Party of California, meetings were held nightly in various parts of the city for the purpose of organizing ward clubs. The earnestness of the agitators in addressing two or three meetings an evening in addition to the Sunday meetings on the sand-lots impressed the people with their sincerity of purpose, and induced hundreds to enroll in the new party, which seemed destined to bring about the expulsion of the Chinese from California. Many who allied themselves with the movement were politicians of the lowest type, although a few were men of more than average ability. Among the early recruits of the organization was Dr. C. C. O'Donnell, a medical practitioner of rather unenviable reputation, but withal a speaker of great force and eloquence. He was later to play a prominent rôle in the affairs of the party.[23]

In the early stages of the agitation unexpected and unasked-for assistance was received from one of the important morning newspapers, the San Francisco *Chronicle*. For years there had been intense rivalry between the *Morning Call* and the *Chronicle;* anything praised by the one was roundly condemned by the other. Consequently, when the *Morning Call* attacked Kearney and his supporters, the *Chronicle* praised them in the most fulsome manner, reported the meetings of the new party at great length, and portrayed Kearney as the savior of the downtrodden working class.

C. C. O'DONNELL

On good authority[24] it has been said that Kearney's earlier speeches were written by a reporter on the *Chronicle* staff, namely, Chester Hull, who delighted in filling them with radical and foolish declarations. However, this was denied by Kearney.[25]

On October 16, 1877, the officers of the Workingmen's Party of California published the following manifesto, in which were set forth the principles of the organization:

We have made no secret of our intentions. We make none. Before you and the world, we declare that the Chinamen must leave our shores. We declare that white men, and women, and boys, and girls, cannot live as the people of the great republic should and compete with the single Chinese coolies in the labor market. We declare that we cannot hope to drive the Chinaman away by working cheaper than he does. None but an enemy would expect it of us; none but an idiot could hope for success; none but a degraded coward and slave would make the effort. To an American, death is preferable to life on a par with the Chinamen. What then is left to us? Our votes! We can organize. We can vote our friends into all the offices of the state. We can send our representatives to Washington. We can use all the legitimate means to convince our countrymen of our misfortune, and ask them to vote the moon-eyed nuisance out of the country. But this may fail. Congress, as you have seen, has often been manipulated by thieves, speculators, land grabbers, bloated bond holders, railroad magnates, and shoddy aristocracy—a golden lobby dictating its proceedings. Our own legislature is little better. The rich rule them by bribes. The rich rule the country by fraud and cunning; and we may say that fraud and cunning shall not rule us. We call upon our fellow workingmen to show their hands, to cast their ballots aright, and to elect the men of their choice. We declare to them that when they have shown their will that "John" shall leave our shores, and that will shall have been thwarted by fraud or cash, by bribery and corruption, it will be right for them to take their own affairs into their own hands and meet fraud with force. Is this treason? Then make the most of it. Treason is better than to labor beside a Chinese slave. . . . The workingmen know their rights, and know, also, how to maintain them, and mean to do it. The reign of the bloated knaves is over. The people are about to take their own affairs into their own hands, and they will not be stayed by . . . vigilantes, state militia, nor United States troops. The people make these things, and can set them aside. The American citizen has a right to express himself as he pleases, as he thinks, and to arm himself as he will; and when organized and strong enough, who shall make him afraid? There is none.[26]

The crowds at the Sunday meetings on the sand-lots increased in size and enthusiasm, the party membership grew rapidly, and in like measure the utterances of the speakers became more radical and incendiary. Finally it was suggested that a meeting be held on Nob Hill, an exclusive residential section of the city, where stood the palatial homes of Crocker, Hopkins, Stanford, and other millionaires. Crocker desired an entire block of land for the site of his mansion, and had succeeded in purchasing all but a small lot owned by a Mr. Jung. Crocker had offered an exorbitant price for the property, but Jung continued to insist upon a still greater sum. Finally Crocker, exasperated by Jung's tactics, built a high board fence on his ground, surrounding Jung's house on three sides. The people looked upon this action as the attempt of a "plutocrat to squeeze a poor person out of his property." When the meeting of the agitators was held in that vicinity on the evening of October 29, several thousand persons were present. Kearney made one of his most intemperate speeches. He is reported to have said:

The Central Pacific Railroad men are thieves, and will soon feel the power of the workingmen. When I have thoroughly organized my party, we will march through the city and compel the thieves to give up their plunder. I will lead you to the City Hall, clean out the police force, hang the Prosecuting Attorney, burn every book that has a particle of law in it, and then enact new laws for the workingmen. I will give the Central Pacific just three months to discharge their Chinamen, and if that is not done, Stanford and his crowd will have to take the consequences. I will give Crocker until November 29th to take down the fence around Jung's house, and if he doesn't do it, I will lead the workingmen up there and tear it down, and give Crocker the worst beating with the sticks that a man ever got.[27]

A few nights later, Kearney addressed a meeting at the corner of Stockton and Greene streets.

When we issue a call [he said], we want you to act promptly. We want to know the man who will discharge any workingmen who turn out to attend these meetings. We will brand him so that every workingman in this city shall know him. . . . But I tell you, and I want Stanford and the press to understand, that if I give an order to hang Crocker, it will be done. . . . The dignity of labor must be sustained, even if we have to kill every wretch that opposes it.[28]

Day also spoke, and said, in part:

Everything must be made subservient to the rights of labor. It must be done even if we have to paralyze nine-tenths of our factories. We intend to emancipate labor. Capitalists must succumb to the workingmen. I caution these men that the people are already on the verge of starvation. Unless the millionaire movement succeeds, we shall be unable to stay the most devastating catastrophe. We intend to move, even though we have to override every figment of the law. The young people will rise in this anti-Chinese movement and deluge this city in blood, if not entirely destroy this city. We shall show them that the days of the capitalists are over.[29]

At a meeting on November 2, Dr. C. C. O'Donnell declared that the Workingmen's Party of California had in its ranks

fully 17,000 workmen, the bone and sinew of the country. . . . They have got to stop this importation of Chinese, or you will see Jackson Street run knee deep in blood.[30]

The agitation had become so threatening that the mayor was unable longer to withstand the insistent demand that something be done to suppress it. Finally, with considerable hesitancy on the part of the city authorities, Kearney and his companions were placed under arrest for using language "having a tendency to cause a breach of peace."[31] Kearney was taken into custody on the evening of November 3, while speaking at a meeting in front of Dr.

KEARNEY SPEAKING TO THE WORKINGMEN ON NOB HILL, SAN FRANCISCO, OCTOBER 29, 1877

O'Donnell's office, just as he was expressing his willingness "to lay down his life in the cause of Freedom."[32] Excitement prevailed throughout the city following the arrest of "the leader of the workingmen," and it was thought that an attempt might be made to storm the jail and release him. In order to guard against such a possibility, and to maintain order, the militia was called out; it remained under arms during the night. The Chinese Six Companies also became frightened, and addressed a communication to the mayor appealing to him for protection. They concluded their request with the significant statement:

As a rule, our countrymen are better acquainted with peaceful vocations than the scenes of strife, yet we are not ignorant that self-defense is the right of all men; and should a riotous attack be made upon the Chinese quarter, we should have neither the power nor the disposition to restrain our countrymen from defending themselves to the last extremity, and selling their lives as dearly as possible.[33]

No outbreak occurred. A mass meeting was held on the following day (November 4) in Horticultural Hall, to protest the action of the city authorities. Warrants had also been issued for the arrest of the other agitators, and while the meeting was being held, J. G. Day, H. L. Knight, James Willey, and William Kennedy were taken into custody. The audience was at once in an uproar. For a few moments it looked as though violence might be done to the police; but Bates succeeded in quieting the disturbance and introduced William Wellock,[34] and after a speech by Wellock the meeting quietly adjourned. The militia was kept under arms all day, but no occasion arose for its use. On Monday, Bates was arrested while visiting the prisoners. Bail for each of them was fixed at $3,000 for each count, and efforts to have it reduced were unavailing.

On November 5, a thousand men marched in the rain from hall to hall, vainly seeking a place in which to hold a meeting. Finding all halls closed to them, they marched to the jail, where it was suggested that an attempt be made to release their leaders. Saner counsel prevailed and the men returned to the sand-lots where they listened to speeches by Wellock, Cronin, McCormick, and Bates, the last-named having been released on bail. The meeting was unusually quiet, considering the circumstances under which it was held; nothing occurred to mar the occasion except the arrest of Dr. O'Donnell, who was charged with having used the following language while addressing a meeting on the evening of October 15:

When thoroughly organized, we could plant our flag on Telegraph Hill, and our cannons, too, and blow the Mail steamers and their Chinese freight out of the waters. . . . We would have a grand parade and march down to the Mail wharf and notify the agents of the steamers not to land any more Chinamen. If they don't listen to us, then we will talk to them in another strain.

A second complaint charged that on October 25 he had said:

There are 76,000 Chinamen in this city, 17,000 of whom are out at work as chambermaids. I do not believe in injuring Chinamen, but those who employ them. This association is now 8,000 strong, and we are going to march down to the Pacific Mail Docks and notify the agent that it does not intend to allow any more Chinese to be landed in San Francisco, and if they persist in bringing them, the association will blow their ships out of the water.[35]

Bail for Dr. O'Donnell was fixed at $9,000 and was at once furnished. Charles Pickett, an eccentric who had taken only a minor part in the agitation, and Abraham Krause were arrested on November 9 for having indulged in incendiary declarations before public gatherings.

On November 7, the executive committee of the Workingmen's Party of California issued an address to the members of the organization, cautioning them to commit no acts of violence and not to interfere with officers of the law. The committee advised them

to have patience in this hour of trouble, and you will see that this martyrdom of our leaders will, in the end, redound to their glory and the liberation of the workingmen of California from the thralldom of capital and the incubus of the Chinese.

Nothing more plainly exposes the true character of the imprisoned "martyrs," or more clearly shows their cowardice, than the letter which they sent to the mayor under date of November 3. It was as follows:

HON. A. J. BRYANT,   City Prison, Nov. 3, 1877.
Dear Sir:

You are doubtless aware that Dennis Kearney and myself are held in the City Prison, charged with misdemeanor. We feel that we have been unfairly reported, that the published extracts from remarks, shorn of the qualifying sentences, put us in an unfair position before the community. We assure you that our anxiety for the peace of Society is as deeply seated as it well can be. We have no design against the peace of the city, either present or future, and we are willing to submit to any wise measure to allay existing excitement.

We do not propose to hold any more out-of-door meetings, or to tolerate any further use of incendiary language, and sincerely hope that our friends will, under all circumstances, obey the officers of the law and uphold the peace of the city.

You may make such public use of these, our sentiments, as to you seem conducive to public safety.

JOHN G. DAY
DENNIS KEARNEY

The sentiments herein expressed by Messrs. Day and Kearney meet our hearty endorsement.

H. L. KNIGHT
THOS. H. BATES
WM. KENNEDY
JAMES WILLEY.[36]

Bail was subsequently obtained for the imprisoned men, and they were released. On November 9, however, Kearney and Knight were again arrested on additional charges of having used incendiary language.

When the leaders of the workingmen came to trial on November 14, the Court dismissed them on the ground that the ordinance under which they had been arrested was invalid because it had not been published the required number of days before being formally passed by the Supervisors. Day, Knight, Kearney, and Bates were at once rearrested, however, and charged with having incited a riot. A week later, the Court again dismissed them, saying that evidence upon which to hold them was lacking. The decisions of the Court were received with great rejoicing by the Kearneyites, and preparations were hastened to make the anti-Chinese parade, which had been set for Thanksgiving Day, a triumphal procession in honor of the liberated leaders.

The evening and Sunday meetings on the sand-lots and elsewhere in the city continued as before, but the speeches of the leaders were in strange contrast to those that had previously been made. This change perhaps resulted in part from the action of the Board of Supervisors in passing the Gibbs "Gag" ordinance, a measure (adopted on November 23, 1877) which had been drafted with the sole intent of prohibiting and punishing the use of incendiary language and the holding of riotous meetings. It was made unlawful for

any person, by word, act, or deed, to advise, advocate or encourage, incite, request, counsel or solicit, endeavor, or propose to another to commit or cause to be committed any felony, misdemeanor, crime or public offense whatever, then or at any other future or indefinite time.[37]

Day, who had been thoroughly subdued and intimidated by his arrest and prosecution, hastened to resign from the party.

On Thanksgiving Day a procession of workers, variously esti-mated as having from 7,000 to 10,000 men in line, marched through the streets of San Francisco as a protest against the presence of the Chinese, and in honor of the liberated sand-lotters.[38] The parade was marked by much warmth of feeling and good behavior on the part of both spectators and marchers. When the marchers reached the sand-lots, they were addressed by Kearney, Knight, Wellock, and O'Donnell, but the speeches were mild and temperate as com-pared to those of former occasions, being limited for the most part to such harmless topics as the currency, public land policy, na-tional banks, and the railroads.

On the same evening, a meeting was held in Charter Oak Hall for the purpose of taking action on a proposal to call a state con-vention of the party, at which it was planned to nominate delegates to the State Constitutional Convention. The meeting was attended by delegates selected from the organizations that had been repre-sented in the afternoon's procession, and from a number of associa-tions in the interior of the State. As early as 1857, the people had asked that either the State Constitution be amended or a new one drafted. Beginning in 1860 the Democratic Party had made the matter a political issue. In 1876, the electorate had voted favorably on the proposition to hold a State Constitutional Convention, and subsequently the legislature decreed that it should convene on April 1, 1878.

Lack of harmony marred the evening meeting of the representa-tives of the Workingmen's Party of California. The Sacramento delegates withdrew, declaring that they would not submit to the dictatorial methods of Kearney, Knight, and Wellock. For some time Kearney had been managing the affairs of the party in a high-handed manner. He had made it a practice, when visiting the vari-ous ward-club meetings, to go accompanied by a crowd of boisterous followers, who proceeded at his command to cry down any speaker and to break up any gathering that did not meet with his approval. Chairmen were deposed, and new club officers were elected, as pleased his fancy. At one time he was even reported to have said: "I am the voice of the people. I am the dictator until the people put some one else in my place. I owe the people nothing, but they owe me a great deal."

Dissension within the ranks of the party continued to grow, finally resulting in the dissolution of some of the ward clubs and the expulsion of several of the prominent members, among whom was Thomas H. Bates. The climax came through accusations of corruption and bribery within the organization. In November, 1877, Carl Browne (who some years later became a lieutenant in Coxey's Army of the Unemployed on its memorable march to Washington, D. C.) had started a weekly paper, *The Open Letter*. He had perceived that the Workingmen's Party of California would undoubtedly become a movement of some importance, and therefore he suggested to its leaders that a company be incorporated to publish *The Open Letter* as the official organ of the movement.[39] The proposal was accepted, and Kearney was chosen president of the board of directors. Browne had personally retained 1,205 shares of the company's stock. It was because of that fact, and also because of the accusation that the party was being used to sell *Open Letter* stock to the members, that charges were preferred against Knight, Kearney, and Wellock by Bates and others, especially the Sacramento delegation. It was also asserted that *The Open Letter*, the Workingmen's Party, and even Kearney himself were "owned and run" by the San Francisco *Chronicle*, and that there had been flagrant misappropriation of the organization's funds. On December 9, O'Donnell and one Crossley declared before a large audience that Kearney had promised to stop the agitation if the merchants and wealthy citizens of San Francisco would give him $5,000. On the same day, the members of the Sacramento branch of the party adopted resolutions calling upon the movement to rid itself of Kearney, Wellock, and other incendiary propagandists. The tactics and dogged determination of a dictator were indeed needed at that critical moment to check the incipient revolt within the party ranks. Kearney's attempt to use such tactics was partly successful; at his command, clubs were disbanded and members expelled until he felt that he had the movement again under his control.

Kearney was fully aware that his greatest strength lay in coarse and vituperative attacks against the moneyed class. Calm, cool discourse was not his forte, and could neither gain him new followers nor retain those already allied with him. Feeling that the situation justified strenuous measures if he were to retain his position at the head of the rapidly growing political party, he again launched forth with most amazing and violent tirades against the rich and the Chinese. While speaking to one of his audiences about the several militia companies that had been organized among members of the ward clubs,[40] he publicly declared:

When the Chinese question is settled, we can discuss whether it would be better to hang, shoot, or cut the capitalists to pieces. In six months we will have 50,000 men ready to go out and shoot pheasants under General Wellock, and if "John" don't leave here, we will drive him and his abettors into the sea.[41]

At a meeting on the sand-lots somewhat later (January 7, 1878) he informed his audience that within

a few months, we will have 1,000 men armed with Springfield rifles, and ready for action.

He also declared:

Now we are ready. We are ready to come right down to the scratch, to expel every one of those moon-eyed lepers. We are ready to do it. If the ballot fails, the bullet. That "if" must come in. If the ballot fails, we are ready to use the bullet. . . . We insist on organizing. We are bent on driving from the State of California these miserable, monstrous, moon-eyed lepers. If they call that a conspiracy, let them make the most of it. We are not to be intimidated by a Grand Jury; we are not to be intimidated by anybody. It would take 50,000 men in the State of California to intimidate the workingmen that are now ready, and if we can get through this without the shedding of blood, so much the better for ourselves. I don't care about dying just now, but if it comes to that, I am ready to carry my point. I don't care who suffers, or who is going to be put down. We are not going to be beat. We are going to carry this thing either to death or victory.[42]

In the latter part of December, Kearney and Knight addressed a number of meetings in the interior of the State, and journeyed as far south as Los Angeles. In that city, Kearney made the threat before one of his audiences that "if we have to destroy the whole city of Los Angeles, we will drive out the Chinese."[43]

On January 3, 1878, approximately 500 unemployed men marched to the City Hall, where their committee, headed by Kearney, demanded that the mayor give them work. Kearney informed the latter that he could not keep his followers under control unless they were given "work, bread, or a place in the county jail," and that he did not care to be held responsible for the consequences if their request was not granted. Reply was made that the city authorities had no power to provide employment, whereupon the men marched to the sand-lots and listened to speeches by their leaders.

As weeks passed, Kearney became increasingly radical in his public utterances. Especially was he eager at all times to recommend the arming of the unemployed in order that they might more readily obtain their demands. At one of the meetings, he is reported to have asked of his audience:

Are you courageous? How many of you have got muskets? Up hands, who have got muskets? How many of you have got about ten feet of rope in your pocket? Well, you must be ready and arm yourselves. This thing has got too hot. There is a white heat in this thing now, and you must be ready when I issue a call for 10,000 men. Come right down to the wharf when the steamer comes in. When I say I want you, will you be ready? Then we will see who are our friends and who are our enemies. Then we will know whether the militia is on our side, or against us. . . . How many of you are willing to meet outside the sand-lots next Sunday to drill? Will you all be there, and bring a stick or something with you? My friend here, Mr. Wellock, is a military man, and he will drill you; but do not waste too much time on the tricks of shouldering, but learn to put a cartridge in, and learn to shoot it off. Let them interfere with us![44]

So threatening became the agitation that another Committee of Safety was secretly formed among the propertied citizens of San Francisco.

On January 5, 1878, the Grand Jury returned two indictments against Kearney and Knight, and one each against Helm, Wellock, O'Donnell, and Pickett, all of whom were charged with riot. They were arrested and at once released on bail. A few days later, Kearney, Knight, and Wellock were again arrested on a charge of having used language tending to create a breach of the peace. The city was in a tumult; excitement prevailed on all sides; threats of violence were publicly made; and for a time it looked as though a serious outbreak might occur. Several companies of militia were kept under arms, and the "Lackawanna" was again anchored in the harbor off the Pacific Mail docks. The *Chronicle*, realizing that it had gone too far in encouraging the sand-lotters, reversed its position and thenceforth was as bitter as its rival, the *Morning Call*, had been in its denunciation of the agitators. The *Evening Bulletin* on January 16, 1878, said:

> There has been no time during the last fifteen years when this city was so badly governed as it is today. In default of a strong, courageous and healthy municipal government, a mob has been breeding and festering, until now it threatens to capture the city, and murder peaceful citizens. . . . The authorities have temporized and apologized to the mob, and have incidentally helped such scoundrels as Kearney, and his confederates become bolder and more reckless and devilish in their proceedings. The Mayor has backed and filled until now the question is raised among the law-abiding citizens, "Has this man any pluck and courage? Dare he execute the law, or is he going down on all fours in the presence of cut-throats who now openly threaten to burn and hang?"

The mayor was finally induced to call a special meeting of the Board of Supervisors, for the purpose, as he said, of

> taking measures whereby the riotous meetings held in this city may be broken up. . . . The time has arrived [he continued] when men get up in our public halls and threaten to destroy property and defy government, and it has become, in my judgment, the duty of this city government to spend every dollar and let the last man be mowed down, in order that these meetings may be broken up, and order preserved in the city for the future.[45]

Resolutions were passed by the supervisors, calling on the legislature to enact measures for the protection of the city. The mayor also issued a proclamation on January 17, declaring unlawful all assemblies of an incendiary or riotous kind, and ordering the arrest of all persons taking part in them. This at first tended but to increase the discontent, but as soon as the sand-lotters realized that the authorities were determined to enforce the order—as they showed by forcibly breaking up a number of meetings—the trouble-makers quieted down and awaited developments.

The legislature also had become thoroughly aroused over the seriousness of the situation and hastened to enact measures for the protection of the city. On January 19, 1878, the governor signed a bill, later known as the "Gag Law," which provided as follows:

> Any person who, in the presence or hearing of twenty-five or more persons, shall utter any language with intent either to incite a riot at the present or in the future, or any act or acts of criminal violence against any person or property, or who shall suggest or advise, or encourage any act or acts of criminal violence against any person, or persons, or property, or shall advise or encourage forcible resistance to any of the laws of this State, shall be deemed guilty

of a felony, and on conviction thereof shall be punished by imprisonment in the State Prison, or in a County Jail, not exceeding two years, or by a fine not exceeding five thousands dollars, or both.[46]

Another bill was passed by the legislature, increasing the police force of San Francisco,[47] while a third appropriated $20,000 "to be expended in the discretion of the Governor for the conservation of the public peace."[48]

The first state convention of the Workingmen's Party of California was to be held in San Francisco on January 21, 1878. Kearney and Knight, therefore, as president and secretary, respectively, addressed a petition to Governor Irwin praying for the protection of their Constitutional rights of free assembly and free speech. In concluding their petition, they said:

We may here assure Your Excellency that in no case have we molested person or property, or proposed to do so. We have advised our party to arm themselves, well knowing the character of our opponents, that when we prevail at the ballot box, we may not be defeated by fraud, by returning boards, or money-purchased commissions. We have never spoken of the use of arms but as a means of rebutting fraud and corruption, keeping our adversaries within the pale of the law, and vindicating the expressed will of the people, expressed at the ballot box.[49]

When the state convention of the party met in San Francisco on the appointed date, it elected Frank Roney temporary chairman.[50] Mayor Bryant had ordered the police to break up the convention if it should assemble, but the delegates outwitted the officers of the law by secretly notifying one another of the place of meeting, and at the same time advertising that the convention would be held in several different places, in widely separated parts of the city. When the police finally found the hall in which the delegates were gathered, the meeting was proceeding in a quiet and orderly manner, and they did not interfere.[51] After the appointment of committees and the election of officers, the convention adjourned to the following day.

In the meantime, the trial of Kearney and his companions, charged with disturbing the peace, had been proceeding in the Criminal Court. On January 22 they were acquitted. The remaining charges were not pressed, and the prisoners were released.[52] The verdict was loudly welcomed by the sand-lotters, and the leaders of the Workingmen's Party again found themselves hailed as "martyrs" of the working class. The militia, however, remained under arms, in readiness for any outbreak that might occur.

An additional impetus was given at this time to the rapid growth of the Workingmen's Party by the election of its candidate to the state senatorship from Alameda County. The death of the incumbent had necessitated a special election. J. W. Bones had been nominated by Kearney's followers, and he was elected on January 22 by a substantial plurality of the votes cast for the three candidates.[53] Bones was an eccentric person, tall and lean, and known as "Barebones," or as "Praise-God Barebones," because of his obviously pious proclivities and perhaps in imitation of the name of that historic Cromwellian follower who presided over the Rump Parliament. At a ratification meeting held before the election, he had publicly declared that he was not a follower of Kearney's. In spite of this public repudiation, Kearney went to Oakland and brought the newly elected candidate to Humboldt Hall, where the state convention of the party was in session. They were warmly received. After electing Kearney permanent chairman, the convention adjourned for the day.

As presiding officer, Kearney continued his dictatorial policy. He would brook no interference from the floor and permitted no person to question the validity or propriety of his rulings. Those who attempted to do so met with the most unparliamentary and brutally discourteous treatment.

Within the next two days a platform was framed and adopted, and various resolutions were passed by the delegates. The convention was then adjourned *sine die*. In brief, the platform declared that the government of the United States had fallen into the hands of capitalists and their willing tools with the result that the rights of the people, their comfort and happiness, were entirely ignored; coolie labor was a curse to the land and should be restricted and forever abolished; land should be held for cultivation and settlement only; a system of finance "consistent with the agricultural, manufacturing and mercantile industries, and requirements of the country, uncontrolled by rings, brokers, and bankers," should be introduced; the eight-hour day should be made the legal workday; the farming out of convict labor was condemned; all labor on public works should be performed by the day and at the current rate of

wages; the accumulation of millions and the existence of monopolies should be made impossible by the adoption of a proper method
of taxation; and the fee system for the payment of public officers
should be abolished.

Another state convention was held in San Francisco on January
18, 1878, by thirty-one delegates who said that they represented
the National Labor Party. This was a local organization with a national name, formed in 1877 by a few local politicians to further
their personal ends. It had no connection with the national party
of the same name. One of the delegates said: "The National Labor
Party is a failure; the movement is not strong enough to enable the
party to organize. It cannot even form its ward clubs without calling on its friends from all the wards in the city to meet and form
a crowd."[54] The convention adopted resolutions strongly condemn-
ing the incendiarism of the Kearney movement.

In the early months of 1878 the Workingmen's Party movement
tended to drift away from its policy of attacking the Chinese. It
began to concern itself chiefly with the condemnation of Capital
and Monopoly. The hostility of the Californians had caused a decline in the number of Chinese entering the State; this, and the
fact that the people had begun to tire of anti-coolie tirades, had
forced the leaders to resort to other issues in order to keep the
populace aroused. They found their new objects of attack in the
abuses of land and railroad monopolies, which had seriously affected the economic interests of the residents of California. It was
asserted by some San Franciscans that the change in the nature of
the campaign carried on by Kearney and his associates was caused
by their desire to levy blackmail on the landed and railroad interests against whom their attacks were directed.

For a while the leaders were more temperate than they had been
in the early stages of the agitation, although some of the lesser
lights of the party continued to use radical and incendiary language in addressing their followers. Charles W. Pope, in speaking
to the Eighth Ward Club, said: "By God, the Chinese must go. We
can easily get a thousand breech loaders, and soon settle this question. I honestly believe, gentlemen, it will never be settled any other
way. I hope you will organize and drill, and get ready for the fight
that is bound to come, if justice is not done us." Another speaker

said: "Now we can talk to each other. Let us have bullets, bullets, bullets. That's the talk."[55]

On February 19, 1878, a special election was held in Santa Clara County to choose a state senator and an assemblyman. The Republican and Democratic parties united under the name of the People's Party and waged a vigorous campaign against the Kearneyites, but the latter elected their candidate for the Assembly. In March, the Workingmen's Party of California elected the mayor and city attorney of Sacramento, and the mayor, police judge, district attorney, and justice of the peace in Oakland.

The decline of the organization may be said to date from about this time.[56] It had become a factor in state and municipal politics, and self-seeking politicians hastened to ally themselves with it so as to use its machinery and membership for their personal advancement. The legislative record of Senator Bones had caused the voters to become suspicious and dissatisfied with the party and its propaganda. Upon taking office, Bones had disregarded the principles of the organization, had voted for a number of objectionable measures, and had participated in the caucuses of the Republican Party. His resignation was demanded, but he refused to be worried by the outcry. Threats to do him bodily harm and even to hang him were made publicly, but he remained indifferent.

At this time the Workingmen's Party was also forced to suffer the ignominy of hearing its leaders accused of accepting bribes. In February and March charges were repeatedly made by persons within and without the organization that Kearney had sold out to the corporations. One speaker asserted that every candidate elected by the Workingmen's Party was a railroad tool, "from Bones down to the Mayor-elect of Sacramento, and it was a notorious fact that all the Sacramento municipal officers were railroad men and elected by the railroad's design, and that Kearney knew it and had known it."[57] At a meeting of the state central committee of the party on April 27, 1878, Kearney was denounced by McCabe, ridiculed by Knight, and called a liar by others. The trouble arose over a resolution which Kearney had introduced, proposing that no officer of the party should be nominated as a delegate to the Constitutional Convention. This naturally aroused strenuous opposition, because, if adopted, the party would be represented on the floor of the convention by its weaker and less capable members, thus seriously lessening its influence in that very important gathering. On the next evening, the lie was again passed between Kearney and the members of the executive committee, and a stormy session resulted. On May 4, Kearney held a meeting of his faction, and received its support. Having picked his crowd, he had no difficulty in getting a resolution passed demanding the resignation of McCabe, Roney, Linehan, Formhals, Johnson, Marchabout, and Knight, all of whom were allied with the opposition group on the executive committee.

The anti-Kearney faction met the following day. Several of its members accused Kearney of having used the party to further his personal ends, and of having accepted money from certain corporations.[58] Amid much excitement and speech-making, the rebellious members of the executive committee deposed Kearney from the presidency of the party. They also drafted and published the following address to the people of California:

Friends and Fellow Citizens:

At last, under an imperative necessity, this Committee has deposed Denis Kearney from the position of President of this party, and as Chairman of this Committee. Henceforth, he is no more than a member of this Committee, and is neither honored nor trusted, even in that capacity.

We have been impelled to this course by the following considerations:

First, Because the said Denis Kearney has, from the first, assumed the rôle of the dictator who would brook no opposition to his will, suspecting everybody of treason who dared to differ with him in opinion.

Second, Because, without specifying a single fact to support his accusations, he has charged all officers of the party with being wire-pullers, political tricksters, traitors, and thieves.

Third, Because, failing to carry out his despotic designs within the Constitution and laws of the party, he has undertaken to set them aside, and of his own will, aided by a few promiscuous meetings at the sand-lots, to revolutionize the party and make himself its dictator, and take control of its affairs.

Fourth, Because he is more than suspected of selling out to the enemy. Grave charges have been made against him, and are now under investigation, which, if proved, place the mark of Cain on his brow, which he is so ready to bestow on the brow of others.

Fifth, Because of late he has displayed a lack of truthfulness and honor, which unfit him for the high position of Chairman of this Committee or President of this Party.

Sixth, Because his language and his manners show him to have no regard for the rights of others, for the decencies of civilized life, and the inalienable rights of American citizens.

Seventh, Because we doubt his perfect sanity; such conduct as his defiance of the law, good manners, republican liberty, and equal rights of man, indicate a disordered mind.

Eighth, Because he is now acting as an irresponsible disorganizer and an enemy of the party, persuading men to folly, riot, and disorder, breaking up clubs, and otherwise damaging and disgracing the party....[59]

Roney was elected temporary chairman by the seceding members of the executive committee.

Because of the dissension within the party, two separate state conventions were held in San Francisco on May 16, 1878, for the purpose of nominating candidates to represent the party in the ensuing election of delegates to the State Constitutional Convention. The representatives of the branches of the party from the interior of the State did not know with which faction they should affiliate. After listening to the arguments of both groups, twenty joined the Kearneyites, ten the seceders, and nine refused to affiliate with either.

The Kearney convention, after a heated discussion, passed a resolution declaring that all officers of the party should be ineligible as candidates for any public office. A long platform was adopted, and a complete list of candidates nominated. The anti-Kearney convention, presided over by Frank Roney, was poorly attended. After adopting a platform, it nominated candidates for the first Congressional district only.

There was no noticeable similarity between the platforms of the two factions. The Kearney faction had accepted a platform characterized by the press as "being as mild as a platform could well be." The spirit of radicalism was "utterly repudiated." With two exceptions, the various planks were such as would ordinarily have been found in a party platform of that period: one of them called for a limitation on the amount of property that one might acquire; the other, for the referring of all laws to the people for approval before they should become effective. The platform of the Roney-Knight faction, on the contrary, was surprisingly radical. It declared that the increasing poverty of the workers resulted from monopoly of the soil; that hours of labor should be reduced as use of machinery increased; that wages should represent the product of labor; that acquisition of land should be limited; that taxation should be graded so as to relieve the workers altogether; and that the principle of the referendum should be established.

In the ensuing campaign, friction continued between the two factions of the party. Roney and Knight attempted to reorganize the movement, but without success. In a few wards each faction had a club. Kearney continued his former tactics of going about from place to place accompanied by a crowd of forty or fifty adherents, who broke up the meetings of his opponents.

In the early days of the Kearney agitation, the Workingmen's Party of California had been opposed by the local branches of the socialistic Workingmen's Party of the United States, but in a relatively short time practically all the members of the latter allied themselves with the Kearney movement.[60] The locally organized National Labor Party group also made a feeble and unsuccessful attempt to oppose the Kearneyites. In May, 1878, it nominated a list of candidates for the State Constitutional Convention, but none was elected. Efforts were made to effect a union between the National Labor Party and the anti-Kearney faction, but to no avail. Somewhat later, the members of the National Labor Party allied themselves with the Greenback Labor Party.

In many districts of the State, the Democrats and the Republicans joined forces and nominated a Non-Partisan ticket, hoping thereby to defeat the candidates of the Workingmen's Party. As the day of the election approached, the old-party politicians appeared to be more hopeful of victory than they had been for many months; the Workingmen's ticket had been defeated in the Stockton municipal election, and in other communities the party was rapidly losing its following because of internal dissensions.

On June 19, seventy-six Non-Partisans, fifty Workingmen,[61] eleven Republicans, ten Democrats, and two Independents were chosen as delegates to the State Constitutional Convention. The Workingmen carried San Francisco, Los Angeles, and Nevada City. In the Los Angeles district, they fused with the Grangers, with the result that the men elected were "more Grangers than Workingmen." In Nevada County they combined with the miners, and nominated a "Miners' and Workingmen's ticket." The defeat of the Kearneyites in Oakland, Sacramento, and San Jose was significant in the face of their victories in the preceding elections.

An analysis of the returns shows that the Workingmen's Party had been successful in the mountain counties, in San Francisco, and in southern California. It was in the last-mentioned part of the State that the greatest outcry had been raised against the abuses of land monopoly and the inequality of taxation. The party polled its largest vote in those counties which had suffered most from the drought of the preceding year.

On July 21, Kearney, accompanied by Carl Browne, who was to act as his secretary, went East to visit his aged mother in Boston, and to see what could be done to organize a national party along the lines of the Workingmen's Party of California. It was said that he had been requested by General Butler to assist in the latter's campaign for the governorship of Massachusetts. If this was true he was soon released from his obligation, for, after Kearney had delivered several incendiary speeches,[62] Butler hastened to disclaim any connection with him. While in the East, he spoke in a number of cities, but nowhere was he accorded the reception to which he had become accustomed in California. On his return to San Francisco on November 26, he was met at the Ferry building by a cheering crowd of adherents, who marched with him to the sand-lots, where speeches were made by himself and others.

The State Constitutional Convention assembled at Sacramento, September 28, 1878. For some weeks preceding, the Workingmen's Party delegates had met regularly to discuss proposed constitutional provisions and decide upon a course of action to be followed in the convention. During the sessions of the convention, they allied themselves with the farmer or Granger element, and introduced unsuccessfully many proposals that at the time were considered extremely radical. The following are typical: the State to build and own a system of irrigation canals; the abolition of the office of lieutenant governor; a single legislative chamber; no Chinese to be given a license to trade, peddle, or carry on any kind of mercantile business; no Mongolians to be hired by any corporation; aliens not to be permitted to own, sell, or acquire by any means, any interest in real estate in California; no person to be permitted to settle in California if unable to become a citizen of the State; "land grabbing" to be stopped; no land or other subsidies to be granted to any corporation; the pardoning power of the governor to be abolished. Many others were proposed, directed for the most part against the Chinese, landowners, and corporations.

The State Constitutional Convention concluded its labors on March 3, 1879. On May 7 the new document was submitted to the voters, and adopted by a vote of 77,959 to 67,134. Many citizens looked upon this as a distinct victory for the Workingmen's Party of California. Kearney and some of the other leaders of the party had toured the State, speaking for its adoption. The anti-Kearney faction, however, had sent Knight to trail behind them and speak against it.[63] With the exception of the San Francisco *Chronicle,* the leading newspapers of the State had vigorously opposed the New Constitution, as had also the business and merchant classes, the landowners, corporations, and other propertied interests.

Child of the Workingmen's Party though it was, such was the agitation and doubt upon the subject of the new constitution that when it came to the vote, San Francisco, the home of the chief instigators of the change, rejected it by a majority of 1,592 out of 38,034.[64]

Throughout the State the vote of the cities was uniformly against its adoption, Los Angeles being the only important city to give it a majority. Oakland rejected it by 1,496 votes, Sacramento by 1,251, Santa Clara County by 679, and San Jose by 574. The largest majorities in its favor came from the northern lumber counties and the southern agricultural counties; the former had suffered from a depression in the lumber trade, and had undoubtedly voted for the New Constitution because of the pressure of "hard times," and the southern counties had suffered for years from the oppression and exactions of land and railroad monopolies. Almost without exception, the more prosperous counties voted against it.

T. H. Hittell aptly summarizes the situation in the following words:

There can be no doubt that the Constitution of 1879 was framed at a very unfortunate time and under very unfavorable circumstances. The people were too angry and desperate to make a good constitution. Railroad and labor troubles, worked up by demagogues, had made them mad. An insane desire to "cinch" capital and expel the Chinese had seized hold of men's minds and driven them into excesses; and the result was a constitution which was intended, mainly, insofar as it differed from the Constitution of 1849, to accomplish these objects, and which, if carried out in these respects as designed, would have made California a sad spectacle to nations. But as it turned out, a conservative supreme court and legislature prevented to a very great extent the intended cinching of capital, and the plain rights of the Chinese under the Burlingame treaty were too solidly established to be very much affected by the unconstitutional clauses of the new constitution against them.[65]

The results of the New Constitution did not come up to the expectations of the people in their desire for relief and reform. Bancroft, a contemporary historian, says:

The effect [of the New Constitution] upon corporations disappointed its authors and supporters. Many of them were still strong enough to defy state power and evade state laws in protecting their interests, and this they did without scruple. The relation of capital and labor is even more strained than before the constitution was adopted.... Legislators were still to be approached by agents of railroads and other corporations.... Chinese were still employed digging and grading. The state board of railroad commissioners was a useless expense to the commonwealth, being as wax in the hands of the companies it was set to watch. The new constitution was framed to make the rich pay their share of taxation, to control corporations, to correct the revenue system, and to equalize the rights of the people altogether. In each of these designs, it failed.[66]

While Kearney had been absent in the East, the party had been torn by internal dissensions and petty quarrels. Wide breaches had been made in the organization. Upon his return, he undertook, in his customary energetic and dictatorial manner, to bring order out of chaos; he went about from ward club to ward club with a devoted group of adherents, disbanding here, reorganizing there, and finally bringing about a semi-satisfactory state of affairs within the party. In February, 1879, there was a slight revival of interest and enthusiasm in the organization. In March, Kearney deposed Wellock from the vice-presidency of the party, and gave that office to Clitus Barbour, a lawyer. Barbour had been active in the ranks of the organization for some time, and had served as one of its delegates to the State Constitutional Convention. Wellock, during Kearney's absence, had been in charge of the Sunday meetings on the sand-lots, but he had not been able to attract or hold the crowds that formerly gathered to listen to his chief. The mantle of leadership which had temporarily fallen upon his shoulders gave him an exaggerated opinion of his own importance; he defied and insulted the state central committee, and lost the support of many of the party members. It was felt that his retention would cost the organization at least 5,000 votes. After being deposed, however, he remained more or less active in the movement until June, 1880, when he was formally expelled for activity within the organization in the interest of the Democratic Party.

On June 3, 1879, the state convention of the Workingmen's Party of California met in San Francisco to nominate candidates for State, legislative, and Congressional offices. Kearney was again elected president of the convention, and in his opening address declared that the party was well organized in forty counties and partly organized in ten others. Delegates were present from the ward clubs of San Francisco and from twenty-nine interior counties. The proceedings were most harmonious and were presided over in a dignified manner by the man who had previously frightened the local authorities and the citizens of San Francisco by advocating a reign of violence and anarchy. A platform was adopted similar to that of 1878, but containing also some clauses taken from the New Constitution. W. F. White, a wealthy rancher, was nominated for governor, and W. R. Andrus for lieutenant governor.[67]

In the campaign which followed, the Workingmen's Party repeatedly fused with other parties and succeeded in electing eleven senators, seventeen assemblymen, and a railroad commissioner. In the legislature the Workingmen's Party representatives were outnumbered only by the Republicans. They accomplished nothing of consequence. For the most part they were neither better nor worse than the average of politicians. They were as easily controlled as, some of them more easily than, those whom they had denounced as the willing and easily purchased tools of the corporations and monopolies. On several occasions they proved decidedly susceptible to corporate influence.[68]

In 1879 the Workingmen's Party of California also nominated its first municipal ticket in San Francisco. A convention was held on June 18, and there was placed before the voters a complete list of candidates, headed by Isaac S. Kalloch for the mayoralty. Kalloch was pastor of Metropolitan Temple, a sort of "People's Church," and had obtained a large following among the masses because of his speeches and sermons against monopolies and the Chinese, and this in spite of the fact that, prior to the popularity of the Workingmen's Party of California, he had had the largest Chinese Sunday School in the city, and had publicly declared that the only way to deal with the mob was by using grapeshot and firing low.

In the mayoralty campaign, a vicious and scurrilous attack was made upon Kalloch's character by the San Francisco *Chronicle,* which said that it had uncovered certain scandals of his early life. Kalloch replied from the pulpit on the following Sunday, and,

ISAAC S. KALLOCH

throwing aside all dignity and caution, went so far as to besmirch the reputation of the mother of the two DeYoung brothers, the owners of the *Chronicle.* They felt that they could not permit such an act to go unavenged, and on August 23 Charles deYoung shot and seriously wounded Kalloch, while the latter was standing in front of his church. The assault created great excitement. DeYoung did not have the esteem of the people of the city, and for a time it was feared that an effort would be made to lynch him. The *Morning Call* on August 24, 1879, declared:

Never, since the news was received of the assassination of Abraham Lincoln, has the city been more excited than over the tragic event of yesterday. Immediately after it was known that Mr. Kalloch had been shot, workmen rushed from their shops into the streets, the merchant abandoned his counting room, the financier his bank; all classes, conditions, ages, and sexes were abroad, inquiring for particulars.... Some called for vengeance, others wept.

Groups of workingmen in various parts of the United States adopted resolutions of sympathy for the victim. Kalloch had suddenly become a martyr, and on September 3 he was elected mayor by a safe majority.[69] The Workingmen's Party also elected the sheriff, auditor, tax collector, treasurer, city and county attorney, district attorney, public administrator, surveyor, police judge, three school directors, and nine of the judges of the Superior Court. However, the names of only three of the nine judges appeared exclusively on the Workingmen's Party ticket.

When the newly elected Workingmen's officials came to take office, they found that various obstacles had been put in their way by the retiring Board of Supervisors. The latter had attempted to exclude them from office by raising the amount of bonds required and by refusing to give up the offices to those who had been elected or who had been appointed to serve out the unexpired terms. They also asserted that the pledge of the Workingmen's candidates to turn over a certain percentage of their salaries to the treasury of the party was a form of bribery, therefore illegal, and sufficient to keep them out of office. The courts were called on to decide the legal points involved, and later gave a decision favorable on all counts to the Workingmen's representatives. Bonds were furnished, and the new officials were sworn in. Here again one finds that those who had been elected by the Workingmen were no different from the officeholders whom they had replaced. They administered the affairs of the city in virtually the same manner as those who preceded them and as those who came after them. None of their acts characterized them as representatives of workingmen.

Kalloch, during his term of office, was continually opposed by the Board of Supervisors. Several times he earned their ill will by vetoing ordinances which were highly objectionable or which had been drafted solely for the purpose of pillaging the city treasury or of assisting corporate interests. By May, 1880, the spirit of hostility existing between him and the Board of Supervisors had become so bitter that an attempt was made to impeach him. The complaint filed with the court charged that

Mayor Kalloch did on divers occasions use incendiary language in public; that he received money from persons for obtaining official positions for them; that he solicited and accepted from the Market Street Railroad a free pass, which he used on said road; that he solicited and received tickets from the City Railroad Company to the number of 300, free of cost; and that he solicited and received from the Southern Pacific Railway Company a free pass to ride from San Francisco to Los Angeles.

The decision of the court, however, was in his favor.

In the early months of 1880 another agitation, unconnected with the Kearney movement and in many respects different from it, was launched among the unemployed in San Francisco. Business had been depressed for some time, and many men were out of work. On January 18, 1880, a meeting of the unemployed was called by the Painters' Union to discuss conditions and devise means of relief. Nothing was accomplished, however, other than the adoption of the customary resolutions. The unrest of the people then found a new outlet by attacking the Chinese problem in a new way. The second article of Section XIX of the New Constitution declared that "no corporation now existing, or hereafter formed under the laws of this state, shall, after the adoption of this Constitution, employ directly or indirectly, in any capacity, any Chinese or Mongolian." The unemployed knew that this clause would not be legally enforced, so they undertook its enforcement. They marched from factory to factory, threatening violence if the Chinese were not discharged.[70] On February 7, 1880, a crowd of fully 1,000 men gathered on the sand-lots and listened to a speech by Thomas Allen, who said that he had worked but two years in the last five, by H. W. Moore, who had previously been the general secretary of the Workingmen's Party of California, and by Mrs. Anna Smith, a representative of the Socialist Labor Party. Resolutions expressing the objects of the movement were adopted, and one of them was as follows:

Resolved, That we have the physical means in our hands to enforce a compliance with the Constitution, and to compel the discharge of the Chinese by corporations, and that we will not hesitate to use these means, if, after due notice, they do not comply with our demands.[71]

Day after day the unemployed met, resolved, and marched, demanding employment and the discharge of the Chinese. In causing the discharge of the Chinese they were partly successful, being aided by the enactment by the legislature in February, 1880,[72] of a law, later declared to be unconstitutional,[73] which prohibited the employment of Chinese by any corporation chartered by the State of California. The Pioneer and the Mission woolen mills discharged more than 500 Mongolians, the Oakland Jute Mills discharged about 300, and many small employers did likewise. The movement, which had begun as a quiet but determined insistence on the part of the workers that they be given the places of the Chinese, gradually tended to become incendiary. The city was again as agitated as it had been in the early period of the Kearney excitement. A secret Committee of Safety was organized, which made preparations to protect life and property. Business was brought to a standstill; building operations ceased. The climax was reached in February, when the Board of Health declared Chinatown a nuisance, and issued a proclamation that it should be abated. This ordinance was condemned by the Committee of Safety as sand-lot legislation. City officials were publicly accused of being in league with the mob. The conservative elements threatened to take the situation into their own hands if any attempt were made to carry out the order of the board. Intense excitement prevailed and for a time it looked as though a serious outbreak might occur.

Kearney added fuel to the flames by declaring to a sand-lot meeting that a plot to assassinate him and Mayor Kalloch had been uncovered. President Hayes was appealed to by various groups to give military protection to the city; an ordinance to increase the police force was passed over the mayor's veto; and preparations were made by both sides for the impending struggle. Each was organized and determined. On the part of the Workingmen, a Committee of Thirteen recommended that the Chinese be driven out of the city, at the point of bayonets if necessary. Among the merchants and propertied classes, a Citizens' Protective Union was formed for "(a) the preservation of public peace, (b) the protection of property, (c) the restoration of confidence in the security of life and property from all violence, and (d) the resuscitation of legitimate commerce, industries, and business of the people."[74]

On March 11, 1880, Kearney was arrested on a charge of having used incendiary language. It was alleged that he had made the threat, "I tell you right here that if I hear of any man plotting to kill me, ———— ————, I will kill him, so help me God." He was also charged with having publicly called Claus Spreckels[75] a thief. Gannon, one of the leaders of the unemployed, was also arrested and charged with having made a statement to the effect that "I understand that some of us have got to go. If they start in, the city will be levelled to ashes and the ruins filled with the roasted bodies in twenty-four hours after." The arrest of these two men and the determined attitude of the authorities appeared to quiet the disturbance. They also aided somewhat in reviving interest in the Workingmen's Party, which had lost much of its popularity. Kearney and Gannon were tried and sentenced to six months' imprisonment and fined $1,000 each. Both cases were appealed to the higher courts. On May 27, 1880, the State Supreme Court reversed the decision in Kearney's case, and ordered him released from the county jail.[76] Gannon was later freed by a similar ruling. The release of Kearney was warmly greeted by his followers, who marched to his home and drew him on one of his drays to the sand-lots, where speeches were made and a salute of one hundred guns was fired.

The Workingmen's Party had lost many of its earlier characteristics and had become a party of and for the politicians. In January, 1880, Kearney had gone to Washington, D. C., to attend a "unity" convention of labor organizations, Grangers, and Greenbackers. On his return to San Francisco he announced his allegiance to the principles of the Greenback Labor Party. The stage was now set for a struggle between the Democrats and the Greenbackers for the control of the Workingmen's Party organization. During the next few months, the contest was most vigorously waged.

On March 15, 1880, the local branches of the Workingmen's Party in San Francisco held a convention and nominated fifteen freeholders for places on the board which was to draft a new charter for the city. Only a few of the men nominated had been leaders in the affairs of the organization, but many were prominent Demo-

crats and a few were Republicans. In opposition to the Workingmen's ticket, a Committee of Two Hundred from the Citizens' Protective Union nominated a group of well-known citizens, subsequently supported by the Republicans. In the hope of preventing a
bitter struggle which might possibly result disastrously for the
best interests of the community, an attempt was made to effect a
compromise between the two opposing parties. No definite agreement was reached, but it was mutually understood that

if the Citizens' Protective Union would give the Workingmen assurance that
there would be no illegitimate interferences with the execution of the order of
the Board of Health providing for the abatement of nuisance in Chinatown,
... in return the Workingmen's military companies would disband and give up
their arms, . . . all violence and incendiary agitation should cease, and things
would be allowed to resume their natural course in the city.[77]

Many of the members of the Committee of Two Hundred were in
favor of repudiating any sort of understanding with the Workingmen short of absolute and unconditional surrender. A few days
later when the lower court declared Kearney and Gannon guilty of
using incendiary language, as noted above, the opposition of the
extremists was so strong that all negotiations were abandoned.

The Workingmen's Party had previously lost the municipal elections in Oakland, Sacramento, and San Jose. It was also overwhelmingly defeated in the election of freeholders in San Francisco. This did much to break the spirit of its followers and to quell
the local excitement. The dissolution of the Kearney movement
seemed merely a question of time.

On April 5, 1880, the executive committee of the Workingmen's
Party met and chose delegates to represent the organization at the
Greenback Labor Party convention to be held at Chicago in June.
This action aroused criticism and opposition among the members of the ward clubs, and many withdrew to affiliate with the
Democratic Party. The state convention of the Workingmen's
Party was held in San Francisco on May 17, 1880, with one hundred delegates present, representing twenty counties. A constitution and platform were adopted. The more important planks of the
platform called for the taxation of United States bonds, the sub-
stitution of greenbacks for national bank notes, the regulation of

railroad rates, and the enactment of restrictive measures designed to prevent monopolies of all kinds. A letter from Kearney, who at the time was still in jail awaiting the decision of his case by the State Supreme Court, urged the selection of delegates to the national convention of the Greenback Labor Party. Discussion arose over this proposal, and finally caused a split among those present. The Greenback-Kearney faction, which was then in control of the party, proceeded with the election of delegates. Kearney and three others were chosen.

In San Francisco, as a result of the action taken by the state convention, the Workingmen's Party organization was disrupted. Democrats and Greenbackers struggled to obtain control of the party machinery and to reorganize the movement with their separate interests in mind. Clubs were disbanded; others were reorganized; and within a comparatively short time nothing remained of the Workingmen's Party of California.

In June, Kearney and his fellow-delegates went east to attend the national convention of the Greenback Labor Party. While he was away the party was further disrupted. On Sundays, two meetings were held simultaneously on the sand-lots, one being addressed by Wellock and others, who advocated the principles of the Democratic Party; the other by Carl Browne, H. W. Moore, and a Mr. Smith, who denounced the Democrats and upheld the principles of the Greenback-Labor Party.

In Chicago, Kearney was made a member of the national executive committee of the Greenback Labor Party, and after his return to California he carried on a vigorous campaign in its interest. On July 1 the Democratic faction of the Workingmen's Party of California held a state convention, expelled Kearney from the organization, and endorsed the national platform and candidates of the Democratic Party. Somewhat later, when he attempted to speak on the sand-lots for the Greenback Labor Party, he encountered so much opposition that he was forced to retire under police protection. In the campaign that followed, the Workingmen did not nominate a separate ticket, but fused either with the Democrats or with the Greenback Labor Party. Several unsuccessful attempts were later made to revive the organization, but the Workingmen's Party of California had become a thing of the past.

From 1881 to 1883, Kearney spoke frequently at the Sunday meetings on the sand-lots, but his remarks were exceedingly temperate, and dealt only with current economic and political problems. There were no attacks on the "bloated aristocrats," or the "leprous Chinese"; nothing but a calm, dispassionate discussion of the issues of the day. After the campaign of 1880, he returned to his drayage business, but in 1881 he again entered politics in the interest of the Anti-Monopoly Party. In 1882 he spoke throughout the State for General George Stoneman, the Democratic nominee for governor. In 1884 he abandoned politics forever, and became a real estate, stock, and ticket broker, and later the proprietor of an employment office. From that time until his death in Alameda on April 24, 1907, he took little or no part in public affairs, giving all his attention to his business interests.[78]

In the history of the labor movement in California, Kearney has a place among the unique leaders. It is difficult for persons unacquainted with the characteristics of the Californians of those days, and ignorant of the economic and political conditions then existing in the State, to understand why an agitator of Kearney's characteristics could arouse the people to such an extraordinary pitch of excitement. Economic and political changes were demanded by the people. Thousands of white men were unemployed, yet hordes of Chinese were at work. Greed and speculation were dominant in business. Corruption stalked in city halls and legislative chambers. Railroad and land monopolies ruled the commonwealth. Under such circumstances a popular uprising was inevitable, and in Kearney the people found the type of leader that suited the occasion.

Had the civil authorities taken a firmer and more determined stand against violence and incendiarism in the early days of the agitation, the reign of anarchy and the sway of Kearneyism might have been short. But politicians have always been politicians, and undoubtedly always will be. In the Kearney affair, their desire to pander to the mob, to show the voters that officeholders are (at least, on the surface) "with the peepul" and opposed to capitalists and corporations, easily explains the laxity of the civil authorities at crises of threatened or actual mob violence. Moreover, the people of California were still living on a frontier; still vivid in memory were the traditions of the Golden Era when the ideals of democracy had prevailed, when all men were considered to be equal in the struggle for wealth, and when the enforcement of the law rested in the hands of each person or in an organized but nonpolitical group. Constituted authority is, as a rule, effective and respected only in older and more settled communities.

The Workingmen's Party movement, riotous and turbulent though it was, was productive of far-reaching consequences. It forced the Chinese question into the foreground as an issue of national importance and compelled the Federal government to abrogate the Burlingame treaty. It was influential in the framing and adoption of a new State Constitution, an instrument so radical that it frightened Capital and greatly hindered the development of the State until its more objectionable features were set aside by decisions of the State Supreme Court or modified by the legislature. It also, temporarily at least, taught the Democratic and Republican parties a lesson, by disclosing what can happen when the workers, betrayed on all sides by politicians, become so dissatisfied that they organize a party and attempt to carry through a program to their own liking. For some years thereafter, the officeseekers and officeholders hearkened a little more attentively to the demands of the common people, although the political reforms needed to ensure freedom from the corrupting influence of railroad and land monopolies were not attained for several decades.

CHAPTER VIII

THE TRADES ASSEMBLY OF SAN FRANCISCO, 1878–1884

CALIFORNIA'S INDUSTRIES were slow in recovering from the depression of 1877, the disastrous consequences of which had been prolonged by the Kearney agitation and the adoption of the new State Constitution. Not until 1881 were signs of returning business activity to be noted. In the intervening years a few unimportant strikes had been called, usually unsuccessful in their outcome, and a few unions had been formed, only to succumb within a short time. Industry had been so demoralized and labor had been so plentiful that the results could not well have been otherwise.[1]

The Kearney movement had received its support mainly from the unemployed and the unorganized. With few exceptions[2] the trade unions did not ally themselves with the Workingmen's Party, nor did the latter concern itself with Organized Labor.[3] Kearney and his followers were ignorant of the principles of trade unionism. It was only indirectly that the sand-lot agitation had any effect upon the union movement in California, and it came about in the following manner.

At the first state convention of the Workingmen's Party of California, held in San Francisco on January 21, 1878, a few of the delegates, members of the unions in their respective crafts, fell to discussing the probable effects of Kearneyism on trade unionism. In the appointment of the executive committee of the party, the union representatives had been given no recognition, and this had aroused dissatisfaction in the ranks of those labor associations which had affiliated with the Kearney movement. Some of the delegates accordingly called a meeting to discuss the situation and, if possible, map out a plan of action. Fifteen to twenty persons were present at the conference, which was held on February 24. A few suggested that a federation of unions be formed; others desired to seek representation on the executive committee; still others were opposed to taking any action whatever, for fear that it would lead to dissension within the Workingmen's Party. After some argument, in which W. Clack, a union printer, and C. W. Pope, a union boot- and shoemaker, took the lead, it was agreed that, in order to protect the few existing labor organizations, and at the same time to aid in the spread of union principles, a central labor body of some sort should be formed. A provisional executive committee was accordingly appointed to carry on a campaign of organization.

In April, 1874, a resolution had been adopted at a picnic of the Journeymen Tailors' Union, urging all labor associations to send delegates to a meeting which that union had called for the purpose of organizing a city federation. At the meeting thus called, which was held on April 21, 1874, only six unions adopted the proposed constitution. A few meetings were held subsequently, but otherwise nothing was accomplished toward carrying out the tailors' proposal.

In 1878, however, the results were far more encouraging. A committee from the tailors' and printers' unions visited other labor organizations, and succeeded in interesting ten of them in the proposed federation.[4] Their representatives were present at the first meeting, held on March 10, 1878. Formal organization was postponed until March 31. On that date, C. W. Pope was elected chairman of the group.[5] The outcome of the meeting was the formation of the Representative Assembly of Trades and Labor Unions, with H. B. Warner, president, J. W. Jamison, vice-president, A. H. Morrison, secretary, and J. Robinson, treasurer. It was voted not to "endorse or support any party or parties, nominee or nominees of any party in the name of the said Convention."[6]

The Trades Assembly, as it was popularly known, met monthly. On July 6, 1879, it adopted resolutions to the effect that "it would unite its efforts with those of the Chicago Trades' Unions . . ." and would support "any feasible plan looking towards the centralization of labor organizations."[7] Two years later it sent C. F. Burgman, a union tailor, as its representative to the Pittsburgh conference of trade and labor unions, out of which came the Federation of Organized Trades and Labor Unions of the United States and Canada, which later changed its name to the American Federation of Labor. In 1882, the San Francisco unions of tailors, cigar-

makers, bookbinders, and harness-, collar-, and whip-makers affiliated with the new national labor federation, as also did the local
Trades Assembly.

The officers of the Trades Assembly were conscientious in the
performance of their duties, and the delegates were regular in attendance, yet there was no enthusiasm, virility, or real leadership.
But when, on July 21, 1881, Frank Roney was admitted as a delegate from the Seamen's Protective Union, things changed.[8] Roney
had been active in the early councils of the Workingmen's Party of
California and had been one of its most intelligent and resourceful
leaders. He had rebelled against the dictatorial methods of Dennis
Kearney, and had presided over the anti-Kearney convention of
May, 1878. After severing his connection with the sand-lotters, he
became interested in socialism, and joined the socialistic Workingmen's Party of the United States, which later became the Socialist
Labor Party. As a Kearneyite, he had been an ardent advocate of
the rights of the masses; as a socialist, he was even more so. He
made speeches at meetings in various parts of the city and was in-
defatigable in his efforts to spread the doctrines of socialism among
the workingmen.

One evening, at a water-front meeting at which he was the
speaker, Roney met a fellow-countryman, J. P. Devereux. Devereux, born in Cork, Ireland, in 1844, had shipped to sea at the
age of fifteen years. He had learned by bitter experience the miserable condition of sailors, and he told Roney of their wretched existence. If ever a man lived who was intensely sympathetic, that
man was Roney. Devereux's stories caused him to resolve that he
would do all in his power to better the lot of the sailor. Night after
night found him under the light of some friendly street-lamp along
the water front talking to small groups of seamen. Socialism was
his theme, but when the steamship sailors and firemen gathered to
discuss their grievances, he was among the first to advocate the organization of a union.

Three other men were closely associated with Roney in spreading
the doctrines of socialism—S. Robert Wilson, T. F. Hagerty, and
A. J. Starkweather.[9] These four men soon became familiar figures
along the water front. One evening in September, 1880, when the
sailors gathered to discuss their grievances, Roney, Wilson, Hag-

erty, and Starkweather were called in as counselors and advisers. As an active member of the ironmolders' union, Roney appreciated the benefits of organization and knew that much good could result

FRANK RONEY

from the unionization of the sailors. With this in mind, he and his associates succeeded in forming the Seamen's Protective Union on September 4, 1880. The union survived for about a year and a half, but failed to accomplish anything of consequence for its members.[10]

Roney was sent as a delegate from the Seamen's Protective Union to the Trades Assembly in July, 1881. His executive ability was at once recognized; within a month he was elected its president.[11] The Trades Assembly now took on new life. An active and successful campaign of organization was started, resulting in the formation of many unions which later affiliated with the central body.[12]

The Trades Assembly also took an active interest in other matters affecting the laboring class. One of the first problems with which it concerned itself was convict labor. Mention has been made of the earlier agitation against the farming out of convict labor.[13] In the years 1872–1874 the disastrous competition of convict-made goods had again brought the issue forcibly to the attention of the workingmen, who forthwith made strenuous efforts to restrict the use of convict labor and to prohibit the sale of prison-made goods. The San Francisco *Chronicle* on January 27, 1872, commented editorially upon the situation in the following words:

Under the present system as practiced at San Quentin, the labor of the prisoners is let out at forty cents a day, or one-sixth of the average remuneration received by good workmen. The practical effect of this is to discourage free labor and to place premium on crime. It has already driven away from the city some of the best workmen, in several industries, and left many a shop idle and deserted. In the manufacture of kegs, barrels, and casks, and in that of saddlery and harness, it has been particularly mischievous, having almost destroyed the former industry in this city, and monopolizing one-third of the value of the latter.

In 1873 the cabinetmakers' union had taken the initiative in waging the campaign against the evils of convict labor. In the latter part of that year, a committee from the Mechanics' State Council reported that out of 931 prisoners, 531 were working under contract, 50 being employed as shoemakers, 200 as cabinetmakers, 125 as harness-makers, 63 as brickmakers, and 200 as wagon-makers. No data were given on the rest. The yearly output of the convict cabinetmakers was valued at $150,000 to $200,000, and that of the convict shoemakers at about $50,000.[14] The agitation against the injurious competition of convict labor subsided in the next few years because of the unstable conditions in industry. In 1881 it was revived by the Trades Assembly. Article X, Section 6, of the new State Constitution[15] decreed, as did a statute enacted in 1880, that the contract system of prison labor should be abolished when all contracts then existing had expired (January 1, 1882). Thereafter, the convicts were to be employed for the benefit of the State only. This appeared to be a step forward, but it did not remove the competition of prison labor. The convicts continued to manufacture the same products that had been made under the old contract system, and the private contractors, to whom the prisoners had previously been farmed out, were given the privilege of furnishing the materials, hiring and paying the foremen, and purchasing the finished goods. The evils of convict labor therefore remained, and although the Trades Assembly called mass meetings and published condemnatory resolutions, nothing was accomplished at the time toward removing the abuse.

Another question with which the Trades Assembly concerned itself was Chinese immigration. The anti-Capital, anti-Monopoly attitude of the Workingmen's Party of California in its later years, and a decline in the number of Chinese entering the United States, had caused the people to lose interest in the agitation against the Orientals. The cry, "The Chinese must go," had been forgotten in the virulent attacks of the sand-lotters on Capital and Monopoly. The immediate results of the ratification of the treaty of 1880 between the United States and China, however, greatly changed the situation. This treaty, as previously noted, permitted the United States "to regulate, limit, or suspend" the immigration of the Chinese or their residence in the United States whenever it was felt that the coming of the Chinese laborers or their residence in this country affected or threatened to affect the interests of the United States or the "good order of the said country." But the immigration of the Chinese or their residence in this country could not be absolutely prohibited. The limitation or suspension had to be reasonable, and was to apply only to the Chinese who entered as laborers; other classes were not included in the limitations imposed by the new treaty. Every vessel crossing the Pacific was filled with Chinese hastening to enter, fearful lest the gates should be closed permanently against them. In the three years 1880–1882, inclusive, more than 57,000 Chinese were admitted. In the ninety days preceding the date on which the Exclusion Act of 1882 (prohibiting the immigration of Chinese laborers for a period of ten years) was to become effective, 15,769 arrived in California. Under the circumstances it is not strange that the anti-Chinese agitation broke out anew. But it was entirely different in character from that of preceding years. Instead of incendiary language and threats of violence, the boycott was resorted to in an effort to prevent the sale of Chinese-made goods.

A campaign had been carried on in earlier years to induce the public to buy the products of white labor only, but it had not succeeded. The consumer had no way of knowing whether the goods which he bought were made by white labor or by Chinese labor. In 1874 the cigarmakers, who had suffered most seriously from the

LABEL OF CIGAR MAKERS' ASSOCIATION OF THE PACIFIC COAST

effects of Chinese competition, originated the idea of attaching a label to their products by means of which it would be possible to distinguish white-labor cigars from Chinese-labor cigars.[16] The label was white and was pasted across the box.[17] Shortly thereafter the shoemakers also adopted a white-labor label. In March, 1878, the Shoemakers' Protective Union incorporated so that it "could own a particular stamp of its own." The stamp was a steel die and was used to imprint the label upon the products of the white shoemakers. The union also appropriated a sum of money to pay for the hire of a horse and wagon, a blackboard, fife, drum, and transparencies, for "two hours every Saturday night, to pass around the town and cry down enemies and advertise friends."[18]

The labels of the cigarmakers and the shoemakers were frequently imitated by unscrupulous merchants and manufacturers. It is asserted that, in order to get needed protection, the shoemakers had a bill introduced in the legislature of 1876 making it an offense to counterfeit such labels, but that the measure was quietly suppressed.[19] In February, 1878, the Order of Caucasians proposed that a law be enacted compelling all boot and shoe manufacturers to place a label or stamp on their goods, stating whether or not they had been made by Chinese labor. A week later (February 18) the cabinetmakers', the carpenters', and the boot- and shoemakers' unions held a well attended mass meeting and petitioned the legislature to enact a law providing that "all manufacturers be required to mark their goods or wares by stamps or label with these words, namely: 'manufactured by white labor' or 'manufactured by Mongolian labor,' or in accordance with the class or kind of labor so employed by said manufacturers; failure to comply constituting a misdemeanor."[20] In order to satisfy the popular demand, and yet not give the workers the desired legislation, a bill was introduced in the legislature of 1877–1878 compelling "boot and shoemakers in this state to brand their names on the goods they manufacture." The deceit was discovered by the unions, and the bill was killed.[21] Two years later, a bill which embodied their demands failed of passage in the legislature.[22] Laws protecting the union label were not enacted by the State legislature until 1887.[23]

At first no effort was made to advertise the label extensively or to push the sale of labeled goods. The label was a new weapon and it was some time before it began to appeal to the people as a practical method of meeting Chinese competition. An appreciation of the present difficulties attendant upon inducing customers, even though they are union members, to purchase label goods, provides a basis for surmising that the union-label advocates of those early years must have found the task of popularizing the label most discouraging. By means of persistent agitation and as a result of the dogged determination of the trade unionists, a number of firms were induced to adopt the label, and a fair-sized demand was created for label products. At a meeting of the Seventh Ward Club of the Workingmen's Party of California on October 2, 1878, William Wallaz, an ardent trade unionist and later one of the leaders of the local union movement, said that the adoption of the cigarmakers' label had thrown more than 1,000 Chinese out of work and had made room for 200 or 300 additional white cigarmakers in San Francisco.

Label goods, however, were not necessarily union-made goods. For some years after the introduction of the label, it was not required of the employer, as a condition of his having the use of the label, that all his workers be members of the union. Provided that white labor exclusively was employed, the presence of one union member in a shop would obtain the label for that shop. In December, 1878, four years after the cigarmakers had originated the label, their organization adopted the following resolution : "No manufacturer shall be entitled to receive the union label for the work of any cigarmaker in his employ over thirty days, unless he be a member of the union in good standing."[24] This practice was in effect for some time, but was finally superseded by a rule that the label could only be used by an employer when all his employees were members of the union. Another early regulation of the Cigar Makers' Association prohibited the use of the union label by manufacturers who did not have the cigar made entirely by one person. In many shops it was customary to have one worker, usually a boy or girl, roll the bunch, and a journeyman put on the wrapper.

In 1879, the cigarmakers' union attempted to copyright its label so as to protect it against imitation. The United States Patent Office, however, refused the application "on the ground that the label was not a trade-mark within the purview of the act, since it did not appear that 'the members of the Association all manufacture the same goods, or propose to apply the mark to any particular kind'."[25]

For the purpose of advertising label goods and thus creating a demand for white-labor products, the Sacramento cigarmakers' union in 1879 suggested that the unions of the State have a display of their labels and of label goods at the State Fair. The plan was approved by the unions concerned, but it was not carried out.

The Shoemakers' Protective Union of San Francisco, which had been disrupted by the Kearney agitation, was reorganized in 1881 as the Boot and Shoemakers' White Labor League. It introduced a new stamp for its products, consisting of a paper label which was pasted across either the toe or the

LABEL OF BOOT AND SHOE-MAKERS' WHITE LABOR LEAGUE

heel of the shoe. This organization remained active for some years, and waged a vigorous campaign against Oriental competition.

The sudden influx of Chinese in 1880–1882 brought about a determined though rather conservative opposition by the white workers of California. The Trades Assembly interested itself in the matter, and from time to time appointed committees to investigate the actual conditions in the trades in which the Chinese were serious competitors. In 1882, one of its committees reported that in San Francisco 8,500 Chinese and only 179 whites were employed in cigar manufacturing. Of the 187 cigar factories using Chinese labor, only 37 were owned by white proprietors, and of the 62 slipper factories, only 12 were owned by them. Twenty-five clothing factories employed 6,010 Chinese workers, and an additional 1,500 were employed in manufacturing custom work and underwear. Five hundred and ten Chinese laundries gave employment to 7,650 Chinese, and 615 were employed by the proprietors of white laundries.

Resolutions and petitions were sent to Congress praying for relief, but nothing was done until 1882. In March of that year a bill was introduced in the United States Senate calling for the prohibition of Chinese immigration for a period of twenty years. So eager were the Californians for the enactment of the measure that the governor of the State declared March 4 a holiday, so that they might adequately express their approval of the bill and their encouragement of those Congressmen and Senators who had announced their willingness to support it. Large demonstrations were held in San Francisco and in other cities. The bill was approved by the Senate on March 9, and by the House of Representatives on March 23, and sent to the President for his signature. President Arthur vetoed the bill on April 4 as being a breach of national faith, asserting that neither the United States nor China, in drafting and approving the treaty of 1880, had contemplated the approval of a twenty-year period of exclusion. The people of California were indignant. Protest meetings were held in many places and for a while it looked as if the agitation against the Chinese might again take on an incendiary character.

In the hope of shaping the opposition of the people so as to make it more effective, the Trades Assembly called a state convention of labor and anti-Chinese organizations to meet in San Francisco on April 24, 1882. The meeting was well attended.[26] The outcome of the convention was the formation of the League of Deliverance with Frank Roney as president and W. F. Eastman as secretary. Branch leagues were organized in several localities, especially in San Francisco; in less than a month, 13 branches had been formed with a membership of more than 4,000. Branches were also established in Nevada.[27]

The League of Deliverance employed several methods to make effective its opposition to the Chinese. First, it began a vigorous boycott of Chinese-made goods. Large placards advertising white-labor goods were placed in the windows of stores that dealt in such wares exclusively. The manufacturers of Chinese-made goods, and the dealers in them, were similarly advertised. A certain shoe-store proprietor of San Francisco had been a persistent champion and seller of Chinese-made products. The league employed a boy to stand in front of this merchant's store and distribute handbills asking the public not to buy from him. The police frightened the boy away, but his place was taken by A. J. Starkweather, who volunteered to parade in front of the store with a placard on his back advertising that the dealer was a friend of the Chinese. The novelty of the situation attracted a large crowd, which blocked the sidewalk. At noon Starkweather was replaced by John Monroe, whom the police arrested. Starkweather, upon his return, repeated the morning's performance, and he also was arrested. On being released on bail, some hours later, he donned an old coat on which was painted the statement which the placard had borne, and again walked back and forth in front of the store. About that time Frank Roney appeared with a transparency upon which was printed a similar statement. He was arrested, but he turned the transparency over to Isaac Coronson. Coronson also was arrested. The next day, Starkweather was again arrested and his painted coat taken from him. He had no difficulty in obtaining bail, and on his release started once more for the boycotted store, only to be arrested a third time. The actions of the police aroused considerable excitement, especially among the members of the League of Deliverance, and threats of violence were made openly.

Roney and Starkweather were freed after brief trials; the charges against Coronson were subsequently dropped. Starkweather was again arrested, this time on complaint of F. Grass, who charged that Starkweather had libeled him by distributing handbills upon which was printed the following statement:

> Here we are again! Don't patronize Grass or Butterfield; they sell Chinese-made boots and shoes. Avoid them! They are traitors to their race.

Starkweather was later discharged by the Court.

The boycott of the League of Deliverance was carried on so vigorously and with such determination that it had an appreciable effect on the sale of Chinese-made goods and the employment of Mongolians. One factory which had from 500 to 600 Chinese on its pay roll replaced them with white workers, as did many other employers. The *Morning Call* on July 31, 1882, said:

> The effect of this depression in the Chinese factories is seen in an encouraging revival of business in the establishments where Chinese are not employed. Members of the White Shoe-makers' League say that they are running full time. About thirty of our large factories, who were employing Chinese, have discharged them and are now employing white labor exclusively.

Besides the boycott, the League of Deliverance outlined another plan of action, resort to which fortunately never became necessary. It was to the following effect:

> When the Visiting and Information Committee have thoroughly canvassed their district, it will become the duty of the branch to call an executive meeting of all the members to determine from what portion of the district the Chinese shall be removed first. The Executive Committee will then notify the owners of the property rented to the Chinese of the decision of the branch.
>
> Should the owners of the property and the Chinese residents then fail to comply with the request of the Executive Committee, after the expiration of six days it will be the duty of the Executive Committee to declare the district dangerous, and to define its boundaries, and to notify the inhabitants thereof to remove beyond said boundaries within thirty days. Should the Chinese remain within the proclaimed district after the expiration of the thirty days, the general Executive Committee will be required to abate the danger in whatever manner seems best to them.[28]

The Chinese Exclusion Act, which President Arthur had vetoed on April 4, 1882, was reintroduced into Congress, amended so as to restrict Chinese immigration for a period of ten years, passed, and signed by him on May 6, 1882. The League of Deliverance, its mission accomplished, soon dissolved. The agitation against the Chinese, however, was carried on intermittently for about a decade. On May 5, 1892, President Cleveland signed the Geary law, which, among other things, extended the exclusion period for another ten years. Finally, on April 29, 1902, the provisions of the laws to restrict Chinese immigration that Congress had previously passed were extended indefinitely.

The Trades Assembly, besides carrying on an organization program among the workers of San Francisco as well as a campaign against the Chinese, participated to a certain degree in local politics. In 1882 it appointed a legislative committee to draft labor measures, question candidates for office, and lobby for labor legislation at the State capitol. The committee prepared a list of questions covering various topics in which Labor was interested, such as employers' liability, factory inspection, postal savings banks, government ownership, free textbooks, weekly pay day, and the abolition of child labor, and submitted it to the candidates for political office. Union members were then urged to support those who replied to the satisfaction of the Trades Assembly. This committee also caused the introduction of bills in the legislature of 1883, relative to the following matters: establishment of a Bureau of Labor Statistics, introduction of a uniform system of public school textbooks, printed and distributed free by the State, and establishment of a state-owned book bindery. Only the bill creating a Bureau of Labor Statistics was passed by the legislature. It was signed by the governor on March 3, 1883.[29] A similar measure had been passed by both houses in 1878 but had failed to receive the governor's signature.[30] John S. Enos was the first State Labor Commissioner of California. The duties of the office were so numerous and varied and the successive commissioners so little interested in the welfare of Labor that for many years the bureau was a great disappointment to the workers; it was used primarily to reward the political henchmen of the party in power.

Roney, while president of the Trades Assembly, proposed the erection of a labor temple. Incorporation papers were obtained, authorizing the issue and sale of $100,000 capital stock, and options were taken on several sites; but the unions failed to support the project, and it had to be abandoned.

The revival of industrial activity and the efforts of the Trades Assembly to spread the gospel of unionism among the workers had resulted in the formation of many associations in San Francisco and elsewhere.[31] A national charter was obtained by the carpenters' and joiners' union of San Francisco in March, 1882, the third union at that time to have national affiliations, the others being the printers' and the ironmolders' unions of that city. On September 1, 1882, the carpenters demanded and obtained the eight-hour day for Saturday only. On February 1, 1883, they announced that they would work only nine hours a day after May 1, 1883, and that they would abolish piecework. Both demands were granted.

Conditions of employment among the bakers of San Francisco had always been most unsatisfactory: they customarily worked from twelve to eighteen hours per day, also Saturday nights, and for about six hours on Sunday; wages were paid monthly; and employees were compelled to board at "homes" provided by the employers. In 1880 the German bakers' union succeeded in obtaining the enactment of a State law prohibiting Saturday night and Sunday work,[32] but in July of that year it was declared unconstitutional.[33] In 1882 two unions existed among the bakers: one for the Germans, who comprised the majority of the workers in the trade; and one for the English-speaking workers. In February, 1882, an agitation, unsuccessful at the time, was begun for shorter hours, no Saturday night or Sunday work, weekly wage payments, and the abolition of the requirement that employees must board with their employers. The two unions subsequently obtained charters from the national bakers' union, and in later years succeeded in reducing hours and improving working conditions. But the bakers and confectioners (the latter group of workers having become affiliated with the bakers) did not succeed in obtaining one day of rest in seven until the latter part of the year 1900, and in order to get it they agreed to work ten hours for five days, and thirteen hours on the sixth day.

During the latter part of March, 1882, the white employees of Fay's Shingle Mill in San Francisco struck successfully against the employment of Chinese labor. The marble cutters on September 18, 1882, announced that on and after October 2 they would demand $3 per day, a nine-hour day, and wage payments every two weeks. The plumbers and gas fitters demanded $4 per day in October. The ship painters organized a union and announced that on and after November 1 none of their craft would work for less than $4 per day of eight hours, with time and a half for Sunday labor, overtime at the rate of $1 an hour, and that none would labor for even a few hours at less than a full day's pay. These demands were granted by the employers.

The spirit of organization spread to the workers in near-by cities. In April, 1882, the cigarmakers of San Jose organized as a branch of the Pacific Coast White Cigar Makers' Association, and the carpenters of Oakland and of San Rafael organized in December of the same year.

During 1883 the San Francisco clearing-house returns and other indicators showed a slackening of business and industry, but the union movement continued its growth and activity. Agitation by the Knights of Labor and the International Workingmen's Association made an increasingly strong appeal to the members of the working class, especially in the cities of central California. Strikes and demands for higher wages and shorter hours became a lively part of the industrial life of San Francisco and neighboring places. In January, 1883, the plasterers of San Francisco, who had been organized for about a year with wages at $2 per day, decided to demand $5 for an eight-hour day after March 1. Their employers formed the Master Plasterers' Protective Association, and on January 30 agreed to grant the demands of their men, but with the understanding that they were to become effective only after April 1. In March, the plumbers, gas fitters, and bricklayers obtained a nine-hour day, and the painters declared that they would enforce the eight-hour day on and after May 14.

Because of the initiative of the building trades unions of San Francisco in getting the shorter workday, the time seemed propitious for the formation of a united body that should increase the bargaining power of the building trades workers. Accordingly, on June 18, 1883, representatives of the carpenters, painters, metal roofers, bricklayers, and stair-builders met to form a Confederation of Building Trades. Several subsequent meetings were held, a constitution was adopted, and officers were elected, but other unions showed no interest in the project, and the association quietly disappeared in August, 1883. Thomas Poyser was president and J. W. Maher was secretary of this, the first, federation of building trades in San Francisco.

In May, 1883, 500 cigarmakers in the employ of George P. Lees & Company, of San Francisco, struck successfully for an increase in wages. In June, the Chinese shoemakers of that city struck for an increase in wages from $1 to $1.40 per day. In July the sailmakers asked for a nine-hour day and a wage of $4 per day, to become effective on July 16. On July 5, the stair-builders struck for an increase of 50 cents per day. They had been receiving $3.50 to $4 per day. Strike breakers were brought in from the East and the strike of the stair-builders was lost. On June 23, the coopers' union struck for higher wages. The employers appeared to be immovable, and the coopers announced that they would open a coöperative shop. This frightened the employers, and on July 28 they granted the workers' demands. In July the brass molders and finishers struck for an increase of 25 cents per day. The wharf-builders, who had organized in February, 1883, notified their employers in the early part of July, of the same year, that they would work only nine hours on and after August 1. On July 13, thirteen white waiters in the Royal Crown Dining Saloon, of San Francisco, struck against the employment of Negroes. This led to the formation of the White Cooks' and Waiters' Union of the Pacific Coast, which for many years played an important part in union affairs in San Francisco.

On July 19, 1883, the nation-wide strike of the telegraphers reached California. The telegraphers had formed a national union in 1882, and had affiliated with the Knights of Labor. The strike was directed against all commercial telegraph companies, the demands of the workers being for a six-day week, an eight-hour day, and a seven-hour night, with a wage increase of 15 per cent. The strike involved thirty-five men in San Francisco, eleven in Sacramento, and three in Yreka. After about a month, the strike was declared off. In the latter part of July, the longshoremen of San Francisco struck for higher wages. On July 30, the printers struck against the *Morning Call* and the *Evening Bulletin,* asserting that the proprietors of these two newspapers had forced their employees to give up their union cards. The employers, however, declared that the union had struck in order to obtain the discharge of nonunion workers. Approximately sixty printers were affected. An active boycott of the two papers followed. The unions of the city supported the strikers by attempting to induce *Call* and *Bulletin* subscribers to purchase other papers. A handbill in support of the boycott was circulated, signed by the presidents of the Trades Assembly, the Building Trades Assembly, thirty San Francisco unions, five Oakland unions,[34] thirteen Knights of Labor assemblies, and by the Division Secretary of the International Workingmen's Association. These organizations, it was stated, represented 18,347 union men. The circular declared:

> ... we put the stamp of OUR disapproval on these two papers; and we will in the future not only refuse to patronize them, but will so far as possible avoid all places of business which do patronize them, either by subscribing to them or advertising in their columns, until they abandon their present antagonistic attitude to Labor Organizations.

This strike, like the telegraphers' strike, was a complete failure, the two newspapers concerned having no difficulty in obtaining typesetters. About this time the marble cutters decided that they would enforce the closed shop, and notified their employers that they would not work with non-union workers. As the growing strength and activity of the unions became evident, the employers of San Francisco deemed it advisable to form a protective body, and on October 29, 1883, the Merchants' and Manufacturers' Association was organized.

Outside the city of San Francisco there were in 1883 but few occurrences in the labor field that need recording. On March 17, 1883, the Central Pacific railroad informed its shop employees at Sacramento and Truckee that the hours of labor would be reduced from ten to eight per day, but with only eight hours' pay. The men struck for the retention of the longer workday and the previous wage scale. In March, the cigarmakers of Stockton struck against the introduction of a mechanical device which they asserted made it impossible for them to earn their former wages. On May 15, the carpenters of Alameda organized a union. In July, the cigarmakers of San Jose opposed successfully a reduction in wages. In Oakland the Pacific Iron and Nail Works announced a reduction in wages, which caused its employees to form Golden Gate Lodge, No. 1, of the Amalgamated Association of Iron, Steel and Tin Workers of the United States.

Business conditions in California during 1884 were worse than they had been during the preceding year. Bank clearings decreased noticeably. Retailers reported 50 per cent fewer sales than in 1883. Employment was not so plentiful as it had been, and, consequently, affairs in the labor world were quieter than they had been for some time. In February, the trunk- and valise-makers employed in the factory of D. Black & Company, San Francisco, struck against a reduction in wages ranging from 25 to 40 per cent. In the fall of 1883, a union had been organized among the Chinese cigarmakers of San Francisco. In the early part of 1884 they demanded an increase of $1 per 1,000 cigars, which was granted by the employers on February 11. Having so easily won this first skirmish with white employers, the Chinese cigarmakers sought further to enforce certain conditions of employment. On February 28 they struck against the employment of two cigar-packers of their own race, who did not meet with their approval. That afternoon the Merchants' and Manufacturers' Association of San Francisco met and resolved that all cigar factories should lock out their Chinese employees until the men went back to work, that those employers who did not do so should be required to pay a fine of $5 per head weekly for every Chinese employed, and that Chinese-made cigars should not be purchased by the members of the association. The lockout affected 2,800 Mongolians. On March 17, the *Evening Bulletin* announced that the Chinese had returned to work without obtaining any concessions from their employers.

In the early part of February, 1884, the blacksmiths of San Francisco organized a union among their helpers. When the Union Iron Works discharged all helpers known to be members, the blacksmiths struck. In April, the boss painters of San Francisco posted notice of a wage of 33⅓ cents per hour, and a ten-hour day. The journeymen painters promptly met and resolved not to work for less than $3.50 for a nine-hour day. Upon the refusal of the employers to grant these demands, 500 painters in San Francisco and 100 in Oakland struck on May 6. A week later it was announced that the strike had been won. An unimportant strike of molders occurred in June, 1884, among the workers in the plant of the Agricultural Iron Works of San Francisco against the employment of non-union men and the hiring of too many apprentices.

The apprenticeship rule of the union permitted one apprentice to eight journeymen. In the latter part of June, the tailors employed by Sanders & Johnson, of San Francisco, struck successfully against their employers. Forty-three master painters of the Pacific Coast organized an employers' association on March 25, 1884. About the same time thirty master plasterers of San Francisco also organized. The master masons and builders of San Francisco were likewise brought together into a protective association. It is interesting to note that the last-named group agreed, among other things, to employ only those workers who were members of the local bricklayers' union.

In February, 1884, James H. Barry, of San Francisco, began the publication of *The Daily Star*. Barry was a prominent member of the typographical union and for many years played an important part in the local labor movement. It is said that he was the first employing printer in the United States to give his workers voluntarily the eight-hour day. *The Daily Star* proved too costly a venture, and within a short time it was changed to a weekly. It suspended publication in 1921. Although the *Star* was a journal of liberal views and not, strictly speaking, a labor paper, it was nevertheless an ardent champion of the rights of the working class and gave its unqualified support at all times to the cause of Labor.

In August, 1884, a convention of labor organizations met in San Francisco to discuss the advisability of taking political action. One hundred and forty delegates were present. H. C. Kinne was chairman of the meeting. The outcome of the conference was the formation of a temporary organization, known as "The Labor Council of San Francisco," and the adoption of a platform addressed to the workers of San Francisco. The Labor Council played no part in the ensuing election. In September, 1884, the remnants of the old Workingmen's Party of California were brought together by Dennis Kearney, Thomas Maybell, and others, and a platform was drafted, but no ticket was put in the field and no votes were cast by the party in the subsequent election.

During 1883 and the early part of 1884, the interest of the organized workers of San Francisco in the affairs of the Trades Assembly greatly declined. In 1883 the Trades Assembly was composed of representatives from only the printers, bookbinders, tailors, cigarmakers, and coopers, and met only at the call of the president, J. K. Phillips.[35] Toward the close of 1884 it had only a few unions affiliated with it. The exact date of its last meeting is not

JAMES H. BARRY

known, so quietly did it pass from the local labor field. Its end had been brought about chiefly by the growth of two mutually antagonistic organizations, namely, the Knights of Labor and the International Workingmen's Association; men who had been active in its affairs allied themselves with the two newer movements. Lack of vigorous and progressive leadership by the presidents of the

Trades Assembly who succeeded Roney was also a factor in its decline.

The Trades Assembly was a necessary phase of the development of the labor movement of California. Formed in a period of great turmoil and unrest, it did yeoman's service in keeping alive the ideals of trade unionism and in encouraging the formation of labor organizations at a time when, otherwise, the results of the earlier efforts in that direction might have been lost through the Kearney agitation.

For Organized Labor, the years from 1878 to 1884 formed a period of transition. The workers, at least for the time being, were forced to appreciate the fact that they could not secure the satisfaction of their economic demands through political action or through sand-lot propaganda, and that organization in the industrial field was an essential preliminary to higher wages, shorter hours, and improved working conditions. They came to realize that trade-union policies must be formulated and tested, that adjustments must be made, and that conditions must be studied, before it would be possible to know what measures were best suited to their needs. The Trades Assembly and its leaders blazed new trails; they trained the workers to understand the program and policies of unionism. They did their task as thoroughly and as intelligently as was possible under the conditions and with the materials and the experience—or lack of it—that were available. Future years were to see a successful and more stable labor movement built upon the foundations which they laid.

Chapter IX

THE KNIGHTS OF LABOR

IN THE EARLY EIGHTIES, as already noted, there was a gradual revival of business in California. Industry slowly recovered from the depression of the uncertain period of the seventies. Capital, which had been partly driven to cover by the Kearney agitation and by the objectionable clauses of the new State Constitution, came timidly out of hiding in response to encouraging court decisions which softened the harsh clauses of that document, and in response, also, to improved economic conditions in the eastern states. From 1883 to 1885, depression, accompanied by wage reductions, affected seriously the working classes of eastern communities, and many labor disturbances occurred. In California, industry slowed up somewhat. Bank clearings in San Francisco declined from $628,900,000 in 1882 to $562,344,737 in 1885. The wage increases which the California workers had gained following the business revival of the early years of the decade were mostly retained, although the local employers complained bitterly of the competition of eastern plants which were paying lower wages. A few attempts were made to effect reductions, but they were stubbornly resisted by the employees, especially by those who were unionized. A few serious strikes occurred. The years 1886 and 1887, however, were years of recovery both in the eastern states and in California, although a large number of workers remained unemployed in San Francisco even to the closing months of 1886.

The depressed industrial conditions forcibly brought home to the workers of the nation the necessity of collective bargaining and resulted in a rapid growth of the membership of the Knights of Labor and of certain national trade union organizations. It is interesting to note that, as late as the middle years of the eighties, the unions of California were chiefly local, unaffiliated with the national associations in their respective crafts. The only exceptions were the unions of the printers, molders, and carpenters of San Francisco, and the printers' unions of Sacramento and Los Angeles. In general, California organizations had been only slightly influenced by the eastern labor movement. The latter was so completely out of touch with conditions and events in the West that its leaders were apparently quite unaware of the existence of a labor movement in California. This state of affairs caused many of the unions of San Francisco to establish branches in other cities of the Pacific Coast, and brought about, in the early nineties, the organization of a Pacific Coast federation of unions to protect and advance the interests of labor organizations west of the Rocky Mountains.

Although the Knights of Labor had been organized in Philadelphia in 1869, it did not establish relations with the workers of California until 1878. P. S. Dorney, a Knights of Labor organizer, in a speech made in Sacramento on July 9, 1883, said that the first California branch of the order, Local Assembly No. 855, was established in that city on October 14, 1878. The newspapers of the San Francisco Bay region commented on the local Knights of Labor movement as early as March and April, 1879. The Oakland *Times* on March 31, 1879, mentioned the existence of a branch in that city, and called it a "desperate band of conspirators" and "assassins." It asserted that "Patrick McNiff of Harrisburg, Pennsylvania," had been the organizer of the Oakland group, also that McNiff "was here in May and June last year" (1878). The exact date of the establishment of the Oakland assembly is not known.

Officially, the Knights of Labor was a secret organization from 1869 to 1881. In many communities, however, its secrecy was not relinquished until some years later. This partly explains why it is so difficult to get accurate data concerning its growth in California. Its greatest increase in membership and influence occurred in the depression of 1883–1886. This was true not only in California, but also in the rest of the United States, for within that period its national membership ranged from 500,000 to 1,000,000.

The Knights of Labor appealed chiefly to the unorganized workers who had no national unions. It was opposed to the "narrow selfishness" of the trade unions, and laid great stress on the *labor union* form of organization as being ideal for the workers. It preached the importance of the "mixed assembly," which it held to be the essence of perfection. Under the direction of the Knights of Labor, workers of all trades were organized into local assemblies, regardless of trade or craft lines. Occasionally, certain trade unions were admitted to the national organization as members of a particular assembly, but that policy was not encouraged. Persons not of the working class were also welcomed as members of the various assemblies, the only exceptions being saloon-keepers, gamblers, lawyers, bankers, and stockbrokers. Strikes, boycotts, and participation of the organization in politics were not sanctioned. Economic questions, such as the land problem, monopoly, coöperation, and government ownership, provided common topics for debate in the local assemblies.[1]

With the return of prosperity in the late eighties, many of the trade unions revived and rebuilt their national organizations, and many new trade unions were formed. The failure of many unauthorized strikes and boycotts and the growing strength of the trade union movement, which found an outlet through the newly formed American Federation of Labor, resulted in a rapid decline in the importance of the Knights of Labor. A bitter contest ensued between these two national labor organizations, and the Knights of Labor found that it was fighting a losing battle. It remained in existence for some time after the opening of the twentieth century, but its influence in the labor field had come to an end in the early nineties.

For some years after the organization of the first assembly of the Knights of Labor in California, in 1878, the local movement spread very slowly. In April, 1882, Burnette G. Haskell, the editor of *Truth,* announced that there were 5,000 members in San Francisco. In July, 1883, Dorney, in the speech above referred to (p. 152), asserted that the Knights of Labor had 12,000 members in San Francisco alone, and many more in other sections of California. I feel certain that these estimates are gross exaggerations, the first being that of a labor editor with a habit of making extravagant statements, and the latter that of a professional organizer in a speech made for public effect.

District Assembly No. 53, which had supervision over the members of the Knights of Labor in the San Francisco territory (including San Jose and Oakland), was organized on September 3, 1882, with eight local assemblies as constituent members. District

Assembly No. 140, of Los Angeles, had jurisdiction over the local assemblies in the southern part of the State. In August, 1883, the following local assemblies were known to be in existence in San Francisco: No. 1390 (mixed), No. 1573 (mixed), No. 1580 (mixed), No. 1760 (mixed), No. 1903 (painters), No. 2130 (mixed), No. 2188 (patternmakers), No. 2226 (white shoemakers), No. 2383 (harness-makers), No. 2507 (telegraphers), No. 2572 (mixed), No. 2860 (printers, pressmen, and stereotypers), No. 2861 (cigarmakers), No. 2999 (mixed), and a clerk's assembly, the number of which I have been unable to obtain. Local Assembly No. 1554 (mixed) of Oakland, No. 1994 (mixed) of San Jose, No. 855 of Sacramento, and No. 2004 of Los Angeles were also in existence at that date. The Women's Labor League, Assembly No. 5855, of San Francisco, was organized February 24, 1886, and continued in existence until May 13, 1892.

On September 16 and 17, 1888, a state convention of the Knights of Labor was held in San Francisco for the purpose of organizing a State Assembly of California. It was called at the suggestion of Calvin Ewing, one of the local organizers of the Knights of Labor, who for many years had been active as a member of the harness-makers' union of San Francisco. Ewing gave much of his time and energy to furthering the cause of Organized Labor. He was ably assisted by W. W. Stone, J. J. Payne, Thomas Poyser, and others. Ewing, because of his conservatism, early aroused the opposition of the radicals in the local labor movement, who were eager to checkmate his aspirations to become a prominent labor leader; many felt that he and some of his associates were interested in using the movement only for their political advancement. He later became secretary of the State banking commissioners, and in his declining years was employed in the United States Mint at San Francisco.

Delegates from the following local assemblies were present at the state convention: San Francisco, Nos. 1390, 1760, 2752, 2860, 2861, 3657, 4764, 7338, 7546, 7686, 7744; Oakland, No. 4954; Stockton, Nos. 6899, 6900; Petaluma, No. 7169; St. Helena, No. 7267; El Dorado, No. 7684; Georgetown, No. 7685; Hollister, No. 7821; Napa, No. 7838; Boca, No. 7844; and Santa Cruz, No. 7936. Two other assemblies, No. 5764 and No. 7547, whose locations I have been unable to learn, were also represented in the convention. Local assemblies Nos. 2999 (San Francisco), 5674 (Truckee), 6053 (Sacramento), 6898 (Stockton), and 7547 (Vacaville) were in existence at that time, but were not represented.[2]

As results of the two-day session, a state assembly was organized, and a constitution adopted. Volney Hoffmeyer was chosen State Master Workman.[3] No further meetings of the state assembly were held. Shortly thereafter, the influence of the order began to wane, and the workers turned their attention to other forms of organized activity. The passing of the Knights of Labor in California resulted primarily from the declining importance of the national organization. Bitter contests between leaders in the national movement, the increasing opposition of the employing class, and the growth of the rival American Federation of Labor, wrecked the structure which had been built up with much effort throughout the United States.

CHAPTER X

THE INTERNATIONAL WORKINGMEN'S ASSOCIATION

CONSERVATISM marked the Knights of Labor movement in California. Its leaders, as was also true of many men prominent in the national organization, were unduly concerned with using labor support for personal political advancement. Within the ranks of the Knights of Labor in San Francisco, however, there was a small group of extremely active radicals, always at war with the conservative leaders, and fighting energetically for those measures and policies which they felt would better the lot of the common people. These radicals soon gathered under the red banner of a locally organized International Workingmen's Association, and in many ways they aided greatly in laying the foundations of the present California labor movement.

The International Workingmen's Association, the First International, was organized in London in 1864 by Karl Marx and his associates in the British labor movement, for the purpose of opposing the importation of strike breakers from the Continent. The association early abandoned its union activities and became socialistic. The first American branch was formed in New York in October, 1867. One or two branches were later organized in San Francisco.[1] After some years of ineffective activity, the headquarters of the International having in the meantime been moved to Philadelphia, the association was formally dissolved on July 15, 1876, by the action of delegates from nineteen sections. In July, 1881, the followers of Bakunin, the anarchist, organized the International Working People's Association in London. Some of the radical elements in the labor movement of the United States hastened to affiliate with it.[2]

The International Workingmen's Association movement in California, although appropriating the name of the First International, and although patterned along the lines of the two international groups mentioned above, was nevertheless of local origin. It was the brain child of Burnette G. Haskell, of San Francisco, one of the most erratic and brilliant geniuses in the history of the labor movement on the Pacific Coast. Haskell was born in Sierra County, California, June 11, 1857, his parents being among the early pioneers

BURNETTE G. HASKELL

of the State. He attended the University of California, the University of Illinois, and Oberlin College, but was not graduated from any of them. He prepared for the California bar examinations, and in 1879 was admitted to practice in this State. His associates believed that he was to have a brilliant career; but Haskell, erratic and unstable, soon took a deep-seated dislike to the law. As a youth he had had some contact with the printer's trade; so, when his wealthy and politically ambitious uncle was snubbed by local politicians and on January 22, 1882, established a weekly paper, *Truth*, Haskell was put in charge of it.

Several numbers of *Truth* had been issued, when one evening Haskell attended a meeting of the Trades Assembly in search of news. After listening for some time to what was being said, he offered to make his paper the official organ of the Assembly. Bitter opposition to Haskell and his offer was at first expressed by the union delegates, but Frank Roney, who was then president of the Trades Assembly, finally prevailed upon its members to accept Haskell's proposal. To Haskell, trade unionism and its ideals presented an unknown field. His contacts had only been with the wealthy, the legal profession, and the politicians. Yet within a short time he mastered all the available labor and radical literature and became without doubt the best-read man in the local labor movement. He rose rapidly to the position of a prominent though unreliable labor leader, later became in turn a socialist and a communist-anarchist, and finally, in the late eighties, closed his career as a leader of workingmen by attempting to establish at Kaweah, near Visalia, a coöperative colony founded chiefly upon the ideas of Edward Bellamy and Lawrence Gronlund. This colony failed in 1891.[3] For many years prior to his death on November 15, 1907, Haskell lived in poverty, friendless and forgotten.

Truth as a labor paper was short-lived. It remained a weekly until January 1, 1884, when, owing to lack of local support, it was changed to a monthly. In July of that year it suspended publication, and Haskell transferred its good-will to the Denver *Labor Enquirer*, edited by Joseph R. Buchanan.

The story of the founding of the International Workingmen's Association in San Francisco in 1882, as told by Haskell, is as follows:

On January 28, 1882, *Truth* was started by me individually. Through it I began to investigate socialism. In July of that year, we formed an educational group of nearly a score of persons to investigate basic principles. It was called "The Invisible Republic." We weeded out the men who could not go as far as we went in radicalism, and we formed a new organization, "The Illuminati." Then we got into communication with Europe and learned of the status of the two Internationals, and received the suggestion from them that before very long the old Marx International Workingmen's Association would have to be revived, and that we had better organize in its form. We did so organize a Division Executive of nine people,—William Herbert, A. J. Starkweather, S. R. Wilson, T. F. Hagerty, Thos. Poyser, C. F. Burgman, J. H. Redstone, Chas. Moore and myself. At the first meeting, Mr. Herbert resigned and Mr. Danielewicz[4] was put in his place. We then each one started to organize groups.[5]

Haskell's International Workingmen's Association must not be confused with the International Working People's Association (the Black International), an anarchistic association organized by the followers of Bakunin, in London, in July, 1881. The latter established branches in the United States, one of which was in existence in San Francisco in 1884–1885, if not earlier, but it did not at any time affiliate with or work with the Haskell group. The American sections of the Black International met in national convention at Chicago in October, 1881, and again at Pittsburgh in October, 1883. Although its existence was relatively short, it enrolled as members many of the more radical labor agitators in the United States.

The group system, followed by Haskell and his associates in organizing their International Workingmen's Association, was patterned after that of many secret or semi-secret revolutionary societies. Each group was composed of nine members, and each member was expected to form another group of nine. Thus a member ordinarily could know only sixteen other members, unless he disclosed his identity to others. A scheme of red, white, and blue cards was employed to distinguish the three grades of membership.

The holders of the red cards were students of the movement and its principles. The red cards carried the following statements:

... "The Proletarians have nothing to lose but their chains. They have a world to win. Let therefore the workingmen of all countries unite!" ... Karl Marx. To each according to his needs. From each according to his ability. No duties without rights. No rights without duties. Educate, Organize, Agitate, Unite. Our Motto: War to the Palace; Peace to the Cottage; Death to Luxurious Idleness. Our Object: The reorganization of Society independent of Priest, King, Capitalist, or Loafer. Our Principles: Every man is entitled to the full product of his own labor, and to his proportionate share of all of the natural advantages of the earth.

The holders of the white cards were the organizers; they were charged with the task of carrying on the propaganda of the association. The white card merely stated that the bearer (name and occupation, with the member's letter and number) was an organizer of the International Workingmen's Association, and carried the following request: "Let due faith and credit henceforth be reposed in him." It also stated that the white-card bearer had acknowledged himself to be a socialist.

The blue-card members formed the legislative and executive body of the various divisions or territorial sections into which the United States and Mexico were divided. I have been unable to obtain a copy of a blue card, and therefore can give no description of it. The Denver *Labor Enquirer* of May 8, 1886, carried a statement of the principles and policies of the International Workingmen's Association, in which the following appeared:

... so absolutely necessary in action are secrecy, loyalty, devotion, purity, and obedience, that this—its concealed form (in the White and Blue Rank, its membership, plans of action, and special purposes)—is secret, and secret as the grave.

The names of the members of the association were not used in correspondence or in the records of the association. Each membership card was signed with a hyphenated combination of a number and a letter. The letter indicated the parent group from which the subordinate group had come, and the number was the one assigned to the individual member of the group. To illustrate: The United States was divided into the Pacific Coast Division, the Rocky Mountain Division, the Mississippi Valley Division, the Eastern Division, and the Mexican Division. The letters F to N were reserved for the use of the Pacific Coast Division, the letters O to W for the Rocky Mountain Division, and those from A to E for the other divisions. The chiefs or leaders of the parent groups of the Pacific Coast Division were known as F-11, G-21, H-31, I-41, J-51, K-61, L-71, M-81, and N-91. A member of the group headed by the last-mentioned leader might, for example, be designated as N-93. When he in his turn organized another group of nine members, and became chief of that group, his number and letter then became N-931, and the other eight members of the same subordinate group were designated as N-932, N-933, and so on. If a member of this subordinate group should then form a third group of nine persons, the persons in that group would be known as N-9321, N-9322, N-9323, and so on. Thus, to quote from "Circular No. 8, Series B

1883" of the International Workingmen's Association, issued by Haskell as secretary of the Pacific Coast Division,

... the number itself tells where the man that bears it is located. For instance, "R–2947" shows that he belongs to Subdivision "R," that his chief in that Central Committee is "2," of whose group the ninth man was the organizer of the fourth man, in whose group the person R–2947 is the seventh man.

This system of using letters and numbers made it exceedingly easy for the division executives to trace any member through the various groups to the one to which he belonged. It also provided an air of secrecy, which always constitutes a great appeal to many persons. At the same time, the use of large numbers for the members of the separate groups made the uninitiated think that the organization had an extensive membership.

Burnette G. Haskell was the division executive of the Pacific Coast Division, and Joseph R. Buchanan, a prominent leader of the Knights of Labor in the Rocky Mountain region and editor of the *Labor Enquirer,* was the division executive of the Rocky Mountain Division. Many men allied with the labor movement in all parts of the United States enlisted under the banner of Haskell's International Workingmen's Association, and carried their red cards, but for the most part the membership was in California. The strength of the organization was known only to the national executives, and it was never made public. From records which I obtained from Haskell's estate, I feel confident that the International Workingmen's Association had at least nineteen groups in San Francisco, ten in Eureka and vicinity, two in Oakland, and one each in Tulare County, San Rafael, Berkeley, Healdsburg, Stockton, and Sacramento.[6] From a study of the movement and its records, I am led to believe that the extent of its membership was always grossly exaggerated, partly because of the secrecy insisted upon by the association, and partly because of the extravagant statements issued from time to time by its leaders. One such statement was contained in a propaganda circular issued by the Humboldt Federation of Groups, in which it was announced that "we have already over 60 active organizations in the county, with a membership of nearly 300." Another circular, issued by Haskell, entitled "What The I. W. A. Is," declared that the order had "millions of members." Morris Hillquit, in his *History of Socialism in the United*

States,[7] says that the order was estimated to have had about 6,000 members in 1887, grouped as follows: 2,000 in Washington Territory and Oregon, 1,800 in California, 2,000 in Colorado, Montana, Utah, Dakota, and Wyoming, and 200 in the southern and eastern states. I am inclined to believe that Hillquit's figures, which he undoubtedly obtained from Haskell, are also unreliable.

The announced objects of Haskell's International Workingmen's Association were:

> To assist and aid the organization of the Knights of Labor, the various Trades Unions, Granges, Farmers' Alliances, and all other forms of organization in which the producers have organized, or may organize themselves, and after assisting such organization to aid in directing their future action on scientific, educational lines. In addition, it is the object of the I. W. A. to print and circulate proper literature; to hold educational meetings and discussions; to systematize agitation; to establish labor libraries, labor halls, and lyceums for the discussion of labor topics; to maintain the labor press; to protect members from wrongs; to protect all other producers from wrongs; to aid and assist all other toilers; to aid the establishment of unity and the maintenance of fraternity between all labor organizations upon the common ground of Truth; to aid an alliance between the industrial and the agricultural producers; to encourage the spirit of brotherhood and interdependence among all toilers in every state and land; to ascertain, segregate, classify, and study the enemies of the people, their motives, habits, and acts; to secure information of wrongs perpetrated against us, and to record and circulate the same; to arouse and maintain a spirit of hostility to, and social warfare against, and ostracism of, that portion of the capitalistic press which is in any way inimical to the labor movement; to obliterate sectional and racial prejudices, with a view to the International Unification of the producers of all lands.

In the circular entitled "What The I. W. A. Is," Haskell, in extravagant style, as was his custom, wrote as follows about the characteristics of the organization:

> Secret, mysterious, world-wide, quietly honeycombing society, the I. W. A. offers to the daring and devoted men and women of earth, the sole practical means of releasing the wealth-producers from the shackles of tyranny. It does not fear betrayal, since its system of organization prevents the possibility of treason. It does not fear suppression, because it has millions of members, as well qualified as the leaders to assume direction, should those now at the head be removed.
>
> It does not fear failure because it knows its own power and strength, and the justice and truth of its cause.

There was no formal initiation ceremony. Members could be sworn in at any time and place. No initiation fees were imposed. Dues were but ten cents a month, and the money thus collected was used for propaganda purposes. Meetings were held in the homes of the members, at which times various phases of socialism and other radical proposals were discussed.

The organization, as stated earlier, was started with the intent of making it the American duplicate of the Marxian socialistic International Workingmen's Association (the Red International), but if we may judge from data available in its records and publications, it soon shifted its position and became more closely allied with the ideals and purposes of the anarchistic International Working People's Association (the Black International). *Truth,* the official organ of Haskell's International Workingmen's Association, carried many statements advocating the use of violence rather than of educational and political measures to bring about the desired reformation of society. On November 17, 1883, it declared:

War to the palace, peace to the cottage, death to luxurious idleness! We have no moment to waste. Arm, I say, to the death! for Revolution is upon you.

In other issues, it announced:

Truth is five cents a copy, and dynamite forty cents a pound. ... When the laboring men understand that heaven, which they are promised hereafter, is a mirage, they will knock at the door of the wealthy robber with a musket in hand, and demand their share of the goods of this life now.

On December 15, 1883, *Truth* published an article entitled "Street Fighting—How to Use the Military Forces of Capital When it is Necessary! Military Tactics for the Lower Classes." The division executive of Mexico, in writing to Haskell under date of October 17, 1883, inquired of him:

Did you see that article going the rounds of the papers about "ground torpedoes?" ... With a little high grade powder, a galvanic electric battery, and some insulated wire, troops can be blown up in *blocks,* and buildings and roads made impregnable.

In the membership book of the Pacific Coast Division, I find in Haskell's handwriting the following statement of a proposed program:

Seize Mint, Armories, Sub-Treasury, Custom House, Government Steamer, Alcatraz, Presidio, newspapers.

That such a plan was not beyond his fantastic scheming is supported by much evidence. In many of the conversations which I had with him, he told of having manufactured bombs, of secreting valises filled with them in places where they could not be found by the police, of the use he had made of bombs in labor troubles, and of plans to blow up the County Hall of Records and destroy all recorded data on land titles, thus enabling the radicals to seize and claim as their own the more desirable pieces of real estate in San Francisco. These statements were later corroborated by others who were associated with him in the International Workingmen's Association and in the local labor movement.[8]

Haskell's International Workingmen's Association was at the height of its popularity in 1886, but soon thereafter rapidly dissolved. Two reasons may be assigned for its decline: (1) the passing of the depression of 1883–1885, and (2) the withdrawal of Haskell, the moving force in the association, from participation in its activities. In October, 1885, Haskell, with many of his associates in the International Workingmen's Association and in the labor unions of San Francisco, became interested in organizing an ideal communistic colony, the Kaweah Coöperative Colony, on the banks of the Kaweah River, near Visalia. This venture absorbed virtually all his time and efforts during 1886–1891. It seemed doomed to failure almost from the start because of lack of harmony among its members, and because of the opposition of the United States government. Federal officials asserted that the land occupied by the colony had been illegally filed upon. The venture came to an end in 1891. Haskell returned to San Francisco, but was never again connected with the labor movement of that city.

The Pacific Coast Division of the International Workingmen's Association proved an important factor in building up the labor movement of San Francisco and California. Haskell, its recognized head, although erratic and not dependable, was an exceedingly brilliant and resourceful leader. He possessed unbounded ardor, a marvelous gift of oratory, and a daring spirit of an ephemeral sort which flared for a second like lightning at night, to be followed by the most abject and inexplicable cowardice. He would inspire his associates to agree to commit deeds of violence, and then would fail to stand by and assist them. He built up contacts between the Pacific Coast movement and the radical elements throughout the world. His vivid imagination often led him to make extravagant statements. During his prime, which, relatively speaking, was from 1882 to 1885, he held the loyalty of a few devout followers, but for the most part he was a trouble-maker, plotting and planning for power and authority, advocating radical measures which did not make for harmony in the local movement, and always failing to coöperate with other leaders.

Associated with Haskell in the International Workingmen's Association were many who later became leaders in the local labor and radical movements. Some of these men were W. C. Owen, C. F. Burgman, R. A. Gilbride, Thomas Poyser, T. F. Hagerty, S. R. Wilson, Henry Marsden, A. J. Starkweather, J. J. Martin, P. Ross Martin, Sigmund Danielewicz, Alfred Fuhrman, Edward Anderson, and J. B. Johnson. These men were fired with the ideals of the International Workingmen's Association, and most of them unselfishly sacrificed time and money in organizing unions among the workingmen of California. To them the slogan, "Workers of the world, unite!—You have nothing to lose but your chains—You have a world to win," made an appeal that they could not resist. It was through the influence of the members of the International Workingmen's Association and their leaders that an interest in unionism was revived and strengthened among the workers of San Francisco. Many of the activities engaged in and the results accomplished by this group of radicals will be noted in the succeeding chapter.

Chapter XI

THE FEDERATED TRADES COUNCIL OF SAN FRANCISCO, 1885–1892

T HE ECONOMIC DEPRESSION which had begun in 1883 continued into 1885. The decline in stock market quotations affected the fortunes of many Californians. Thousands of workers were unemployed, and many of those who remained at work were forced to accept a decreased wage. Efforts on the part of local employers to reduce wages because of eastern competition and the dullness in various lines of trade, provoked several serious strikes. These happenings, and the activity of members of the International Workingmen's Association, aroused among the workers of the San Francisco Bay district a renewed interest in unionism.

On February 7, 1885, a notice of a 15 per cent wage reduction was posted by the Risdon, the Fulton, the Pacific, the Union, and the Savage iron works. An attempt was made by the molders' representatives to settle the difficulty by conferring with the employers, but in the end a strike was declared affecting approximately 1,400 workers. At that time only the ironmolders and blacksmiths were organized, but immediately thereafter the boilermakers revived their union, which had been inactive for about two years; the machinists formed the Mechanics' Union of the State of California, later changing its title to the Machinists' Union; and the patternmakers organized the Brotherhood of Patternmakers, Section No. 1. On February 10 one of the foundries capitulated, and on the following day the others agreed to return to the old wage-scale. By March 2, all the strikers had been reëmployed. On March 3, the helpers at the Union Iron Works were notified that their wages would be reduced from $2 to $1.75 per day. They struck, and formed the Foundry Laborers' Protective Association, which by March 7 had a membership of more than 400. Being unskilled laborers, however, they could not prevent others from taking their places, and the strike was lost.

The attempted wage reduction in the iron trades forcibly brought

[166]

to the attention of Labor the necessity of organization among the separate crafts and the need for some sort of central federation. On February 15, 1885, a committee of five from each of the iron trades unions had met and conferred on the progress of the strike. This was the first step taken to bring these unions together for a common purpose. On February 25, the ironmolders' union appointed a committee consisting of Frank Roney, Sam McKee, and T. J. McBride, to amalgamate the iron trades unions. In 1869, Frank Roney, who was then employed in the railroad shops of Omaha, Nebraska, published an article in the Chicago *Workingmen's Advocate,* proposing that unions be federated locally and nationally along trade lines. He was, as far as I know, the original proponent of the plan in accordance with which the building trades councils, printing trades councils, iron trades councils, and similar groups are now organized. In 1881, when the Trades Assembly of San Francisco sent C. F. Burgman as its representative to attend the conference of trade unions at Pittsburgh (which resulted in the formation of an association out of which subsequently came the American Federation of Labor), Roney was president of the Trades Assembly. He asked Burgman to urge the delegates at the national convention to adopt his (Roney's) plan of federation. Burgman attempted to do so, but to no avail. The situation in 1885 in the iron trades of San Francisco and the move looking toward the formation of a federation gave Roney his long-awaited opportunity. He proposed his plan to the committee on amalgamation, the members gave it their approval, and on May 11, 1885, the first iron trades council in the United States was formed in San Francisco, with J. B. Johnson,[1] president; S. Gunn, vice-president; J. Mahoney, recording secretary; J. F. Valentine,[2] financial secretary; and J. Turner, treasurer. Roney was a member of the executive committee, but later became secretary of the council. The new organization was first known as the Federated Iron Trades Council, but when it was reorganized in 1890 by J. W. Sweeney, a patternmaker, it adopted its present title, The Iron Trades Council of San Francisco. The original membership of the council consisted of the molders', machinists', patternmakers', blacksmiths', and boilermakers' unions, the Iron Laborers' Protective Association, and the Amalgamated Society of Engineers.

The business depression had seriously affected the local shipping trade. On March 4, 1885, a notice was posted along the San Francisco water front announcing that wages on coasting vessels (as distinct from deep-sea vessels) were to be $25 per month for outside ports and $20 per month for other ports. The sailors gathered in excited groups along the docks to discuss the situation. They also boarded vessels about to depart, and compelled the crews to desert. At noon on March 5, Sigmund Danielewicz, a member of the International Workingmen's Association, passing along the water front and noting the excitement, entered into conversation with some of the men, and advised them to form a union. To the sailors the situation appeared hopeless. Earlier attempts at organization had failed, but Danielewicz, with the ardor of a radical, agreed to obtain assistance from his friends in the International Workingmen's Association and to be on hand the next evening at the Folsom Street wharf. At the time designated, about 200 sailors gathered in the dark to listen to speeches by B. B. Carter, Joseph Kelley (of the Steamshipmen's Protective Association[3]), George Thompson, P. Ross Martin (a Knights of Labor leader from Sacramento), J. J. Martin, Sigmund Danielewicz, Martin Schneider, and Burnette G. Haskell. Cheers frequently interrupted the speakers as they urged the formation of a union. The meeting was adjourned to a near-by lamp post, where virtually all those present signed the roll of the new organization, subsequently known as the Coast Seamen's Union. Meetings were held nightly, and on March 11 the following officers were elected: George Thompson, president; Ed Andersen, J. D. Murray, Michael Sweeney, John Fitzpatrick, and J. D. Thomer, vice-presidents; and Rasmus Nielson, secretary. An advisory committee was appointed, consisting of the following members of the International Workingmen's Association: P. Ross Martin, J. J. Martin, Burnette G. Haskell, Martin Schneider, and Sigmund Danielewicz. The purpose of this committee of landsmen was to give permanency to the organization. Its members would always be in port, while the other officers, of course, were usually at sea. During the next two years, the affairs of the union were carried on chiefly under the direction of the advisory group. Headquarters were opened in the offices of the International Workingmen's Association.

The union grew rapidly in membership; by July 1 it had enrolled about 2,200 out of approximately 3,000 coasting sailors. The Coast Seamen's Union waged a vigorous and at times violent struggle against the proposed reduction and the employers finally agreed to retain the old scale. The union extended its control up and down the western coast and established branches at the more important ports. In November, 1887, it began the publication of the *Coast Seamen's Journal*,[4] which since 1918 has been issued as the *Seamen's Journal*. The editors of this important labor organ have been, successively, Xavier Leder, W. J. B. MacKay, Walter Macarthur, and Paul Scharrenberg.

In the many years that have passed since the organization of the sailors' union, its members and leaders have played a notable part in the labor movement of San Francisco as well as in the councils of seamen throughout the world. It has had many clashes with employers, which have not always resulted satisfactorily for its members. It has also engaged in jurisdictional disputes with other unions in the shipping field, its most serious contest being with the steamship sailors' union, with which it merged formally on July 29, 1891, the resulting organization being known as the Sailors' Union of the Pacific.[5] Its leaders, especially Andrew Furuseth,[6] have been actively engaged in furthering the national and international organization of sailors and in obtaining beneficial legislation for the craft.

A strike which took on significance because of subsequent developments, though it was unimportant by itself, occurred on October 25, 1885, when about forty Chinese cigarmakers employed by Koenigsberger, Falk & Mayer struck in a refusal to work with white cigarmakers. Approximately three-fourths of the workers in the cigarmaking industry of San Francisco were Chinese, about one-half of them being employed by white firms, and the rest by their own countrymen. In the early seventies, the white cigarmakers and a number of their employers had organized the White Cigar Makers' Association of the Pacific Coast, and had incorporated it in May, 1876. Its jurisdiction extended from British Columbia to the Mexican border.[7] The association had resorted to many devices in combating the competition of the Chinese, but without success. In the later seventies the situation was so serious that it was proposed to bring white cigarmakers from the East, the local white factory owners agreeing to provide work for them. The factory owners withdrew their support, however, before the plan

ANDREW FURUSETH

could be put into effect. In 1884 the White Cigar Makers' Association established a school for apprentices, but this was not successful and was abandoned after about $12,000 had been spent on it. On December 13, 1885, some of the members of the association withdrew and organized Local No. 228 of the International Cigar

Makers' Union of America, with C. F. Dinewald, president. The White Cigar Makers' Association, they asserted, protected only the employers.[8] The International Cigar Makers' Union used a blue label in water colors, so that it could not be soaked off empty boxes and pasted on boxes containing Chinese or non-union cigars; the White Cigar Makers' Association, as noted above, used a white label. The latter group did not permit its members to work with the Chinese. The former pursued a contrary policy, merely requiring that its members be employed under white foremen and that their output be kept distinct from that of the Chinese. The two unions fought each other most bitterly, although frequent efforts to bring about an amalgamation were made by representatives of the Knights of Labor.

The strike of the Chinese cigarmakers came at a time of great discontent among the workers of San Francisco, many of whom had been unemployed during the summer and fall of 1885.[9] On October 31, 1885, the local unions held a parade and mass meeting (about 5,000 persons were present at the meeting) to voice their opposition to the Chinese. Frank Roney was grand marshal of the parade. Speeches were made by Calvin Ewing, Frank Roney, Burnette G. Haskell, and Horace Davis. The agitation against the Chinese, which had subsided after the enactment of the exclusion law, flared up again; anti-coolie leagues were formed in many cities;[10] meetings of protest were held at various places on the Pacific Coast. A serious anti-Chinese riot occurred in Seattle, Washington, in February, 1886, in connection with an attempt to expel the Chinese from that city. Five men were shot, many were injured, and martial law was declared. In March, 1886, a state anti-Chinese convention was held in Portland, Oregon, and another in Sacramento, California. The Chinese were driven out of Eureka, Marysville, Truckee, Nicolaus, and other California cities. Petitions were signed by the people and resolutions were adopted by various groups, urging Congress to amend the Chinese Exclusion Act so as to make it more effective in protecting the interests of the white citizens.[11]

On November 3, 1885, Local No. 228 of the International Cigar Makers' Union telegraphed East for 200 white cigarmakers to take the places of Chinese. It also commissioned its president, J. Wolfe, to visit eastern cities and induce white cigarmakers to come to California. Seven arrived on December 21, 1885, 177 on January 3, 1886, and 128 on April 26, 1886. The last two groups were welcomed on their arrival by a parade and mass meeting. It is said that approximately 600 eastern cigarmakers were given employment in San Francisco.

SMOKERS! — SEE THAT THIS LABEL (IN BLUE) IS ON EACH BOX, THE ONLY GUARANTY — SMOKERS!
                  AGAINST CHINESE MANUFACTURED CIGARS

REMEMBER   THE ONLY WAY THAT YOU CAN HELP THE WHITE CIGARMAKER, AND WITHOUT ANY EXPENSE TO YOURSELF, IS
             BY SMOKING ONLY SUCH CIGARS AS HAVE THE LABEL ATTACHED TO THE BOX,

LABEL OF LOCAL NO. 228, INTERNATIONAL CIGAR MAKERS' UNION

In January, 1886, Herman Guttstadt, an officer of Local No. 228 of the International Cigar Makers' Union, announced a new union label, designed for use in California. It was blue; it was a little larger than the one previously used; and it carried a design emblematic of the anti-Chinese fight then being waged. Local No. 228 also began the publication of *The Cigarmakers' Journal,* but discontinued it after a few issues. In its contest with the White Cigar Makers' Association of the Pacific Coast, the local branch of the International Cigar Makers' Union obtained the support of the newly organized Representative Council of the Federated Trades and Labor Organizations of the Pacific Coast. From time to time, efforts were made to amalgamate the rival organizations; finally, on June 2, 1886, a joint committee from both groups recommended consolidation and the adoption of the new label of Local No. 228. On June 22, the members of the White Cigar Makers' Association, 128 in number, were admitted to membership in Local No. 228, and the association disbanded.

Several months later the white employers began gradually to replace their white cigarmakers with Chinese workers. Many of the eastern white cigarmakers, after being discharged, returned to their homes. A few found employment in the coöperative cigar factory which the union established in San Francisco; but this enterprise did not long survive. At a conference of the Knights of Labor,

Cigar Makers' Union No. 228, and the Representative Council of the Federated Trades and Labor Organizations, it was decided to use both the white label of the old White Cigar Makers' Association, which had been widely advertised, and the new blue label of Local No. 228, in order to stimulate a wider consumption of white-label cigars. Lecturers were sent out through the Pacific Coast states to urge the consumption of white-labor goods. The results of the campaign, it was said, were highly gratifying.

Several unions were organized in 1885 as a result of activities of the members of the International Workingmen's Association. The lathers met on March 8, 1885, and agreed to revive their union; the carriage-makers organized in May, the upholsterers on September 10, the Musicians' Protective Mutual Association on September 17, and the tinsmiths in November.

In 1884 and the early part of 1885, there was discussion relative to the possibility of organizing a city federation to succeed the Trades Assembly, which had passed from the field. In 1884 the ironmolders' union issued a call for a labor convention, which was responded to by fifteen organizations, but the meeting adjourned without accomplishing anything. On March 8, 1885, delegates from the iron trades unions met and discussed plans for a federation, but when their proposal was submitted to the labor groups of the city, it was rejected. The iron trades unions then decided to federate, and on May 11, 1885, they formed what was later to become the Iron Trades Council of San Francisco (see p. 167). The Knights of Labor called a conference on March 4, 1884, which was attended by delegates from the following organizations: Knights of Labor assemblies Nos. 1390, 1553, 1903, 2226, 2383, 2962, and 2999, and the unions of ironmolders, brass workers, stevedores, printers, shoemakers, plumbers, tanners, carpenters, cabinetmakers, clerks, harness-makers, and gilders. Out of this conference came the formal organization of the Labor Congress on March 14, with W. W. Stone, president. The life of this local federation was of short duration: on March 27, 1885, the *Daily Report* announced that it had been changed into a parliamentary training school in which its members might be drilled for leadership in the local unions. Undoubtedly the reason for this change in the plans of the Knights of Labor group was that in the meantime another central body had been formed under the guidance of the more aggressive International Workingmen's Association.

In New York, Chicago, and St. Louis the city labor federations were known as Central Labor Unions. Haskell, who was intimately in touch with the eastern labor movement, urged his associates to

WALTER MACARTHUR

form such a group in San Francisco. A call was issued accordingly, and at a meeting held in Irish-American Hall on March 16, 1885, the Pacific Coast Central Labor Union was organized. Delegates were present from International Workingmen's Association groups Nos. 1, 3, 5, 7, 8, 9, 11, 12, 14, 15, 16, 17, 18, 19, 22, 24, 25, 27, 28, 52, 73, 142, 151, 157, 191, and 251. The San Rafael, Tulare, Oakland, Traver, and Berkeley groups were represented; also the Tem-

escal Grange, Eden Grange, Montezuma Grange, Merced Grange,
Contra Costa Grange, Walnut Creek Grange, North Butte Grange,
Knights of Labor Assemblies Nos. 855 (Sacramento), 1573, 2750,
3337 (Eureka), 2999, 1390, and 1903; and delegates were present
from the White Cigar Makers' Association of the Pacific Coast,
and the San Francisco unions of the metal roofers, longshore lumbermen, coast seamen, cabinetmakers, marble polishers, cooks
and waiters, journeymen shipwrights, steamshipmen, blacksmiths,
printers, plumbers and gas fitters, laborers, marble cutters, carpenters, machinists, patternmakers, and boot- and shoemakers;
and from the Tacoma (Washington) printers, and the Tax Reform
League.[12]

The Central Labor Union of San Francisco had brought together
a strange mixture of farmer, labor, and radical elements, which
under no circumstances could have been welded together into a
cohesive body. The meetings of the conference were harmonious,
but nothing tangible resulted from them. The federation was only
a "paper" organization, possessed of an excellent title, which Haskell and his associates employed for advertising purposes. Theodore Holbeck, of the Longshore Lumbermen's Association, was
elected president, and Joseph Kelly, of the Steamshipmen's Association, secretary. The Central Labor Union met with no response from the unions of San Francisco, and subsequently held
but few meetings.

The renewal of the agitation against the Chinese had so aroused
the workers that District Assembly No. 53 of the Knights of Labor
issued a call for an anti-Chinese convention to be held in San Francisco on November 30, 1885. It was openly declared by some of the
local labor leaders that Stone, Ewing, and other officers of the
Knights of Labor planned to use the convention for their political
benefit. Organizations were requested not to send "as delegates
any politician, demagogue, cranks, or lobbyists"—a request that
was aimed directly at Haskell, Owen, and other radicals, who,
as members of the International Workingmen's Association, had
already proved to be thorns in the flesh of the politically aspiring
leaders of the Knights of Labor.

About 200 delegates were present at the first meeting of the
convention. They came not only from San Francisco, but also

from the Knights of Labor group in Sacramento, the Mechanics'
Union of Vallejo, the Carpenters' and Joiners' Union of Alameda,
the Carpenters' and Joiners' Union of Los Angeles,[13] the Los Angeles Trades Council, Knights of Labor Assembly No. 2157, of Los
Angeles, the Stockton International Workingmen's Association,
the San Francisco Turn Verein, and the Socialist Labor Party.

A contest for control of the convention at once arose between the
delegates from the radical International Workingmen's Association and those from the conservative Knights of Labor. The former
were victorious from the first. Frank Roney, the candidate of the
radicals, was chosen temporary chairman and then permanent
chairman over J. J. Payne, the candidate of the Knights of Labor
group. Roney saw in this convention an opportunity to bring about
a permanent federation of the local unions, and threw the weight
of his influence in that direction. At the second meeting of the convention, held on the evening of December 2, the International
Workingmen's Association group, according to a prearranged plan,
introduced a resolution demanding the removal of the Chinese
from the Pacific Coast within sixty days. A bitter debate ensued,
the resolution finally being adopted by a vote of 60 to 47. Many
of the Knights of Labor delegates at once withdrew, leaving the
radicals in control. At the next meeting, held on the evening of
December 5, the resolution was reconsidered, and the objectionable
sixty-day removal clause was rescinded by a unanimous vote.
Having thus rid itself of the leaders of the Knights of Labor, the
convention settled down to consider various proposals that were
placed before it. It held two subsequent meetings on December 7
and 8, and passed resolutions relating to convict labor, the eight-
hour day, and other matters. Before adjourning, it authorized the
appointment of a committee with power to organize a local labor
federation.

The committee met on December 18, drafted a constitution and
by-laws, and called a meeting to be held on January 12, 1886, for
the purpose of organizing the Representative Council of the Federated Trades and Labor Organizations of the Pacific Coast. Haskell
and others, representing the proposed federation, set out on a tour
of organization. A Committee of Nine was also appointed to
visit local unions and obtain their support. Haskell formed a Fed-

erated Mechanics' Trade and Labor Union at Stockton on January 2, 1886, which a week later announced a membership of 197 workers. He established similar organizations at Visalia with 50 members, at Oakland with 160 members, at Sacramento with 250 members, and at Traver with 30 members. On January 30, 1886, he announced that plans were under way for other federations at Tulare and Hanford. His reports relative to membership were undoubtedly exaggerated. These local groups agreed to affiliate with the Representative Council of the Federated Trades and Labor Organizations of the Pacific Coast, which was known subsequently as the Federated Trades Council.

At the first meeting of the council on January 12, 1886, the following officers were elected: Frank Roney, president; Patrick McGreal, vice-president; T. W. Parkin, recording secretary; G. Wenzel, financial secretary; E. McKinley, corresponding secretary; W. C. Owen, statistical secretary; P. F. Murphy, treasurer; Ed G. Anderson, sergeant-at-arms; and Burnette G. Haskell, P. Ross Martin, W. C. Owen, Patrick McGreal, L. Ahrens, and H. Hutton, members of the organizing committee. As the reader will note, the leaders of the International Workingmen's Association were liberally represented among the officers.

Almost the first matter to come before the new council was the contest between the two rival cigarmakers' unions (see p. 172). After an acrimonious debate, it was voted to support Local No. 228 of the International Cigar Makers' Union.

Roney, who had been blacklisted by the foundries of San Francisco for his activities as a labor leader, was at that time employed in the City Hall as assistant to the City Engineer. This kind of employment permitted him, as president of the federation, to give a generous amount of time to the organization of the workers of San Francisco. Under his direction and with the assistance of members of the International Workingmen's Association, many unions were formed, while others which had lain dormant for some time were revived. On January 25, 1886, the Federated Trades Council had a membership of thirty-one organizations, and three months later the number had been increased to fifty-four.[14]

On February 11, 1886, the plasterers', plumbers' and gas fitters', and painters' unions, and the Laborers' Protective Benevolent Association (hodcarriers) met and formed a building trades council. Another meeting was held on February 15 at which delegates were also present from the lathers', metal roofers', and bricklayers' unions. A constitution was framed, and later submitted to all building trades unions. Formal organization of the Representative Council of Building Trades of San Francisco was effected on May 17 by the adoption of a constitution and the election of the following officers: J. D. Campbell, president; J. Nicholson, vice-president; J. D. deGrear, recording secretary; P. H. Kebrigan, treasurer; and B. Daggett, financial secretary. The organization included, however, only the carpenters', painters', lathers', metal roofers', and plumbers' and gas fitters' unions. The Representative Council of Building Trades, which was the second federation to be formed among the building trades unions of San Francisco, was ineffective, and soon disbanded. At this time there was also some discussion relative to the advisability of organizing similar federations among the water-front unions and the printing trades unions, but nothing was accomplished in that direction.

All this time the campaign against the Chinese was being actively carried on. In February, 1886, the tailors' union of San Francisco obtained an agreement from thirty-nine employers, according to the terms of which the latter pledged themselves to hire no Chinese. A group of white women opened a coöperative factory to manufacture underwear on which a white-labor label was to be used. The Boot and Shoemakers' White Labor League incorporated in order the better to protect its label. The league also adopted a new style of label, a steel die to be used in impressing the union insignia on the sole of the shoe, just in front of the heel. In March, 1886, the league announced that all but two of the boot and shoe factories of San Francisco had agreed to adopt its label. Several attempts were made by employers to use the label without the league's consent, but in each attempt the offending party was restrained by a court order. Plans for an extensive Chinese boycott campaign were also made by the cigarmakers, the shoemakers, and the Federated Trades Council; and accordingly, on March 5, 1886, a mass meeting was held, and the Anti-Coolie Boycotting Association of San Francisco was organized. It was planned to extend the activities and influence of the Association to all sections of the

State. At the suggestion of the representatives of the executive committee of the state Non-Partisan Anti-Chinese Convention, which had recently adjourned its meetings in Sacramento, another mass meeting was held in San Francisco on March 20, and resolutions favorable to the proposed Chinese boycott were adopted "with a roar heard for blocks." The San Francisco association printed and distributed thousands of circulars requesting the people of that city to purchase only white-labor goods.

In January, 1886, the Boot and Shoemakers' White Labor League asked the State Labor Commissioner to investigate the employment of Chinese in the boot and shoe trade, and to suggest a method whereby they might be eliminated. The investigation was made, and the publication of the Labor Commissioner's findings greatly aided the campaign against the Chinese. The Labor Commissioner suggested that a law be passed requiring that all goods be marked so as to disclose the kind of labor used in their production.[15] At the request of the cigarmakers' union, the Labor Commissioner in October, 1886, made a similar study of the employment of Chinese in the cigarmaking trade.[16] On December 23, 1886, a state anti-Chinese convention was held in San Francisco under the direction of the Federated Trades Council. Only a few delegates were present. After the customary speeches had been made, anti-Chinese resolutions were adopted and the meeting adjourned. The popular interest in Chinese boycotting was on the wane, and the anti-coolie clubs which had been organized in various parts of the State quietly disbanded.

One reason why the San Francisco unions showed little interest in the anti-Chinese agitation was the fact that they were at the time carrying on a boycott against the *Morning Call* and the *Evening Bulletin*. Loring Pickering and George K. Fitch, the owners of these newspapers, had as early as 1870 crossed swords with the local typographical union, and had been defeated in a strike when they had attempted a reduction in wages. They later announced a non-union policy in their composing rooms, which was followed successfully for many years. The printers were defeated when, in July, 1883, they struck for the closed shop. On February 28, 1886, they decided to make another try for the closed shop. They obtained the support of the Federated Trades Council and the local assemblies of the Knights of Labor. Pickering and Fitch refused to accede to their demands, whereupon a city-wide boycott of the two papers was declared on March 12, 1886. It was heartily supported by more than fifty of the unions of San Francisco. More than

PAUL SCHARRENBERG

40,000 copies of a strike sheet, *The Pacific Coast Boycotter,* were distributed throughout the city. Advertisers and subscribers were urged to withdraw their custom from the two newspapers. After a contest of about a month, the proprietors of the *Call* and *Bulletin* admitted defeat, and the men returned to work.

To celebrate the victory so decisively won, and to show the strength of the local movement as an inspiration to the unorganized trades, a grand "toilers' holiday" was planned by the Federated Trades Council for April 13. Rain forced postponement to April 17, and then to May 11, the date of the first anniversary of the founding of the Iron Trades Council of San Francisco. On that occasion more than 10,000 men, representing about forty unions, marched in a procession that was said to be about ten miles long. Frank Roney was grand marshal. Governor Stoneman had declared the day a legal holiday, and accompanied by his staff he marched with the workers. A celebration at Woodward's Gardens concluded the day's program.

The eight-hour-day agitation, which swept through the eastern industrial centers in the spring of 1886, received virtually no support from the organized workers of California. On May 1, the date set for the nation-wide inauguration of the shorter workday, only the cigarmakers and the furniture workers of San Francisco were able to put the new schedule of hours into effect.

For some time a serious situation had been developing in the iron trades of San Francisco. On January 26, 1886, thirty boilermakers of the Union Iron Works had struck against the employment of helpers on journeymen's work. The controversy was settled to the satisfaction of the men, and they returned to work on February 15. On May 14, the boilermakers demanded that the Union Iron Works discharge members of the Iron and Wood Shipbuilders' Union. This union had been formed by four men, who had been expelled from the shipwrights' union, and other non-unionists and helpers. Its members had agreed to work longer hours and for lower wages than required by the scale of the boilermakers' union. A strike was called without the approval of either the Iron Trades Council or the Federated Trades Council. In spite of this violation of the rules of both of these federations, the Federated Trades Council attempted to settle the difficulty. It did not succeed. The Iron Trades Council thereupon notified the management of the Union Iron Works that, unless the non-union men were discharged, a strike would be called involving all the union men employed in the plant. The management refused to grant the council's demand, and a strike affecting about 400 employees was declared on June 19. Unions were then organized among the coremakers and the boilermakers' helpers. Arbitration was proposed by the workers on June 26, but was refused. The strike continued through July and August. Non-union men were imported from the East. The Federated Trades Council had ordered out the boilermakers at the Risdon Iron Works because the management had directed them to work on the boilers of a steamboat owned by the Spreckels Company, against which the sailors were at that time on strike. This did not meet with the approval of some of the unions in the Iron Trades Council; it was asserted that the Federated Trades Council had exceeded its jurisdiction. On July 30, the ironmolders withdrew from the Federated Trades Council and recommended that the boilermakers return to work at the Risdon Iron Works. Shortly thereafter, the boilermakers[17] and the shipwrights also withdrew from the Federated Trades Council. The proprietors in the iron trades of San Francisco now thought the time favorable for the organization of an employers' association, and they formed the Engineers' and Iron Founders' Association. The patternmakers broke with their associates and returned to work on August 19. They were followed a few days later by the machinists. On September 3 the strike was called off, after having cost the ironmolders' union approximately $14,000. The Union Iron Works strike had virtually disrupted the Iron Trades Council; only five organizations—the patternmakers', blacksmiths', machinists', and stationary engineers' unions, and the Amalgamated Engineers—remained affiliated with it. About a month after the strike, the stationary engineers also gave notice of intention to withdraw from the Iron Trades Council.

The strength and activities of the cooks' and waiters' union of San Francisco brought about the formation of the Eating House Keepers' Association in the spring of 1886.[18] On June 15, 1886, the members of the Association posted a set of rules to which the union took exception. A strike was called and won within a few hours, the employers agreeing to withdraw the objectionable parts of the new regulations.

In June the firemen employed on the "Mariposa," one of the boats of the Oceanic Steamship Company (owned by the Spreckels Company), complained that the fire room was undermanned, and asked for the employment of three more men. The Spreckels Company refused to grant the request, and the men, who were members of the Pacific Marine Firemen's Union, went on strike. They appealed to the Federated Trades Council, which unsuccessfully proposed arbitration. The council then called on all union men, including the sailors, to strike against the Spreckels boats, and ordered a general boycott against the company. The results were disastrous for the workers, especially for the sailors, who, as required by maritime law, forfeited their back wages. This strike brought about the organization of the Ship Owners' Protective Association of the Pacific Coast on June 7. The association at once established a shipping office and a system of "grade books" by means of which employers were able to force sailors to relinquish membership in the union if they wished to obtain employment. On August 26, 1886, a mass meeting of the San Francisco water-front unions was held, and a general city-wide strike was proposed by Haskell, but was voted down. It was then suggested that a strike of all water-front unions be declared, but that proposal also was rejected. Finally, the members of the Coast Seamen's Union, who remained after the meeting adjourned, voted to call out the coasting sailors in a contest with the employers' association. About 3,500 men were affected.[19] Haskell was put in charge of the strike. He proposed arbitration, which the employers rejected; he urged joint control of the shipping office, and this proposal also was rejected; he then recommended a general strike of all trades in San Francisco, but the unions would not support such a radical measure. On September 20, 1886, the Coast Seamen's Union established its own shipping office, but with no noticeable effect on the situation. Non-union men, longshoremen, and others continued to ship as sailors. The strike, although never formally called off, ended in the early part of October in the complete defeat of the union. It had cost the sailors approximately $12,000. As a consequence of competition for employment, wages fell rapidly, as low a rate as $15 per month being paid to some sailors. It was not until the latter part of 1890 that the sailors' union succeeded in building up its membership to the numbers it had had before the strike. In the meantime, the "grade book" system had been abolished, and the Ship Owners' Protective Association had passed from the field.[20]

On September 5, 1886, the organized workers of San Francisco held a Labor Day celebration. There was a parade with banners and floats, and afterward a dance at Woodward's Gardens. W. A.

Bushnell, president of the Federated Trades Council, was the grand marshal of the day. The celebration was not so impressive, however, as the one of the preceding May.

The wave of organization that swept over the San Francisco workers in 1885 and 1886[21] gathered in the horse and cable street-car employees, numbering about 1,000 men. In the latter part of 1885, they had secretly formed the Carmen's Association, Knights of Labor Assembly No. 7338. Great care had been taken to keep the organization under cover until it should be strong enough to enforce its demands. They worked from thirteen and a half hours to fifteen hours per day, and received low wages. The employers, on learning of the existence of the association and the unrest of the men, decided to anticipate the demands of their workers, and the Omnibus line reduced the hours of labor to twelve per day. Somewhat later the company posted a notice requiring all employees to abandon their union affiliations. A vigorous protest was made against this, and the order was rescinded without the necessity of a strike. However, the North Beach and Mission line and the City Railroads Company discharged their Knights of Labor employees, and 200 men struck on July 13, 1886. The next evening the cars were pelted with rocks, and more than 1,000 people gathered at the car barns to jeer the strike breakers as the cars were run in for the night. Some rioting and violence followed. One car exploded some powder, which had been placed on the tracks, and another exploded a cartridge, but no damage resulted. Several cars were overturned by the mob, and the police arrested seven men for rioting. At the end of the fourth day the employers granted the demands of the strikers, promising that membership in the Knights of Labor would not bar anyone from employment.

This strike was the second to be called on the street-car lines of San Francisco, the first having occurred in January, 1874, in protest against excessively long hours of labor. The carmen had been accustomed to work from fourteen to sixteen hours per day for a daily wage of $2.50. The strike was lost, but the San Francisco *Chronicle* carried the cause of the men to the State legislature. A bill limiting the hours of employment to twelve per day was passed by both houses, but it was vetoed by the governor on March 25, 1874, as constituting special or class legislation.[22]

Following the successful conclusion of the street-car strike of Juy, 1886, the wages of the employees of the Sutter Street Car Company were increased from $2 to $2.25 for a thirteen-and-a-half-hour day, while the employees of the other street-car lines, except those on the Geary Street line, received $2.50 for a twelve-hour day. This difference in wage scales was a source of irritation; and on December 8, 1886, the employees of the Sutter Street Car Company struck for $2.50 a day for carmen, $60 a month for hostlers, and preference of meal relief for the men longest in the service. On December 13 the employees of the Geary Street line struck for similar conditions. Much violence ensued. Cars were stoned and damaged, strike breakers were beaten, one person was killed, and the local newspapers recorded eight explosions of dynamite by the street cars. Bus lines were started by the strikers, but they proved a losing venture and were abandoned in March, 1887. The strike lasted eighty-six days, and ended in the defeat of the workers. It had cost them approximately $47,000 in lost wages. The other local unions had contributed $11,000.[23] John E. Stites and Charles A. Dean were arrested and charged with dynamiting. Stites was found guilty.

The strike was lost, but it attracted so much attention to the working conditions of the carmen, especially to the long hours of labor, that the State legislature was induced to pass a law, signed by the governor on March 11, 1887, limiting the working time of gripmen, drivers, and conductors to twelve hours per day.[24] This is one of the first examples of protective legislation enacted in California for the purpose of regulating the conditions of employment of a particular class of workers. Considering the circumstances and the time, it is surprising that the bill was not vetoed by the governor as constituting class legislation, as had been done in 1874.

The Federated Trades Council was represented at the legislatures of 1886 and 1887 by a Labor lobby, maintained in the hope that some of the measures in which Labor was vitally interested might be enacted into law. Demands were made for an anti-convict labor law, a boiler inspection act, a law licensing street-car conductors and gripmen, and another requiring the stamping and tagging of manufactured products with the name of the place of origin. The Labor lobby, headed by Peter Roberts, was only successful in obtaining the passage of a bill prohibiting the mislabeling of goods with respect to the kind of labor employed in their production.[25]

In September, 1886, a Workingmen's Convention was called to nominate candidates for city and legislative offices. H. C. Kinne, District Master Workman of the Knights of Labor, was in the chair. About 150 delegates were present from the local unions and the various Knights of Labor assemblies. The convention, under the title of the United Labor Party, put a complete list of candidates for local offices before the voters. In the ensuing fall election, the party cast only a few votes and elected none of its nominees.

Chapter XII

THE FEDERATED TRADES COUNCIL OF
SAN FRANCISCO, 1885–1892
(Concluded)

U NDER THE PRESIDENCY of Frank Roney, the Federated Trades Council had brought renewed life to the labor movement in California. Toward the close of Roney's third term of office, however, it became increasingly difficult to hold the group together. Many small unions had been formed among workers unacquainted with the ideals and practices of Organized Labor. The continual appeals of these organizations for the authorization of strikes and boycotts caused much dissension among the delegates. Complaint was also made that the radicals of the International Workingmen's Association were in control of the council and that they had formed a number of "paper" unions so as to be able, through the latter's delegates, to dictate its policies. Another cause of irritation was the council's assertion of its authority to levy assessments on the constituent unions for the support of local strikes. It was also said that the basis of representation in the council resulted in gross unfairness; for example, the carmen's association, with a large membership, had but one delegate, while the bakers' union, with less than half the membership of the former, had four delegates because there happened to be four branches of the bakers' national organization in San Francisco. Objections were made to the political activity of some of the local labor leaders. There were protests against the practice of the council in permitting mixed assemblies of the Knights of Labor to send delegates to its meetings and to vote upon matters affecting other unions. These mixed assemblies were frequently composed of lawyers, doctors, and others who were not actually members of the working class, yet who took a prominent part in the affairs of the council.

A bitter struggle on a national scale between the Knights of Labor and the Federation of Organized Trades and Labor Unions of the United States of America and Canada, which later became the American Federation of Labor, was then at its height. The Knights of Labor was trying frantically to hold its constituent organizations together and to prevent them from affiliating with the newly formed Federation of Organized Trades and Labor Unions. It had accordingly ordered the Cigar Makers' International Union to sever relations with the federation. The cigarmakers' union of San Francisco had joined in the fray, and, following the lead of its international union in opposing the edict of the Knights of Labor, had attacked the status of the local assemblies of the Knights of Labor as members of the Federated Trades Council. The local branches of the Knights of Labor and of the Federated Trades Council had also clashed in a dispute involving the employees of Bloch & Company, local trunk and bag manufacturers. The Bag and Satchel Workers' Union was a member of the council. At the request of that union, the council had ordered a boycott on Bloch & Company. Kinne and Hoffmeyer, Knights of Labor leaders, thereupon organized the non-union employees of the firm into a Knights of Labor assembly, and a struggle ensued between the two antagonistic groups of organized workers. This local contest was similar to others then being waged throughout the nation. The iron-molders, patternmakers, shipwrights, boilermakers, and steamship stevedores withdrew from the council, and other unions were on the point of doing so. Roney was worn out, physically and mentally, from his efforts to build up the labor movement of San Francisco and to maintain harmony among the council's members. He declined to be a candidate for reëlection to the presidency of the council,[1] and was succeeded by W. A. Bushnell.[2]

Dissatisfaction with the tactics and policies of the Federated Trades Council soon took tangible form. The agitation was led by the cigarmakers' union, which felt especially aggrieved because the council had ceased its campaign against the Chinese. Herman Guttstadt, president of the cigarmakers' union and vice-president of the council, presided at a secret meeting held on January 14, 1887, at which plans were discussed calling for the organization of a more vigorous and efficient central body. It was decided to call a general meeting for April 24, 1887. In the meantime, the members in control of the council attempted to prevent the revolt from spreading. Although not requested to do so, the council chose delegates to represent it at the meeting of the rebellious elements. The Knights of Labor also had not been asked to send representatives.

About forty delegates, representing twenty-five unions, were present at the first meeting of the insurgent group. Fifteen other organizations had accepted the invitation to send delegates, but were not represented on the floor of the convention. The delegates of the Federated Trades Council were not seated, although a vigorous contest was waged in their interest under the leadership of E. W. Thurman, of the Typographical Union. Herman Guttstadt was chosen president of the new council, which adopted the title of "The Trades Union Mutual Alliance." Representatives of all legitimate unions were eligible for membership. Its object was to carry on the fight against coolie and "scab" labor. No vote for an expenditure of money was to bind any union except with the latter's consent. The original membership included about thirty unions.

The existence of a rival organization frightened the Federated Trades Council into revising its constitution. In May, 1887, it voted to allow one delegate for each union with a membership of less than 200, two for those with a membership ranging from 200 to 500, and three for those with more than 500; to exclude all delegates from the mixed assemblies of the Knights of Labor and from spurious or "paper" organizations which had no membership; and to continue the agitation of the cigarmakers against Chinese competition. The sources of irritation thus removed, the Trades Union Mutual Alliance, after an indifferent existence, quietly dissolved at some time in the following September, its constituent unions again affiliating with the Federated Trades Council.

Another matter which aided in reviving the influence of the Federated Trades Council was its connection with the successful outcome of the first strike and boycott declared by the brewery workers' union. The conditions of employment in the breweries were unsatisfactory. The employees were Germans who had learned their trade in the Fatherland, where unions were practically unknown. For the most part they were socialists, and had no faith in trade unionism; they looked upon it as designed to obtain nothing better than piecemeal reform, and preferred to wait until they could obtain the "whole loaf" under socialism rather than to take "part of a loaf" under capitalism by trade union activities. The principles and practices of Organized Labor had therefore made no appeal to them. In 1886, however, the results obtained by the unions of San Francisco began to make an impression on some of the brewery employees, and in May they requested the Federated Trades Council to organize their craft. Alfred Fuhrman, a German and one of the leaders among the sailors, undertook the task, and in June, 1886, succeeded in forming the Brewers' and Maltsters' Union of the Pacific Coast.[3] Approximately nine months later the organization became Local No. 16 of the National Union of United Brewery Workmen of the United States. Fuhrman organized branches of the San Francisco union in San Jose on October 2, 1886, in Boca in September, 1887, and in Sacramento in the spring of 1888. Branches were also established later in Portland, Tacoma, and Seattle.

Fuhrman, testifying before the Labor Commissioner of California relative to the conditions of the brewery workers as he had found them when he first became interested in organizing the craft, said:

> The men were compelled to turn out at 4 o'clock in the morning, the usual time being from 4 to 5. When I first addressed the men at Turn Verein Hall, about two-thirds of the men were drunk, and the balance were asleep. I found that owing to the fact that these men were compelled to work early in the morning without having any breakfast, and naturally, being compelled to work at the beer business, they drank beer, and it happened many times that the men were drunk in the forenoon; that they were, in fact, drunk before they had eaten breakfast. The men were compelled to sleep in the brewery, which had a demoralizing effect upon them, and very few of them were married because they could not afford to maintain families.[4]

The working time for the brewers and maltsters ranged from sixteen to eighteen hours per day. The men worked in the high temperature of the malt house or in the low temperature of the cellar. Wages were about $15 per week, with board and sleeping quarters provided by the brewery, but at the expense of the employees. There were about 800 brewery workers in San Francisco at the time. The membership of the new union is not known; various statements give figures ranging from 124 to 325.

The union made no demands for improved conditions until May 4, 1887, when a committee representing it and the Federated Trades Council served notice on the employers that, in future, (1)

ALFRED FUHRMAN

only union men should be hired, and only through the employment office of the union; (2) employees should be permitted to live and board where they pleased; (3) wages should range from $15 to $17 per week, with a ten-hour day, a six-day week, and only unavoidable work, for not more than three hours, on Sunday; (4) employees should have free beer, and (5) a board of arbitration should be established with authority to settle all difficulties. The employers were willing to grant almost all the demands of the union, but were united in opposition to the closed shop. This brought about the declaration of a strike on May 7 against the Philadelphia Brewery, affecting 38 employees. Because of the union's lack of strength, it was deemed advisable to confine the contest to but one brewery at a time, and thus wear down the opposition piecemeal. Cities on the Pacific Coast and even those of Australia were circularized and urged to boycott the beer of the Philadelphia Brewery. On May 10, 72 union employees of four other breweries also went on strike. The local union, having become Local No. 16 of the national organization, was assisted by the payment of strike benefits ranging from $6 to $10 per week. On July 22 the employers admitted defeat, and signed an agreement granting all the demands of the union, except that wages were to range from $14 to $16 per week.

This, the first struggle of the brewery workers for improved conditions, had been won through the leadership of Fuhrman, and through the coastwide boycott declared at his suggestion against the products of the San Francisco breweries. Future years were to see additional victories, bringing to the brewery workers a control over the business of their employers more complete than was ever obtained by any other group of San Francisco craftsmen. In August, 1887, Fuhrman was elected secretary of the brewery workers' union, and he held the position until 1892. In November, 1887, the German Coopers' Union and the Beer Wagon Drivers' Union became branches of the local brewery workers' union.

On August 25, 1887, Furniture Workers' Unions Nos. 15 and 25, which had become affiliated with their national union, demanded the nine-hour day with no reduction in pay, and the abolition of piecework. The Wood Carvers' Union joined in making similar demands. Their employers, twenty-nine in number, thereupon organized the San Francisco Furniture Association. All but one of the local firms, however, assented to the conditions demanded, and the one exception agreed to a compromise settlement. The request of the ironmolders for a Saturday half-holiday was refused by their employers on July 13, 1887. A month later the molders asked for a nine-hour day (they had been working ten hours), but this also was not granted.

In March, 1887, the German bakers of San Francisco organized for the purpose of shortening their hours of labor and improving their employment conditions. They had been accustomed to work fourteen hours a day and seven days a week. San Francisco was the only city in the United States in which the members of that craft worked on Saturday nights. An investigation of the San Francisco bakeries made by the State Labor Commissioner in 1889 revealed most objectionable sanitary and working conditions. The workers slept in the bakeries, in tiered bunks, with neither adequate light nor ventilation. Twelve of the bakeries were in filthy, low-ceiled basements, adjacent to stables, and foul with sewer gas. Again, as late as 1896, the State Labor Commissioner, following another investigation of the bakeries of San Francisco, reported:

No other industry presents the same conditions or carries with it the life of drudgery that this one does ... [whose employees] are confined to a foul-smelling, disease-breeding cellar, working over the kneading-board or before a hot oven from ten to sixteen hours per day, seven days each week.[5]

In March, 1887, organization proceeded rapidly among the bakers; four branches of the national union were formed in San Francisco, with a total membership of approximately 800.[6] The following demands were then made upon the master bakers of San Francisco and Oakland: (1) weekly pay day; (2) six days' work, with Saturday night off; (3) ten hours' work per day except on Friday, when fourteen hours' work were to be permitted; (4) bakers not to be compelled to carry and shovel coal; (5) employees not to be required to sleep in the home or bakery of the employer; and (6) bakers to be employed solely through the union office. By strikes, and threats of strikes and boycotts, the union was able to obtain its demands from all but a few employers.

In January, 1888, however, the boss bakers, through their employers' association, decided to break the hold of the union and selected one of their members, W. Westerfield, to carry on the fight against it. The employers posted bonds, promising not to employ union men. The union struck against Westerfield on January 12, and then against all other members of the employers' association. The cooks' and waiters' union, although not directly affected by the controversy, struck in sympathy with the bakery employees. More than 160 bakeries, 50 restaurants, and 40 confectionery shops were closed, involving more than 2,000 men. The unions were finally defeated and their members were forced to return to work as best they could. Many were unable to find employment.[7] The cooks' and waiters' union was disrupted and the bakers' unions were greatly weakened. Reorganization of the former as the Cooks' and Waiters' Progressive Union was effected in the closing months of 1888. In the spring of 1889 it carried on a successful boycott against a number of San Francisco eating houses, and regained much of the ground which had previously been lost. The bakers resorted to an appeal to the legislature, and in 1893 succeeded in having a statute enacted providing one day's rest in seven, but it was subsequently declared unconstitutional by the lower courts.

In May, 1887, the brakemen and conductors on the freight trains of the Visalia division of the Southern Pacific railroad struck against the railroad's practice of requiring its men occasionally to work eighteen to twenty-three hours per day. Six branches of the Brotherhood of Brakemen had been formed in California up to that time, one each in San Francisco, Oakland, Tulare, Los Angeles, Needles, and Sacramento. I have not been able to ascertain the outcome of the strike. On September 12, 1887, the candy-makers of San Francisco struck unsuccessfully against the employment of non-union foremen by L. Sarioni & Company.[8] On October 24, 1887, 321 glove-makers, comprising virtually all the employees of the glove factories of San Francisco, struck against a reduction in wages and organized a union. The strike was lost. The sailors and longshoremen at San Pedro struck on December 1, 1887, against the discharge of union men by the Ship Owners' Protective Association. The strike was lost, being called off on December 15.[9]

A number of unions were organized throughout California in 1887, the carpenters being especially active in unionizing their craft. Carpenters' unions were formed in Riverside in January, in Santa Monica and Pomona in June, in Oceanside, Ontario, and Ventura in July, and in Grass Valley, San Jose, Stockton, Santa Rosa, and Santa Cruz in September. In San Jose the printers organized in September, the bricklayers and painters in October, and the plasterers and stonecutters at some time within the year. The stonecutters of Rocklin organized in March, the printers of Oakland in June, the stonecutters of Vallejo and the plumbers and gas fitters of San Diego in September, and the upholsterers of San Francisco in December.[10]

The brewery owners of San Francisco soon became dissatisfied with the conditions imposed on them following the victory of the brewery workers' union in July, 1887. A national Brewers' Association had been formed in 1884.[11] The members of the latter finally rebelled against the growing power of the National Union of United Brewery Workmen, which had been organized in 1886. In 1887, the national Brewers' Association began a nation-wide fight against the union. After two years of bitter warfare it succeeded in destroying virtually all branches of the national union except the San Francisco branch. Here it met with determined and intelligent resistance. On March 26, 1888, the national Brewers' Association issued a manifesto against unionism, and declared that its members would enter into no agreements, either with the national union or with any of its branches. Nevertheless, in the following May the San Jose branch of the San Francisco Brewery Workers' Union obtained an agreement from the Fredericksburg Brewery, similar to that signed in the preceding year by the San Francisco employers. At the request of the national Brewers' Association, the brewery employers of San Francisco broke their agreement in the summer of 1888. Union members were locked out and replaced by non-union men. The union, planning an attack, again decided to concentrate on one brewery at a time. The United States Brewery was selected as being the most vulnerable, and in September, 1888, a boycott was levied on its products, and a life and death struggle for the union began. The boycott was approved by the Federated Trades Council and by virtually all San Francisco unions. The breweries joined forces and blacklisted union employees. The union was compelled to board, house, and clothe its members, at one time having to care for more than 200 men. Fuhrman, in testifying before the State Labor Commissioner in 1892, declared that "hoodlums were engaged to intimidate, to browbeat, and to attack our members; and at a picnic we held at San Jose, attacks were made upon our men."[12] Herman Schlüter, in his history of the national brewery workers' movement, comments as follows upon the San Francisco situation:

The bosses now used corrupt practices. As in the East, they attempted bribery. In some of the unions—those of the coopers and the boilermakers—they were successful in procuring the passage of the anti-boycott resolutions. Various attempts to bribe delegates to the central labor body were made known.[13]

The members of the brewery workers' union carried on the boycott by personal appeals to fellow-workers, saloon keepers, and restaurant keepers, by speeches, and by circulars. Union beer was provided by the Fredericksburg Brewery of San Jose and by a brewery in Sacramento. The Brewers' Association attempted to crush both of them, but the beer-consuming public supported the union to such a degree that the two union breweries prospered to the discomfiture of the member of the employers' association. After a nine-months' struggle an agreement was signed on June 5, 1889, bringing victory to the union. The Brewers' Protective Association of San Francisco, although supported by the national organization, had been disastrously defeated, at least for the time being.[14]

The victory of Brewery Workers' Union No. 16 brought Fuhrman into national prominence among the members of the craft. He was sent as a delegate to the national convention, but he broke with the national organization over various matters, among them the legality of an assessment levied for the purpose of building up the national body more securely and ensuring the publication of its official journal. At his suggestion, the San Francisco brewery workers' union, which he completely dominated, defied the national organization. It was accordingly suspended on January 14, 1890. Fuhrman then set about to form the United Brewery Workmen's Union of the Pacific Coast, with himself as general secretary. He organized branches in various coast cities, made connections with unions already in existence, and succeeded in bringing into his association the brewery workers of Seattle, Tacoma, Portland, Sacramento, Boca, San Francisco, and San Jose. The closed shop was established in all these places, and the employers, no matter where their breweries were situated, were forced to hire their men through the headquarters of the union in San Francisco.

Some of the San Francisco brewery workers, however, became dissatisfied with the policies of the local union and its leaders, and applied for and received Charter No. 16 from the National Union of United Brewery Workmen. The Federated Trades Council, of which Fuhrman was then president, refused to seat the delegates of the new organization. The national officers of the United Brewery Workmen appealed to the American Federation of Labor, asking that the San Francisco Federated Trades Council be suspended,[15] and this was done by the convention of the American Federation of Labor in 1890. Fuhrman, facing the opposition of both the National Union of United Brewery Workmen and the American Federation of Labor, organized a federation of all Pacific Coast unions. He notified the officials of the American Federation of Labor that his organization would exercise jurisdiction over all unions lying in the territory west of the Rocky Mountains and that the American Federation of Labor would have to be content with the rest of the United States. The federation became aroused over the prospects of serious competition in the western states and took steps to make effective its order that the San Francisco Federated Trades Council be suspended, the order not having been enforced in the intervening period. In 1891 the San Francisco Federated Trades Council asked to be reinstated. Its request was granted only on condition that all brewery unions of the Pacific Coast again affiliate with the National Union of United Brewery Workmen. This was finally done in 1892.[16]

In 1888 a labor paper, *The People,* was established in San Francisco, but it suspended publication in May of that year after only a few issues had appeared. It was followed some months later by the *Pacific Union Printer,* which was the official organ of the printing trades unions in the San Francisco Bay region. For eleven years this paper not only championed the cause of the printing trades but also supported that of all branches of Organized Labor in California. It suspended publication in 1899 because the San Francisco Labor Council had decided to issue its own official organ. In July, 1890, E. W. Thurman[17] and W. A. Bushnell began the publication of a labor paper, *The Pacific Coast Trades and Labor Journal.* It did not long remain in the field.

With the exception of the brewery strike and boycott, the working class movement in San Francisco and in other parts of the State was relatively peaceful in 1888.[18] The State Labor Commissioner in his biennial report published in the latter part of that year announced that in San Francisco and vicinity there were then 81 unions with 19,379 members, but of that number only 18 unions with about 5,700 members were affiliated with the Federated Trades Council.[19] Among the local organizations the influence of the central body was slight, its prestige having declined for causes already mentioned (see pp. 187–188).

On April 27, 1888, a Federated Council of Wharf and Wave Unions was organized by representatives of the following unions whose members were employed on the water front of San Francisco: the steamship stevedores', Stevedores' Protective Union, Marine Firemen's Union, Coast Seamen's Union, Steamship Sailors' Union, Independent Longshoremen, Riggers' Protective Union, stevedore engineers', brick-handlers', shipwrights', wharf-builders', longshore lumbermen's, and ship caulkers'. This, the first federation of the water-front crafts, was active for about a year. It was the forerunner of several similar organizations.

In the opening days of 1888 it was said that there were about 2,000 union men in San Jose. On January 22 of that year a meeting was held with the coöperation of the officials of the San Francisco Federated Trades Council at which the Santa Clara County Federation of Trades was organized. Representatives were in attendance from the unions of the painters, carpenters, brewers, stonecutters, cigarmakers, printers, and bakers. The following officers were elected: J. N. Barcel, chairman; T. M. Richert, vice-chairman; G. A. Ferris, secretary; G. Turner, financial secretary; Albert Schoenberg, treasurer; and John Schubert, sergeant at arms. In November, 1889, the Santa Clara Federation affiliated with the San Francisco Federated Trades Council.

In 1889 the organization of the workers of San Francisco proceeded rapidly. Unions were formed among the barbers, stonecutters, car-builders, candy-makers, wire-workers, box sawyers and nailers, sausage-makers, and stereotypers. The Benicia Fishermen's Association was organized, and applied for membership in the San Francisco Federated Trades Council in September, 1889. The tanners of Redwood City formed a union in the fall of that year. In January, 1889, the bakers of San Francisco organized a local union separate from the national organization. In the latter part of the year Bakers' Union No. 51 (composed of Americans) of San Francisco established a branch in Los Angeles. The San Bernardino Central Labor Union was in existence in January, 1889, but I have been unable to ascertain the date of its organization or the number of its members.

During the early months of 1889 the industrial field was comparatively peaceful,[20] but in the fall of that year the stage was set for what was to prove one of the most disastrous conflicts in the history of the iron trades of San Francisco. On August 30, 1887, an agreement had been entered into by the ironmolders' union and the Engineers' and Iron Founders' Association relative to conditions of employment. One of the provisions of the agreement required that all modifications of the terms of employment should be referred to a conference of the representatives of both parties. On September 16, 1889, the molders notified all local foundry employers that foremen had to join the union. The firm of McCormick Brothers refused to accede to the demand, whereupon the molders employed by this shop struck. The Engineers' and Founders' Association then requested a conference between McCormick Brothers and the union, but the latter refused. On December 13 the employers' association announced that the agreement of August 30, 1887, would be abandoned on January 1, 1890. A conference was then held between the association and the union. The employers protested that local wages were too high, as compared with wages paid in eastern communities ($3.50 as against $2–$2.75 per day); that competition with eastern shops was impossible; and that the depressed condition of the trade required a modification of the employment conditions then existing. But the union would not agree to any revision in wages or hours, whereupon the employers' association declared that on and after March 10 wages would be $3 per day, payable on an hourly basis, and that the non-union shop would prevail. The union then called a strike at twelve of the largest foundries, involving more than 1,000 men. The coremakers went out in support of the molders. The employees of the Vulcan Foundry, which was not in the employers' association, soon returned to their jobs. The machinists' union, whose members had been given a wage reduction of 25 cents per day, also went on strike.

Strike breakers were imported from eastern points in special trains with guarded coaches. To meet this action many who were union members in the East agreed to work in California as strike breakers and were successful in persuading a number of the non-union men to desert along the way. It is said that "during the first nine months of the strike, about two hundred strike breakers were returned to their eastern homes by the union."[21] Men continuing on the job were housed and fed in the foundries or were guarded as they went to and from work. Many obtained permission to carry firearms for protection. As early as July 3, prosecutions were pending in the local courts against several strikers charged with the use of violence. The employers and strike breakers were in turn accused by the union men of similar outrages. Two lives were lost in the struggle. The strike lasted for twenty months and cost the foundrymen $5,000,000, the union $200,000, and the strikers $300,000 in wages. Both sides were exhausted. At the conclusion of the strike the employers agreed not to reduce wages or to discriminate against those who had taken part in it. The union was practically disrupted, and for a year enrolled only about forty members. Although the ironmolders had the support of many of the local unions, which levied strike assessments upon their members and assisted in many ways in carrying on the fight, they were handicapped in their contest by not being affiliated with the Federated Trades Council, from which they had earlier withdrawn. The strike paralyzed many coast industries. Orders for shipbuilding and house-building materials were sent East. "The molders lost their strike and San Francisco lost a lively infant industry. The infant industry went East; the molders simply followed it."[22]

Mention has been made (p. 181) of the campaign begun by the American Federation of Labor for the eight-hour day. At the convention of that body held in 1884 it was voted that members should ask for the eight-hour day in 1886. Out of the 340,000 workers who then made the demand, 200,000 were successful in obtaining the shorter workday. At the convention held in December, 1888, and at the suggestion of the National Brotherhood of Carpenters and Joiners, the American Federation of Labor again decided to try for the eight-hour day, and named May 1, 1890, as the date. At the 1889 convention it was proposed that one union be selected to make the demand, with the understanding that it was to be supported by all the members of the federation. Accordingly, in March, 1890, the executive committee of the federation chose the carpenters. Assessments were levied and funds collected from Organized Labor throughout the country to provide a campaign chest. Eighthour leagues were organized and a vigorous campaign was carried on. The carpenters' struggle for the shorter workday was successful in only 137 cities. In the greater number of other cities a ninehour day was accepted as a compromise.

In San Francisco, the Federated Trades Council called a labor convention on March 17, 1889, chiefly to make plans for starting the eight-hour day on May 1, 1890, but incidentally to urge all local unions to affiliate with the American Federation of Labor. At the second conference, held on June 2, 1889, an Eight-Hour League was organized, with Joseph F. Valentine as president. The league held mass meetings, sent speakers to the local unions to urge unity of action, and published a monthly paper, *The Eight-Hour Herald*. In May, 1890, the *Herald* was succeeded by *The Future,* published weekly by John H. Collins, of the molders' union, and approved by the Eight-Hour League. The Labor Day celebration of September 2, 1889, was entirely given over to furthering the cause of the eight-hour day. A parade of 5,000 union members and a celebration at Woodward's Gardens, were the chief events of the occasion. In November a movement was started to organize a Building Trades Federation to assist in the eight-hour campaign. On December 16, delegates representing more than 2,000 building trades workers met in convention and voted to work eight hours on and after May 1, 1890.[23]

As May 1 approached, preparations were made not only in San Francisco but also throughout the United States and northern Europe for the inauguration of the shorter workday. In many places riots and serious outbreaks occurred, but in San Francisco there was almost no disturbance; about fifty carpenters struck to enforce demands. In Los Angeles, Redwood City, and Oakland, as well as in San Francisco, the eight-hour day was generally granted by the employing carpenters. The mill machine and bench hands of the San Francisco planing mills, numbering about 500, had wished to be included in the eight-hour agitation, and accordingly had organized a union in April, 1890. The Millmen's Protective Association refused to grant their request, and on May 2 the employees struck, only to be defeated because they had to wage their strike single-handed. The Eight-Hour League of San Francisco formally disbanded shortly after May 1, its work being taken over by an eight-hour committee of the Federated Trades Council, which continued the agitation for many years. Miles L. Farland, a union printer, served as the committee's first chairman.

The wave of organization which swept over San Francisco in 1889 continued into 1890. Fuhrman, who became president of the Federated Trades Council in June, 1889, followed an aggressive organization policy. The upholsterers were organized in the latter part of January, 1890; the tin and sheet-iron workers, the sheep butchers, and the sewing machine agents in March; the blacksmiths and horseshoers in the summer months (and in four weeks' time this union had 220 members); the first branch of the Deutsch-Amerikanische Typographia with 30 German printers of San Francisco and Oakland in July; the wood molders and machine men in the planing mills of San Francisco in July, and the hat clerks in November.

A group of musicians in San Francisco seceded from the Musicians' Mutual Protective Association and received Charter No. 5775 from the American Federation of Labor. They installed officers and asked for recognition by the Federated Trades Council, but the Musicians' Mutual Protective Association protested against what it called a "scab union," and the charter of the new group was subsequently revoked. The printers', bookbinders', and pressmen's unions of the State formed a Printers' and Bookbinders' Alliance of California in the fall of 1890 for the purpose of uniting all printing trades unions of California into a state federation. Two years later (January 11, 1892), this organization having succumbed in the meantime, the California Federation of Typographical Unions was formed by eleven unions in the printing trades throughout the State. It held its first convention in Los Angeles on May 26, 1892. The tanners and curriers, the shoemakers, and the harness-makers of San Francisco formed a Leather Federation in April. Carpenters' Union No. 22 issued a call in the spring of 1890 urging the various building trades unions to organize a local federation, but nothing came of the suggestion, although later in that year a building trades labor bureau and reading room were opened. Following the example of the brewery workers, the butchers in August, 1890, and the carpenters and joiners in October set up their own employment offices. In November the boot- and shoemakers established a burial fund, and in December the brick handlers a sick and accident benefit fund which paid $10 weekly to members, and the butchers a sick and burial fund.

In the closing months of 1890, plans were made by the long-shoremen, lumbermen, and steamship sailors of San Francisco to organize the maritime unions into a federation, but nothing came of the proposal. The early-closing campaign was still being carried on by the store clerks of San Francisco. An attempt was made to induce the dry-goods storekeepers to close at 6 o'clock on Saturdays, the shoe stores at 7 o'clock except on Saturdays and holidays, and the millinery stores at 6 o'clock except on Saturdays and holidays. A number of dry-goods and millinery stores granted the request, but the shoe stores refused to do so. Both the retail shoe dealers and the dry-goods merchants formed an association for the purpose of resisting the demands of the union.

From notices in the newspapers, it is evident that a Labor Council was in existence in Stockton as early as 1890. The Sacramento Federated Trades Council was affiliated with the San Francisco Federated Trades Council, and in March, 1890, had ten constituent unions. In December, 1890, a Bay Counties District Council of Carpenters and Joiners was organized with headquarters in San Francisco. It has been in continuous existence since that time, and has exercised great influence in protecting the interests of the carpenters of the Bay region.

Several strikes occurred in San Francisco in 1890. In January the boot and shoe workers employed by Porter, Slessinger & Company, and those employed by Buckingham & Hecht, struck successfully against a reduction in wages. The activity of the boot- and shoemakers' union caused four of the largest employers to organize a protective association which declared for a non-union shop, a policy of dealing directly with employees, no Chinese to be employed, and the closing of all shops if a strike should be declared against any member. On November 12, the shoemakers carried to successful conclusion a two days' strike at Lewis Murr's factory, for the recognition of the union. A strike of the harness-makers employed at O'Kane's harness shop against the employment of girls on journeymen's work was also settled in favor of the workers. In May the tailors' union struck against H. S. Bridge & Company for higher wages.

In Sacramento the printers employed on the *Bee* struck against the discharge of a stereotyper. A vigorous boycott of the paper followed. The strikers started their own newspaper, *The Trades Union*. The proprietor of the *Bee* asked for an injunction against the union and the local Federated Trades Council, and this was granted, but on March 1, 1891, the *Bee* admitted defeat and the men returned to work.

In 1886, shortly after the San Francisco Federated Trades Council was founded, its members had begun an agitation for the adoption of the Australian ballot, but without success. In 1888 and 1889 a campaign was again waged unsuccessfully. Early in 1890, however, under the leadership of Alfred Fuhrman, the council renewed its propaganda for ballot reform. More than 50,000 copies of the proposed measure were printed and circulated, speeches were made, and candidates for political office were pledged to its adoption. In securing the enactment of this much needed political reform in California, finally obtained in 1891,[24] the council was the most important factor.

When the Representative Council of the Federated Trades and Labor Organizations of the Pacific Coast was formed in 1886, the plan was that it should be a federation of all western unions, exercising jurisdiction over them similar to that of a national union over its local organizations. For several reasons that ideal was never attained. Most of the San Francisco unions, although not affiliated with the national organizations of their respective crafts, were not willing to accept supervision or dictation from a central body. Only two unions in the Federated Trades Council, namely, the brewers' and the sailors', had branches in Oregon and Washington, although the musicians', cooks' and waiters', carpenters', bakers', and a few other unions had branches in some of the cities of California. The other unions on the Pacific Coast had not felt the need of affiliating with the council. The central labor councils of Alameda County, Santa Clara County, Stockton, Sacramento, and Los Angeles, although members of the San Francisco Federated Trades Council, were only nominally affiliated with it because it was impossible, owing to transportation difficulties, for them to be represented at its meetings. At no time did the council attempt in any way to control their activities.

In 1891, however, conditions were favorable for the organization of a bona fide Pacific Coast federation. Fuhrman, the outstanding leader in the union movement of the Coast, had broken with the National Union of United Brewery Workmen, and had organized the United Brewery Workmen's Union of the Pacific Coast. The American Federation of Labor had suspended the Federated Trades Council because it had supported Fuhrman and his rebel union. Furthermore, the Pacific Coast labor groups had always felt neglected by the eastern movement, which had never shown any interest in their welfare. At this particular time there were in existence on the Coast the following central organizations: *California*—Federated Trades Councils in San Francisco, Stockton, Sacramento, Los Angeles, Santa Clara County, San Diego, San Bernardino, and Alameda County; the San Francisco Building Trades Council, and the City Front Labor Council of the same city; *Oregon*—Portland Federated Trades Assembly, Salem Trades Assembly, Albina Federated Trades; *Washington*—Seattle Western Central Union, Spokane Federated Trades Council, Tacoma Federated Trades Council, Olympia Trades Council, Port Townsend Federated Trades, Bellingham Bay Central Labor Union, Whatcom Trades Federation; *British Columbia*—Provincial Trades Assembly of British Columbia, Victoria Trades and Labor Club, General Assembly of Miners and Mine Laborers of Nanaimo, Wellington, and other places. These organizations represented in all about 40,000 to 45,000 organized workers. They had accomplished much for their members, but it was felt that more effective action and greater mutual benefit might be secured by welding them into a Pacific Coast association. Fuhrman, with characteristic energy and ardor, set about to accomplish the desired object. As president of the San Francisco Federated Trades Council he called a meeting in San Francisco on September 21, 1891. Delegates were present from the central labor councils of San

Francisco, Sacramento, Seattle, Alameda County, Santa Clara County, and Portland, and from the San Francisco Building Trades Council and the San Francisco City Front Labor Council. As a result of the convention, which lasted three and a half days, the Pacific Coast Council of Trades and Labor Federations was organized with Alfred Fuhrman, president, W. G. Armstrong, of Seattle, vice-president, and W. B. Soule, of Alameda County, secretary and treasurer. The main object was to unite only the local councils, not the individual unions, into a federation which, it was planned, should exercise jurisdiction over the western unions to the exclusion of the American Federation of Labor.

The second convention of the Pacific Coast federation was held in Seattle on June 5, 1893. Twelve central bodies were represented. Fuhrman had resigned from the presidency in March, 1893, and W. G. Armstrong, the vice-president, who had been elevated to his place, was reëlected president at the Seattle meeting. Walter Macarthur, of San Francisco, was chosen secretary-treasurer. A number of resolutions were adopted dealing with matters of concern to Organized Labor.

The third and last conference of the Pacific Coast federation was held at Sacramento on January 8, 1894. An agreement was entered into at that time between the federation and the Farmers' Alliance, pledging mutual assistance in working for certain common ends. The Pacific Coast Council of Trades and Labor Federations succeeded temporarily in developing a closer relationship among the coast labor councils, thereby bringing the American Federation of Labor to see that it should take a livelier interest in the welfare of the western unions. It was also active in carrying on effectively the Wellington, Roslyn, and Coeur d'Alene mine boycotts. Had Fuhrman continued his active association with the labor movement, it is possible that the federation might have been a much more effective and longer-lived body than it was.

The labor situation in San Francisco became increasingly serious in 1891. The retail clerks' union continued to demand early closing, and with some success. Fifty box-sawyers employed by Carrick, Williams & Company struck against a 10 per cent wage reduction. The firm was at once boycotted by the Federated Trades Council. Shortly thereafter the box sawyers of the city demanded the nine-hour day with ten hours' pay and the closed shop. The Box Manufacturers' Association refused to grant the demands and a bitter contest ensued. The mill carpenters of San Francisco and Oakland struck for the eight-hour day, but on June 1 they went back to work on the old basis. The painters had carried on successfully an eight-hour day campaign in Oakland and in San Rafael, and in April they turned their attention to the situation in San Francisco, and had some success there, too. The printers of Los Angeles had obtained the eight-hour day as early as 1887, and it was also in force in Fresno and in the State Printing Office in Sacramento. The International Typographical Society decided to make a try for the national eight-hour day on October 1, 1891. Throughout California steps were taken to attain the desired goal. The results, however, were disappointing. Many years were to pass before the eight-hour day should become the rule in the printers' trade.

In 1891, unions were organized in San Francisco among the peddlers, steam engineers, trunk-makers, marine cooks and stewards, and the horse-collar makers. On March 21, 1891, a Building Trades Council was formed by the following unions, representing about 2,000 members: carpenters', Nos. 304, 483, 616, 707; painters', Nos. 140, 175; stonecutters', granite cutters', bricklayers', plumbers', metal roofers', cornice workers', plasterers', woodcarvers', and the local branch of the Amalgamated Society of Carpenters and Joiners. Some of these unions at once withdrew from the Federated Trades Council, preferring to have but one affiliation, while others remained members of both central bodies. It was inevitable that in this divided allegiance there should lie the seed of future trouble between the two councils. On April 19, 1891, a second attempt to form a maritime federation among the water-front unions in San Francisco resulted in the organization of the City Front Labor Council, composed of the coast seamen, steamshipmen, longshore lumbermen, steamship stevedores, engineer stevedores, riggers and stevedores, and wharf-builders. So many discordant elements, however, could not be welded together, and the group soon disbanded.

There was also some activity in the ranks of Labor in other parts of the State. The barbers of Stockton formed a union in July,

1891. A Federated Trades Council was organized in San Diego in the spring of that year. The victory of the printers' union of Sacramento in its struggle with the *Bee* gave renewed life to the labor movement of that city, and in the twelve months ending with July, 1892, thirteen unions were organized and became affiliated with the local federation, bringing its membership to thirty unions. One of the unions formed at the time was composed of the newspaper writers; it is said to have been the third association of that craft organized in the United States. The stonecutters' union from the near-by town of Rocklin was also affiliated with the Sacramento federation. In January, 1892, the stonecutters employed on the State Capitol building at Sacramento struck successfully for the eight-hour day and a wage of $8.

On January 29, 1891, the women employees of the shoe factories of San Francisco, numbering about 800, were organized into the Boot and Shoe Fitters' Protective Union. At about the same time, 39 boot- and shoemakers struck against the Kutz-Marr factory and within a few days obtained their demands. A few weeks later seven shoemakers of Orin-Jones & Company, struck for higher wages. In April, 200 employees of the Buckingham & Hecht shoe factory struck because that company had refused to abide by union rules, had reduced wages, and had hired non-union men. The boot and shoe manufacturers of San Francisco, as previously noted, had formed a protective association and had announced that they would not operate union shops; also that they would close all their plants if strikes should be called against any of their members, or if they should be boycotted by the union. The Buckingham & Hecht strike precipitated a general lockout, affecting about 1,000 employees, and in less than two weeks the union was defeated.[25] The victory of the employers did not, however, prevent 30 shoemakers of Jones & Glanville from striking against a reduction in wages in the latter part of August, to no avail. In January, 1892, the women shoe fitters of Cahn, Nickelsburg & Company struck against a wage reduction, and a boycott was levied against that firm by the Federated Trades Council. The Boot and Shoe Manufacturers' Association then locked out all union employees and said that, if any of them wished to return, they might do so if they should first give up their union membership. This the employees did, and there remained in San Francisco only one union boot and shoe factory, employing about 105 persons.

In the months from February to September, 1891, strikes were declared in San Francisco by the printers of Crocker & Company, for the closed shop; by the broom-makers of Zann Brothers & Company, against a reduction in wages; by the street pavers, for higher wages; by the horseshoers, for the nine-hour day; by the coopers, for higher wages and against employment of Chinese; by the stevedores, for an increase in wages; and by the upholsterers, for the nine-hour day. In May, the granite cutters struck for the eight-hour day and a wage of $4, this move being part of a campaign of the national union for the shorter workday and higher wages. The strike dragged on for many months and met with most determined resistance on the part of the employers. Many granite cutters left San Francisco for eastern cities, where the strike had been partly successful.

During the years 1889–1891 the unrest, strikes, and boycotts among the organized workers of San Francisco frightened the employing class. As has been noted, unions had been formed in many trades, both skilled and unskilled, and strikes and boycotts had been declared in endless succession in connection with demands for higher wages, shorter hours, and the closed shop, and against reductions in wages. Fuhrman, in his annual report as president of the Federated Trades Council, stated that in his two terms of office (1890–1891) twenty unions and one federation (Los Angeles) had affiliated with the council, and that seventeen boycotts had been levied, of which twelve were for union recognition. Twelve had been won and five remained undecided.

Faced with what appeared to be a situation demanding unity of action, the employers of San Francisco formed associations in their various fields to combat the demands of the unions. The Engineers' and Iron Founders' Association, as has been noted, waged a twenty-months' struggle with the molders. The Boot and Shoe Manufacturers' Association locked out its union workers. The Millmen's Protective Association opposed successfully the eight-hour day demanded by its employees. The growing strength of the building trades unions had forced the Masons' and Builders' Association and the Builders' Association (composed of carpenter contractors) to discuss together the advisability of amalgamation so as to gain greater bargaining strength. Other employers' associations had been organized among the master bakers, cigar manufacturers, brewers, retail boot and shoe dealers, dry-goods merchants, boss granite cutters, boss coopers, and shipowners. On June 11, 1891, a large group of San Francisco employers met to discuss the situation. In August of that year the Board of Manufacturers and Employers of California was organized by firms employing about 40,000 workers. The new association announced that it had been

formed to promote the manufacturing interests of the Pacific Coast. Its policy is not dictated by a spirit of aggression, but it shall be the earnest endeavor of its members to prevent friction, and to peacefully settle all disputes that may arise between employers and employes.

We ... have no wish to interfere with the indisputable right of labor to organize, but believe in the organization and the federation of employers of labor, to the end that neither party shall tempt the other to overstep the bounds of right, reason, and justice.

We believe that the arbitrary spirit shown by the unions, ... and the frequent strikes and boycotts ... are dangerous to its [the community's] industries. ...

We recognize the urge of labor to organize ... , but we reserve to ourselves the right to decide as to whom we shall or whom we shall not employ.[26]

George C. Williams was chosen secretary of the association. Williams, whose real name was Walthew, had been elected to the Michigan legislature in 1882. On June 12, 1889, a warrant had been issued for his arrest on the complaint that he had offered bribes to some of the legislators of that state in connection with the passage of a voting machine bill. He fled to San Francisco and became a labor reporter on the *Daily Report*. The *Examiner*, in its issue of October 9, 1893, exposed his previous record, whereupon he resumed his correct name.

The Manufacturers' and Employers' Association, as it was commonly called, waged a campaign of extirpation against the unions of San Francisco. It was so successful that three years later its president declared:

The general success of this Association can best be understood by the light of the fact that among the industries of San Francisco there remains but one single union which enforces its rules upon its trade. That union is the Typographical Union. The reason why this union still continues to dictate terms is because the employing printers have never combined to resist its demands.

Evidences of the activities of the association and its powerful influence will be noted in succeeding pages.

The old conflict between the brewery workers' union and the local brewers' association was renewed in January, 1892. The former, realizing that it would undoubtedly be attacked by the Manufacturers' and Employers' Association, levied an assessment of $20 on each of its members in October, 1891, in order to have a war chest ready. Seven beer wagon drivers refused to pay the assessment (it is said that their refusal was made at the behest of their employers) and they were suspended by the union. At first both the Hibernia and the Jackson breweries refused to discharge the drivers as requested by the union. On January 10 the Hibernia Brewery reversed its position. On January 16 a boycott was levied against the Jackson Brewery.[27] A struggle followed, in which all breweries joined forces to defeat the union.[28]

The California Brewers' Protective Association, a reorganization of the former association among the local brewers, obtained the support of the Manufacturers' and Employers' Association and carried on the fight aggressively. Hundreds of union men were discharged and blacklisted. The union had hoped to get union beer from a local brewery, but at the last moment the latter cast its lot with the Brewers' Protective Association. Plans were then made to get beer from St. Louis, but that city was too far distant. The union then established the Coöperative Brewery with $500,000 capital, but this brewery made only steam beer and the beer-consuming public could not satisfy its thirst with that beverage alone. The Coöperative Brewery, after operating for several years, was disposed of at a heavy loss. The conflict spread to Oakland, where all brewery employees were paid off and told to return as non-union men. Forty-five beer wagon drivers in San Francisco withdrew from the union and went back to work. The strike and boycotting activities of the brewery workers' union continued until May, 1899, when the breweries were completely unionized.[29]

The policy early adopted by the San Francisco brewery workers' union, of exercising jurisdiction over the entire State, was continued. In San Francisco all the union brewery workers were grouped into three separate local unions, namely, the brewers and maltsters, the bottlers, and the wagon drivers and stablemen.

Union members of these crafts in any city were organized in local branches of the San Francisco unions, and their relations with the brewery owners were subject to approval by the joint local executive board of the three San Francisco unions, and of the international union. Thus, in 1915, Brewers' and Maltsters' Union No. 7, of San Francisco, had about 600 members, of whom 210 were in San Francisco, 30 in Oakland, 64 in Los Angeles, 76 in San Diego, 47 in Fresno, and 54 in Sacramento. Beer Drivers' and Stablemen's Union No. 227 had 625 members, of whom 325 were in San Francisco and 300 in the other cities above mentioned. Beer Bottlers' Union No. 293 had about 450 members, of whom 238 were in San Francisco, 140 in Los Angeles, 50 in Sacramento, and 40 in Oakland. So far as I know, the beer bottlers of Los Angeles were for some time the only exception to this plan of organization. They at first formed a local union, but after the Los Angeles strike and boycott of 1910–1911, they became a branch of the San Francisco Beer Bottlers' Union. With the possible exception of the sailors' union, it is doubtful if any local union was as successful as that of the brewery workers in improving the economic status of its members.

Another of the noteworthy struggles in which the influence and financial backing of the Manufacturers' and Employers' Association played a deciding part in the final outcome was the sailors' strike of 1891. In the latter part of November of that year, the Ship Owners' Association, which had been revived, notified the sailors of a 25 per cent reduction in wages. Shipping was then at a low ebb, and along the San Francisco water front were to be found many unemployed men, most of whom were non-union sailors. The union struck and used every available means to defeat the employers. Much rioting and violence ensued. One life was lost, ropes and hawsers were cut, and dynamite was several times found in the holds of vessels. The struggle continued through 1892, neither side being able to wear down the resistance of the other. In the spring of 1893, however, when the Ship Owners' Association was about to acknowledge defeat, the Manufacturers' and Employers' Association came to its rescue. Walthew, the secretary of the Manufacturers' and Employers' Association, was lent to the shipowners and made the secretary of their association. The shipowners now had a trained executive, and under his direction they proceeded ruthlessly to crush the union by fair means and foul. They established a shipping office and again installed the "grade book" system. Union sailors who signed up as non-union men and then abandoned the vessel before it left port, or who left it when the first port was reached, were arrested for desertion. On December 25, 1893, a valise containing dynamite was exploded in front of Curtin's Boarding House in San Francisco, a non-union house, killing six men and injuring several others, two of whom later died. The outrage was naturally charged to the sailors' union. One of its members, John Tyrell, was arrested and tried, and found not guilty. Burnette G. Haskell defended him. The union offered $1,000 reward for any information leading to the arrest of the real culprit, asserting that the valise had been "planted" by an agent of the Ship Owners' Association. This episode climaxed the struggle, the union being forced to admit defeat. The membership of the union declined from about 4,000 to 1,650, and following the depression of 1893 it further decreased to about 800. In October, 1894, the union made a feeble attempt to increase wages, but a few months later it was again defeated. Not until the spring of 1899 was the union strong enough to wring any concessions from the shipowners. After a strike of more than three months, the sailors obtained an increase of $5 per month for men employed on ships engaged in the Mexican trade. Thereafter the membership increased rapidly, rising in two years to 3,465. The resentment of the sailors against conditions imposed by the Ship Owners' Association in the nineties was stored against the day of wrath and found full vent in the tragic and violent contest which arose in connection with the teamsters' strike of 1901.[30]

In spite of the organized opposition of the employers of San Francisco, the workers continued to make demands for improved conditions. In April, 1892, the cigarmakers struck for higher wages. The employers formed an association, but finally were forced to grant the workers' demands. The coopers carried on successfully a five months' struggle against an increase in the hours of work with no increase in pay. A coöperative cooperage shop which they established aided in bringing them victory. In August, the bakers' unions forced all but twenty-five employers to grant the six-day week. A coöperative bakery was started, in order to bring pressure to bear on employers who held out against their demands. Their success was short-lived, however, for the depressed state of business in the next few years brought back the seven-day week. It was not until November, 1900, that they finally obtained the one day's rest in seven, which they had been demanding since 1852. The tile setters organized in March, 1892; the cooks, waiters, and bar tenders in April; and the wiremen in the latter part of July or the early part of August. The San Francisco Building Trades Council, of which some of the member unions were politically inclined, called a state convention of all unions in San Francisco on May 20, 1892, to consider the formation of a third party, the drafting of labor laws, and the waging of a campaign for their enactment. More than 100 delegates were present, but the only action taken was the adoption of resolutions favoring certain labor measures. The newspapers contained notices of the Building Trades Council of Oakland, which was represented in the Federated Trades Council of San Francisco as early as March 11, 1892.

Because of the large number of boycotts levied by the Federated Trades Council of San Francisco, the Manufacturers' and Employers' Association issued a manifesto on that subject which appeared on May 6, 1892. In part it was as follows:

The boycott is a crying evil of our times.... Walking delegates have been bribed to boycott competitors, and walking delegates have exacted bribes for immunity from boycotts.... When Cahn, Nickelsburg & Company introduced new machinery in their factory, a committee of expert manufacturers reported that the new rate on the new machines actually increased the wages of the operator, yet a boycott was levied. The "Abend Post" is boycotted after the Typographical Union declared the boycott untenable, and asked to have it raised. Wellington coal is boycotted long after the Wellington strike is declared off.[31] Breweries are boycotted, notwithstanding that the beer drivers, in a body, protested against the wrong, and declared that they would not longer permit the Federated Trades to dictate what they should eat, drink, and wear, or read. Drygoods houses are boycotted, although all their clerks declare against it....

This condition of things should no longer be tolerated. The boycott should be stopped.... Watch your employees, and discharge boycotters. Patronize boycotted firms.[32]

The Federated Trades Council faced a serious situation both within and without its ranks. It had to cope with the active and powerful Manufacturers' and Employers' Association and with the various employers' associations in the separate trades. It was carrying on strikes and boycotts in the brewery, shoe, cooperage, cigarmaking, printing, and other industries, for the most part not very efficiently. Equally serious was the conflict within its own ranks. When the Building Trades Council was formed in March, 1891,[33] some of the unions had withdrawn from the Federated Trades Council in order to affiliate with the former group only; and that action created a division among the local forces of Organized Labor. Moreover, some of the building trades unions that had remained in the Federated Trades Council proved a source of dissension. Furthermore, the Nationalist Party movement attracted many of the trade unionists of San Francisco, who had grown discouraged with the results of unionism and who felt that the salvation of the working class lay in political action only. Especially prominent in this latter group were the furniture workers' union, some of the carpenters' unions, and particularly those unionists who were socialists. In March, 1892, the Federated Trades Council had, in no uncertain words, resolved against political action. This was the chief reason why the Building Trades Council had called a labor conference in San Francisco for the following May, to which reference has been made above (see p. 214). The seriousness of the clash between the two councils was further heightened in May by a resolution of the Federated Trades Council approving the strike of the granite cutters, which the Building Trades Council had refused to sanction. Another source of irritation was the dictatorial policies and methods followed by Fuhrman and some of his associates in their direction of local labor affairs.

Many unions had severed their connections with the Federated Trades Council, and in the winter of 1891 the Federated Trades Council of Sacramento had also deemed it advisable to withdraw. The labor movement of San Francisco, which had been the inspiration for that of the rest of the State, was facing a crisis. Many felt that, if it collapsed, trade unionism in California was doomed. Fortunately, the Federated Trades Council of Sacramento was at the time an active body composed of about thirty unions. In July, 1892, it offered to act as arbiter of the internal difficulties which had disrupted the San Francisco Federated Trades Council. Wal-

ter Macarthur, president of the latter body, and others associated
with him, being greatly concerned over the situation, gladly accepted the offer. Accordingly, on August 21, 1892, John Joost and
J. A. Sheehan, of Sacramento, met with a joint committee representing the Building Trades Council and the Federated Trades
Council. Joost and Sheehan stayed in San Francisco several weeks,
visiting the various unions, consulting with labor leaders, and
seeking a solution of the many local problems. They first asked a
number of the prominent labor leaders, especially Fuhrman, to
resign, and these leaders did so.[34] They then requested the two antagonistic councils to unite in one federation, but the Building
Trades Council refused to accept the proposal. Their next suggestion, that a new federation be formed, met with approval, and both
groups, the Federated Trades Council and the Building Trades
Council, disbanded. Thirty-one unions were represented in the
meeting of November 20, 1892, at which the first steps were taken
to form a new federation. At subsequent meetings a new constitution and by-laws were discussed. Finally, in December, 1892, the
San Francisco Trades and Labor Council was formally launched.
On February 4, 1893, it shortened its title to the San Francisco
Labor Council. F. H. Staule, of the barbers' union, was the first
president, and M. L. Farland, of the printers' union, the first secretary of the new body. Since that time it has had a continuous,
occasionally tempestuous, existence.

The Labor Council went on record as favoring a judicious use
of strikes and boycotts and of independent political action. Several
of the more radical and politically inclined unions accordingly refused to affiliate with the Labor Council, preferring to stake their
future on political action through the medium of the Nationalist
Party or the Socialist Labor Party. One of the first official acts of
the new council was to call off virtually all strikes and boycotts
then in effect. Its members expressed the hope that never again
would the local movement become entangled in disputes, both internal and external, which it had neither the power nor the ability
to bring to a satisfactory conclusion.

CHAPTER XIII

SUPREMACY AND DEFEAT

THE LABOR COUNCIL OF SAN FRANCISCO entered upon its career at a most inopportune time. Many of the local unions had been forced out of existence by the vigorous attacks of the Manufacturers' and Employers' Association and the individual employers' associations in the various crafts. Unemployment was general; in San Francisco about 35,000 men were out of work. The *Coast Seamen's Journal* as early as March 30, 1892, had said that "not for over twenty-five years has San Francisco witnessed such destitution, misery and suffering." Nor did conditions improve : they became even more discouraging. The panic of 1893, originating in New York City in the first week of May, began to be felt in California in June. Bank and business failures occurred in rapid succession in spite of the receipt of $2,500,000 in gold sent from the East for the relief of the critical situation. Twenty-seven banks (six national and twenty-one state) closed their doors, and ten of them never resumed operations. Industry and agriculture were at a standstill. Sacramento drove its unemployed out of the city limits and many of them made their way to San Francisco. Free employment bureaus, soup kitchens, public wood-yards, street sweeping, and charitable ventures of various sorts were resorted to in attempts to help the hungry and desperate population. Carl Browne, who had been one of Dennis Kearney's lieutenants in the anti-Chinese agitation of the seventies, helped to organize the California contingent of Coxey's Army and to direct its march toward Washington.

The heavy wheat crop of 1893, which sold for a fair price, relieved the situation somewhat for the agricultural population. An uneven rainfall in 1894, however, with resulting light crops for 1895, contributed in part to the continuation of the depression into that year. The Chinese-Japanese War of 1894–1895 brought about a slight upturn in the exporting trade of the Pacific Coast, especially that of California. Business in general, however, remained depressed until the discovery of gold in the Klondike, the rush of gold seekers to the Yukon in 1897–1898, the Spanish-American War, and the annexation of Hawaii brought about renewed industrial and commercial activity. Concurrently came the development of oil and hydro-electric resources as well as the opening of the Imperial Valley to irrigation and settlement. Prosperity once more gladdened the hearts of Californians.

From 1893 to 1898 the labor movement of the State reflected a depressed industry and a depressed agriculture. The San Francisco Labor Council was kept alive with the greatest difficulty and only through the tireless efforts of its loyal leaders. In 1895 its membership had declined to 16 affiliated unions; in 1897 this number was further decreased to 15, the lowest in its history. At that time there were about 4,500 union members in San Francisco.[1]

The Los Angeles County Council of Labor apparently fared much better than the San Francisco federation, for in May, 1896, it was said to have 23 affiliated unions, representing approximately 5,400 workers. The Sacramento Federated Trades Council also was in excellent condition during 1893 and the early part of 1894. In that city's directory were listed 41 unions, the greater number of which were members of the council. The defeat of the American Railway Union strike in 1894 greatly discouraged the Sacramento unions, and many of them disbanded. In 1900 only 12 organizations were listed in the Sacramento city directory.

In the years 1893–1895 there were very few strikes, and only a small number of unions were organized.[2] The most important labor dispute of those three years was the strike of the American Railway Union against the Southern Pacific railroad. Some of the employees of the Pullman Palace Car Company, of Pullman, Illinois, had struck on May 11, 1894, for the restoration of a previously existing wage scale. They had affiliated in March of that year with the American Railway Union. This organization was an industrial union of all railway employees, and its leader was Eugene V. Debs. On June 26, 1894, the union declared a sympathetic strike against all railroads using Pullman cars. On July 7, Debs and the principal officers of the union were arrested for contempt of court for having disobeyed an injunction. United States troops were ordered out by President Cleveland to keep the mail trains moving; and after a short but violent struggle, centering chiefly in Chicago, where property valued at more than $80,000,000 was destroyed, the union was disastrously defeated.

It is surprising that California, so far removed from the center of the conflict, should have become involved. Debs and his associates, however, in order to give greater strength to the strikers, had ordered all local and overland trains to be tied up. Although legally the Central Pacific Railway and the Southern Pacific Railway of California were separate corporations, they were owned by the same interests and both were known popularly as the Southern Pacific. Seldom has any railroad been so generously hated by the citizens of any state. A contemporary writer said:

According to the common report, the Southern Pacific runs political conventions, influences elections, controls legislatures, owns railroad commissioners, and frustrates justice. It is the arbiter of trade, fixes the prices of most commodities, determines who (if any) shall prosper and who shall go to the wall, dictates the waxing and waning of prosperity in every community within its grasp. It pursues individuals with petty spite, from which great corporations are supposed to be free. . . . Some of these charges are proved, more of them are known to be true, all of them are believed.[3]

Nevertheless, the relations of the Southern Pacific railroad with its employees had been uniformly harmonious, and at the time of the strike the latter had no grievance of any sort against the company.

The strike in California centered at Sacramento, an important terminus of the railroad, at which its largest railroad shops were located. Serious disturbances also occurred at Oakland and Los Angeles. In Oakland, on June 27, union crews refused to take out east-bound trains because Pullman cars were attached. All local trains were handled as usual on that day and the succeeding day. On July 29, however, the local traffic, including the ferry service from Berkeley, Oakland, and Alameda to San Francisco, was tied up. The strikers raided the Oakland roundhouse and shops, killed the engines, jammed the switches, obstructed the tracks, and stopped all trains. Chaos reigned. Order was restored ten days later by the intervention of the State militia, which had been called out and sent to various scenes of trouble. Two regiments were sent from San Francisco to Sacramento. The State militia, being unaccustomed to handling critical labor situations, occasioned many needless and irritating clashes. At Sacramento one person was shot. Under military guard a train was run out of Sacramento, but a bridge had been tampered with, the train was thrown off the track, and the engineer and four soldiers were killed. Other attempts to wreck trains operated by strike breakers fortunately entailed no serious consequences. On July 14, intermittent railway service was restored; two days later the strike was over.

The damage to business, agriculture, and industry in California was very great. The strike affected 11,537 railroad and other employees, who lost about $1,000,000 in wages, while the railroad losses aggregated approximately $545,000.[4] Grapes and other fruits rotted on the ranches because farmers were unable to ship their crops. Mail was held up for about two weeks. Thousands of persons were unable to get to their places of work. Nevertheless, in spite of the loss and inconvenience caused by the disturbance, the public's sympathies in California were with the strikers because Californians so hated the railroad. Only one newspaper in San Francisco defended the railroad's position. From the first it was evident that the strike could not succeed, for railroad employees on strike in other parts of the United States rushed into California, where they would not be known, to take the places of their union brethren.

Much bitterness and resentment followed the conclusion of the strike. One hundred and thirty persons were arrested, charged with killing engines, damaging property, and obstructing the mails. Two of the accused were selected and tried in San Francisco. More than a hundred witnesses testified at the trial, but in the end the jury disagreed. The cases were kept in the courts for about a year, and then, through the intervention of the State Labor Commissioner, E. L. Fitzgerald, they were dismissed by the United States District Attorney. One S. F. Worden, however, an American Railway Union organizer of Sacramento, was convicted of the murder of S. A. Clark and condemned to be hanged; but the unions of California rallied to his cause and successfully petitioned the governor to commute his sentence to life imprisonment. All union members were blacklisted by the Southern Pacific railroad, irrespective of what part, if any, they had played in the strike. In June, 1896, however, the railroad announced that it had removed from its blacklist the names of those who had not damaged its property at the time of the strike.[5]

In January, 1895, the Barbers' Protective Union of San Francisco began a campaign for the enactment of a State law requiring barber shops to close at noon on Sunday. The barbers had been forced to work seven days a week and from ten to fourteen hours a day. In February the journeymen met with their employers and organized a Barbers' Association for the purpose of furthering this much needed reform. There were then about 540 barber shops in the city, employing 2,800 journeymen. The bill was passed by the legislature and signed by the governor on March 29, 1895.[6] Steps were taken to see that the law was enforced, but in April, 1896, the barbers were grievously disappointed when the State Supreme Court declared the act unconstitutional.[7] Through their union they then levied boycotts on certain employers, hoping to force them to close their shops at noon on Sunday and at eight o'clock every evening except Saturday. Success finally attended their efforts, and in the fall of 1900 they announced that virtually all shops had agreed that after December 1, 1900, they would close at 8 P.M. on weekdays and at noon on Sundays.

In 1894, M. McGlynn and one Johnson began the publication of *The New Union,* which was soon succeeded by *The Voice of Labor,* with McGlynn[8] as editor. *The Voice of Labor* was the official organ of the San Francisco Labor Council and the San Francisco Building Trades Council, but when the latter withdrew its support in 1900 and made plans to issue its own official paper, *The Voice of Labor* suspended publication.

In May, 1895, the carpenters' unions of San Francisco began an active campaign for members. By August they had organized about five-sixths of their craft and stated that they had a membership of about 2,000. They then felt strong enough to demand the following working rules, effective September 15: (1) a working card to be carried by all union members in good standing; (2) the closed shop; and (3) an eight-hour day, with time and a half for overtime. The demands were granted, the employers offering little opposition, although some of the building contractors objected to the enforcement of the working card regulation.

The painters' and decorators' union had disbanded early in 1895, but, encouraged by the success of the carpenters, reorganized in August and September of that year. On September 4 it followed the example of the carpenters and adopted the working card system. It also urged the formation of a building trades' council. In December it voted not to work on any job that had been struck by the carpenters' union. The painters' and decorators' union also decided to ask for a wage of $3 for painters and $4 for decorators. It had about 700 members, but the employing painters also had a strong, vigorous organization. On March 1, 1896, the day set for putting the new working rules into effect, about twenty-five employers refused to grant the increased wage and the closed shop. On March 18 the Master Painters' Association voted not to recognize the union. A strike resulted, lasting for about two weeks and ending in a partial victory for the union.

The need of a central federation in the building trades had been felt following the dissolution of the earlier organization at the time of the formation of the San Francisco Labor Council. On December 5, 1895, a preliminary meeting to discuss the matter was attended by representatives from the various carpenters' unions, the painters', the granite cutters', and the plasterers'. On February 6, 1896, permanent organization was effected by delegates from Carpenters' Unions Nos. 22, 304, and 483, and from unions of the painters and decorators, plasterers, cornice-makers, and granite cutters, representing approximately 4,000 craftsmen. Henry Meyers, of Carpenters' Union No. 22, and R. T. McIvor, of the painters' and decorators' union, were elected president and vice-president, respectively, with Alexander Murray, financial secretary, J. W. Rose, recording secretary, and John McCartney, treasurer.[9] The Building Trades Council grew rapidly. The lathers, glaziers, plumbers, shinglers, varnishers and polishers, sandstone cutters, marble cutters and finishers, and metal roofers affiliated with it in the next few months. Almost from the first, the council was a militant, successful body, winning victory after victory for its members. Nothing is so contagious as success—and in a short time many unions were organized in the building trades and admitted to the council. In the summer of 1901 it had 36 component unions with about 15,000 members. In 1905 its secretary, O. A. Tveitmoe, informed the State Building Trades Council that there "was nothing more to organize in the building industry"[10] in San Francisco, so completely did the local federation dominate the situation.

Shortly after its formation, the Building Trades Council of San Francisco was faced with the possibility of a serious split over the matter of representation. All the constituent unions, irrespective of size, had the same number of delegates; thus the smaller organizations were able to dominate its affairs. Some of the larger unions, including the organizations of the carpenters, plumbers, cornicemakers, and painters, withdrew from the council and refused to have anything further to do with it until the basis of representation should be changed. In October, 1897, its constitution was modified so as to grant to each union a number of delegates that bore a fixed relation to the size of its membership. The seceding organizations then reaffiliated.

The first task of the newly organized Building Trades Council was that of supporting the demands of the carpenters and painters for the introduction of the working card system. It soon realized, however, that an insistence on having working cards for each craft would result in confusion and make enforcement extremely difficult. Accordingly it announced that on April 1, 1896, it would introduce its own working card to be used by all affiliated unions to the exclusion of their separate working cards. It was necessary to call strikes on a number of jobs in order to enforce the new regulation, but by the use of pickets, walking delegates, and similar means, and through the loyalty of all the constituent organizations, the council was successful in waging this its first contest with local employers. During the next few years the San Francisco Building Trades Council continued its campaign for the adoption of the working card system. By 1899 virtually every building trades job in San Francisco had been unionized, and by 1901 every building trades worker found it necessary to carry the working card of the council. The council announced at that time that it controlled the building industry from the foundation to the roof.

The lathers organized in February, 1896, and at once struck for an increase in wages. The strikers committed many acts of violence. Charles A. Mars, a non-unionist, was so severely man-handled that he died a few weeks later. Six lathers were tried for murder, but the jury announced a verdict of "involuntary manslaughter, not amounting to a felony."[11] The case was appealed and the sentence of a year's imprisonment was confirmed by the higher courts. The convicted unionists, after serving the greater part of their sentences, were pardoned in November, 1897.

The spirit shown by the building trades unions through the new central body aroused the delegates to the Labor Council from their lethargy. The delegates decided that they would try to bring back into the council the unions that had withdrawn, and to carry on a campaign of organization. Accordingly a call was issued by the Labor Council for a convention to be held on February 14, 1896, at which there was to be a "full and free discussion of any and all matters pertaining to the labor movement." The meeting was well attended, but instead of unifying the labor movement, it succeeded only in dividing it more sharply into two bitterly antagonistic factions. The Labor Council leaders were for non-political action, but the leaders of the radical unions, which in the early nineties had been the cause of much dissension in the ranks of the Federated Trades Council, remained loyal to their belief that in political action lay the salvation of the workers. The meeting was virtually controlled by the socialists, who gave to the conference the appearance of a convention of the Socialist Labor Party rather than of trade unionists. The platform which was adopted called for government ownership of all public utilities, the imposition of income and inheritance taxes, and the adoption of the initiative, the referendum, the recall of judges, universal and equal suffrage, proportional representation, and other reform measures. The Labor Council, having steadfastly upheld a non-political program, suggested that it be permitted to function solely as a trade union body, and that a separate organization be formed to work in the political field. Before a referendum on the proposal could be taken, the radical unions of the Labor convention had formed a new federation, the Central Trades and Labor Alliance, the objects and announced program of which were socialistic, for it was openly affiliated with the Socialist Labor Party. It vigorously condemned the principles and policies of the American Federation of Labor and as vigorously voiced its opposition to the San Francisco Labor Council. To the latter organization, the future appeared hopeless. It held several meetings at which it considered whether or not it should disband. Its constituent unions were asked to express their wishes in the matter, and all but two, namely, Bakers' Union No. 24 and the Wood Workers' Union (the old furniture workers' union), voted to remain affiliated with the Labor Council.

The Central Trades and Labor Alliance was short-lived. Composed chiefly of the younger, less experienced unions, its radical proposals did not appeal to the older, more conservative organizations. Renewed life came to the Labor Council because its adherents realized that its very existence was threatened and that they had to put forth determined efforts if they were to increase its strength and influence. From that time to the present, it has had to meet the opposition of only one rival federation, namely, the local Building Trades Council, with which it has been in almost continuous conflict. The demand that Labor enter the political field either directly or indirectly, proved too strong, however, to be resisted by the Labor Council, and since 1896 the council has taken an interest in such matters, but always (officially) through other channels than a Labor party.

The fall elections of 1896 were approaching. A Labor convention, called at the suggestion of the carpenters' and joiners' unions of San Francisco, met on October 11 to draft needed labor legislation and to plan a campaign for its enactment. Every union in San Francisco, as well as the Labor Council and the Building Trades Council, was represented at the meeting. Eighteen different bills were subsequently drafted, approved, and submitted to candidates for state office. Of the candidates successful in the ensuing campaign, almost all had agreed to vote for the passage of the proposed measures, but when the legislative session of 1897 adjourned, not one of the bills sponsored by Organized Labor had been adopted. In subsequent elections the same policy was followed, for the most part without success. In 1910, however, the Progressive Party of California succeeded in overthrowing the "Southern Pacific machine," and elected Hiram W. Johnson governor. He was ably supported by a liberal legislature. In 1911, thirty-nine out of forty-nine labor measures placed before that body were enacted into law, and a similar record was made in 1913 and 1915, with the result that California took a prominent place among states interested in conserving the welfare of the working class. At the time of the World War and in all the years since, Organized Labor in California has had great difficulty in retaining the progressive legislation adopted from 1911 to 1915. Yet, though slight modifications of certain laws have been made, the labor and factory laws of the State have survived unchanged, for the most part, since 1915.

The period 1896–1898 was comparatively quiet. There was still much unemployment in the larger cities, although in many places, especially in San Francisco, business was slowly improving, particularly in the building trades. There were several unimportant strikes,[12] and a few unions were organized or reorganized.[13] A state convention of cigarmakers' unions was held in San Francisco in March, 1897, to discuss matters of interest to the craft. The most important event in the local labor field in the years 1896–1897 was the formation of an Allied Printing Trades Council. From the earliest days of the gold rush, the printers' union had steadfastly supported the cause of Organized Labor in San Francisco. It had also engaged in some serious clashes with employers, and not always successfully. In July, 1888, the pressmen, bookbinders, and printers had discussed the possibility of strengthening their positions by forming a central body, but evidently they were unable to do so, for nothing further is heard about the matter until April 28, 1889, when Typographical Union No. 21 voted to revive the proposition. Nothing resulted from this effort. A third unsuccessful attempt was made on July 27, 1890. During the next few years employment relations in the printing trades were thrown into a confused condition by the introduction of the linotype machine. Many printers lost their jobs and were forced to seek employment in other trades. It was useless to oppose the linotype, but, in order to protect the interests of the printing trades employees, it was deemed advisable to stress the adoption and use of the union label. In order to make this plan effective, it was proposed that all the printing trades unions be brought together into a trades council. On February 23, 1896, the pressmen issued a call for a meeting, which resulted in the organization of the Allied Printing Trades Council, composed of the pressmen, the bookbinders, and the printers. On

July 1, 1896, the council voted to issue a union label and to urge its adoption in the local offices. For many years thereafter much time and money were spent for that purpose, as well as in fighting for the closed shop, higher wages, and better working conditions. At first, counterfeit labels were used by unscrupulous employers, but the council succeeded in a campaign against them. In March, 1897, the Board of Supervisors of San Francisco was induced to pass an ordinance requiring that all city printing bear the union label. Several suits were filed in the State courts to test the constitutionality of the measure, but it was always upheld. The unions were also successful in suits which they filed against employers who used imitation labels.[14]

The newly organized Allied Printing Trades Council was soon involved in a serious contest with the employing printers and bookbinders over a reduction in the hours of labor. In October, 1896, the delegates to the convention of the International Typographical Union had voted to adopt the nine-hour day. The proposal was submitted to the constituent unions and approved by them. In January, 1897, the national convention of the pressmen also went on record as favoring the nine-hour day. In the San Francisco Bay region, after much discussion, only a few employers acceded voluntarily to the demands of the unions. The printers of Berkeley struck on March 10, 1898, for the closed shop and an increase in wages. Meeting with determined resistance, they started a local newspaper, but it did not receive public support. The strike fever spread to San Francisco, and on April 4, 1898, the Allied Printing Trades Council called out the members of the affiliated unions in an effort to make the nine-hour rule effective. More than 400 employees were involved. On June 12 the unions admitted defeat. Many employers in the jobbing plants forced the men to give up their union cards before they would reëmploy them. Later in the year Oakland Typographical Union No. 36 obtained the nine-hour day for hand typesetters, effective on November 1. The eight-hour day had previously been granted to the linotype operators.

In June, 1898, the photo-engravers of San Francisco organized a union, thus increasing the bargaining power of the printing and bookbinding office employees. The defeat of the nine-hour campaign in 1898 did not signify that the campaign was ended: it was vigorously carried on, especially against the book and job printing offices. The printers employed in the newspaper offices of San Francisco obtained the eight-hour day in 1899, but those in the book and jobbing plants continued to work ten hours. As time passed, a number of offices were induced to grant the shorter work-day. In May, 1900, the unions struck and obtained a concession from the book and jobbing plant employers whereby fifteen minutes were to be cut off the working day each month until the nine-hour day was reached. This goal was attained on October 1, 1900. The eight-hour day was not granted in the book and job printing plants, however, until January 1, 1905. The 1906 report of the State Bureau of Labor Statistics disclosed the fact that at that time virtually all printers in California, except those of Los Angeles, had obtained the eight-hour day.[15]

For California, the years at the close of the nineteenth century and the beginning of the twentieth were a period of state-wide prosperity. In 1899 the newspapers were decidedly cheerful about the upturn in business conditions. They said that the year had broken all previous records in volume of trade and amount of profits. Bank clearings were 74 per cent greater than in 1897; business failures were fewer than in twenty-five years past; and railroad mileage constructed was the greatest since 1890. The farmers had prospered, too. Heavy seasonal rains had brought large crops, and the rising price-level had yielded increased returns to the agriculturists.

The city workers, determined to share in the returning prosperity, organized unions in virtually all trades and in various parts of the State. In 1900, the State Labor Commissioner announced that he had received returns from 217 unions, representing about 37,500 members. Ninety of these unions—about 41 per cent—were "in San Francisco; 26, or about 12 per cent, in Los Angeles; 23, or about 10 per cent, in Oakland; 20, or about 9 per cent, in Sacramento; 6 in San Diego, 5 in Vallejo, 5 in San Jose, and the remainder scattered. . . . [Some] 81 distinct avocations or callings [were] represented." Of the 217 local unions, 127 were affiliated with their national or international organizations, and 103 with local central bodies. The commissioner also reported the existence of nine central labor bodies.[16]

In 1901, unionization progressed at an even more rapid pace. It is doubtful whether any other state in the Union has ever felt the ardor for organization that characterized the workers of California during the period 1899–1901. In 1902 the State Labor Commissioner reported that there were 495 labor organizations in California, 125 of which were in San Francisco, 68 in Los Angeles, 45 in Sacramento, 36 in Oakland, and the rest in other centers of population. Many localities which had never known any labor movement, reported that virtually all trades were organized. In the years 1900–1902 the number of unions had increased about 75 per cent and the total membership[17] had increased about 125 per cent. The separate vocations or trades that were organized had increased in number from 81 to 149. Labor councils existed in San Francisco, Los Angeles, Oakland, Sacramento, Bakersfield, San Jose, Stockton, Santa Rosa, San Diego, Fresno, San Bernardino, Eureka, and Vallejo. San Francisco, Oakland, Los Angeles, Sacramento, San Jose, Stockton, and Fresno each had a building trades council; San Francisco, Oakland, Los Angeles, and Sacramento each had an allied printing trades council, and San Francisco and Los Angeles each had a district council of carpenters. San Francisco, which was the most thoroughly unionized city in the State, also had an iron trades council, a retail trades council, a sheet metal workers' council, and a city front federation composed of unions on the water front.[18]

The California labor movement in its earlier years had concerned itself almost solely with the organization of the skilled workers. In the years 1899–1901, however, unions were formed among groups of workers that had been neglected, such as the butchers, stablemen, teamsters, hackmen,[19] hodcarriers, cement workers,[20] pipe and boiler coverers, felt and composition roofers, carpet workers, laundry workers, house movers, and window-shade workers. National and international unions sent professional organizers into the local field. Most of the newly organized unions in San Francisco affiliated with the Labor Council, although a few joined the Building Trades Council. In July, 1900, the Labor Council had a membership of 34 unions; in July, 1901, 90; and in October, 1901, 98. San Francisco became to all intents and purposes a closed-shop city, and so remained for many years. The more conservative Building Trades Council, however, was outspoken in its condemnation of the policy of the Labor Council in encouraging the formation of unions among the unskilled. Its official publication, *Organized Labor*, declared:

Probably the [Labor] Council will not be able to protect all the children it takes in. Organize only those who will stay organized. Educate first and strike afterward. San Francisco is experiencing a union Pentecost breeze. It passes; the air is charged with union electricity, but beware of the storm.[21]

A few months later the editor announced that his warning had fallen on deaf ears. Instead of exercising caution,

the professional organizer doubled his efforts and the Labor Council increased its organizing committee. Unions were formed—that is, very few of them were trade unions, but there were many, many unions of divers occupations and callings. Charters were signed for and hung in meeting houses until they covered the four walls. . . . The Labor Council gathered under its wings a most varied collection of eggs and hatched some curious ducklings and labeled them trade unions.[22]

These "curious ducklings" were soon a cause of serious trouble to the Labor Council, which was compelled to face a situation not unlike that which had brought about the disruption of the Federated Trades Council. The newly organized unions were unacquainted with the principles and practices of trade unionism. Their members had been led to believe that salvation was to be obtained through organized effort, and they at once set out to get it. As soon as a union was formed, its delegates went to the Labor Council and announced that they desired the council to boycott some firm against which they had declared a strike. The Federated Trades Council had had a rule to the effect that none of its constituent unions should strike without its approval, and then only after the union had been affiliated with it for at least six months. An effort was made to have the delegates to the Labor Council adopt a similar regulation, but those who represented the recently organized unions of the unskilled prevented its passage. "New Unionism," namely, the organization of the unskilled, was rampant in San Francisco. Demands were made for shorter hours, higher wages, and the closed shop, and almost all the employers granted the demands without a struggle. There were some noteworthy contests, shortly to be referred to, but the rising tide of business prosperity and the rising price-level provided a setting which was extremely favorable to the organized workers. More than twenty-five unions successfully made demands upon their employers in the years 1899–1901. The retail dry goods clerks and the shoe clerks obtained the six o'clock closing of stores; the laundry workers, a shorter working day,[23] improved working conditions, and an increase in wages; the hackmen, shorter hours; and the stablemen and upholsterers, increased wages and the shorter workday. The beer bottlers, beer wagon drivers, sand teamsters, electrical workers, fixture hangers, carpenters, millmen, marble cutters, painters, art glass blowers, structural ironworkers, elevator constructors, sailors, boot and shoe workers, milkers, milk wagon drivers, foundrymen, garment workers, cloak-makers, picture frame workers, blacksmiths, barbers, butchers, bakers, and carriage and wagon workers, were all able to obtain concessions of shorter hours or higher wages or both from their employers.

In March, 1900, the Oakland painters and paperhangers obtained an increase in wages, and in June of that year the Oakland building trades unions announced jointly that the eight-hour day would prevail on and after August 13. On October 21, 1900, the Alameda County Federated Trades Council was organized, with headquarters in Oakland. Similar developments were to be noted in other parts of the State.

Although, as stated above, by far the greater number of the gains mentioned were obtained without a struggle, there were several establishments against which strikes and boycotts had to be levied. In San Francisco, the Techau Tavern was boycotted in June, 1899, because of the employment of non-union musicians; the Pedro X L Dairy and the firms of Owens & Varney and L. A. Morse & Son were also boycotted; and in the summer of 1900, boycotts were levied against the shoe store of G. M. Kutz, the Popular Restaurant, Whelan Brothers, and the cloak manufacturing concerns of the city. One hundred marble cutters of San Francisco struck in March, 1899, against a reduction in wages. The strike was supported by the local Building Trades Council. In March, 1899, the shipwrights struck against Boole & Son's shipyard because of the employment of an objectionable foreman. Non-union

men were called in to take their places. The painters and caulkers
in the shipyard then quit their jobs, and the Labor Council threatened to declare a general boycott against the firm. The latter then
discharged the foreman and the strikers returned to work. On
April 4, 1899, the Sailors' Union of the Pacific demanded an increase in wages, and obtained it after a guerrilla warfare of some
months. The boilermakers employed on government transports
demanded the eight-hour day with ten hours' pay, asserting that
legally all work on government contracts should be on the eight-
hour day basis. Conferences were held in September, 1899, by representatives of the workers, the employers, and the government,
but no settlement was arrived at. A strike was therefore declared,
with what outcome I have been unable to learn. Two small strikes
occurred at the Union Iron Works in 1899: in August, fifteen patternmakers struck because their demand for a 25 per cent increase
in their daily wage was refused; in September, seventy brass and
iron foundry workers also struck for increased wages.

The cloak-makers' union of San Francisco had been organized in
May, 1899. Three of the largest cloak manufacturing firms of the
city combined to crush the organization. From January 13 to January 17, 1900, they locked out all union employees, although no
demand had been made for shorter hours or higher wages. Efforts
were made by the Labor Council and by the retail cloak dealers to
settle the difficulty, but in vain, whereupon a boycott was declared.
On May 29 the employers' combination was broken when Meyer
Brothers signed an agreement with the union. The boycott against
the other firms was continued until late in December, 1900, when
they too surrendered to the union. This victory enabled the union
to obtain control over approximately 90 per cent of the workers in
the trade.

It will be recalled that the shoemakers' union of San Francisco
had been disrupted in the early nineties by the employers' association which had been organized in that trade. In the early part
of 1900, the employees reorganized as the Lasters' and Shoemakers'
Union. On April 2, 1900, a strike was declared against G. M. Kutz
& Company, ostensibly as a protest over a reduction in wages, but
actually because the company was gradually weeding out all union
members. A most effective boycott was levied by the Labor Council,

and in the latter part of July the company acknowledged defeat.

A union was organized among the electrical linemen of San Francisco in October, 1900. Similar unions, branches of the International Brotherhood of Electrical Workers, existed or were formed in other parts of California. In December, 1900, a statewide strike was declared for higher wages, but in only a few localities did it end satisfactorily for the union.

By far the most important contest of 1900 was the one waged by the San Francisco Building Trades Council in support of the local mill workers. In July, 1900, the council had notified the building trades employers that on and after October 1, 1900, its members were to work but eight hours a day for the standard wage of $3. All the twenty-seven unions concerned, except those of the millmen, the woodworkers, and the varnishers and polishers, gained the new conditions of employment, and somewhat later the varnishers and polishers and the woodworkers gained them, also. It was therefore decided to make a fight for the millmen. In order to present a united front to the employers, the mill workers of San Jose, Santa Clara, and other cities of the San Francisco Bay region were unionized, and they too demanded an eight-hour day. On August 13, 1900, the Master Builders' Association proposed a lockout. The Millmen's Association of San Francisco, representing nineteen mills, locked out its employees, as did the planing mills at Oakland, Berkeley, Hayward, San Jose, and Santa Clara, 8,000 men being affected.

Arbitration was suggested by the unions but was refused, the planing mill employers insisting that under the proposed conditions they could not compete with outside mills working nine and ten hours a day. The Building Trades Council then said that it would refuse to allow its members to work on outside material if the demands were granted, but that offer too was rejected by the employers' association. The council ordered all its affiliated unions to "refuse to handle, place or work on any building where said unfair mill work constitutes a part of the structure." The employers' association then announced that its members would not figure on any new work or sell material to any contractor employing union labor. The Building Trades Council thereupon established a union planing mill, Progressive Mill No. 1, the second largest in the city, stock in this enterprise being held by the affiliated unions. Union contractors were thus able to obtain union material. More than $25,000 was raised by the unions to support the millmen in their struggle. Late in February, 1901, at the request of the Mill Owners' Association, the controversy was submitted to arbitration. The award provided that an eight and one-half hour day should prevail for three months, after which the eight-hour day was to become effective.[24] The employers were not to be required for six months to employ union men, but thereafter all skilled workers with the exception of foremen were to be members of the millmen's union. In return for these concessions, the building trades unions agreed not to work on any material produced in mills not having the eight-hour day. All the firms but one signed the award, and this firm finally signed it in April, 1901.

The effective manner in which the Building Trades Council had advanced the economic interests of its affiliated unions, especially the interests of the millmen, gave it great influence in the building trades not only in San Francisco but elsewhere in California. It completely dominated the local situation and continued to do so until 1922, when its hold was broken, at least temporarily, by the vigorous opposition of the Industrial Association, the employer-members of which were advocates of the open shop. In its period of mastery, the council aided in establishing building trades unions in various parts of northern California. Its success inspired the organization of many local building trades councils. As a result of the initiative of its leaders, a State Building Trades Council was formed at a meeting held in San Francisco on December 16, 1901, by delegates from the building trades councils of San Francisco, Alameda, Santa Clara, and San Joaquin counties (it was the policy then, as now, to have the councils exercise jurisdiction over an entire county). The first president of the new federation was P. H. McCarthy, who served continuously until 1922. Its influence spread rapidly, and in 1911 it had a membership of nineteen local councils.

In December, 1900, a committee of the San Francisco Labor Council issued a call for a meeting of the unions of California to consider the formation of a state federation. The meeting was held in San Francisco, January 7–9, 1901. One hundred and sixty-three delegates were present, representing 61 unions, 5 central bodies, and approximately 10,000 members. The outcome of the convention was the organization of the State Federation of Labor, with

P. H. McCARTHY

the following officers: C. D. Rogers (Oakland), president; J. C. Netz (Los Angeles), first vice-president; Guy Lathrop (San Francisco), secretary; and B. W. Smith (San Francisco), treasurer. The various building trades unions and building trades councils of the State refused, however, to affiliate with the State Federation, asserting through their leaders that they had special interests to conserve and that they were not concerned with the activities, demands, or policies of unions in other trades. Their attitude was additional evidence of the bitter struggle which had been going on for some years between the Labor Council and the Building Trades Council of San Francisco for domination over the labor movement in that city. The Labor Council insisted that it was the central body with which all local unions should affiliate; the Building Trades Council refused to permit any of its constituent unions to affiliate with the Labor Council. The two antagonistic bodies even held separate Labor Day celebrations. The issue was sharply drawn.[25]

From 1896 to 1901 a large number of the building trades unions had withdrawn from the Labor Council and had affiliated with the Building Trades Council. Carpenters' Unions Nos. 304, 483, 616, and 1032, however, refused to obey the orders of the latter council and for four years, in spite of bribery and the use of violence, carried on their struggle for a united labor movement in San Francisco. In 1904 and 1905 they finally joined the Building Trades Council, but retained their membership in the Labor Council. Efforts to arbitrate the difficulty between the two councils were made by various parties, but without success. The national officers of the United Brotherhood of Carpenters and Joiners, and the executives of the local Builders' Protective Association as well as those of the San Francisco Planing Mill Owners' Association also intervened, but were unable to make peace between the warring factions. When the State Building Trades Council and the State Federation of Labor were formed, the contest involved a wider area and many parts of the State. On July 2, 1902, the executive committee of the American Federation of Labor met in San Francisco, made an extended investigation, and suggested a plan of settlement; but the plan was rejected. Apparently there could be no harmony between the two antagonistic bodies—the one dominated by P. H. McCarthy, whose policy was avowedly that of "rule or ruin," the other led by a group of men interested in the worthy object of attaining a united labor movement in San Francisco. Finally, at the annual convention of the State Building Trades Council, in January, 1910, the breach was healed by the announcement of its president, Mc-Carthy, that in the future the building trades unions would be permitted to join the Labor Council in their respective communities, and to affiliate with the State Federation of Labor. McCarthy was, at the time, a candidate for the mayoralty of San Francisco and evidently desired the backing of a unified labor vote. It was also said that he aspired to be governor and hoped to have the state-wide support of Organized Labor. An equally important factor in the restoration of harmonious relations between the two groups was the great pressure brought to bear upon him by the officers of the American Federation of Labor. Since that time the labor movement of San Francisco, and of the State generally, has not had to contend with any similar internal dissension among its constituent unions.

In the closing years of the nineteenth century, the San Francisco Building Trades Council began to feel the need of an official publication, through which the members of its affiliated unions might be kept more closely in touch with one another and with the labor movement in general. Accordingly, on February 3, 1900, *Organized Labor* made its bow to the public. Olaf A. Tveitmoe was its first editor.[26] Two years later (February 28, 1902) the San Francisco Labor Council, which had never issued an official journal, began the publication of a weekly, the *Labor Clarion,* with Joseph J. O'Neill as editor. At his death in August, 1908, he was succeeded by Will J. French, who resigned in September, 1911, and was followed by James W. Mullen.[27]

The rapid growth and heightened activity of the organized labor movement in San Francisco made increasingly evident the need of a central meeting-place, a labor temple. The initiative toward its acquisition was taken by the Building Trades Council on November 11, 1899. Committees were subsequently appointed by both this organization and the Labor Council, for at that time the two central bodies were on fairly harmonious terms. Plans were drawn up for a joint meeting-place; but the old contention for domination broke out anew, and both councils decided to proceed with plans for separate headquarters. The Labor Council in 1906 erected a frame structure on leased ground, but in 1912 formally opened an imposing five-story brick structure, costing approximately \$250,000. The Building Trades Council opened its building on April 20, 1908.

During this period of great organizing activity among the workers of California (1899–1901), there also developed a widespread

OLAF A. TVEITMOE

interest in the adoption of the union label as a means of ensuring a demand for union-made products. In October, 1899, Union Label League No. 1 was established in San Francisco by representatives of the printers, pressmen, stereotypers, photo-engravers, and web pressmen. The brewery workers' union obtained the adoption of its red label by the local breweries; the milkers' union introduced a "union milk" sign among the dairies; and the cigarmakers continued the campaign for their blue label. In a few years there was scarcely a product originating in San Francisco which did not bear a union label of some sort, so thoroughly were the workers of that city organized into protective associations.

The progress of Organized Labor in San Francisco and the seeming inability of the employers to resist separately the demands of the unions, inevitably brought about the formation of another Employers' Association in April, 1901. Its officers and membership were kept secret in the hope that it might thereby be more effective. A huge war chest was collected and plans were drawn up for a life and death struggle with the unions over the issue of "closed shop" or "open shop" in San Francisco. Similar campaigns were being waged in virtually every industrial center in the United States under the leadership of the National Manufacturers' Association and other national employers' organizations.

The influence and strength of the Employers' Association of San Francisco was soon felt by the labor organizations. On April 1, 1901, the metal polishers struck for the eight-hour day with ten hours' pay. Many of the smaller employers would gladly have granted the demands, but they were notified by the association that their supplies would be cut off if they did so. The strike was a failure and the men returned to work in July. On May 1, the cooks' and waiters' union, one of the newer organizations and scarcely a year old, struck for an increase in wages, shorter hours, one day's rest in seven, the closed shop, and the display of the union card in all restaurants. The strike affected approximately 2,000 members of the craft. About 300 of the smaller eating places acceded to the demands of the union. The proprietors of the larger restaurants, however, organized a Restaurant Keepers' Association and, assisted by the Employers' Association, waged a vigorous battle against the union. Again, supplies were cut off from those places that accepted union conditions. This in turn brought on a fruitless sympathetic strike by some of the bakery employees.[28] The retail butchers were forced to sell supplies to union restaurants by the threat of a strike by their employees, but the wholesale butchers announced that they would refuse to sell to those retail butchers who displayed the union card in their shops. This move caused about 1,500 journeymen butchers to quit their jobs. The butchers' union, having just been organized and possessing no funds, was forced to admit defeat at the end of the fourth day. On May 1 the members of the Carriage Makers' Association agreed to grant the demands of the carriage and wagon makers' union for the closed shop, shorter hours, and increased wages, but before the agreement could be signed the Employers' Association announced that supplies would be withheld from all shops that recognized the union, while those that did not do so would receive financial assistance to wage a fight against the union. On May 8, 500 men struck. A few of the smaller concerns granted the union's demands, but their supplies were at once cut off. The teamsters' union now announced that its members would not haul for firms that refused to sell supplies to union shops. On May 22 the carriage and wagon makers' strike was declared off because the employers acceded to the terms laid down by union and the latter voluntarily waived its demands for a signed agreement.

At this time of turmoil, the local machinists' union was preparing to ask for the nine-hour day in the iron trades.[29] This was part of the nation-wide program of the American Federation of Labor, which had voted to concentrate on one trade at a time in its fight for the shorter day, so as to have a better chance of attaining its object. A strike fund had been collected, and the employers had been given a six months' notice. The waiting period was extended for another twenty days, and when the employers refused to grant the demands, a strike was declared on May 20, 1901, involving more than 4,000 men in all branches of the local iron trades. Again the Employers' Association cut off the supplies of the smaller firms that yielded, and the strike appeared lost. The struggle was continued, however, for the next ten months, at a cost of $69,000 to the machinists. The results were partly satisfactory for the union and for the other iron trades organizations—many of the smaller firms granted the shorter day; and in another year the iron trades workers had gained the nine-hour day from all. In 1907 a campaign was begun for the eight-hour day. After a six weeks' strike an agreement was signed by the employers and the unions which introduced a sliding arrangement whereby the hours of work were to be gradually reduced until the eight-hour day should be reached on June 1, 1910.

But to return to the events of 1901. On July 26 the breweries of San Francisco notified the beer bottlers' union that thenceforth they would have no relations with it; a lockout was declared by all the breweries but one. Shorter hours were promised to the box-makers, provided they gave up their union membership. When they refused, they too were locked out. The Employers' Association was daily gaining greater control over the local situation; an increasing number of the newer and weaker unions were being forced out of existence; and the San Francisco labor movement faced the possibility of extinction at the hand of "the powerful and mysterious Employers' Association."[30] Conditions became increasingly serious. The *Coast Seamen's Journal* on July 24, 1901, remarked: "It is a dull morning now-a-days that doesn't bring news of a new labor trouble." The more seasoned and experienced labor leaders feared a catastrophe. They realized that the policy of the new unions, typified by the slogan, "Organize, demand, strike," was bringing about a state of affairs which threatened the very existence of the local labor movement. They acknowledged that "at least 75 per cent of the strikes of 1900 and 1901 could have been avoided by sensible and judicious action on the part of the unions engaged in the trouble."[31] Yet they seemed unable to direct the activities and policies of their followers in such a way as to avoid the impending disaster. Some even declared that it was advisable to bring on a city-wide struggle before the Employers' Association should succeed in completely wrecking the labor movement by its method of attacking and destroying one organization at a time—the same tactics that had been followed so successfully by Fuhrman and the brewery workers' union in their contests with the brewery owners. In May the Labor Council asked for a conference with the Employers' Association, but the latter replied that there was nothing it desired to confer about. Under the circumstances a crisis was inevitable. When finally the fight began— and the inciting event was not long in appearing—Labor and Capital rushed at each other's throats like angry dogs. Regardless of the consequences to themselves or to the economic, political, and social interests of the community, each was intent only on destroying the other.

In the latter part of July the Epworth League held its national convention in San Francisco. The contract for handling the baggage of the delegates was given to a non-union firm, the Morton Special Delivery Company. The task proved too large for it to handle satisfactorily, and another drayage firm was called in, the Morton Draying Company, owned by a brother of the manager of the Morton Special Delivery Company. The Morton Draying Company was a member of the Draymen's Association, which had an agreement with the teamsters' union[32] granting the closed shop, but also requiring that the union men work only for the firms that were members of the association. The union teamsters of the Morton Draying Company refused to handle the Epworth League baggage, asserting that to do so would be a breach of the contract existing between their union and the Draymen's Association. This decision led to a lockout of the union teamsters by the Morton Draying Company, which then resorted to non-union help. Other members of the Draymen's Association, encouraged and supported, no doubt, by the Employers' Association, locked out their teamsters. Approximately 6,400 employees were affected.

The crisis had arisen over the old issue of the workers' right to organize and bargain collectively with their employers. The local labor leaders faced the problem of calling a general strike or calling out only those trades which were closely allied with the work of the teamsters. The latter policy was finally agreed upon, and on July 30 the unions that were affiliated with the City Front Federation were thrown into the fray as shock troops.

The City Front Federation had been organized on February 2, 1901, among the water-front unions of San Francisco.[33] Many earlier attempts had been made to weld these unions into a federation, but without lasting success. It was undoubtedly the fear of the growing strength of the employing class that had induced these unions again to attempt federation in 1901. The City Front Federation was the most powerful group of workers that could have been called on for assistance, for its affiliated unions had a membership of from 13,000 to 16,000 workers and their treasury funds aggregated about $250,000. The dock laborers at Oakland, Redwood City, and Benicia and the warehousemen at Crockett and Port Costa also quit their jobs.

Shipping was completely tied up, boats being unable to leave the harbor or to unload their cargoes. Business in the San Francisco Bay region, and indeed in many other parts of California, was at a standstill. Goods and produce could not be moved. Agricultural districts suffered from lack of necessary supplies and of means to get their products to the Bay region. Factories closed because drayage facilities were not available. It was estimated that 5,000 workers not on strike were forced to remain idle because of the disturbed conditions,[34] and that the total daily loss to the State amounted to approximately $1,000,000.[35]

Such a state of affairs could not long continue. It soon became evident that the teamsters and water-front unions were waging a losing battle. Farm hands flocked to San Francisco eager to take the places of the strikers. Many Negroes were brought in and put to work. Employment was given also to university students and to former army teamsters lately returned from the Philippines. The good nature of the strikers vanished, and acts of violence were committed; 5 deaths and 336 assaults were recorded, and 250 of the assaults required surgical attention. Arrests were so numerous that the courts were unable to handle the cases brought before them. Many complaints were dismissed. Some of the trials were held without notice, and witnesses and arresting officers were not notified to be present. Of 110 men arrested only 15 were convicted, and in almost all the convictions only short sentences or small fines were imposed. The judges of San Francisco were quite obviously eager to keep the good will of the labor vote. The police force, however, acting under orders from Mayor Phelan, strove valiantly to protect the interests of the employing class. A large number of special officers were sworn in, and many of these, because of their inexperience, were sources of trouble. Two policemen were put on each dray to guide and protect the non-union drivers. On the water front the police were especially energetic, and, it was asserted, unnecessarily rough, in clearing the docks and in making arrests. They aroused much resentment among both the strikers and their supporters. The presence of State militia was requested, but the request was refused by the governor.

Repeated attempts at arbitration and conciliation were made by city authorities and by public-spirited citizens, but to no avail. The Employers' Association always answered that it "had nothing to arbitrate." It asserted that it was waging a battle for the

WILL J. FRENCH

employer's right to run his business without interference from Organized Labor. It could not arbitrate the demand for the closed shop or for the right to strike and use the boycott. The uncompromising attitude of the association turned the public against it, but, as August and September passed, it was apparent that its tactics were slowly wearing down the resistance of the strikers: union treasuries were depleted; strike breakers were enabling business to be carried on at perhaps half its usual volume. The strike was first called off in Oakland. The port facilities at Crockett and Port Costa were opened up with non-union men, and farm products began to flow through the customary channels. On October 2, Governor Gage arrived in San Francisco and called a conference of the representatives of the Draymen's Association, the teamsters' union, and the City Front Federation. Within an hour an agreement was reached, the terms of which have never been made public. The strikers, however, had lost the objective for which they had fought, for on the next day they returned to work beside the non-union men.

The final chapter in that memorable and violent struggle was yet to be written. As early as August, some of the smaller unions of San Francisco had started an agitation for the organization of a Union Labor Party, saying that, if it once got into office, it could then control the police department and more easily enforce Labor's demands. At first the older unions in the Labor Council vigorously discouraged the proposal, but as the teamsters' and waterfront strike continued, they either openly or tacitly supported it. The building trades unions, under the domination of P. H. McCarthy, who was then holding a municipal appointment under a Democratic administration, declared that such a party would be a menace to the welfare of Organized Labor, and that unions should never advocate or support political action along class lines. The Union Labor Party was formed, however; candidates for local offices were nominated; and an energetic campaign was got under way. No newspaper or labor journal except the *Coast Seamen's Journal* gave the movement any support. In its issue of October 30, 1901, the *Coast Seamen's Journal* clearly stated the position of those who felt that resort to political action was necessary. It asked:

Who can forget the policy pursued by the police department under the Commissioners and Chief Sullivan, all appointees directly or indirectly of Mayor Phelan? Who can forget the shooting and clubbing of strikers, the wholesale arrests of hundreds of inoffensive men, the surrender of the entire police force to the Employers' Association, the employment of special policemen, and the call of Police Commissioner Newhall for the National Guard?

Those were matters that union men and their sympathizers could not and would not forget. Nor could they forget the methods resorted to by the Employers' Association in carrying out its avowed intention of destroying trade unionism, root and branch.

When the November election returns were tabulated, consternation reigned among the so-called "better classes" of San Francisco. Eugene E. Schmitz, a union musician and candidate of the Union Labor Party, had won the mayoralty by a vote of 21,806 to 17,699 for Wells, Democrat, and 12,684 for Tobin, Republican. Had either of the other parties put up a more suitable candidate (one was decidedly unpopular and the other had to bear up under the reputation earned by a previous administration which had pretty much run counter to the wishes of the public), the results might have been different and San Francisco might have been saved the scandals of graft and corruption which followed in the wake of the Schmitz administrations. The Union Labor Party also elected three out of eighteen supervisors. In 1903 Schmitz was again elected and in 1905 he and the entire Union Labor Party were swept into office. In his second term, Mayor Schmitz and his associates were openly accused of graft, but it was not until after the disastrous fire and earthquake of 1906 that a most startling state of affairs was uncovered. Graft, extortion, corruption, bribery—in short, all the abuses of a totally unprincipled city administration—were exposed. Indictments were brought against the mayor, sixteen of the eighteen supervisors, the political boss of the Union Labor Party (Abraham Ruef), and against many prominent business men who were accused of bribing city officials. The prosecution dragged on for six years and the final result was that Ruef alone was sent to prison. The public soon tired of the attempt to clean up the political life of the city, and when public support is lacking in such situations, little can be accomplished.

Many of the labor leaders who had supported the Union Labor Party in the elections of 1901 and 1903 were soon "forced, first into silence and finally into open repudiation of the methods of the Union Labor Party administration."[36] A number of them subsequently joined whole-heartedly in the efforts of the Graft Prosecution to "clean up" the city. Another interesting incident in the short history of the party was the complete reversal in the attitude of P. H. McCarthy and the building trades unions toward it. Starting from a position of uncompromising hostility in 1901, 1903, and 1905, McCarthy and his cohorts actually became *the* party in 1909, because McCarthy was then its candidate for the mayoralty. Although opposed by the leaders of the Labor Council, he was elected by 29,455 votes to 19,594 for Leland, Democrat, and 13,766 for Crocker, Republican. The Labor Council leaders, who had been called "scabs" by the building trades group in 1901 and 1903 because they had supported the Union Labor Party, were again called "scabs" in 1909 because they then openly opposed it and its candidates. McCarthy again ran for the mayoralty in 1911 and in 1915, but was defeated in both campaigns. Interest in the Union Labor Party waned, and it passed from the field. Since then the unions of San Francisco have been content to work politically through the regular party organizations, disregarding party lines but giving their support to favored candidates.

The Employers' Association disbanded shortly after the conclusion of the teamsters' and water-front strike of 1901. Its functions were later taken over in part by a rather ineffective local branch of the national open-shop organization known as the Citizens' Alliance.[37] The water-front unions, no longer having to present a united front to a common, powerful enemy, fell to quarreling among themselves. The old jealousies, submerged during the period of stress and strain, again came to the surface and made their disrupting influence felt. The first clash occurred in 1902 between the sailors and the longshoremen, and continued for several years. On June 4, 1905, the riggers and stevedores were expelled from the City Front Federation because of a jurisdictional dispute. In June, 1906, the shipowners locked out the sailors, firemen, and cooks and waiters of steam schooners, who had asked for an increase in wages. In order to prevent a general lockout of all the unions which were members of the City Front Federation, the three unions affected voluntarily withdrew from that body, thus further handicapping its usefulness and shortening its life.[38] The lockout of 1906 lasted for five months and resulted in a victory for the unions. It was marked by frequent acts of violence. One sailor was killed and three were seriously wounded. The strike cost the sailors' union approximately $25,000. Comparative peace reigned along the San Francisco water front until 1921 when, owing to depressed business conditions, the employers sought to lower wages. On May 1, 1921, a strike was declared which was broken by the Ship Owners' Association after much violence and some acts of sabotage by the unions. Besides having to accept a reduction in wages the men had to agree to work under open-shop conditions, while the employers again introduced the "grade book" system and hired their men through the employment office of the Ship Owners' Association only.

The formerly powerful Sailors' Union was also forced to contend against internal dissension which had been developing for some time. A group of radical members associated with the Industrial Workers of the World attempted to gain control of the organization and oust the conservative leaders who had been in power for many years. At the time of the strike in 1921 the radicals succeeded in electing one of their members to the editorship of the *Coast Seamen's Journal*. They also forced the adoption of radical policies. In the end, however, Furuseth and his conservative colleagues crushed the revolt and regained control, but not before the union had been badly rent by dissension from within and weakened by attacks on the part of the open-shop employers from without. Since that time the union has been steadily but slowly rebuilding its membership, steadfastly keeping before it Furuseth's motto, "Tomorrow is also a day."

The teamsters' union fared much better than its associates, the water-front unions. Following the defeat of 1901 it greatly increased its membership and on October 1, 1902, signed an agreement with the Draymen's Association. By this agreement the former wage scale was retained, but Sunday work was abolished. Since then the relations between the two groups have been for the most part harmonious. With the signing of each new agreement, the union obtained additional concessions until its members finally received privileges and working conditions formerly accorded to the most skilled craftsmen only. The union was also strongly influential in the formation of associations among other branches of the teaming trades, such as the milk wagon drivers, chauffeurs, material teamsters, ice wagon drivers, laundry wagon drivers, retail delivery wagon drivers, soda and mineral water wagon drivers, and stable employees. These organizations were later brought together into a central federation known as the Team Drivers' Local

Joint Executive Council, to which were submitted practically all matters of importance to the teaming trades.

The defeat of the teamsters' and water-front strike of 1901 did not react unfavorably upon the interests of other groups of workers in San Francisco. The organization of unions proceeded at a rapid pace, and in a short time San Francisco became the only closed-shop city in the United States. It was virtually impossible for a non-union worker to obtain employment. Naturally the Union Labor Party's administration of the city's affairs greatly strengthened the hold of Organized Labor on the industrial and business interests of the city. The labor movement received a temporary setback because of the chaotic conditions which existed immediately after the earthquake and fire of 1906, but it soon got under way again and continued its forward march.

Demands for higher wages, shorter hours, a half-holiday on Saturday, and the closed shop were made in endless succession. Scores of strikes were declared, some of which, notably the street-car strike of 1907,[39] were characterized by violence and the importation of strike breakers. The labor situation became unbearable for the local employers and attempts were made to bring them together into an open-shop association. On March 26, 1914, the Merchants' and Manufacturers' Association of San Francisco was formed, similar to organizations then active in Los Angeles[40] and Stockton,[41] which had been successful in combating Organized Labor. The association was avowedly "open shop in its attitude, its announced object being to free San Francisco from the domination of Organized Labor and the labor boss." The San Francisco unions, however, were too strongly entrenched for the association to change the local situation materially. In 1916 the longshoremen broke the terms of an agreement with their employers and struck for a 35 per cent increase in wages. There was much violence along the water front, and this so thoroughly aroused the employing class of San Francisco that the Chamber of Commerce, which had previously taken no part in matters affecting local labor disputes, announced that the mercantile and industrial interests of the community must be freed from union domination. Through its efforts a Law and Order Committee was organized in 1916 with the intention of making San Francisco an open-shop city. For some years thereafter the Committee carried on a vigorous and active campaign, but war conditions in industry, the scarcity of labor, and the necessity of industrial peace stressed by Federal authorities,

JAMES W. MULLEN

all conspired to minimize the results of its attack on trade unionism. Shortly after the United States entered the World War, the Law and Order Committee became the Industrial Relations Committee of the Chamber of Commerce. During and immediately following the war, there were numerous strikes by shipyard workers,

machinists, electricians, telephone employees, riggers and stevedores, ferry boat employees, and other crafts. Prices were rising
rapidly, and the workers felt compelled to demand higher wages
if they were not to accept a lowered plane of living. More than
1,000 strike breakers were brought into the city in 1919.

In February, 1920, the plasterers, hodcarriers, painters, and
metal roofers of San Francisco struck for an increase in wages,
and a general walkout of all the building crafts seemed imminent.
The dispute, however, was submitted to arbitration, with the understanding that the claims of thirteen other building trades
unions would also be considered by the arbitration board. While
the arbitrators were sitting, prices began to fall at an astonishing
rate, so that when the award was finally made on March 31, 1921,
the arbitration board announced a 7½ per cent reduction in wages
to become effective at once. The unions refused to accept the award,
asserting that the board had no right to announce a decreased wage
scale when the only issue placed before it by both the unions and
their employers was whether or not wages should be increased.
The question of a reduction in wages had not entered into the controversy which had been submitted to the board. On May 9, 1921,
a general lockout was declared by the Builders' Exchange (the
employers' association in the building trades). The San Francisco
Chamber of Commerce, which had been instrumental in bringing
about the arbitration, obtained the support of bankers, material
men, and other local employers in making the lockout effective.
Union employers could not obtain an adequate supply of materials.
The Building Trades Council again attempted to provide the
needed supplies, as it had done at the time of the millmen's strike
of 1900, but it was soon forced to retire because it was unable to
obtain them. The council tried to break the contractor-material
dealer combination by court action, and failed. On June 10 the
Building Trades Council voted to accept the award, but the employers notified their employees that they could only return to
work under open-shop conditions. This resulted in a general strike
of the building trades unions on August 3, which tied up all building activities in San Francisco. The strike was soon lost, however,
and on August 28 most of the men returned to work under open-
shop conditions. Not only did the failure of the strike result in

the complete overthrow of the closed-shop policy which for more than twenty years had been dominant in the San Francisco building trades, but it also further wrecked the local movement by bringing about the suspension of the charters of those unions which had participated in the strike contrary to the orders of their national and international officers. Hostility to the leadership of P. H. McCarthy became so strong and outspoken among the building trades unions that he was forced to resign the presidency of the local Building Trades Council on January 12, 1922. He was succeeded by Lawrence J. Flaherty, of the cement finishers' union. In a short time, McCarthy also resigned the presidency of the State Building Trades Council, and was succeeded by Frank C. MacDonald, of San Francisco.

On November 8, 1921, the Industrial Association of San Francisco was organized to continue the campaign for the open shop which had been started so favorably by the Chamber of Commerce. It was signally successful. It raised a war chest of $1,250,000; obtained pledges of support from almost every major division of business and industry; took under consideration, if it did not actually adopt, a policy of urging bankers not to lend funds on building projects unless the projects were operated on the open-shop basis; and coöperated with the Builders' Exchange in running an employment office for the registration of non-union men and in maintaining a hotel for them. It started a training school for plasterers, bricklayers, and plumbers, and advertised for non-union mechanics. It has been estimated that by the close of 1932 the Industrial Association had placed more than 87,900 men on local jobs, had trained more than 1,700 boys in various building crafts, and had brought approximately 5,000 non-union men to San Francisco. These latter data do not take account of the labor turnover, which undoubtedly was high.[42]

In order to make the open-shop policy effective and to safeguard the non-union men against violence, the Industrial Association formed an inspection and protection department under the direction of a nationally known strike breaker. It also introduced the permit system, which was effectively enforced in the years 1921–1923 and again in 1926. Only those consumers, dealers, and contractors who had been given a permit by the Builders' Exchange could obtain building materials. According to the terms of the permit, the construction job had to be operated on the open-shop basis and in conformity with certain other principles of the association. The unions tested the legality of the permit system in State and Federal courts, but it was upheld as not being in contravention of the anti-trust laws of California or of the United States. The Industrial Association has also appointed wage boards which have held hearings and set local wage rates in the building trades at various times since 1921. For the most part the unions concerned have refused to be represented at the hearings of the wage boards.

The opposition of the building trades unions to the introduction of the open shop resulted in the calling of strikes in the spring of 1922 by the bricklayers, plasterers, plumbers, and steamfitters. In April about 2,100 members of these crafts were on strike. The Industrial Association brought in non-union men from other cities and opened training schools for bricklayers, plasterers, and plumbers. The unions were defeated, all the strikes being declared off at various dates from March to August, 1923.

In the summer of 1922, the San Francisco molders' union asked for a wage increase of 60 cents a day. Negotiations dragged on for some time, a few of the shops not being willing to grant the molders' terms. The controversy developed into an open-shop fight, with six shops, employing about 100 men, taking the initiative. The aid of the Industrial Association was obtained, and twenty-four additional plants in San Francisco, Oakland, and Sunnyvale, employing about 450 men, became involved in what turned out to be one of the longest and most serious conflicts in the labor history of the San Francisco Bay region. In December, 1922, the molders' union officially went out on strike against the open shop, and the contest was waged bitterly for several years. Sixty-three acts of violence were reported. Three men were killed and fifteen were seriously injured. In September, 1926, a union molder of Oakland was convicted of assaulting a strike breaker. In San Francisco in May, 1928, five union molders, arrested on charges of murder and conspiracy, were freed by the court for lack of evidence. The strike was never officially declared off. Some of the establishments are now (1933) working as open shops, others as closed shops. All the plants have increased the wage scale over that of 1922.

The third, and to date (May, 1933) the last, serious attempt to question the dominance of the Industrial Association in the local labor field occurred on April 1, 1926, when the carpenters' unions, with the approval and coöperation of their national organization, struck for the closed shop and the return of the old practice of collective bargaining with the General Contractors' Association. From 4,000 to 5,000 carpenters were involved in the struggle. The strike was declared off February 17, 1927, the men returning to work under open-shop conditions. The Industrial Association spent about $400,000 and brought in approximately 1,100 strike breakers. Several hundred non-union men also drifted into San Francisco and took the places of strikers. The local and national carpenters' unions spent a sum considerably larger than that expended by the Industrial Association. It is said that the material yards opened by the strikers for the purpose of supplying materials to union contractors involved an expenditure of approximately $250,000. These yards were later sold to local material dealers. One death and more than 300 acts of violence were recorded.

As a result of the effectiveness of the campaign of the Industrial Association, San Francisco became to all intents and purposes an open-shop town. The control of Organized Labor over the mercantile and industrial life of the community was definitely broken. Union membership declined, and many of the associations became mere skeletons of their former selves. The results of the efforts and sacrifices of scores of leaders and thousands of union members were swept into the discard. Twenty years of supremacy had ended, at least temporarily, in defeat.

THE GENERAL STRIKE IN 1934

[While the manuscript of this chapter was in the hands of the printer, the industrial, shipping, and mercantile life of San Francisco and the Bay area was prostrated on July 16, 1934, by the declaration of a "general strike" by 65,000 trade unionists; ultimately about 100,000 workers were involved. The strike was so unusual in kind and so important in the history of the labor movement of the State that the following has been added even though the book is now in page proof.—I. B. C.]

It may be recalled that in June–July, 1916, the riggers and stevedores, collectively known in later years as "longshoremen," broke an agreement with their employers and struck for higher wages. They were defeated. The strike, as is usual in water-front labor conflicts, was marked by violence, forty-five cases of assault being recorded. The San Francisco Chamber of Commerce then reversed its policy of non-interference in labor disputes and organized a Law and Order Committee, hoping that by this means it might free the employer interests of the city from union domination. In September, 1919, the longshoremen again struck and again were defeated. A large number of assaults and one death marked that strike. A split then occurred in the ranks of the union, and a company union, the Longshoremen's Association of San Francisco, was formed with the aid of the shipowners. During the next fourteen years this was the only longshoremen's union recognized and dealt with by the shipping interests.

Dissatisfaction of the men with the functioning of the company union led to an intensive membership campaign in the fall of 1933 by national organizers of the International Longshoremen's Association (ILA). The campaign was unexpectedly successful. In October, 1933, 400 members of the ILA struck against the Matson Navigation Company, asserting that union workers had been discriminated against. The discharged men were reinstated. The success of the ILA in its first brush with the employers marked the passing of the company union, surprised the officers and members of the new union, and astounded the employers.

On March 7, 1934, the ILA voted to strike on March 23 for higher wages, shorter hours, a wider distribution of the work, a coast-wide agreement, and control of the hiring hall. An appeal to President Roosevelt brought from him a request that both sides submit their differences to a Fact Finding Committee to be appointed by him. This was agreed to. Will J. French, a former local labor leader, Judge M. C. Sloss, formerly of the State Supreme Court, and Professor Ira B. Cross, of the University of California, were asked to serve, but Judge Sloss and Professor Cross asked to be excused. The heads of the Regional Labor Boards of Seattle (C. A. Reynolds), San Francisco (Dr. H. F. Grady), and Los Angeles (J. L. Leonard) were then appointed. It was found impossible to compromise the differences between the contending parties. On May 9, the ILA called a coast-wide strike.

On August 31, 1933, the Sailors' Union of the Pacific, the Pacific Coast Marine Firemen, Oilers, Watertenders, and Wipers Association, and the Marine Cooks' and Stewards' Association of the Pacific Coast had unsuccessfully presented demands to their employers concerning wages, hours, and the closed shop; and on November 10, 1933, similar demands were made at the Shipping Code hearings in Washington, D. C., but with no results. They now threw their support to the longshoremen and on May 15 voted a coast-wide strike. They were later joined by the Ship Clerks' Association, the Marine Engineers' Beneficial Association, and the Masters', Mates', and Pilots' Association.

Boats entering coast harbors were unable to load or unload. More than ninety vessels were tied up in San Francisco harbor, and a smaller number in other ports. It is said that more than 1,000 strike breakers were put to work in San Francisco and an even larger number in San Pedro (the Port of Los Angeles). On May 15, 300 strikers stormed the stockade at San Pedro. One person was killed, six were wounded by gun-fire, and scores received bodily injuries. Two days later, six strike breakers were seriously beaten in San Francisco. When 1,000 strikers paraded along the water front of the latter city on May 28, a clash occurred with the police, and seven persons were badly injured.

On May 13, the truck drivers (Teamsters' Union) of San Francisco refused to haul from the docks to the warehouses, cargo which had been unloaded by strike breakers, and on June 14 refused to handle it under any circumstances. The water front was completely tied up; cargoes could not be moved.

Joseph P. Ryan, the national president of the ILA, arrived in San Francisco on May 24 and with the help of district officers of the union, succeeded in drawing up an agreement with the employers, but when it was submitted to the members of the union it was overwhelmingly repudiated because its terms did not include the members of the marine unions which had gone out on strike with the longshoremen.

The Fact Finding Committee having failed to effect a settlement, President Roosevelt was requested to appoint a mediation board, which he did on June 26. This National Longshoremen's

Board consisted of Archbishop Hanna, Assistant Secretary of Labor E. F. McGrady, and O. K. Cushing, a San Francisco attorney. The board labored unceasingly for some days, but without results. Wages and hours could be compromised, but neither side would agree to arbitrate control over the hiring hall. The union feared that unless it had control, its members seeking employment would be discriminated against. The employers feared that unless they had control, they would have to contend with closed-shop conditions, to which they were unequivocally opposed. The union subsequently announced that it would arbitrate control of the hiring hall, provided the employers would agree to arbitrate with all unions then on strike. This the employers refused to do.

Conditions at the Port of Los Angeles were such that boats and cargo moved more freely there than at San Francisco. Railroad tracks went directly onto the docks, so that passengers and freight could be taken care of without interference. Such being the situation, many boats that customarily entered San Francisco harbor put into the southern port, and passengers and freight were thus lost to San Francisco and gained by San Pedro. Under these circumstances, the San Francisco Chamber of Commerce asked the Industrial Association to "open the port," and it started to do so on July 5. Police protection was promised by the mayor. With trucks manned by strike breakers, goods were moved from the docks to the warehouses; but no farther. Strikers and their sympathizers were too active. Trucks were overturned; some were burned; goods were dumped into the street; police and pickets clashed; a riot occurred. Tear gas and pistols were met with cobblestones and brickbats. Two union men were killed; more than a hundred were seriously wounded; other hundreds were injured. A few days later, 10,000 union men marched in the funeral procession of their slain comrades.

The Junior Chamber of Commerce presented to the governor a petition bearing 10,000 names, requesting the declaration of martial law. The governor refused, but instead sent 5,000 of the California National Guard to protect State property—the entire water front of San Francisco, including the docks and the Belt railroad serving them, being owned by the State of California. The strikers had attempted to prevent the operation of the Belt railroad because it served the interests of the employers. The governor, however, announced that he would not permit any group of individuals to interfere with State activities or to damage State property. With the arrival of the militia all rioting ceased.

Paul S. Taylor and Norman L. Gold, in an article entitled "San Francisco and the General Strike," which appeared in the *Survey Graphic* in September, 1934, state that "to the strikers, confident and more impassioned than ever, the situation seemed clear; the employers had finally used their last resource—their own strength first, then the police, the Industrial Association, and the militia; now the men must win enforcements for the final test of power. From the waterfront through the ranks of organized labor and to the public went the appeal for support of a general strike." Organized Labor in San Francisco was fighting for its right to exist.

The Labor Council appointed a Strike Strategy Committee on July 6, to investigate the situation. The committee recommended that a general-strike vote be put to the unions. One hundred and twenty out of approximately 175 organizations voted to strike or to stand ready to obey orders from the General Strike Committee which had been formed to direct the struggle. Similar action was taken by the members of the Alameda County Central Labor Council, across the Bay.

The employers now announced their willingness to arbitrate all phases of the controversy with the longshoremen, but only to bargain with the marine workers' unions. Again the longshoremen refused to abandon their associates.

The truck drivers quit work on July 12. The general strike was announced to take place on July 16. Panic seized the citizens of the Bay region. Grocery stores, and vegetable and meat markets, were jammed by persons eager to obtain supplies to carry them over the crisis. No one knew how long it might last. Long lines of automobiles blocked service stations, their owners begging for a few gallons of gasoline. Hysteria gripped the populace of not only the cities near by, but also of those hundreds of miles distant.

On July 16, all theaters and liquor stores were closed; street railways and interurban service ceased operating; building activities were halted; only 19 of San Francisco's 2,000 restaurants were permitted to remain open. The city's industrial and commercial life was at a standstill. Only emergency trucks (hospital, scavenger, fire, and police) were permitted to operate without restraint; all others were forced to carry a union permit. Roads entering the Bay cities were picketed so as to prevent the passage of food trucks, but the governor immediately gave orders to the State Highway Patrol to convoy all food trucks to their destination. There was never any real shortage of food in the affected area. The strike spread across the Bay to the cities of Berkeley, Oakland, and Alameda.

On July 16, the General Strike Committee authorized the municipal street-car employees to return to work, because they faced the loss of civil-service status. On the second day, fifty-nine restaurants were permitted to open. A day later, gasoline and fuel-oil trucks were allowed to move freely and the ban was removed from all eating-places and meat shops. By July 19, the strike was over. The truck drivers then voted to return to work, irrespective of the wishes of the water-front unions.

The shipowners, on July 21, agreed to arbitrate all issues with all water-front unions, provided the longshoremen would submit all points in controversy to arbitration. By a vote of about 4 to 1, the union agreed to accept the terms of the employers, and returned to work on July 29. The maritime unions also accepted the shipowners' proposals and went back to work on July 31.

The National Longshoremen's Board now became an arbitration board. Hearings were held at all coast ports. On October 12, 1934, the board announced its award, affecting only the longshoremen, the seamen still being engaged in voting to determine whether the Sailors' Union of the Pacific or the company union should represent them in the arbitration proceedings. Compromises were effected with respect to hours and wages. The control of the hiring hall was vested in a Labor Relations Committee composed of three representatives of the ILA, three representatives of the Ship Owners' Association, and a seventh member to be appointed by the Secretary of Labor or by some authority designated by that official. The dispatching officer in the hall was to be a union man.

During the period of the water-front strike and the general strike, the local newspapers unceasingly whipped up the hysteria of their readers by asserting that the community faced an "insurrection" led by "communists" or "reds," who were being "financed by Moscow" and who were under "the control of the Third International," intent upon overthrowing the Constitution of the United States and establishing the dictatorship of the proletariat. It is true that some of the strikers, a very small number, were members of the Marine Workers' Industrial Union, a communist organization, which was given much undeserved publicity and an importance out of all proportion to its small membership and influence. In vain did the Strike Strategy Committee of the Labor Council declare that it most strenuously objected to "the attitude of the newspapers in constantly asserting that communists have been in direction of the strike. That has never been the case." The strike was not a communist demonstration, but the public, aroused by the statements of the press, believed that the fundamental issue at stake was that of Communism versus Americanism. Communist places of meeting and the hall of the Marine Workers' Industrial Union were raided and wrecked; in some raids the police lent assistance. Several hundred communists and sympathizers were thrown into jail. Groups of "vigilantes" were organized in the East Bay cities and armed with pick-handles; meeting places of radicals and liberals were wrecked; brickbats carrying a written warning were thrown through the windows of the homes of radicals and union sympathizers. The librarian of the Alameda County Library was ordered to prepare a list of books dealing with communism, which were to be destroyed. Radical literature disappeared from the shelves of city libraries. Scarcely a person dared voice a protest against the acts of the "vigilantes," for fear of personal violence or public condemnation. The hysteria still continues. In many cities and rural districts of California, far removed from the Bay area, groups of "vigilantes" have been organized, ready to swing into action and take "law into their own hands" whenever a labor conflict appears probable.

The immediate cause of the general strike of July 16–19, 1934, was the presence of the militia on the water front. The fundamental cause, however, was the fear that the remnants of trade unionism in San Francisco might be destroyed by the Industrial Association. An intense feeling of bitterness and resentment against the latter had existed from its inception and as a consequence of its success in breaking the hold of Organized Labor upon the industrial, commercial, and mercantile life of San Francisco.

The results: A prominent citizen of San Francisco was quoted in the press on July 20 as saying:

This strike is the best thing that ever happened to San Francisco. . . . It's solving the labor problem for years to come, perhaps forever. . . . When this nonsense is out of the way and the men have been driven back to their jobs, we wont have to worry about them any more. . . . Labor is licked.

To which the *Seamen's Journal* of August 1, 1934, replied:

The fact is that the unions of San Francisco are stronger today and more firmly established than for many years past. . . . A further fact is that every union in San Francisco and vicinity has increased its membership during the strike and since the strike. . . . There is more active interest in trade-union affairs, in tactics, in policy, than has ever been known. . . . So far from being "licked," organized labor in California is just beginning to perform.

The *Labor Clarion*, the official organ of the Labor Council, took occasion to point out that every time Labor has been "licked," it has come back stronger than before. Such in truth has been the fact, as shown by the preceding story of the labor movement in California. In the early seventies, the employers crushed the eight-hour day movement, but in the eighties the workers of San Francisco were better organized than before. In 1893, the Manufacturers' and Employers' Association disrupted the local labor movement and announced that only one union was left to enforce "its rules upon the trade." That crushing defeat of trade unionism was followed by an even more thoroughgoing organization of the workers during the remainder of the decade. The Employers' Association "licked" the unions in the water-front and teamsters' strike of 1901, but in a few years San Francisco became the most completely closed-shop community in the United States.

The results of the general strike of 1934 are still in the making. There has been a surprising amount of organizational activity among the workers. Labor leaders say that almost every trade is insisting upon unionization as in 1900–1901. Prior to the general strike of 1934, the unions had become more active because of the collective-bargaining provision of the NIRA, and they are now more militant than in many years past.

THE ANTI-JAPANESE MOVEMENT[43]

During the closing years of the nineteenth century, the antagonism of Californians to the presence of Oriental labor began to reassert itself, directed, however, against the Japanese. Prior to the late nineties, there were so few Japanese in California that their presence was unnoticed. According to the United States Census, the Japanese population of the nation in 1870, 1880, and 1890 was respectively 55, 140, and 2,039. In 1885 the Japanese government reversed its traditional policy and permitted the emigration of its subjects. Three years earlier, the United States had adopted its first Chinese Exclusion Act. When the immigration of Chinese was thus prohibited, many of the Chinese in California gradually moved into the cities and there became factory hands, domestic servants, or storekeepers and employers on a small scale. This shift of the Chinese from the country to the city created a shortage of cheap agricultural labor and resulted in increased costs of production for the farmers. There then arose an insistent demand for some kind of cheap labor to supply the shortage. California could not look to Europe for aid because few immigrants from that part of the world made their way to the Pacific Coast, and the Europeans who did come to California were unwilling to work under conditions which had been acceptable to the Chinese. California agriculturists therefore turned to the Japanese, and employed an increasingly large number of them. The United States Census of 1870 listed only 33 Japanese as residents of California. By 1880 this number had increased to 86, and by 1890 to 1,147. In the later nineties, immigration increased so rapidly that in 1900 the Japanese population of California had risen to 10,151, and in 1910 it was 41,356.

Many of the Japanese came from the Hawaiian Islands, where they had been employed on large plantations. Higher wages, superior employment conditions, and better economic opportunities were the chief reasons for their migration to the mainland. Practically all of them were members of the poorest and most ignorant classes, and more than one-half were agriculturists. The same abuses that had characterized Chinese immigration were also present in the Japanese immigration. Emigration from Japan and Hawaii was encouraged through advertising, by steamship companies, and by labor contractors. Many Japanese came on funds advanced by fellow-countrymen who, as labor contractors, bound them by agreements similar to those that had been used formerly in the eastern states in connection with the importation of European contract labor.

At first the Japanese were warmly welcomed. They constituted a colorful addition to the State's already cosmopolitan population. They were clean in personal habits, ambitious, hard working, eager to adopt American standards and practices, and desirous of becoming socially and industrially assimilated. They bought or rented barren land and turned it into berry ranches, vegetable gardens, orchards, and vineyards, and soon were successful in growing and harvesting crops produced under conditions of intensive cultivation. It did not take long, however, for opposition to arise, and it came from many sources. The Japanese were quicker and steadier workers and willing to labor longer hours than the Chinese or other laborers. The Chinese soon gave up the contest and the greater number of them moved to the cities. The whites, both on the farms and in the cities, began a campaign of opposition. The farm owners found that the Japanese were not so easily controlled as the Chinese had been : the latter were docile, seldom protested against housing or employment conditions, abided by their contracts, seldom if ever struck, and as a rule had no desire to become landowners; but the Japanese demanded better employment and housing conditions, insisted on controlling the job, violated contracts, struck when the strike would be most inopportune for the farmer, and were eager to become landowners. Not once but many times, white farmers were forced to lease or sell their ranches to the Japanese because the latter, having a monopoly of the farm labor in the community, employed that monopoly most effectively in bringing financial loss to farmers who resisted their demands. By these and other methods the Japanese obtained control over some of the most fertile sections of the State. They worked fourteen to sixteen hours a day; their wives and children labored beside them in the fields; their plane of living was low; their ambition to advance economically was unquenchable. Soon they were virtually in control of the berry, potato, flower, and garden truck markets in almost every community of any size. Antagonism could not but grow more bitter.

In the cities, the Japanese became small merchants, restaurant proprietors, laundrymen, domestics, and gardeners. They worked on railway section gangs and in mines and canneries. In general they followed in the footsteps of the Chinese, although they were seldom to be found in factories or workshops. They possessed a spirit of aggressiveness quite foreign to the Chinese. They cut prices and wages, and thus aroused the antagonism of the merchant and working classes. They refused to live in a city's Oriental quarter, preferring to mingle with the white population. They not infrequently paid excessively high prices or rentals for a few pieces of city property in a locality where they wished to live. When they moved in, white families in the adjoining or neighboring properties moved out; property values were thereby reduced and the Japanese were frequently enabled to buy or rent buildings and residences on their own terms. These practices aroused the white landlords, who by various means attempted to prevent the Japanese from spreading into all parts of a city.

As early as 1896 the State Labor Commissioner of California gave an entire section of his biennial report to the results of an investigation of Japanese immigration, which had been made by his staff.[44] In 1900, the increasingly antagonistic attitude of the people was publicly voiced. On May 7, 1900, a mass meeting was held in San Francisco to petition Congress to reënact the Chinese Exclusion Law, which was about to lapse because of the expiration of the ten-year period. A resolution to that effect was adopted, as was also one requesting Congress to exclude all Japanese other than members of the diplomatic staff. The increase in Japanese immigration was startling. In 1899 only 3,395 Japanese entered the country, but in 1900 the number was 12,628. Congress, however, took no action. In 1901, 5,249 Japanese arrived; in 1902, 14,455; in 1903, 20,041; and in 1904, 14,382. In 1905 the San Francisco

Chronicle began a vigorous campaign against them. In May of that year the Asiatic Exclusion League was organized by the local labor leaders. For many years thereafter the League carried on an energetic campaign against the "little yellow man," using every means, political and otherwise, to attain its ends. The cooks' and waiters' union was especially active in the agitation because many Japanese were employed in the city restaurants, while others had opened small eating houses. They had also entered the laundry business, as had the Chinese many years before them. This aroused the united opposition of the laundry workers' unions and the laundry proprietors. An Anti-Japanese Laundry League was organized in San Francisco in 1908, and one in Oakland somewhat later. Attempts to form similar leagues in other communities were not successful.

The presence of Japanese children in the public schools was another source of irritation. In a few of the rural districts they constituted the greater number of the pupils. On May 6, 1905, the San Francisco Board of Education ordered the establishment of an Oriental school to which all Chinese and Japanese pupils were to be sent. At that time there were only ninety-three Japanese in the twenty-three public schools of the city. The order was not to become effective until 1906. The government of Japan filed a protest with the Department of State of the United States, alleging discrimination against the children of her subjects. An investigation was made by the Federal authorities, which was followed by a conference between President Theodore Roosevelt and the officials of San Francisco. The school order was subsequently rescinded.

Opposition to the Japanese grew more determined and outspoken. In 1907 Congress granted to the President power to suspend the immigration of Japanese and Korean laborers into the continental United States when such laborers came from Canada, Mexico, or American insular possessions.[45] On March 14, 1907, President Theodore Roosevelt issued an order under the authority thus granted. Japan then agreed to grant no passports to skilled or unskilled laborers who wished to emigrate to the United States. Exceptions were made of Japanese who had been residents of the United States, or who were parents, husbands, wives, and children of those who were then residents thereof. This was the so-called

"Gentlemen's Agreement." At first it seemed to offer the desired solution of a difficult problem. In 1905, 11,021 Japanese had entered the United States, and in 1906 the number had increased to 14,243. In 1907, when strained relations between the two countries seemed likely to bring about a policy of further restriction or total exclusion, thousands of Japanese hastened to sail for the continental United States. In 1907, the year in which the Gentlemen's Agreement was promulgated, 30,824 Japanese arrived. It took about a year to perfect the administration of the agreement so as to make it effective. Within that period there was a further immigration of 16,418. In 1909, the number declined to 3,275, but it did not long remain at that low level; on the contrary, the number of Japanese immigrants again increased rapidly. In 1918, 10,168 were officially admitted to the United States, and in 1919 the number was 10,056. So far as the residents of the Pacific Coast were concerned, the Gentlemen's Agreement was not working satisfactorily. They asserted that Japan, through various subterfuges, was permitting its evasion. The anti-Japanese agitation again flared up; protests were made to Congress; hearings were held; and on May 26, 1924, the Federal Immigration Act was amended to the effect that "no alien ineligible to citizenship shall be admitted to the United States," with the exception of government officials, tourists, seamen, traders, students, and clergymen: these were to receive temporary residence permits.[46] Immediately thereafter Japanese immigration decreased noticeably. Whereas in 1924, 8,481 Japanese had arrived, in 1925 only 682 were admitted. Since 1925 the yearly total has been below 800.

The adoption of the Gentlemen's Agreement had virtually no effect on the anti-Japanese attitude of the Californians. In succeeding sessions of the State legislature, bills were introduced to abolish "Japanese language" schools, to authorize the segregation of Japanese school children, to prohibit Japanese from engaging in commercial fishing, and to forbid their ownership of farm land or their leasing of farm land for more than a short term of years. Almost all the proposed measures were defeated, often under pressure from Federal authorities. In 1913 an alien land law had been adopted which forbade the ownership or leasing of land by any person ineligible to American citizenship.[47] The law applied to all aliens excluded from citizenship, but it was chiefly of concern to the Japanese. Means were found, however, whereby its provisions were easily evaded. In 1920 an initiative measure, which had been drawn with the intent of making evasion impossible, was adopted by a 3 to 1 vote of the electorate.[48] Cases were subsequently carried into the State and Federal courts questioning the law's constitutionality and its conflict with treaty rights, but in all instances the act was upheld. In 1923 the State legislature amended the law of 1920 so as to make its provisions even more drastic.[49]

After the amendment of the Federal Immigration Act in 1924, the agitation in California against the "little yellow man" subsided. Since that time, and partly as a consequence of the events mentioned above, the relations between the Japanese and the United States governments have been more or less strained. Japan, as a modern progressive nation, continues to feel that her subjects have been unjustly discriminated against by the legislation enacted not only by California, and by other western states which have adopted measures similar to those of California, but also by the 1924 amendment to the Federal Immigration Act. The attitude of the Californians is still distinctly anti-Japanese, but it is not so openly voiced as it was from 1905 to 1924.

Since 1900 there has also been some agitation against the immigration of Hindus and Filipinos. The former have never been numerous, have never presented a serious problem, and have now (1933) almost ceased coming to American shores. The Filipinos are citizens of an American administrative possession, and only during the past decade have they been coming in appreciably large numbers to the continental United States. Although there have been several violent outbreaks against them, it is to be doubted that the opposition will ever assume the intensity of the anti-Chinese and anti-Japanese agitations of the earlier years.

Chapter XIV

THE LABOR MOVEMENT IN LOS ANGELES

SELDOM, IF EVER, in any state of the Union have there been two communities of such contrasting types as San Francisco and Los Angeles. Differing in origin, causes of growth, civic spirit, and climate, they have also shown a strangely different attitude toward Organized Labor. San Francisco was predominantly pro-Labor from the early days of the gold rush until after 1922, when the vigorous, determined campaign for the so-called "American" or open-shop plan resulted in an anti-union success. In Los Angeles almost a century passed before unions appeared, and at no time have they played an important part in the industrial or political life of the community.[1]

Los Angeles was founded by Spain on September 4, 1781. Its original population consisted of forty-four persons. As late as the eighties it retained its sleepy, non-aggressive Spanish and Mexican characteristics; but from 1850 to 1870 it had the reputation of being the toughest frontier town in the United States. Its Vigilance Committee of 1857 executed four times as many persons as did the Vigilance Committee of 1856 in San Francisco. In October, 1871, the Chinese quarter was pillaged by a mob which killed nineteen Chinese and stole or destroyed more than $40,000 worth of their property.[2] This event sobered the citizens, and no similar outbreaks occurred thereafter. It is interesting to note that even in the heyday of the Kearney movement in the later seventies there was no rioting or violence such as characterized the agitation in San Francisco.

It is not known when the first union was organized in Los Angeles. The November, 1862, issue of *The Printer*, published in New York City, carried an item from San Francisco, dated September 25, 1862, saying that a printers' union was then in existence in Los Angeles. The next mention of organized activity among the workers of that city is found in the *Weekly Los Angeles Republican* of

July 18, 1868, which announced that the Mechanics' League, composed of carpenters, bricklayers, stone masons, plasterers, and painters, had notified the local employers that the eight-hour day without a reduction in wages was to be observed on and after August 10. The Mechanics' League had undoubtedly been formed as a result of the influence of the Mechanics' State Council of San Francisco, which was then carrying on an active campaign for the eight-hour day. It is not known whether the trades listed as members of the Mechanics' League were actually organized into unions, or whether the League was a bona fide labor federation. Nor is it known whether the League was successful in obtaining its demands. Los Angeles was then a town of small population, and it is to be doubted that there was a sufficient number of workers in any of the trades mentioned to start an organized labor movement. The first union of which there is definite record is that of the printers (Typographical Union No. 174), chartered on October 1, 1875, with nine members.[3]

In September, 1876, the completion of the construction work on the Southern Pacific railroad between San Francisco and Los Angeles invited an intensive agricultural development in the southern part of the State. The population of Los Angeles grew from 5,728 in 1870 to 11,183 in 1880. The first labor dispute arose in this decade. The proprietors of the *Daily Star,* the only local newspaper, employed non-union printers. On October 6, 1876, the typographical union demanded that the plant be unionized, and this was done without the necessity of a strike. It is significant that the printers were the first to organize and the first to make demands upon their employers. Out of a similar conflict fourteen years later the seeds were sown for the most bitter and continuous open-shop war that has ever marked the economic life of any community.

In August, 1881, Harrison Gray Otis purchased the Los Angeles *Times,* and this newspaper subsequently became an effective medium for a campaign against Organized Labor. The *Times* and its job printing office, the Times-Mirror Publishing Company, operated in the same room. The union employees of the former were paid by the piece and the non-union employees of the latter by the week. Dissension arose among the printers, but after some negotiations harmony was secured by having the employees of the jobbing office join the union. On August 17, 1883, the union employees struck in an effort to unionize the *Times* staff completely and to obtain the reëmployment of a union printer. On October 2 a compromise was reached, the *Times* agreeing to employ a union foreman and the union approving the employment of non-union men.

In 1881, the Southern Pacific railroad began construction on its line from Los Angeles to New Orleans. The population of Los Angeles began to grow rapidly, increasing from 11,183 in 1880 to 15,000 in 1882. Real estate values rose 25 per cent in 1882 and doubled in 1883. On November 1, 1885, the Santa Fe railroad entered the city. A rate war was at once declared between the two railroads, and this rate war, combined with the florid advertising of climate and of the unparalleled agricultural and industrial possibilities of southern California, resulted in the most astounding local real estate boom of the nineteenth century. In 1887 the population of Los Angeles was estimated at 80,000. It is said that more than 200,000 persons arrived in that city in the years 1885–1887, and that many of them settled permanently in the southern part of California. Real estate values reached dizzy heights; subdivisions for a population of 10,000,000 were laid out in and near the city, in valleys, on steep mountain sides, and in the wash of the San Gabriel Valley, which was filled with "rocks so rugged and so hot withal that they are reputed to have burnt the corner stakes." The more inaccessible the land, the more numerous the buyers. Twenty-three hundred lots were sold in Chicago Park, which no person was ever able to locate. Sales in 1887 approximated $200,000,000. In the fall of that year the ardor for real estate speculation waned, but it was revived again in the spring of 1888. By July the boom had burst. In its wake were blasted hopes, poverty, suicides, unemployment, and business failures. Strangely enough, not a bank closed its doors. Although in 1888 and 1889 more than a thousand persons per month had departed from Los Angeles, the census of 1890 disclosed a population of 50,395, approximately a five-fold increase in a decade. Since that date the rate of population growth has been unparalleled, the figures by ten-year periods being as follows: 1900, 102,479; 1910, 319,198; 1920, 576,673; 1930, 1,238,048.

Much of the increase between 1920 and 1930, however, was obtained through the annexation of near-by cities and towns which agreed to annexation in order to obtain from Los Angeles an adequate water supply for their rapidly expanding populations.

The land boom of the later eighties led to extensive building operations and the establishment of small industries and stores. Under such circumstances one would expect that many labor organizations would be formed and that they would become an important element in the economic life of the community. It was the contrary, however, that actually occurred. The mild climate attracted invalids, many of whom were able to work at light jobs. Eastern farmers came, eager to escape the discomforts of winter weather. Others, who had small incomes or small savings and who were therefore willing to sell their services for almost any wage, also arrived in great numbers. Husbands and fathers, wives and mothers, came with their sick ones and made their contribution to the local labor supply. Added to this condition of an unusual competitive labor situation, there has always been present the relentless opposition and widespread influence of almost all the local newspapers, which have steadfastly fought against Organized Labor and the principles for which it stands. In spite of these overwhelming odds, however, a few courageous souls have battled for trade unionism even though the results in general have been disappointment and defeat.

Concomitant with the growth in population, increase of property values, and expanding building operations in the early eighties, Carpenters' and Joiners' Union No. 56 was organized with eleven members, and chartered on March 11, 1884. On April 8 of the same year the painters organized as Knights of Labor Assembly No. 3167, with twenty-five members. Three other branches of the Knights of Labor, namely, Assemblies Nos. 2004, 2157, and 2405, were also started about the same time. From occasional items in the local newspapers, it appears that unions also existed among the tailors (who struck in October, 1884), hodcarriers, plasterers, bricklayers, barbers, and cigarmakers.[4] The last-mentioned group became affiliated with the International Cigar Makers' Union in 1885, but apparently soon disbanded; it reorganized on April 24, 1886, with nine charter members.[5]

On September 6, 1884, the painters notified their employers that a nine-hour day would be in effect on and after September 8. About the same time the carpenters made a similar demand, effective on May 1, 1885. It appears that the bricklayers and plasterers were also active in the campaign for shorter hours, but evidence is lacking to support the belief that these two crafts were unionized. After a vigorous campaign the nine-hour day became general for the building trades in January, 1886. This was undoubtedly made possible in large part because of the prevailing "boom time" conditions.

On October 15, 1884, the first bona fide labor federation, the Los Angeles Trades Council, was organized. The names of its charter members and first officers are not known. In July, 1885, it had eight constituent unions. The Trades Council was not a militant body, possibly because the local labor movement was still in its swaddling clothes and therefore unacquainted with union tactics. It passed from the field with the collapse of the real estate boom in the later eighties.

There was some unemployment in Los Angeles in 1885 and this led to an unsuccessful attempt to revive the anti-Chinese movement. In the summer months the Anti-Chinese Union was organized, which agitated for the discharge of all Chinese laborers and their removal from the city; but the Chinese issue made no appeal to the people of Los Angeles. In February, 1886, the Trades Council started a boycotting campaign against the Mongolians, and again there were no results.

In July, 1885, the printers struck against the *Express* because of an announced reduction in wages and the use of "boiler plate." They had the support of the local unions and the Trades Council, and even went so far as to establish a daily newspaper, the *Evening Union*. On October 25 the issue was compromised, the printers returned to work, and the publication of the *Evening Union* was stopped.

During the boom period the city was virtually free from labor disputes. Wages rose, employment was general, and a few unions were organized. In 1888, the *Third Biennial Report of the California Bureau of Labor Statistics* reported[6] the unions then in existence and their membership as follows: bricklayers', 120; Amalgamated Brotherhood of Carpenters, 60; carpenters' and joiners', 907; stonecutters', 54; plasterers', 150; plasterers' helpers', 100; lathers', 75; plumbers', 100; plumbers' helpers', 40; sheet metal

ARTHUR VINETTE

workers', 200; painters', 75; sandstone cutters', 20; wage workers' union, 150; Knights of Labor Assembly, 153; cooks' and waiters', 48; typographical union, 212; pressmen's, 40; ironmolders', 50; cigarmakers', 10; tailors', 87; bakers', 50; total number of unions, 21; total membership, 2,701. It is not known how many of these organizations were affiliated with the local Trades Council or with their respective national unions. The cooks' and waiters' union and the bakers' union were branches of San Francisco organizations. The cigarmakers had organized on April 24, 1886, the stonecutters in May, 1887, and the bricklayers on March 8, 1888. In addition to these associations, there was a local branch of the Brotherhood of Locomotive Engineers, of the Brotherhood of Locomotive Firemen, and of the Order of Railroad Conductors. The railroad unions, however, did not affiliate or coöperate in any way with the local labor movement.

When the real estate boom broke, the union movement collapsed. The Trades Council disbanded in the fall of 1888. Only four or five craft organizations were able to maintain themselves with a handful of loyal members. In April, 1889, the time seemed favorable for the establishment of another federation and the Los Angeles Council of Labor was formed, of ten unions, namely, the tailors', bakers', printers', cigarmakers', carpenters', painters', cooks' and waiters', bricklayers', stonecutters', and the Eight-Hour League. On July 1, the following officers were elected: P. H. Hurley (printers), president; H. Schubert (cigarmakers), vice-president; W. C. Akerman (printers), secretary; J. Sharf (bakers), treasurer.

The Eight-Hour League had been organized on February 22, 1889, in connection with the national movement for the eight-hour day, receiving its inspiration more directly from the San Francisco group. Arthur Vinette, a carpenter and secretary of the Los Angeles Council of Labor, was one of the moving spirits in the agitation,[7] and was assisted by W. C. Owen, formerly of San Francisco, T. E. Cross, president of the league, E. Bailey, R. Hunter, and L. D. Biddle.[8] On April 30, 1890, a mass meeting was held, following a parade, and resolutions were adopted calling for the eight-hour day in the building trades from and after May 4; no reference was made to wages. On May 10 another parade of about 1,000 to 1,500 was held, representing the cigarmakers, carpenters, bakers, tailors, printers, bricklayers, stonecutters, ironmolders, painters, plasterers, barbers, the County Coöperative Association, and the Laborers' Coöperative Construction Association. There is no record of the results of the eight-hour agitation in Los Angeles, but it seems that, because of the abundant labor supply and the relative scarcity of jobs, they were of no consequence.

On August 2, 1890, the proprietors of the *Times, Express, Tribune,* and *Herald* requested the typographical union to consent to a

LEMUEL D. BIDDLE

wage reduction. The union was not willing to do so. On August 5 its members, numbering somewhat more than 100, were locked out. Two days later the *Tribune* and the *Express* compromised the issue, but the *Herald* and the *Times* refused to compromise; the latter two newspapers imported strike breakers and prepared for a long struggle. In October the *Herald* capitulated, but the *Times* carried on the fight single-handed. It was especially outspoken in its denunciation of the union and of trade union policies in general. Since that time it has stood before the people as the champion of non-unionism and the open shop. Its bitterness of attack has never been matched by any other newspaper in the United States or elsewhere. Without doubt it has been the most important factor in the creation of an almost universal hatred of unionism among the residents of southern California.

To meet the *Times'* lockout, the printers' union declared a boycott, which was ineffective although it was supported by the organized workers of Los Angeles. The aid of the International Typographical Union was asked for, and M. McGlynn, a San Francisco labor leader, was sent to assist in the contest. He at once ordered a boycott on the People's Store, the largest advertiser in the *Times*. In April, 1892, the proprietor of that store arranged a conference between the union and the *Times*, at which it was agreed that the union men should be gradually reëmployed provided the boycotts against the *Times* and the People's Store were lifted. Four union men were reëmployed by the *Times*, but it soon became evident that the newspaper was not living up to the agreement. The two boycotts were then reimposed, and additional assistance was obtained from the International Typographical Union. In December, 1903, W. R. Hearst, at the request of the union, established the Los Angeles *Examiner* as an offset to the *Times*. Eight months later, at the suggestion of the manager of the *Examiner*, the boycott against the People's Store was lifted so that the latter's advertisements might be accepted by that paper. The fight against the *Times* continued, however, and has been intermittently but unsuccessfully carried on since that time.[9]

In April, 1892, the Los Angeles Council of Labor comprised eight unions. In 1892 unemployment was rather widespread. The painters and the plumbers, however, had an eight-hour day, and the newly organized clerks' union was able to reduce the working hours of its members. In a labor parade on June 27, eleven unions were in the procession. On May 21, 1893, fifty members of the bakers' union struck to retain the ten-hour day with no night work, an arrangement which had been in effect for several months. The boss bakers asserted that hotels and restaurants insisted upon receiving fresh bread in the morning and that night work was therefore necessary. The strike and boycott were lost within a few weeks. The activity of the printers' union in waging its battle against the *Times* was the incentive for the organization of several unions. In September, 1893, eighteen unions were affiliated with the Council of Labor. There were also in existence four Knights of Labor assemblies and three railway brotherhood unions.

The depression of 1893 seriously affected Los Angeles and the vicinity; low prices for farm products put many farmers in straitened circumstances and affected the liquidity of local banking institutions. The failure of the Riverside Banking Company on June 14, 1893, so frightened Los Angeles depositors that they started a run on three banks. On June 20 and 21, six local banks closed their doors, unable to withstand the strain. One was later declared insolvent; two others went through voluntary bankruptcy, paying all claims in full; and the rest subsequently reopened. Many of the local unemployed were cared for by public works; others joined the southern California contingent of Coxey's Army. The "Army" did not get far on its journey toward Washington, D. C., before it met the stern hand of the law in Colton, California. One hundred and seventy of its members were arrested for disturbing the peace and sentenced to four months in jail.

The American Railway Union strike against the Pullman Company in June, 1894, seriously affected the shipping interests of southern California. Not a train left Los Angeles on June 27. An injunction was issued by the Federal courts against the strikers, but it did not prevent many acts of violence. On July 2 six companies of United States infantry were sent from San Francisco to maintain order. Several trains were moved under guard on July 6, and by July 15 the strike was broken. On July 21 it was officially declared off. Two of the officers of the local union and two of its members were tried, found guilty of conspiring to obstruct the passage of United States mail, and sentenced to eighteen months' imprisonment.

In the latter part of March, 1895, the plumbers struck against a reduction in wages. Only seven unions were in the Labor Day parade of 1895. In June, 1896, the Los Angeles Council of Labor affiliated with the American Federation of Labor. It was planned to make the council a county rather than a city federation, so its name was changed to the Los Angeles County Council of Labor. At that date it was composed of 23 unions with a membership of about 5,400 workers. In the Labor Day celebration of 1896, 600 men were in line, representing 21 unions, a notable increase over the number of the preceding year. In January, 1897, the first local building trades council was organized,[10] and in July the Allied Printing Trades Council was formed.[11] In October a boycott was declared which greatly increased the local opposition to Organized Labor. The San Francisco brewery workers' union had branches in various cities of the State. The Maier & Zobelein brewery of Los Angeles had no objection to the unionization of its employees, but the latter had refused to join the organization, asserting that they worked union hours and received higher than union wages. Many of them were stockholders in the firm. A boycott was declared by the San Francisco union and supported by the Los Angeles labor groups. The controversy aroused the members of the Merchants' and Manufacturers' Association, and they opposed the union so vigorously that the boycott failed. The Merchants' and Manufacturers' Association, usually referred to as "The M. & M.," now became an ardent supporter of the non-union campaign of the *Times*, and has remained so to this date. Its influence has always been extremely powerful. For twenty-seven years its secretary was F. J. Zeehandelaar, who up to the time of his death was intimately associated with Harrison Gray Otis in the fight against the unionization of the workers of southern California. The M. & M. was formed on June 23, 1896, by a merger of the Merchants' Association organized in 1894 and the Manufacturers' Association organized in 1895. Both were at first concerned with a campaign to encourage the use of local products and to further the business interests of their members. It was not until the brewery boycott was declared that the M. & M. entered upon the union-breaking open-shop career which, steadfastly and successfully, it has followed ever since.

The later nineties were for Los Angeles a period of prosperity. Employers voluntarily raised wages; building operations were active; and local industries were busily engaged in manufacturing various products. There were no labor disturbances, and the number and strength of the unions remained nearly constant. With the opening of the twentieth century, however, the local labor movement began to assert itself. In 1900 the State Labor Commissioner of California reported that there were twenty-six unions with about 2,100 members in Los Angeles.[12] Two years later he reported sixty-eight unions (an increase of 150 per cent) and an increase of 125 per cent in membership.[13] This noteworthy growth had in great part resulted from the efforts of John C. Ince, a union organizer who had been sent to Los Angeles by the American Federation of Labor.

The first important strike of this period occurred on October 3, 1900, among the linemen of the telephone, telegraph, and electric lighting companies. The linemen had been receiving $2.50 for a ten-hour day; they demanded the closed shop, eight hours, a minimum wage of $3, and a one-year trade agreement. Sympathetic strikes occurred at Pasadena, Santa Ana, and Riverside. About ninety employees were involved. In February, 1901, the employers acknowledged defeat and the men returned to work. The available records do not disclose whether or not the closed shop was granted. On July 1, 1901, more than 300 members of the shirt waist and laundry workers' union struck for the closed shop, but were defeated. In July several minor strikes and walkouts occurred in the building industry, but in all of them the employers were victorious.

In the Labor Day parade of 1901, 29 unions were represented by about 2,500 marchers; twelve unions were not represented in the procession. As soon as the parade was over, the Building Trades Council declared a general strike on all construction work where non-union men or members of the bricklayers' and hodcarriers' unions were employed. The latter two organizations had refused to affiliate with the Building Trades Council, and their members were therefore classed as non-union workers. About 500 men went on strike. Four days later they returned to work, defeated. On September 25, the Millmen's Association agreed to grant the demands of the woodworkers' union for an eight-hour day, but with the provision that it be introduced on a sliding basis in order to permit the employers to meet outside competition. This proposal was rejected by the union, and 77 workers struck on November 1. The strike was lost.

During 1902 Los Angeles was virtually free from labor troubles. In September a small strike by the molders for higher wages and the closed shop was successful only in obtaining the former demand. The foundry proprietors were determined to remain on a non-union basis. There were also several petty strikes among the building trades workers and the machinists. Organized Labor found itself face to face with a growing and extremely hostile opposition. It was unable to make any noticeable impression on the local situation. In the spring of 1903 there were several strikes in the building trades. The only important result was the organization of the Master Builders' Association and the Master Electrical Contractors' Association. On May 5 about 200 linemen of the telephone, lighting, and power companies struck for the closed shop and higher wages. On June 23, 1,500 linemen of the Pacific States Telephone and Telegraph Company in California, Oregon, Washington, and Arizona struck for similar reasons. In Los Angeles the strike, after dragging on for several months, was finally abandoned. On June 7 the butchers' union struck in an attempt to force Maier's Packing House to operate as a closed shop. The meat cutters' union went out on sympathetic strike, but defeat was again the result. In the Labor Day parade of 1903, seventy-six unions were in the procession. The movement was growing numerically, partly as a result of the presence of national and San Francisco organizers, but its influence and effectiveness were not increasing proportionately. The opposition of the *Times*, the M. & M., and the various employers' associations, together with local public sentiment, was still too powerful a factor in the situation.

In 1904 the Pasadena unions expressed a desire to withdraw from the Los Angeles County Council of Labor and to form their own federation. This provided the occasion for a change in the name of the central council, which on May 19, 1904, was chartered by the American Federation of Labor as the Central Labor Council of Los Angeles. Later, charters were issued to federations in Pasadena, San Pedro, Santa Monica, Long Beach, and Glendale.

From 1905 to 1910 a number of minor labor disputes occurred, but none was of sufficient consequence to record in this place. The year 1910, however, will not soon be forgotten by either the employers or the unions of Los Angeles. During the early months of that year a widespread feeling of discontent was evident among

FRANK B. COLVER

the workers of the city. In March the Mexican laborers of the Los Angeles Pacific Railway and the Los Angeles Railway Company struck for higher wages. The leather workers struck on March 22 for higher wages and shorter hours. On May 19, 454 brewery workers struck for an increased wage. After a long and bitter struggle, the brewery proprietors surrendered to the demands of the union in August, 1911.

In June, 1910, the unions of San Francisco were warned by their employers that, unless they unionized Los Angeles and thus equalized wages and working conditions between the two cities, the open shop would be introduced in San Francisco. With a determination not to sacrifice the principles for which they had fought through so many years, nor the gains which they had won, they made plans to unionize the workers of Los Angeles. To assist their own organizers, they obtained the services of George Gunrey, national organizer of the International Molders' Union. It was deemed advisable first of all to support the metal trades employees who were then on strike. The Metal Trades Council[14] had made demands for the eight-hour day and a minimum wage. The Founders' and Employers' Association had refused to meet with the union representatives or to communicate with them by mail. On May 29, the employees of one small shop had been locked out, and by June 1 every metal trades plant in Los Angeles had either locked out its men or had been struck against. Some 1,200 men were affected. Picketing and occasional acts of violence followed. With the brewery and the metal trades strikes in full swing, the City Council was prevailed upon by the employers' organization to pass an anti-picketing ordinance on July 16. In a short time, more than 470 strikers were arrested for violating its provisions.[15] Injunctions against the strikers were also issued by two of the local judges. Offers to arbitrate the difficulty were refused by the employers. In February, 1911, a small group of brass molders struck, out of sympathy for the ironworkers. The strike and lockout continued until February 26, 1912, when the men returned to work, defeated. The outside organizers went back to their homes, leaving the Metal Trades Council disrupted. It remained a skeleton organization until 1917, when it took on renewed life because of the industrial activity that followed in the wake of the World War.

On the morning of October 1, 1910, the Los Angeles *Times* building was dynamited, with the loss of 21 lives and a property damage of $500,000. The cry was at once raised that the crime was the work of the local unions, which for years had suffered under the vigorous and bitter attacks of the *Times*. A number of local labor leaders were arrested and subjected to the "third degree," but no evidence was uncovered to connect them or the Los Angeles labor movement with the outrage. For some months the search for the guilty parties proved fruitless. On December 25, 1910, the Llewellyn Iron Works was dynamited and certain bits of evidence were then obtained which on April 12, 1911, resulted in the arrest of James B. McNamara and Ortie McManigal. On April 23, John J. McNamara was arrested also. He was a brother of James B. McNamara, and secretary of the International Association of Bridge and Structural Iron Workers, as well as a prominent official in the American Federation of Labor. Throughout the United States and even abroad the cry was raised that the arrested men were innocent; that they had been "framed"; that they were being made "martyrs" to the cause of Labor. The labor and the radical groups of the nation rallied to their support and collected a large defense fund. Clarence Darrow and a staff of able attorneys were employed to defend them. McManigal turned state's evidence. He confessed to having taken part in a number of similar dynamitings in connection with the open-shop fight in other parts of the United States, which had resulted in the loss of 112 lives and property to the value of approximately $7,500,000. In his confession he implicated a number of prominent national labor officials.

While the jury was being chosen to try the McNamara brothers, the leading defense attorney, Clarence Darrow, was accused of attempting, through an agent, to bribe a juror. He was twice tried, but the jury disagreed both times and the charges against him were finally dismissed. Following the accusation of jury tampering, the two McNamaras changed their plea from "not guilty" to "guilty." John J. McNamara was sentenced to fifteen years' imprisonment for complicity in dynamiting the Llewellyn Iron Works, and James B. McNamara was sentenced to life imprisonment for his connection with the *Times* explosion. McManigal, freed because he had turned state's evidence, dropped from sight. In a pamphlet issued by the Los Angeles *Times* under date of October 1, 1929, entitled "The Forty-Year War for a Free City," it is stated that " . . . he is still living in an American city under a different name. . . . About a year ago he was arrested on a minor charge and only quick work on the part of persons acquainted with the facts prevented his identity becoming known."

On the basis of evidence which had been gathered in connection with the McNamara case, the Federal grand jury at Indianapolis brought indictments against fifty-four persons connected with the labor movement of the United States, who were charged with the transportation of dynamite and nitroglycerin on passenger trains for unlawful purposes or with conspiring to cause such violations of Federal laws. Thirty-nine convictions were obtained, and among the convicted men were O. A. Tveitmoe, secretary of the California State Building Trades Council and editor of *Organized Labor,* and E. A. Clancy, business agent of the San Francisco structural steel workers' union. Both were sentenced to six years' imprisonment. On July 3, 1914, a higher Federal court reversed the decision in Tveitmoe's case, and he was granted his freedom. The publicity given to Tveitmoe's connection with the dynamiting group seriously weakened his influence among the trade unionists of California. Although his usefulness was at an end, he retained his official connection with the building trades movement until shortly before his death in 1922.

The arrest of McManigal and the McNamaras made it impossible to carry out effectively the proposal for a general strike in the building trades on May 1, 1911. Only about 300 men struck, 200 of whom returned to work after being out for only a few days. The other hundred were easily replaced by the employers. In September, 1911, a short and unsuccessful strike was declared by the local shopmen of the Southern Pacific railroad and the San Pedro, Los Angeles, and Salt Lake railroad as part of a national strike against the Harriman lines.

In June, 1912, another attempt at a city-wide strike was made by the building trades unions. It was stated that about 20,000 men were engaged in building construction work at the time, but that only 5,000 were unionized. The local labor leaders said that between 1,500 and 2,000 men quit work, but the employers said that not more than 300 artisans were involved. Building activities were not interfered with, and the strike was a failure.

The years 1913–1915 were a period of industrial peace for Los Angeles, only a few minor labor disturbances taking place. In

1915, Samuel Gompers, president of the American Federation of Labor, and a group of professional organizers journeyed to Los Angeles determined to unionize the city. The organizers were most energetic and were partly successful, with the result that 1916 was marked by several serious outbreaks. On April 30 about 300 employees of the California Shipbuilding Company at Long Beach struck for the closed shop and a 25 per cent increase in wages. In a month the strike was lost. On May 29 a strike was called against the Gordon bakery because of a dispute which had arisen between the proprietor and some of his union bakers. Several of the nonunion employees were kidnapped, others suffered manhandling from union sympathizers, and certain acts of violence were committed against the property of the employer. In the end the strike was lost. On June 1, 1916, 12,000 members of the riggers' and stevedores' union struck in all Pacific ports for an increase in wages. More than 1,200 men employed at the Los Angeles harbor were affected. Arbitration was attempted, but was refused by the men because it did not include lumber handlers. Much violence occurred, about sixty assaults by strikers being recorded; but the lumber companies carried on with strike breakers and under police protection, and an injunction restraining acts of violence and picketing was issued by a local judge. By August 4 the local strike was lost, the men returning to work on the open-shop basis.

During the months that the United States was engaged in the World War, Los Angeles was comparatively free from labor troubles. The most serious strike was that of about 700 of the 1,500 employees of the Pacific Electric Railway (a suburban electric railroad system), who made an unsuccessful demand for the closed shop. Armed sailors from United States battleships were put on the cars to keep them running. There were also several small strikes in the local ironworking plants and among the carpenters, mill workers, roofers, icemen, packing house employees, and rattan workers. The demand for the closed shop, where made, was invariably defeated.

On May 2, 1919, the entire day and night crew of the Los Angeles Shipbuilding and Dry Dock Company, which employed some 6,000 men, struck for what actually amounted to the closed shop. The strike dragged on for months. On October 1 the employees of the Long Beach Shipbuilding Company and of the Southwestern Shipbuilding Company struck because their employers refused to grant certain demands relating to hours, wages, and conditions of work. About six weeks later the strike of the shipyard workers collapsed and the men, in a panic, clamored at the gates for their old jobs. In 1919 there were strikes by the tailors, the painters, and the telephone company employees, all of which were defeated. The painters' strike, involving about 1,000 men, began on April 1 and lasted for about six weeks. The telephone strike was called on June 17 as part of a nation-wide attempt to unionize the telephone systems of the country. About 1,200 linemen and switchboard operators went out, but they were forced to acknowledge defeat on July 20. The tailors' strike was intermittent, breaking out, being settled, and breaking out again at various times in the summer months. In November, the difficulty was brought to a conclusion by the employers' conceding a wage increase, although they retained the open shop. On August 16, 1919, about one-half (1,500) of the employees of the Pacific Electric Railway and about one-third (700) of the employees of the Los Angeles street-car company went on strike. On August 21, 800 yardmen, switchmen, and train handlers of the Southern Pacific, Union Pacific, and Santa Fe railroads struck out of sympathy for the employees of the electric transportation companies. The strike was lost.

The labor press of Los Angeles has not had the varied history which has marked that of San Francisco. The labor movement of San Francisco has had a much longer history and that fact by itself explains the many attempts that have been made to establish a labor press. But even so, success, as has already been noted, did not attend those efforts until the *Coast Seamen's Journal* began publication in 1887. In Los Angeles, where the following of Organized Labor has been much less numerous and where at all times the movement has been weaker, very few labor papers have been established. The first of which we have any record was *The Union Printer*, which was issued in 1890. It was followed by the *Los Angeles Workman* in 1891, the *Industrial Age* in 1892,[16] the *California Federationist* in 1894, and the *Labor World* in 1896. The *Labor World* was published by Frank B. Colver, who, from 1888 to 1898, was one of the most prominent figures in the labor movement of Los Angeles.[17] In 1901, L. W. Rogers began the publication of the *Union Labor News*. In 1904 it became *The Citizen*. The Central Labor Council voted to purchase the journal, but a satisfactory arrangement could not be made with its owners. The Union Labor Temple Association, which had been organized to erect and finance the local union headquarters,[18] established its own paper, *The Labor Press*, on January 21, 1916. It was soon discovered, however, that it was unfortunate to have two labor papers dividing the support of the unions. On May 1, 1916, they were merged and continued as *The Los Angeles Citizen* under the ownership and management of the Union Labor Temple Association. On October 1, 1917, the paper was taken over by the Central Labor Council, of which it still remains the official organ.

Following the example set by the building trades unions of San Francisco, the Los Angeles County Building Trades Council and the local District Council of Carpenters decided in 1924 that they would publish their own labor journal, and accordingly started the *Southern California Labor Press*. On February 3, 1928, it was merged with the *Los Angeles Citizen*. The latter is now owned and controlled by the four local councils, namely, the Central Labor Council, the Building Trades Council, the Metal Trades Council, and the Allied Printing Trades Council, which share alike in its management and ownership. It has been ably edited and has been a source of information and inspiration to the labor movement of southern California.

The Los Angeles unions have steadfastly refused to enter politics as a separate party. Beginning in 1911 and for several years thereafter, they supported the Socialist Party municipal candidates, but for some time they have pursued the non-partisan policy advocated by the American Federation of Labor and have merely expressed their preferences for candidates of the parties regularly in the field. In 1923 an effort was made to go into politics by nominating candidates from their own ranks at the primary election of that year, but all these candidates were defeated.

The story of the labor movement of Los Angeles after 1919 is virtually similar to that of the preceding years. There have been continuing and costly attempts to unionize the workers in various occupations, but for the most part with no tangible results. Strikes, usually insignificant in extent, have been called only to be lost because of the overwhelming supply of laborers and the anti-union attitude of employers, the newspapers, and the community. The contest has been, and for some years yet is likely to be, productive of discouraging results for the advocates of collective bargaining. Nevertheless, those who believe in the fundamental principles of Organized Labor still hopefully carry on, remembering Furuseth's rallying cry, "Tomorrow is also a day."

NOTES

NOTES FOR CHAPTER I

¹ Cf. Frank W. Blackmar, *Spanish Institutions of the Southwest*, Johns Hopkins University *Studies* (Baltimore, 1891), X: 85–86; H. E. Bolton, *Fray Juan Crespi* (Berkeley, California, 1927), pp. xvii–xix; C. E. Chapman, *A History of California, the Spanish Period* (New York, 1921), chap. 20; R. G. Cleland, *A History of California, the American Period* (New York, 1922), chap. 3; Robert Greenhow, *The History of Oregon and California and the Other Territories on the Northwest Coast of North America, etc.* (Boston, 1845), pp. 182–183.

² Frank W. Blackmar, *Spanish Colonization in the Southwest*, Johns Hopkins University *Studies* (Baltimore, 1890), VIII:143.

³ See map on p. 5.

⁴ The ruins of many of the missions still remain. The chapels of several have been restored sufficiently to permit the holding of religious services. These relics of the early life of California supply many pictures of beauty and color for artists and innumerable tales of romance for writers of fiction.

⁵ For an excellent description of the mission system, see Blackmar, *Spanish Institutions of the Southwest*, chap. 7.

⁶ For a general description of the life of the padres in their relation to the Indians of California, see H. H. Bancroft, *California Pastoral* (San Francisco, 1888), chap. 6; Fr. Zephyrin Engelhardt, *The Missions and Missionaries of California* (4 vols.; San Francisco, 1912), II, chaps. 15–16; F. Soulé, J. H. Gihon, and J. Nisbet, *Annals of San Francisco* (New York, 1855), chap. 4.

⁷ T. H. Hittell, *History of California* (4 vols.; San Francisco, 1897), I: 728–729, 744.

⁸ Alexander Humboldt, *Political Essay on the Kingdom of New Spain* (4 vols.; London, 1814), IV:301–303, states that in 1802 there were 15,562 neophytes connected with the California missions, of whom 7,945 were males. E. Duflot de Mofras, *Exploration du territoire de l'Orégon, des Californies, et de la mer Vermeille, etc.* (2 vols.; Paris, 1844), I:320–321, states that there were 30,650 Indians connected with the missions in 1834, T. H. Hittell, *op. cit.*, II:207, places the number at 30,000, while H. H. Bancroft, *History of California* (7 vols.; San Francisco, 1886–1890), IV:62, places it at but 15,000. Alexander Forbes, *California, a History of Upper and Lower California* (London, 1839), p. 201, states that in 1831 there were 18,683 Indians in the missions.

⁹ Bancroft, *California Pastoral*, p. 236. Captain F. W. Beechey, *Narrative of a Voyage in the Pacific and Beering's Strait, etc.* (2 vols.; London, 1831), II:18–19, says: "Thus there are in almost every mission [Indian] weavers, tanners, shoemakers, bricklayers, carpenters, blacksmiths, and other artificers. Others again are taught husbandry, to rear cattle and horses; and some cook for the missions; while the females card, clean, and spin wool, weave and sew; and those who are married attend to their domestic concerns."

¹⁰ "About twenty of these artisan instructors were sent to California, chiefly in 1792 and 1795. Their contracts were for four or five years and some of the *maestros* received $1,000 a year, while the journeymen received from $300 to $600. The married ones were given a male and female servant for each family with the understanding that they were to be fed and educated."—Bancroft, *History of California*, I:615–616.

¹¹ In 1791 "we hear of a convict blacksmith teaching the natives at San Francisco. In 1798 the Concepción brought twenty-two convicts. . . . They were

set at work to learn and teach trades."—Bancroft, *History of California,*
I:606. Cf. *ibid.,* pp. 605–607.

¹² Cf. J. F. de G. LaPérouse, *Voyage round the World, 1785–1788* (3 vols.;
London, 1798), II:213, 215–218; W. H. Hudson, *The Famous Missions of California* (New York, 1901), pp. 63–64; J. S. Hittell, *History of San Francisco*
(San Francisco, 1878), p. 55; Blackmar, *Spanish Colonization in the Southwest,* p. 152; Bancroft, *History of California,* II:164; Bancroft, *California
Pastoral,* p. 234; E. Hughes, *The California of the Padres* (San Francisco,
1875), p. 23.

¹³ Some authors maintain that the workday of the neophytes ranged from
six to nine hours, varying with the season and with extra work on special occasions, as at harvest time. The friars, however, affirmed that "working hours
were from four to six hours; that not more than half the natives worked at the
same time, the rest escaping on some reason or pretext, for they were always
excused, even when their plea was doubtful; that many did little even when
pretending to work; that tasks were assigned whenever it was possible, and so
light that the workers were usually free in the afternoon or on a day or two in
every week."—Bancroft, *History of California,* I:591–592.

¹⁴ Duflot de Mofras, *op. cit.,* I:265, states that "les femmes recevaient tous
les ans deux chemmes, une robe, et une couverture."

¹⁵ *Ibid.,* pp. 320–321.

¹⁶ Soulé, Gihon, and Nisbet, *op. cit.,* p. 70.

¹⁷ Forbes, *op. cit.,* p. 220, says, "It is obvious from all this, that these poor
people are in fact slaves under another name." A. Robinson, *Life in California,*
p. 26, in writing of the San Luis Rey Mission, declares that "in the interior of
the square might be seen the various trades at work, presenting a scene not dis-
similar to some of the working departments of our state prisons." In commenting upon the enforced attendance of the Indians at religious services, he writes
that " ... it is not unusual to see numbers of them driven along by alcaldes,
and under the whip's lash forced to the very doors of the sanctuary." Cf. Bancroft, *California Pastoral,* p. 237; Bancroft, *History of California,* I:593;
Beechey, *op. cit.,* II:31–32, 47, 320; Mary Cone, *Two Years in California* (Chicago, 1876), p. 38; Engelhardt, *op. cit.,* II: 27; LaPérouse, *op cit.,* II:
212–213.

¹⁸ Blackmar declares that " ... there has always been a lack of colonizing
material of the right sort in Spain; there has been a lack of that sterling middle class, so useful in all lands, who represent the bone and sinew of all rational
development."—*Spanish Institutions of the Southwest,* p. 84.

¹⁹ *Op. cit.,* II:308.

²⁰ *History of California,* II:158.

²¹ F. Tuthill, *History of California* (San Francisco, 1866), p. 153, asserts
that in 1846 there were 15,000 white people in California.

²² Some authors state that Captain John Sutter frequently acted as an inter-
mediary in supplying, to his friends and others, Indian ranch laborers and domestic servants. Sutter came to California in 1839.

²³ Bancroft, *History of California,* II:415.

²⁴ Bancroft, *California Pastoral,* p. 438. Duflot de Mofras, *op. cit.,* p. 459,
commenting upon the employment of Indian laborers by Sutter, writes that
"maintenant, M. Sutter est en paix avec les Indiens, dont une centaine envi-
ron travaillent chez lui. Ils sont nourris, et reçoivent par jour deux réaux en
marchandises, telles que grains de verre, colliers, mouchoirs, étoffes et autres
articles."

²⁵ Bancroft, *California Pastoral,* pp. 347–348. The following statement from
Blackmar, *Spanish Institutions of the Southwest,* p. 321, is of interest in con-
nection with this matter: "Some of the ranchos were like the old feudal estates.
The ranchero lived like a lord. He had his retainers and servants, his flocks and

herds, as well as great landed estates. The land owned was great in extent, and it was not uncommon for a ranchero to have several thousand horses, ten to fifteen thousand cattle, and from fifteen to twenty thousand sheep."

26 Bancroft, *California Pastoral*, p. 438. "Many Indians of San Diego Mission went to the presidio to sell a variety of small articles and the padres wished them arrested if they had no pass."—Bancroft, *History of California*, II: 420–421, n.

27 Bancroft asserts that in 1840 only 6,000 neophytes remained in the missions.—*History of California*, IV:62. Duflot de Mofras says that there were but 4,450 in 1842. He also comments upon the greatly decreased possessions of the missions.—*Op. cit.*, I:320.

28 T. H. Hittell, *op. cit.*, II:116. Cf. Walter Colton, *Three Years in California* (New York, 1850), p. 21.

29 Bancroft, *California Pastoral*, p. 438.

30 *Ibid.* Cf. Bancroft, *History of California*, II:666; IV:71, 138.

31 L. W. Hastings, *A New Description of Oregon and California* (Cincinnati, 1857), p. 155. Early in 1848 wages in San Francisco ranged from $1 to $3 per day.—*The Californian*, San Francisco, July 15, 1848.

32 San Francisco had a population of about 460 in August, 1847.—*California Star*, San Francisco, March 18, 1848.

33 In commenting upon the penalty imposed by this ordinance, the *California Star* on September 18, 1847, said: "The punishment for desertion of six months labor hardly atones for the disabling effects produced upon the ship-owners and masters, and it is not in our estimation sufficiently checking to the deserter himself. Any worthless fellow, to escape the discipline of the shipboard and exchange a life of confinement for the liberty of the land, would consent to hazard a chance of six months drudgery at the public work."

34 For an account of the ordinance and its enforcement, see two articles by I. B. Cross, "The Sailors of the '49's," *Coast Seamen's Journal*, June 19, 1907, and "First Seamen's Unions," *ibid.*, July 8, 1908.

NOTES FOR CHAPTER II

[1] *The Californian* suspended publication on May 29, 1848, and the *California Star* on June 14, 1848. An observer said, " . . . the blacksmith dropped his hammer, the carpenter his plane, the mason his trowel, the farmer his sickle, the baker his loaf and the tapster his bottle. All went off to the mines, some on horses, some on carts, and some on crutches, and one went in a litter."—Colton, *op. cit.,* p. 247. Cf. *ibid.,* pp. 247–255.

[2] T. H. Hittell, *op. cit.,* II:689.

[3] T. O. Larkin, naval agent at San Francisco, under date of June 1, 1848, wrote to the Secretary of State at Washington: "Clerks' wages have risen from $600 to $1000 per annum and board." Quoted by F. Robinson, *California and Its Gold Regions, etc.* (New York, 1849), p. 19.

[4] T. H. Hittell, *op. cit.,* II:700, estimates that 3,000 sailors deserted at San Francisco in 1849. "Sailors who have $400 or $500 due them forfeit the whole and escape to the mines."—J. E. Sherwood, *California, Her Wealth and Resources* (New York, 1848), p. 29. In July, 1849, five hundred vessels were anchored in the harbor of San Francisco, having been deserted by their crews.—Bancroft, *History of California,* VII:125.

[5] "Sailors' wages were two and three hundred dollars per month."—J. D. Borthwick, *Three Years in California* (London, 1857), p. 66.

[6] Cf. especially the Rev. W. Taylor, *Seven Years' Street Preaching in San Francisco* (New York, 1857), chap. 44.

[7] For a history of the sailors' organizations, see I. B. Cross, "First Seamen's Unions," *Coast Seamen's Journal,* July 8, 1908; P. S. Taylor, *The Sailors' Union of the Pacific Coast* (New York, 1923).

[8] "From the sunny climes of Spain and Italy, from the fairylands of Persia and Arabia, from the regions of snow and ice in Norway and Russia, from the corn and vinelands of pleasant France, from the British Isles and colonies, from the green South America, from the imperial dominions of the near relative of the sun and moon, and from the golden islands of the Pacific, have they come in myriads to California. In our streets the fair European jostles with the swarthy Kanaka or the darker Hindoo; the pious Mussulman says his daily prayers as he passes the churches of the Christian; the calculating German drives hard bargains with the volatile French, and the stiff-made Yankee daily deals with the long-tailed Chinaman. Such an *omnium gatherum* of humanity has never before been witnessed in the world's history."—*Alta California,* San Francisco, February 7, 1851. Cf. especially a series of articles on the Jews, French, Germans, Spanish, Peruvians, and Chileans which appeared in the *Alta California,* December 11, 1851, May 13, 16, 22, 24, 1853. San Francisco still remains a most cosmopolitan city. "Every country on the globe, every state and principality, almost every island of the sea, finds here its representatives."—*Sunset Magazine,* XXV:612.

[9] In 1849, 35,000 came by sea and 42,000 by land. In 1850, 27,000 came by sea and 55,000 by land. In 1851, 27,000 came by sea; and in 1852, 66,000 arrived by the same route. In 1852, 23,000 left the State. In 1853, 33,000 came by sea, and 55,000 by land, although during the same year 31,000 returned by sea. In 1854, 48,000 came by sea. Cf. J. S. Hittell, *op. cit.,* pp. 139–140, 216; Bancroft, *History of California,* VII:696, n.; T. H. Hittell, *op. cit.,* II:700, III: 403; Tuthill, *op. cit.,* p. 357.

[10] Prices in the fall and winter of 1848: flour, $25–$27 per bbl.; wheat, $4 per bu.; beef, $20 per bbl.; pork, $60 per bbl.; sugar, 20–25 cents per lb.— Bancroft, *History of California,* VII:103, n. Dried beef, 50 cents per lb.; coffee, 50 cents per lb.; shovels, $10 each; tin pans, $5 each; crowbars, $10

each; common shirts, $5 each; flannel shirts, $5 each; boots, $16.—E. G. Buffum, *Six Months in the Gold Mines* (Philadelphia, 1850), pp. xxiii–xxiv.

11 "There were comparatively few miners at the end of their first two years in California who had $1,000 laid by."—H. H. Bancroft, *Inter Pocula* (San Francisco, 1888), p. 230.

12 Bancroft, *History of California*, VI:424.

13 Cf. T. H. Hittell, *op. cit.*, III, chaps. 1–9, for an excellent description of the life of the early miners; also Bancroft, *History of California*, VI, chap. 16.

14 Sutter took 100 Indians and 50 Hawaiians into the diggings with him, but his venture proved to be unsuccessful because of their fondness for liquor.—*Hutching's Illustrated Magazine*, II:194–198.

15 Borthwick, *op. cit.*, pp. 163–164.

NOTE.—California was especially fortunate with respect to Negro slavery. The industries of the State were not suited to Negro labor, and therefore slavery never became a question of any importance. The Constitution of the State, adopted in 1849, provided: "Neither slavery nor involuntary servitude, unless for punishment of crime, shall ever be tolerated in this State." In spite of this prohibitory clause, evidence gathered from many sources "proves that many Negroes continued in the state of slavery in California for shorter or longer periods after 1849. In unusual instances this involuntary servitude seems to have persisted even until the period of national emancipation."—C. A. Duniway, *Annual Report of the American Historical Association* (1905), I:244.

The following advertisement appeared in the Sacramento *Transcript*, April 1, 1850:

TO FAMILIES

For Sale—A valuable NEGRO GIRL aged eighteen, bound by indentures for two years. Said girl is of amiable disposition, a good washer, ironer, and cook. For particulars apply at the Vanderbilt Hotel of
J. R. HARPER.

The slavery question was brought before the legislature at various times as a result of messages submitted by the governors, bills introduced by the legislators, and petitions presented by the Negro population of the State, but no action worth noting was taken, other than the passage of a bill on April 15, 1852, the fourth section of which was especially pro-slavery.—*Assembly Journal*, 3 Sess., pp. 95, 146, 147; *Senate Journal*, 3 Sess., pp. 257, 274–285; *Cal. Stats.*, 1852, p. 77. It declared that all slaves brought into the State previous to the adoption of the Constitution, who refused to return with their masters to the state in which they owed labor, should be deemed to be fugitives from labor, and that the owners were to be given power to reclaim them in the same way as was provided for the recovery of such fugitives entering California from any other state. In several cases tried before the State courts in the fifties it was held that slavery in California was a legal institution. One of the more important decisions was that of the State Supreme Court in October, 1852, *In re Perkins* (2 Cal. 424). Perkins had come to California in 1849, and had brought three slaves with him to work in the mines. Later, when he wished to return to his native state, the Negroes refused to accompany him. The case was subsequently carried to the State Supreme Court, which held that he could compel the slaves to return with him. Another case of importance, *Ex parte Archy* (9 Cal. 147), was decided by the State Supreme Court in 1858. In that case the court held that the master, not having acquired a domicile in California, was entitled as a visitor or traveler to hold his slave while temporarily residing within the State or to remove him if he (the master) wished to go elsewhere.

The best discussion of the subject of slavery in California is to be found in Lucile Eaves, *A History of California Labor Legislation* (Berkeley, California, 1910), chap. 2.

16 *Evening Bulletin*, San Francisco, January 7, 1860.

17 "Kanakas get $1.00 an hour for the commonest of labor; mechanics from $8 to $10 per day; clerks and salesmen as high as $2,500 [per year] with board; head waiter in one of the hotels, $1,500 a year; other waiters, $1,200 to $1,500."—Letter from J. L. Folsom, dated October, 1848, published in the New York *Journal of Commerce*, December 27, 1848. Cooks' wages were $300 per month.—Bancroft, *History of California*, VI:64. "Rather an anomaly is now presented in this territory in the relative conditions of men. The capitalist is in reality the least independent of persons among us, and the laboring man is the one most sought after and respected. This state of affairs extends into all occupations and trades."—*The Californian*, October 7, 1848.

18 "There are a large number of laborers here [October, 1848], but many refuse to work on any terms, while those who labor do so at exorbitant rates."—Folsom, *loc. cit.* "The prices paid for labor [August, 1849] were in proportion to everything else. The carman of Mellus, Howard and Co. had a salary of $6,000 a year and many others made from $15 to $20 daily. Servants were paid from $100 to $200 a month, but the wages of the rougher kinds of labor had fallen to about $8. Yet notwithstanding the number of gold miners who were returning enfeebled and disheartened from the mines, it was difficult to obtain as many workmen as the enforced growth of the city demanded."—Bayard Taylor, *Eldorado* (New York, 1850), I:58. At Benicia in 1849 the government paid laborers $16 per day. Sailors received $150–$200 per month.—Bancroft, *History of California*, VI:110. Carpenters, tinsmiths, bricklayers, paperhangers, and other building-trades men got from $12 to $20 per day.—Buffum, *op. cit.*, p. 121. Men received $10 per day pushing a wheelbarrow.—Walter Colton, *Deck and Port* (New York, 1850), p. 401. In 1849–1850 rough labor received $8 per day, carmen $15–$20, domestics $100–$200 a month.—Tuthill, *op. cit.*, p. 329. Doctors received $32 for a single visit, and, for each hour detained, $32 additional; advice, $50–$100; night visits, $100; operations, $500–$1,000.—Bancroft, *Inter Pocula*, p. 351. At Stockton [December, 1849] common labor received $5–$10 per day, and mechanics $10–$16.—J. H. Audubon, *Western Journal* (Cleveland, 1906), pp. 189–190.

19 "The winter [1849–1850] having set in, thousands were returning sick and impoverished from the mines. The arrival of so many laborers soon affected the rate of wages, and the points were daily crowded with men unable to obtain work.

"As this influx of labor caused a great diminution of wages, the prices of provisions remaining the same, discontent and indignation prevailed among the lower orders, and nightly meetings took place, attended by crowds of the rabble, ripe for pillage or riot, but luckily without a leader.... Violent speeches were made, and secret leagues formed in every quarter, and had an O'Connell arisen from amongst them, order might have been subverted and terms dictated by the mob to the storekeepers and houselords; as it was, these meetings ended in furious tirades forbidding foreigners to seek employment, or people to hire them, accusing foreigners of being the cause of a fall in wages, and holding out a deadly threat to all who dared labor under the fixed rate of payment, ten dollars per day.

"These nocturnal assemblies had in them something appalling, being composed of between three hundred and one thousand cut-throats, armed with bowie-knives and fire-arms, and often intoxicated.... Both master and men felt themselves subject to an inquisition and control making them fearful of entering into any contracts together lest they should be betrayed or endangered; consequently workingmen, who would have willingly worked for a reasonable sum, were almost destitute for want of employment and nigh starving, being deterred from engaging themselves at lower wages by a mob of malcontents, the majority of whom could not or would not work under the fixed rate. ... The detention of crews on shipboard was another grievance which the mob took upon themselves to redress by rowing out and delivering the men from captivity. . . . There was a high cliff near Miller's Point, which I carefully avoided at night, as from this Tarpeian Rock three poor fellows had been hurled who had worked under wages or were suspected of having done so."— William Shaw, *Golden Dreams and Waking Realities* (London, 1851), pp. 170–175.

20 1849. Shave and haircut, $4.—Colton, *Deck and Port*, p. 395. 1849–1850. Beefsteak and cup of coffee, $1; eggs, 75 cents to $1 each; washing, $8 per dozen pieces.—Tuthill, *op. cit.*, p. 326. "Towards winter [1849–1850] the price of board rose from $20 to $35 per week. A moderate charge for board and lodging was $150 per month. . . . Rooms at ordinary hotels cost from $25 to $100 per week."—Bancroft, *History of California*, VI:191, n. Boarding varied from $25 to $80 per week.—Shaw, *op cit.*, p. 168. Potatoes cost $16 per bu.; turnips and onions, 25–62 cents each.—T. B. King, *California, its Population, Climate, etc.* (London, 1850), p. 74. May, 1850. Flour cost $6.50 per cwt.; bread, 2–9 cents per lb.; rice, 8 cents per lb.; jerked beef, 2½–5 cents per lb.; mess beef, $14–$16 per bbl.; pork, $25–$35 per bbl.; coffee, 28 cents per lb.; sugar, 27–50 cents per lb.—Bancroft, *History of California*, VII:106, n. At Stockton, the prices in December, 1849, were: flour, $40 per bbl.; pork, $65 per bbl.; pilot bread, 20 cents per lb.; rubber boots, $50–$60 per pair; flannel shirts, $6–$8 each; shot, 30 cents per lb.; powder, $1–$1.50 per lb.; tents, $40; washing and ironing, $6 per dozen pieces; board, $3–$6 per day without lodging.—Audubon, *op. cit.*, p. 189. Real estate in 1849 advanced from five to ten times its former price.—*Evening Bulletin*, April 22, 1877.

21 At certain times in 1849 and 1850, employment in the building trades of San Francisco was plentiful, because of the destruction wrought by the fires of those years. On December 24, 1849, property valued at $1,000,000 was destroyed, while on May 4 and June 14, 1850, fires again caused estimated losses of from $3,000,000 to $4,000,000. Smaller conflagrations occurred on September 14, October 31, and December 14, 1850.—Soulé, Gihon, and Nisbet, *op. cit.*, pp. 598–603.

22 The outcome of this strike, as well as that of many others mentioned in this study, is not known. It is seldom that newspapers and other sources of information enable one to trace such events to their conclusion.

23 Somewhat later its name was changed to The Pacific Typographical Society.—*Alta California*, November 5, 1853.

24 *Ibid.*, June 24, 1850. It must have been organized only a short time before that date, because the officers who signed the announcement attached the phrase "pro tem." to their office. The temporary officers mentioned in the notice were A. Skillman, chairman, and H. C. Williston, secretary. Ben F. Foster as president and B. H. Monson as secretary were the first regularly chosen officers of the union.—*Ibid.*, July 27, 1850. A short time after its organization it was said to have about seventy members.

25 The *Ninth Biennial Report, California Bureau of Labor Statistics, 1899–1900*, p. 111, says that the Amalgamated Society of Engineers established a branch in San Francisco in 1850. I have found no trace of the association at that early date.

26 Some of the printers slept in the composing rooms and were charged $8 per week for the privilege. For data and reminiscences concerning the pioneer printers of San Francisco, see *The Pacific Union Printer*, San Francisco, April, 1899, June, July, 1890; *The Labor Clarion*, San Francisco, December 18, 1908; *Alta California*, July 1, 1852, November 5, 1853.

27 *Alta California*, July 13, 1850.

28 The boatmen manned the scows and lighters used in transporting passengers and cargoes from the ships to the shore.—*Alta California*, October 26, 27, 1850, February 8, July 6, 1851.

29 Bancroft, *History of California*, VII:110, n., makes mention of a strike in 1850 by the masons of San Francisco, for an increase in their wages from $12 per day to $14. I have been unable to find any data bearing upon the matter.

30 The sailors boarded some of the vessels and drove off men who had agreed to ship for lower wages.—*Alta California*, August 12, 1850.

31 On the anti-foreigner movement see especially J. Royce, *California* (New York, 1886), pp. 356–368; T. H. Hittell, *op. cit.*, III:262–265, 705–711; J. S. Hittell, *op. cit.*, pp. 185–187; Bancroft, *History of California*, VI:402–408; Bancroft, *Inter Pocula*, pp. 232–236; C. H. Shinn, *Mining Camps* (New York, 1885), chap. 18; Mary R. Coolidge, *Chinese Immigration* (New York, 1909), chap. 2. The last-mentioned volume contains a wealth of valuable data on the Chinese question.

32 T. H. Hittell, *op. cit.*, III:706.

33 The situation would have been sufficiently regrettable had only the native Americans taken part in the agitation against the darker-skinned foreigners, but the leaders in the movement were generally Irish, Germans, and English, who themselves had been only a short time in America.

34 In this brief sketch of the "anti-foreigner movement," the word "foreigner" will be used to designate the darker-skinned races against whom the movement was directed.

35 *Cal. Stats.*, 1850, pp. 221–223.

36 One of the bills posted on the trees in the diggings near Columbia carried the following:

"NOTICE: It is time to unite: Frenchmen, Chileans, Peruvians, Mexicans, there is the highest necessity of putting an end to the vexations of the Americans in California. If you do not intend to allow yourselves to be fleeced by a band of miserable fellows who are repudiated by their own country, then unite and go to the camp of Sonora next Sunday: there will we try to guarantee security for us all, and put a bridle in the mouths of that horde who call themselves citizens of the United States, thereby profaning that country."—*Alta California*, May 28, 1850.

37 A large number of the Latin people went into gardening.—Bancroft, *History of California*, VII:28–29. Many Frenchmen joined the filibustering expeditions into Sonora, Mexico, in 1851–1852.—T. H. Hittell, *op. cit.*, III:727. "We infer with tolerable certainty that from fifteen to twenty thousand Mexicans, and perhaps an equal number of Chileans, are now leaving or preparing to leave California for their own country."—*Daily Evening Picayune*, August 14, 1850. "The Mexicans who a few months ago crowded to the mines by the thousands have mostly packed their mules and started back to their own country. . . . The Chileans also have been gradually disappearing, being taken back free in vessels chartered by their government."—L. Kip, *California Sketches* (Albany, 1850), p. 56.

38 *Cal. Stats.*, 1851, p. 424.

39 *Ibid.*, 1852, p. 84. Approved May 4, 1852.

40 *Ibid.*, 1853, p. 62. Approved March 30, 1853.

41 *Ibid.*, 1855, pp. 216–217. Thus for the first year the law decreed a rate of $6 per month, for the second year $8 per month, for the third year $10 per month, etc.

42 *Ibid.*, 1856, p. 141. "The income from the Foreigner Miners' licenses in the decade from 1854 to 1865, amounted to one-eighth, and for the whole period from 1850 to 1870, to one-half of the total income of the State from all sources."—Coolidge, *op. cit.*, p. 36. Coolidge states that the revenue yielded by the tax totaled $5,094,078.42.—*Ibid.*, p. 37.

43 Cf. Coolidge, *op. cit.*, pp. 498–500, for statistics on Chinese immigration and emigration.

NOTES FOR CHAPTER III

1 Tuthill, *op. cit.*, p. 325.

2 I. B. Cross, *History of Banking in California* (2 vols.; Chicago, 1927), I:92.

3 Soulé, Gihon, and Nisbet, *op. cit.*, p. 366, say that "in 1850 real estate was assessed at the value of $16,849,024; while in 1851 it was only $10,518,273; and this notwithstanding the vast improvements that had taken place in the interval."

4 The *Evening Bulletin*, April 21, 1877, places the loss at $15,000,000.

5 "One would scarcely believe it possible in this golden land where every ravine and hillside is full of treasure, that so many persons were to be found entirely out of employment."—*Alta California*, August 20, 1851.

6 *Ibid.*, October 12, 1851.

7 From the data at hand it does not appear that these workers attempted a formal organization at that time.

8 C. D. Murray and C. H. Bailey, respectively, were president and secretary of the Teamsters' and Draymen's Association of San Francisco in 1851.—*Ibid.*, July 1, 1851.

9 *Ibid.*, May 13, August 1, 1852.

10 The *Alta California* of August 4, 1852, mentions the following organizations that were to participate in the ceremonies held in San Francisco to pay "the last sad tribute of respect to the memory of Henry Clay": boatmen, draymen, lightermen, Pacific Typographical Union, and mechanics.

11 J. B. De Voe was president of the association.—*Alta California*, March 7, 1852.

12 *Ibid.*, February 12, 1853.

13 *Democratic State Journal*, Sacramento, May 30, 1853. Cf. *Ibid.*, June 4, 1853.

14 It is estimated that in 1852–1853 approximately 54,000 persons left the State.

15 Bancroft, *History of California*, VI:782–783.

16 The following table of wages paid in San Francisco is merely an estimate compiled by George Gordon, of the Vulcan Iron Works of that city, and published in the *Alta California* of March 3, 1853. It is probably inaccurate in some items. Seamen, $45–$55 per month; carpenters and machinists, $5–$7 per day; blacksmiths, $1,000–$1,500 per year with board; bricklayers and masons, $6–$9 per day; printers, $1.50 per 1,000 ems; pressmen, $10–$12 per day; female cooks, $600–$800 per year; housemaids, $500–$700 per year; laundresses, $600–$900 per year; nursemaids, $400–$600 per year. The *Alta California* of May 2, 1853, published the following rates of wages: printers, $1.50 per 1,000 ems; carpenters, joiners, shipwrights, caulkers, patternmakers, engineers, molders, machinists, $7 per day; wagonmakers, wood turners, coopers, $4–$6 per day; sawyers, stonecutters, plasterers, cart with horse and driver, $8 per day; brass founders, millers, $6 per day; bricklayers, $8–$10 per day; tinners, $4–$8 per day; blasters, shoemakers, tailors, common laborers, $4 per day; painters, paperhangers, $5 per day; jewelers, lapidaries, $9 per day; musicians, $20 per day; teamsters, hack and stage drivers, brewers with board, $100 per month; gardeners, $60 per month; cooks, $60–$100 per month; housemaids, $35–$70 per month; waiters, sewing women, chambermaids, $40–$70 per month; nurses, $40 per month and board. Soulé, Gihon, and Nisbet, *op cit.*, p. 459, give the following scale of wages as prevailing in July and August, 1853: bricklayers, stonecutters, ship carpenters and caulkers, $10 per day; plasterers, $9 per day; carpenters, blacksmiths, and watchmakers, $8 per day; tinners and

hatters, $7 per day; painters and glaziers, and longshoremen, $6 per day; tenders, $5 per day; tailors, $4 per day; shoemakers, $100 per month without board; teamsters, $100–$120 per month without board; steamship firemen, $100 per month; coal passers, $75 per month; farm hands, $50 per month with board.

17 C. C. Plehn, *Yale Review*, IV: 420, says: "The Hat Finishers' Union of San Francisco is said to date from 1853." I have found no trace of the existence of that association prior to 1857.

18 The following strikes occurred in San Francisco in the summer months of 1853: In June and August the employees of the Mountain Lake Water Company, engaged in digging ditches and laying pipes for San Francisco's first water supply, struck unsuccessfully for an increase in wages. The hodcarriers demanded and obtained $6 per day. The carpenters demanded $8 per day; 400 of them paraded the streets; the strike lasted several weeks, and was finally won. The coopers demanded an increase in wages. The longshoremen struck successfully for $6 per day and a nine-hour day with $1 per hour for overtime. The shipwrights and caulkers obtained $10 per day. The steamboat firemen struck for $100 per month, and the coal passers for $75 per month. The blacksmiths struck for $8 per day, the plasterers for $10 per day, the tinners for $8 per day, the bricklayers for $12 per day, and the stonecutters for $10 per day.

19 The bricklayers of Sacramento struck successfully for $10 per day in July, and in September were able to prevent a reduction to $8 per day. In August the hodcarriers of that city demanded $6 per day, the plasterers $10 per day, and the street workers $75 per month, an advance of $25.

20 In August the carpenters of Marysville struck for and obtained $8 per day.

21 In August the hodcarriers of Stockton struck unsuccessfully for $6 per day, an increase of $1.

22 The *Alta California* of August 2, 1853, in discussing an attack made upon a group of workers by a band of strikers, said, "This is not the first time that violence has been used and threatened by the strikers, and it is high time that something be done to preserve a little better order for the future." On August 14, 1853, it announced, "This is a free country, and every man that wants to work for nothing and board himself has a perfect right to do so in peace."

In the closing months of 1853 an agitation was begun in San Francisco looking toward the reduction of the wages of domestic servants. For some years thereafter, frequent mention is made of this matter in the newspapers. The presence of the Chinese, and, in later years, of the Japanese, helped somewhat to solve, but not completely, the servant problem for the Californians. See especially the *Alta California*, November 12, 1853; *California Daily Chronicle*, June 27, 1857; *Evening Bulletin*, various issues of February, 1862.

23 *Alta California*, July 1, 1852.

24 James O'Meara, "Pioneer Printers," *Pacific Union Printer*, June, 1890.

25 The San Francisco Typographical Society survived until January, 1854.

26 Alexander M. Kenaday was president, and William Jauncey secretary, of the union at the time it received its national charter.

27 "Carried away by the hallucinations of the brilliant days of '49–'50, and the exorbitant rents of houses of every kind, the city has been extended beyond its natural wants, both in the number of its buildings and the extent of its population, many of the latter being without employment."—*Evening Bulletin*, January 2, 1857. Out of 1,000 buildings, at least 300 were unoccupied.— J. S. Hittell, *op. cit.*, p. 217.

28 Cross, *History of Banking in California*, I:181–197.

29 The *Evening Bulletin* of December 30, 1859, published the following "Insolvent Calendar":

Year	Number	Liabilities	Assets
1855	197	$8,377,827.00	$1,519,175.00
1856	146	3,401,042.00	657,908.00
1857	128	2,696,865.00	264,707.00
1858	94	1,609,534.00	70,603.00
1859	56	827,641.00	96,831.00

30 The *Evening Bulletin*, January 4, 1858, gives an excellent sketch of "The Present Conditions of Our Mining Population," and presents a detailed historical review of mining methods that had been used in California up to that date.

31 Bancroft, *History of California*, VII:114.

32 J. S. Hittell, *op. cit.*, p. 217.

33 For an excellent statement concerning gold rushes and their influence upon California life, see J. S. Hittell, "The Mining Excitements of California," *Overland Monthly*, II:413 ff.

34 In 1854, common laborers received $3 per day, while artisans were paid $5–$6 per day. In January, 1855, the daily wages for carpenters were $6 per day; for masons, $8; for laborers, $3. Deckhands received $60 per month. In 1856, masons received $4–$5 per day; carpenters, $4–$5; laborers, $2–$2.50; deckhands, $40–$50 per month, and sailors $20 per month. Wages in the mines were $35 per month with board. In 1857 the average pay of laborers in San Francisco was $2.25 per day, with employment hard to get. Ranch hands received $30 per month and board.

35 There were very few wells in San Francisco, and for some years after the gold rush all the city's water had to be carted in from near-by springs. Water was sold by the watermen at about $1 per cask. A cask was sufficient for the needs of an ordinary family for a week. In 1856, although San Francisco had a water system, some sections of the community still relied upon the service of the watermen. Cf. Isabelle Saxon, *Five Years within the Golden Gate* (Philadelphia, 1868), pp. 107–108.

36 In 1857 the *Morning Call* frequently took occasion to encourage the formation of unions among the various crafts. In its issue of December 8, 1857, it declared that "it is only through combinations that labor can expect to succeed in the contest with capital, and to that end a thorough and complete union should be effected throughout all branches of industry." Langley's *Directory of San Francisco*, 1858, gives the following information concerning the unions then in existence in that city: Coopers' Association, organized August 4, 1857; Eureka Typographical Union, organized November 24, 1854; Hatters' Association, organized in 1857; Journeymen House Painters' Benevolent and Protective Society, organized in October, 1857, 52 members; Riggers' and Stevedores' Association, organized July 25, 1853; Ship Caulkers' Association, organized February 9, 1857; Journeymen Shipwrights' Association, organized April 26, 1857, 86 members; Ship and Steamboat Joiners' Association, organized March 21, 1857.

37 Strikes in 1854: The hodcarriers and helpers of Sacramento on July 25 demanded an increase in wages from $5 to $6 per day. The printers of San Jose struck for higher wages in January.

Strikes in 1855: In San Francisco, the sailors in March, the stevedores in April, and the longshoremen in August all demanded higher wages.

Strikes in 1856: In July the longshoremen of San Francisco again struck for higher wages.

Strikes in 1857: In September the ballastmen in San Francisco struck for $4 per day; in May the brickmakers of Sacramento struck for an increase of $10 per month; and in December the miners at Monte Cristo, Sierra County, struck against a reduction in wages.

[38] For an excellent discussion of the campaign waged against convict labor in California see Eaves, *op. cit.*, chap. 15.

[39] The sailors were successful in obtaining wages ranging from $30 to $50 per month.

[40] Half the draymen of San Francisco had departed for the Fraser River. Whereas they had formerly been getting $40 per month, "they now get $100 and are hard to obtain at that."—*Morning Call*, June 24, 1858.

[41] The wages of the sawmill and planing mill employees were increased by $1 per day.—*Morning Call*, June 9, 1858.

[42] The tinners organized a union and demanded a 20 to 30 per cent increase in wages. The union also provided sick and death benefits.—*Ibid.*, June 18, 1858.

[43] The *Evening Bulletin* of January 11, 1870, said that "business was excellent in 1858 and improved steadily until 1863."

[44] The reorganization of the printers' union was accomplished primarily through the efforts of George H. Pettis. The officers chosen were as follows: president, A. D. Jones; recording secretary, G. H. Pettis; corresponding secretary, H. Havelock; treasurer, P. J. Thomas.

[45] This organization was the first Pacific Coast union to send a delegate to a national convention of any craft; the delegate was Jeremiah Gray, and he was sent in 1861.

[46] *Cal. Stats.*, 1850, pp. 211–213. The law was not satisfactory, and was later amended. *Ibid.*, 1853, pp. 202–203; 1855, pp. 156–159; 1857, p. 84; 1858, pp. 225–227. Eaves, *op. cit.*, chap. 8, presents an excellent discussion of "The Laws for the Protection of the Wages of Labor" in California.

[47] *Cal. Stats.*, 1853, p. 187.

[48] Children were employed in the cigar factories of San Francisco as early as 1851.

[49] The *Morning Call* of December 22, 1857, editorially took a vigorous stand against what it called "a stimulated population that would cast upon our shores thousands of workmen, who would be compelled to enter into competition with those already here, and the result of which would be an undue depression in the price of labor."

NOTES FOR CHAPTER IV

¹ The organization of stock companies for the purpose of exploiting mining properties did not come into practice in California until the Comstock lode excitement in the later fifties. From 1860 to 1863, these companies multiplied in number out of all proportion to the needs of the situation. In 1863 "more than 3,000 companies were incorporated . . . in California and adjacent territories, for the ostensible prosecution of mining enterprise, to say nothing of a still larger number formed under the regulations of the various districts for the same purpose."—*Evening Bulletin*, January 11, 1865.

² *Ibid.*, January 11, 12, 1865.

³ In 1864 more than 1,000 houses and stores were built in San Francisco.—*Evening Bulletin*, October 21, 1864.

⁴ *Ibid.*, January 11, 1870.

⁵ 1860. The draymen and cartmen reorganized in March. Unions existed in the following trades: printers, journeymen ship carpenters and caulkers, riggers and stevedores, and cigarmakers. In August, 1860, the laborers employed in the construction of the San Francisco gas factory struck successfully for a ten-hour day. In the same month, day laborers employed in leveling some of the sandhills of San Francisco were not successful in making the same demand.

1861. Unions existed in the following crafts: ship joiners, ship carpenters, shipwrights and caulkers, teamsters, riggers and stevedores, draymen and cartmen, printers, plasterers, coopers, cigarmakers, hodcarriers, and hairdressers. In November, 1861, the plasterers of San Francisco struck successfully for $5 per day. On several jobs the day laborers of that city also struck for higher wages. Sometimes they were successful, sometimes not.

1862. Notices appearing in the local press and in Langley's *Directory of San Francisco*, 1862–1863, give evidence of the existence of unions in the following trades in San Francisco in 1862: cigarmakers, hackmen, hodcarriers, draymen, teamsters, riggers and stevedores, watermen, plasterers, printers, hat finishers, coopers, shipwrights and caulkers, and ship and steamboat joiners. *The Printer*, New York, November, 1862, has a letter from San Francisco, dated September 25, 1862, in which it is stated that the printers' union of San Francisco had 165 members at that time, that of Sacramento about 60, and that of Stockton about 25. Sacramento Typographical Union, No. 46, had been chartered November 12, 1859. It is also stated that a typographical union existed in Los Angeles in 1860.

⁶ About fifty men were said to be employed in the coopers' shop of the state prison at San Quentin in June, 1862.—*Alta California*, June 6, 1862.

⁷ *Daily Herald*, July 18, 1861.

⁸ The immediate cause for the organization of the bakers was a request on their part for a twelve-hour day, the abolition of Sunday work, and an increase in wages. The wages demanded were $85–$90 per month for ordinary journeymen, an increase of $30 per month, and $120 per month for foremen and superior journeymen, an increase of $45. The demands were granted.

⁹ Eaves, *op. cit.*, p. 11, says that "as this organization was conducted as a secret society, it is difficult to find contemporary information about it. . . . John M. Days, a state senator, was the first president of this Trades' Union. He was succeeded by A. M. Kenaday, who had been secretary." The fact that notices of the meetings and reports of its activities appeared regularly in the San Francisco papers seems to be sufficient evidence that it was not so secret as Miss Eaves would have us believe. The first president of the Trades' Union was J. M. McCreary, and not Senator J. M. Days; Days was not a resident of San Francisco until 1872. The second president of the organization was John A. Russell. A. M. Kenaday was its third president. The source of information from which

Miss Eaves drew her data was undoubtedly the inaccurate article which appeared originally in the San Francisco *Daily Report* of May 11, 1886.

10 *Evening Bulletin*, January 28, 1864.

11 The *Morning Call* under date of February 23, 1864, said that the legislature would undoubtedly have repealed the Specific Contract Law had it not been for the petition of the Trades' Union.

12 The *Alta California* of June 2, 1868, said that "the Trades' Union devoted all its energies to the passage of a mechanics' lien law in which it failed." This is inaccurate, for the published reports of the activities of the Trades' Union seldom refer to an interest in a mechanics' lien law.

13 In January, 1866, only seven unions were represented in the San Francisco Trades' Union.

14 "Striking seems to be much in fashion in New York, Philadelphia, and Boston."—*Evening Bulletin*, December 11, 1863.

15 Commons and Andrews, "Labor Movement, 1860–1880," in J. R. Commons, V. B. Phillips, E. A. Gilmore, and J. B. Andrews, *A Documentary History of American Industrial Society* (10 vols.; Cleveland, 1910), IX:22–23.

16 *Ibid.*, p. 23.

17 Some of the less important strikes were as follows:

1863. In November the bricklayers demanded an hour for lunch. In June the laborers employed in laying street-car rails on Folsom Street struck for a ten-hour day. The contractor had insisted on eleven hours. The men employed by the Federal government on construction work at Fort Point struck in June against a reduction of wages.

1864. In April the ship and steamboat joiners demanded $5 for a nine-hour day on old work, and $4.50 on new work, and the painters struck for double pay for overtime and for Sunday work. In October the printers "ratted" the offices of the *Argus* and the *Daily American Flag* for paying less than the customary wage scale.

1865. In March the hotel waiters struck against a reduction in wages, and the boilermakers of Donahue, Booth & Company demanded higher wages.

18 The hotel waiters demanded and obtained $40 per month and board, an increase of $10 per month. The restaurant waiters demanded $50 per month and board. The employers were not willing to grant the increase and formed a "Restaurant Proprietors' Association" to oppose the Waiters' Union Benevolent Society.

19 The Grooms' Society had a membership of 240 at that time. The treasurer of the society attempted to abscond with the funds of the strikers, approximately $500, but was caught before boarding a steamer for Panama.

20 Cf. Eaves, *op. cit.*, pp. 198–215.

21 Commons and Andrews, *op. cit.*, p. 277.

22 Alexander M. Kenaday was born of Irish parentage at Wheeling, Virginia, on December 8, 1824. Somewhat later his parents moved to St. Louis, where he learned the trade of a printer. After spending some months in a Jesuit college, he gave up his studies and worked on a Mississippi River steamboat. He enlisted in the United States Army at the time of the Mexican War and distinguished himself by reckless daring and bravery under fire, for which he was promoted to the rank of sergeant. After the war, he returned to New Orleans, but when the news of the discovery of gold reached that city, he set out for California. He met with no success in the placer mines, and finally returned to San Francisco, where he worked at his trade. He assisted in organizing the Typographical Union, and later served as its president. In 1861 he married a Miss Conniff, of New York. In 1863 he took an active part in the formation of the San Francisco Trades' Union, and was subsequently chosen its president. It was while serving in the latter capacity that he began the agitation for the eight-hour day. Shortly thereafter he published the first labor

paper on the Pacific Coast, *The Journal of Trades and Workingmen*. In 1866 he was instrumental in bringing about the formation of a local society of the veterans of the Mexican War, and was made its secretary. In 1868 he went to Washington to ask Congress to establish an old soldiers' home on the Pacific Coast, but in this he was unsuccessful. In 1874 he aided in organizing the National Association of Mexican War Veterans, and served as its secretary until his death on March 26, 1897.

23 Much of the material presented herein on the unsuccessful attempt to obtain the passage of the eight-hour day law in 1865–1866 is based upon a small pamphlet with the rather high-sounding title of *The Record of the Eight-Hour Bill in the California Legislature, Session 1865–66; Embracing an account of the preliminary agitation of the subject by the Workingmen of the State, the Debates in the Senate and Assembly, the means resorted to by its enemies to defeat the measure, and the record of its friends and opponents. Prepared and published at the request of Theophilus Tucker and Jere J. Kelly, Special Committee of the Trades' Union, by A. M. Kenaday, Special Agent Selected by the Mechanics and Workingmen, and Late President of the Trades Union of San Francisco. San Francisco, 1867.* As far as I know, the only copy in existence is in the State Historical Library at Sacramento, California.

24 *Senate Journal,* 16 Sess., p. 287.

25 *Assembly Journal,* 16 Sess., pp. 316–317.

26 *Senate Journal,* 16 Sess., pp. 419–420.

27 *Assembly Journal,* 16 Sess., p. 578.

28 *Senate Journal,* 16 Sess., pp. 513–515; *Evening Bulletin,* March 22, 1866.

29 A law establishing an eight-hour day on all government work was passed by Congress in June, 1868.—40 Congress, 2 Sess., chap. 72.

30 Eaves, *op. cit.,* p. 201, says erroneously that "the journeymen ship and steamboat joiners gave notice that on January 1, 1867, they would adopt the new time schedule." The *Times* of January 4, 1868, said that they had obtained it in December, 1865, although in its issue of February 24, 1868, it gave January, 1866, as the date.

31 In October, 1866, for example, several hundred plasterers struck for an eight-hour day, although some of them had been working eight hours since the preceding August. The *Morning Call* of January 30, 1867, said that the plasterers, shipwrights, ship joiners, ship painters, and caulkers were working eight hours at that time.

32 A. M. Winn was born at Punkinville, Virginia, April 27, 1810. He later moved to Vicksburg, Mississippi, where he took up the carpenter's trade, and became a member of the Master Carpenters' and Joiners' Society. He was also a brigadier general in the state militia of Mississippi. Arriving in California in the early days of the gold rush, he engaged in business at Sacramento. In 1850 he was appointed brigadier general in the state militia of California, and was reappointed in 1854. He later served as president of the State Board of Swamp Land Commissioners. Moving to San Francisco in the sixties, he married the widow of James King, of William, the martyred publisher of the *Evening Bulletin,* and for some years thereafter engaged in the real estate business. He took a prominent part in the temperance movement of the State. After withdrawing from active participation in the labor movement, in connection with which he became a nationally known figure, he spent his declining years in the organization and advancement of The Native Sons of the Golden West and The Society of the Sons of Revolutionary Sires. He died in Sonoma County, August 26, 1883.

33 Six months after the organization of Carpenters' Eight-Hour League, No. 1, it was said to have about 2,000 members.—*Evening Bulletin,* June 3, 1867.

34 Eaves, *op. cit.,* p. 201, says that "in April, 1866, as soon as it became evident that the law would not pass, the carpenters gave notice that on June 3,

1867, they would demand the eight-hour day." As noted above, the carpenters did not meet to discuss the matter until January, 1867, and consequently could not, as she says, have taken "a year in which to prepare for the change."

35 The *Morning Call* of June 4, 1867, gave that position to the foundrymen, numbering 300 men, and failed to mention the gas fitters. The foregoing list is from the *Evening Bulletin* of June 3, 1867. The ship caulkers' union, which was the first organization to obtain the eight-hour day, did not appear in the procession.

36 The *Morning Call* of September 29, 1867, announced that in the various crafts the number of members working eight hours per day were as follows: riggers, 50; ship and steamboat joiners, 150; stonecutters, 100; plasterers, 60; lathers, 40; gas fitters, 90; hodcarriers, 225; carpenters, 1,530; ship carpenters, 300; total, 2,495.

37 R. A. Marden, an ironworker who had been active in the agitation for the eight-hour bill of 1865–1866, is said to have been the founder of the league.— *Morning Call*, May 10, 1867.

38 *Alta California*, June 2, 1867.

39 *Times*, February 5, 1867.

40 *Morning Call*, April 2, 1867.

41 *Ibid.*, February 7, 1867.

42 *Ibid.*, February 26, 1867. Cf. Eaves, *op. cit.*, pp. 16–19.

43 *Morning Call*, March 30, 1867. At a later meeting of the league the following were reported as being represented: House Carpenters' Leagues, Nos. 1 and 2, coopers, ship caulkers, shipwrights, ship painters, stone masons, stonecutters, tinsmiths, metal roofers, bricklayers, curriers, Laborers' Protective Benevolent Association, anti-coolie clubs from the twelve districts of San Francisco, machinists, riggers and stevedores, plumbers, and boilermakers.— *Times*, April 10, 1867.

44 *Dispatch*, April 3, 1867.

45 *Morning Call*, June 22, 1867.

46 *Ibid.*, June 4, 1867.

47 *Ibid.*, June 5, 1867.

48 The Industrial League and the Mechanics' Eight-Hour League were not the earliest examples of the participation of labor unionists in politics in California. The action of the teamsters in 1850 has already been noted. On September 2, 1851, a notice appeared in the *Alta California* warning workingmen not to vote for Judge Shepperd, a candidate for office, because he had decided against some laborers in a mechanics' lien suit. He was reëlected. In September, 1853, two tickets, made up of candidates nominated by the Whigs, Democrats, and Independents, were announced by two separate groups of workingmen as favorable to the interests of Labor. On August 30, 1858, the teamsters', draymen's, and watermen's unions supported a Mr. Bigelow as a candidate for the office of Superintendent of Streets, but in the subsequent election he was defeated. In the fall elections of 1860 and 1861, the People's Protective Union, an anti-Chinese association, played an active part in both campaigns. In the latter year it joined with the Mechanics' League, an anti-convict labor association, hoping thereby to elect men favorable to their mutual demands.

49 *Alta California*, July 20, 1867.

50 *Ibid.*

51 The statements which follow are based in part on data contained in a pamphlet entitled *The Annual Message of General A. M. Winn to the Mechanics' State Council*, dated 1869.

52 The unions in the following trades were represented at that conference: shipwrights, caulkers, ship painters, ship joiners, house carpenters, stonecutters, plasterers, plumbers and gas fitters, house painters, bricklayers, riggers and stevedores, and wood turners.

53 Representation in the council was determined on the following basis: three delegates from each union, the members of which were working eight hours a day; and one from each of those which were planning to do so, with five delegates allowed to the House Carpenters' Eight-Hour League because of its large membership.

54 Sec. 5 and Sec. 8 of the by-laws of the Mechanics' State Council were as follows:

"Sec. 5. Whenever satisfactory evidence of the necessity of having a correspondent in any of the inland towns of this State, or on this Coast, has been brought before this Council, they may, upon proof of the fitness of any person known to be friendly to the laboring interests, elect the same as a corresponding member of the Mechanics' State Council."

"Sec. 8. Whenever a corresponding member visits the city, he shall be allowed a seat in the Council, may speak on questions under debate, but shall not be allowed to vote on any question.

55 Commons and Andrews, *op. cit.*, pp. 231, 258, 270.

56 The eight-hour day bill was signed on February 21, 1868, and became effective sixty days later. For the eight-hour law see *Cal. Stats.,* 1867–1868, p. 63; *Assembly Journal,* 17 Sess., pp. 146, 221, 312–313, 477; *Senate Journal,* 17 Sess., pp. 218, 379–381. For the mechanics' lien law, approved March 30, 1868, see *Cal. Stats.,* 1867–1868, p. 589; *Assembly Journal,* 17 Sess., pp. 358, 814; *Senate Journal,* 17 Sess., p. 945. For the act "to protect the wages of labor," approved March 21, 1868, see *Cal. Stats.,* 1867–1868, p. 213; *Assembly Journal,* 17 Sess., pp. 151, 263; *Senate Journal,* 17 Sess., p. 690.

57 The council purchased a fog whistle which could be heard for twenty miles, to be blown at eight, twelve, one, and five o'clock for the eight-hour men. It was installed at Miller & Haley's mill, but was soon abandoned because too much steam was required to operate it.

58 A similar ordinance was passed over the mayor's veto in Oakland on July 27, 1868.—*Dispatch,* July 28, 1868.

59 *The Annual Message of General A. M. Winn to the Mechanics' State Council* (1869).

60 A. M. Winn, *Valedictory Address,* pamphlet dated at San Francisco, 1871.

61 While in the East, General Winn became greatly interested in a secret labor organization, "The Ecumenic Order of United Mechanics," which had just been formed. The order was similar in many respects to the Masons and the Odd Fellows, but was to be "more extensive in its intention of action." It was to consist of local, state, national, and international branches, and was to interest itself in the welfare of the working class. Several local lodges were started in San Francisco, but the order survived for only a few months.

62 *Dispatch,* May 8, 9, 1868. The *Alta California* of May 13, 1868, said: "Several thousand able-bodied men from Pennsylvania and New York, accustomed to labor on public works, have arrived here within a few days by steamer, and went to work with alacrity at the wages offered."

63 *Dispatch,* June 12, 1868.

64 *Drew & Carroll v. Smith,* 38 Cal. 325.

65 *Cal. Stats.,* 1869–1870, p. 777.

66 The *Evening Bulletin* of July 19, 1870, said: "There is much competition for work among the various mills, and hundreds of men stand ready, and not only ready, but anxious to get employment in the place of any who may be discharged or who think proper to withdraw voluntarily."

67 The ten-hour day was established in the planing mills of San Francisco and Oakland on March 1, 1872, following an agreement to that effect among the employers. The *Daily Report* of May 11, 1886, said that the bricklayers of San Francisco maintained the eight-hour day until 1875, when, owing to their refusal to work longer hours at the request of a contractor, who desired to

hasten the completion of the Palace Hotel, a hundred men were imported from the East to take their places. It also said that the local plasterers retained the eight-hour day until 1877, when their union disbanded as a consequence of the failure of a strike for higher wages. The article from which the foregoing is taken is erroneous in so much of what it says that one cannot rely upon any part of it without verification from other sources. On April 26, 1875, Golden Gate Lodge, No. 1, United Plasterers, adopted the following resolution, which tends to show that its members still worked but eight hours per day at that time:

"Whereas: In the *Evening Post* and *Alta* of today, there appeared articles . . . tending to injure the present eight-hour system,

"Therefore be it

"Resolved, that we, the officers and members . . . are perfectly satisfied with our present rate of wages and number of hours work, and do not propose to work ten hours under any consideration or on any building not covered by special rule."—*Evening Bulletin*, April 27, 1875.

68 The members were to pledge themselves "to strike for eight hours on the day that may be fixed by the Mechanics' State Council at the request of the delegates from any trade association." There were to be no fees or regular meetings.—*Chronicle*, June 5, 11, 1872.

69 *Alta California*, August 9, 1875.

70 1866. In March the steamboat firemen and coal passers in San Francisco struck for a twelve-hour day and $70 per month, but their places were taken by Negroes and Kanakas. In October the plasterers demanded and obtained the eight-hour day. In November the iron door and shutter workers struck for higher wages and shorter hours, and the sailors opposed a reduction in wages from $30 to $20 per month.

1867. In May the laborers at Mare Island struck against a reduction in wages from $2.50 to $2 per day. In June the mechanics of the San Francisco and San Jose railroad struck for an increase in wages. In July the lumber stevedores demanded $5 for a nine-hour day, with 75 cents an hour for overtime.

1868. In March the firemen on the boats of the Pacific Mail Steamship Company struck against a reduction in wages, as did also the workmen at the Almaden quicksilver mines. A month later the freight hands of the California, Oregon, and Mexican Steamship Company struck for shorter hours and 50 cents an hour for overtime.

1869. In June the ironmolders employed at Booth & Company's foundry, San Francisco, struck because of a violation of apprenticeship rules by the employers. In the following October, the ironmolders in the Union Iron Works and in the Risdon Iron Works struck against a reduction in wages. Non-union men were hired to take the places of the strikers. The strike failed, although it was continued in a desultory manner for almost a year. It resulted in the disruption of the Iron Molders' Union, No. 164, which was not reorganized until some years later. In July the bakers struck against Sunday work and for a twelve-hour day, but were defeated. Five hundred and twenty-five members of the Miners' League of Grass Valley struck in April against the introduction of Giant powder for blasting purposes, asserting that it was injurious to health and was extremely dangerous. The league, composed for the most part of Cornishmen and Irishmen, waged a bitter but unsuccessful struggle.

71 It was in connection with this strike that the word "scab" first appeared in a San Francisco paper. In the *Morning Call* of February 8, 1867, the Shoemakers' Protective Union published an advertisement in which the word "scab" was used to designate any person who took the place of a striker.

72 The Knights of St. Crispin, a national association of journeymen boot- and shoemakers, was organized in Milwaukee in 1867. At the height of its power it had a membership of from 40,000 to 60,000. It began to decline in 1871 and

finally passed out of existence in 1878. Cf. D. D. Lescohier, *The Knights of St. Crispin* (Madison, Wisconsin, 1910) ; Commons and Andrews, *op. cit.*, pp. 84–88. The *Daily Report* of January 14, 1886, says that the San Francisco lodge of the Knights of St. Crispin was formed in 1868 with James Butler as sir knight and William Griffin as secretary. At one time the local lodge was said to have a membership of 800.

[73] The *Evening Bulletin* of June 16, 1870, printed the following data concerning the coöperative boot and shoe factories in San Francisco : The Journeymen's Coöperative Boot and Shoe Manufactory, started in September, 1867, employed twelve men and four women. The United Workingmen's Boot and Shoe Factory, started January 15, 1868, employed about sixty men and eight women. The St. Crispin's Coöperative Boot and Shoe Factory, started in October, 1869, employed thirty men and twelve women. The Metropolitan Boot and Shoemakers' Union started July 16, 1868, with thirty coöperators. The California Coöperative Boot and Shoemakers started in October, 1869, with 120 coöperators. Cf. C. H. Shinn, "Coöperation on the Pacific Coast," Johns Hopkins University *Studies*, Ser. VI (Baltimore, 1888), pp. 459–463.

[74] "The experiment of employing Chinamen in boot and shoe factories was first tried in 1869, on account of the unreasonable demands of white labor, and within less than 2 or 3 years from that date at least one-half of all the goods manufactured in California were made up by Chinamen."—J. S. Hittell, *The Commerce and Industries of the Pacific Coast* (ed. 2 ; San Francisco, 1882), p. 509.

[75] Copy of the closed-shop agreement between the Painters' Union and the employers :

"December 7, 1863 : The Journeymen Painters' Association of the city of San Francisco, having fixed an established rate of wages for all kinds of work required of them, and having formed said association for mutual protection and assistance, and for the protection of the trade, now, therefore, the undersigned Boss Painters of the city of San Francisco, for the encouragement of said association, agree to employ no journeyman painter under us who is not a member of said association, or who cannot procure a certificate of such membership. In witness of which agreement, and that we may be in all honor bound thereby, we hereunto set our signatures. . . . "—*Evening Bulletin*, March 4, 1864.

On May 4, 1864, the Journeymen Painters' Union adopted the following resolution :

"Resolved, That no member of this Association shall be allowed to work with any person, working as a journeyman, who is not a member of this Association, such person having been notified of the existence of this society, and who has failed to become a member after the first meeting."—*Morning Call*, May 8, 1864.

[76] The following note appeared in the *Morning Call* of November 8, 1867 :

"At a meeting of the Metal Roofers' Protective Union held October 30, it was resolved that upon the 13th day of November, no member of this Association will work with any Journeyman Roofer who is not a member of the Union. By order of the Metal Roofers' Protective Union.

J. C. ROBERTS, President,
WM. CRONAN, Secretary."

[77] Cf. I. B. Cross, "Labor Papers of the Pacific Coast," *Labor Clarion*, June 5, 1908.

[78] Besides the connections established by Kenaday and Winn, there is little to record. The San Francisco and Sacramento printers had affiliated with the National Typographical Union in the fifties, and the ironmolders had joined their national organization in 1867, but intimate relations between the local unions of California and the national bodies were not established until the eighties and nineties.

NOTES FOR CHAPTER V

1 Royce, *op. cit.*, p. 113.

2 *Overland Monthly*, I:298 ff.

3 About 10,000 Chinese and betwen 2,000 and 3,000 whites were employed in building the Central Pacific railroad.

4 *Chronicle*, June 12, 1870.

5 According to the *Evening Bulletin* of June 11, 1870, in 1869 there were 1,163 men employed in the foundries of San Francisco at an average wage of $4 per day. "The business commenced to decline early in 1869, and before the year closed, four large establishments failed, involving a loss of not less than $200,000. The other foundries lingered." In January, 1870, about 500 men were employed in the local foundries, at an average wage of $3 per day. For additional data on the business conditions of the time, see the *Evening Bulletin*, January 17, 22, February 11, 24, 26, March 1, 1870; *Chronicle*, January 20, 30, June 12, 1870.

6 Rainfall in California taken at San Francisco.—*Alta California Almanac*, San Francisco, 1877, p. 22:

Year	Inches	Year	Inches
1864–65	24.53	1868–69	21.35
1865–66	22.93	1869–70	19.15
1866–67	33.69	1870–71	12.57
1867–68	38.83		

7 "The year 1869 was a most remarkable one for real estate transactions. For the first nine months of it, prices ran rapidly upward, and sales increased amazingly. Then came the monetary stringency, at times, indeed, almost bordering upon a panic, and the monthly real estate transfers dropped from nearly $5,000,000 to $1,000,000 and $2,000,000."—*Evening Bulletin*, January 1, 1870. The same paper on January 3, 1871, declared: "The total value of [real estate] sales of 1870 was only a fraction more than half that of 1869."

8 "It has been officially stated, and perhaps with some degree of accuracy, that there are 7,000 men in the city out of employment."—*Evening Bulletin*, January 22, 1870. "It is idle to deny that the present times are dull. The industrial situation is not encouraging. Things look gloomy."—*Chronicle*, January 20, 1870. "Hundreds and thousands [are] out of employment, hopelessly out of employment week after week, and month after month."—*Ibid.*, March 31, 1870. For the first time in the history of the State, a meeting was called "of those interested in the establishment of a soup house for the poor" of San Francisco.—*Ibid.*, March 13, 1870.

9 See the *Evening Bulletin*, March 31, 1870, for a statement of the measures proposed.

10 *Cal. Stats.*, 1869–1870, p. 130.

11 In 1870, the boot and shoe workers in San Francisco had two lodges of the Knights of St. Crispin, one for the male and the other for the female workers, and a local union composed of custom workers not affiliated with any national organization. They had also formed a semi-military company, "The Crispin Guard." In May, 1871, another lodge of the Crispins was organized. In that year a delegate was sent East to the national convention of the association. In California the Crispins were not successful in their fight against the Chinese in the boot and shoe industry. A large number of boot and shoe workers subsequently returned to eastern states. The decline of the national organization was a factor in the dissolution of the local lodges.

12 For a detailed discussion of the anti-Chinese agitation of this period, see Chap. VI.

13 "The real estate market was dull and depressed during all of the year 1871."—*Evening Bulletin*, January 3, 1872. "It is safe to say that one-half of the mechanics are idle or are working on half time."—*Chronicle*, June 17, 1871. The *Evening Bulletin* of March 24, 1873, published the following data relative to business failures in 1870–1872:

Year	Number	Liabilities
1870	60	$2,423,000
1871	89	4,279,000
1872	80	2,434,000

14 "In this city the mechanics have had hard times for several months, but with the number that have left, and the improvement of business, they are nearly all employed."—*Chronicle*, December 10, 1871. "The spirits of our people have recovered and now we look forward with hope and confidence to the future."—*Ibid.*, December 13, 1871.

15 J. S. Hittell, *History of California*, p. 392, gives the market value of silver stocks for the months January to May, 1872, as follows: January, $17,000,000; February, $24,000,000; March, $26,000,000; April, $34,000,000; May, $81,000,000.

16 *Evening Bulletin*, May 7, 1872.

17 *Ibid.*, May 20, 1872.

18 1870. In July the two rival plasterers' unions of San Francisco decided to consolidate. "The Carpenters' and Joiners' Union . . . is a branch of the National Union of Carpenters and Joiners, and is fast absorbing the members of the [Carpenters' Eight-Hour] League."—*Chronicle*, July 31, 1870. The latter was meeting but once a month, then it met semi-annually, and finally, in January, 1873, merged with the Ecumenic Order of United Mechanics. A local branch of the Amalgamated Society of Carpenters and Joiners was formed in San Francisco on August 17, 1872.

1871. The house carpenters, bricklayers, and laborers of Sacramento were organized in 1871.

1872. In July the painters and plasterers of San Jose organized eight-hour leagues. The painters of San Francisco organized on April 27, 1872, with the object of demanding a nine-hour day. Some were working nine hours and some ten hours. They finally decided that nine hours should prevail on and after May 13. In May the journeymen cabinetmakers of San Francisco formed a union with 400 members. Organization was perfected among the lumber stevedores of San Francisco in 1872, as well as among the boot- and shoemakers, the tanners and curriers, the longshoremen, and the German bakers. In June the Musicians' Union fined two of its members for playing with amateurs.

19 The platform as adopted made the following demands: the disenthrallment of labor by the equalization of the wages of labor with the income of capital; the establishment of an equitable rate of interest; the abolition of the national bank system; the creation of a national paper currency; the payment of the national debt exactly according to contract; the maintenance of the protective tariff as long as necessary; the eight-hour day; the establishment of a Federal labor bureau; governmental lands to be held for actual settlers; the government to be restored to the complete sovereignty of the people; compulsory citizen suffrage and compulsory secular education; government regulation of the rates of all chartered and subsidized corporations; a constitutional convention to limit the powers of Congress to the disposition of Federal lands to actual settlers only, to provide for the direct election of the President and Vice-President of the United States, and their election for one term only; and the direct election of United States Senators; Congress definitely to be given the power to issue paper money, which should be legal tender for all debts, public and private; the prohibition of Chinese immigration; and the practical incorporation of the Golden Rule into the social and political system.

20 In the next few years one finds occasional mention in the California press of the National Labor Union and the National Labor Party. Neither had any close connection with the local working-class movement. In May, 1877, some of the men in California who had been associated with the National Labor Union in 1871–1872 formed a state political party under the title of "The National Labor Party," and through an executive committee nominated candidates for the different offices. It played an insignificant part in the ensuing campaign. The party was not a working-class organization but was composed mainly of Greenbackers, Grangers, anti-Chinese agitators, Laborites, and reformers of all sorts. It was especially active at the time of the Kearney anti-Chinese agitation; for, although opposed to that movement, it hoped to ride into power on the wave of popular discontent. It failed most signally, and somewhat later merged with the Greenback Labor Party.

21 1870. In January the marble cutters struck against the use of too many apprentices; the boot- and shoemakers employed by Wentworth & Company demanded higher wages, and the telegraphers opposed a reduction in wages. In October the lumber stevedores struck against a reduction in wages. They had been receiving $4 per day, and it was proposed to reduce the wage to $3. The strike failed.

1871. In February the sailors struck against a reduction of wages from $30 to $25. Violence marked the strike.

1872. Strikes were declared in the following trades for an increase in wages: street laborers in February, lumber stevedores in April, the employees of the North Pacific Transportation Company in April, the employees of the Wool Exchange in May, the hodcarriers on the City Hall of San Francisco in July, and the stevedores of the Central Pacific railroad in July.

22 Unsuccessful efforts were made to reorganize the printers of San Francisco in January, 1872. It was finally accomplished in August of that year.

23 *Constitution and By-Laws of the Amador County Laborers' Association.*

24 This, so far as I have been able to learn, is the first occasion on which the State militia was called out to protect property and strike breakers in California.

25 The *Evening Bulletin*, December 22, 1874, characterized the year 1874 as "in some respects one of the most prosperous in the history of California."

26 The journeymen boot- and shoemakers had formed an association in June, 1872, but it must have passed out of existence before 1873, since in June of that year they again organized to oppose the encroachments of the Chinese in their trade. These associations, together with the Crispin lodges, were the precursors of the White Boot and Shoemakers' League which later played such an important part in the agitation against the Chinese. In October, 1873, the journeymen tailors also formed an association for the purpose of combating the employment of the Mongolians in the clothing trades. At this time they demanded and obtained a ten-hour day.

27 The *Evening Bulletin* of August 27, 1875, said that "the collapse . . . was . . . most terrible. The market has not since recovered from the setback it then [January and February, 1875] received, although some of the ground has been partially regained."

28 The savings banks fell back upon the legal right of demanding thirty days' notice. "The three Stock Boards suspended, one has since resumed."— *Evening Bulletin*, September 23, 1875. "The bank trouble, which started in August, 1875, left baleful influences in operation for the next four years."— B. C. Wright, *Banking in California, 1849–1910* (San Francisco, 1910), p. 108. Cf. I. B. Cross, *History of Banking in California*, I:398–412.

29 "The partial destruction by fire of Virginia City caused a loss of $5,000,000, and lowered stocks by $35,000,000."—Bancroft, *History of California*, VII:688, n.

30 Passengers by rail to and from San Francisco, 1869–1875.—*Evening Bulletin,* May 10, 1875:

Year	Arrived	Departed
1869–70	27,200	15,100
1870–71	30,600	24,300
1871–72	28,700	20,700
1872–73	38,100	22,800
1873–74	52,900	26,100
1874–75	63,300	25,700

Arrivals and departures by rail and sea for January–April, 1872–1875.—*Ibid.*

Year	Arrived	Departed
1872	11,000	7,500
1873	18,000	8,100
1874	18,900	8,200
1875	30,900	9,500

Gain in population of the State through immigration.—*Ibid.,* January 10, 1876.

Year	Gain	Year	Gain
1858	12,700	1867	15,300
1859	13,800	1868	34,900
1860	16,200	1869	24,400
1861	16,900	1870	15,100
1862	14,800	1871	10,300
1863	15,900	1872	18,700
1864	9,800	1873	34,800
1865	3,800 (loss)	1874	47,300
1866	4,800	1875	65,500

"The arrivals for the past year were more numerous than for any previous year in the history of the city."—*Ibid.*

31 The *Evening Bulletin* of May 17, 1875, said: "The city is at present overflowing with newly arrived immigrants from the East, waiting and searching for employment."

32 "We learn from the officers of the San Francisco Benevolent Association that there is more destitution in our city than has existed for many years."— *Evening Bulletin,* November 16, 1875.

33 "It is noteworthy that during an unusual period of financial depression, incident to the failure of the Bank of California in August [1875], real estate values" were "steadily maintained" to the end of the year, although they declined during 1876.—*Evening Bulletin,* January 3, 1876.

34 A strike of little significance occurred among the street-car employees of San Francisco in January, 1874. An attempt was made a few months later to obtain the passage of a State law limiting their hours of labor. It was voted upon favorably by both houses, but failed to receive the governor's signature. The early store-closing movement again got under way in March, 1874. In April, 1874, an unsuccessful attempt was made to organize a city federation of trade unions. A meeting of "mechanics and trades" associations on May 18, 1874, protested against the proposed repeal of the Federal eight-hour law, and approved the platform of the Industrial Congress, which had been adopted at Rochester, New York, on April 14, 1874. In September, 1874, a San Francisco ordinance prohibiting the employment of women as waitresses in saloons was declared to be constitutional. The bricklayers, lathers, and plasterers employed on the Palace Hotel struck during the closing months of 1874. In 1874 there was also some agitation against the employment of convict labor.

No events of any consequence occurred in the labor world in 1875 or 1876.

35 Rainfall at San Francisco, 1870–1877.—*Alta California Almanac* (San Francisco, 1878), p. 22.

Year	Inches	Year	Inches
1870–71	12.57	1874–75	18.00
1871–72	28.18	1875–76	25.39
1872–73	15.90	1876–77	9.84
1873–74	22.69		

36 As early as September 26, 1876, the *Evening Bulletin* had well described the situation in an article entitled, "Is the Bonanza Giving Out?"

37 It is virtually impossible to describe the eagerness with which workingmen, capitalists, farmers, business men, miners, widows, chambermaids, and others invested their funds in the stock market at that time. The speculative spirit still characterizes the people of California, and it is the exceptional family which today does not possess at least a few shares of stock.

38 Hittell, *op. cit.*, p. 424.

39 The number of unemployed in San Francisco at that time was estimated at about 15,000.—H. H. Bancroft, *Popular Tribunals* (2 vols.; San Francisco, 1887), II:704.

40 *Evening Bulletin*, April 14, 1877.

41 *Ibid.*, July 24, 1877.

NOTES FOR CHAPTER VI

[1] Among the more substantial discussions of Chinese immigration, not to mention countless pamphlets and magazine articles, are the following: the Rev. O. Gibson, *The Chinese in America* (Cincinnati, 1877); G. F. Seward, *Chinese Immigration in its Social and Economical Aspects* (New York, 1881); H. H. Bancroft, *Essays and Miscellany* (San Francisco, 1890), pp. 309–418; Bancroft, *Inter Pocula*, pp. 561–582; Bancroft, *History of California*, VII:335–348; T. H. Hittell, *op. cit.*, IV:98–113; Coolidge, *op. cit.* (an excellent discussion from the pro-Chinese point of view); Eaves, *op. cit.*, chaps. 3–6 (unbiased, and the most satisfactory brief treatment of the subject in print, although it contains a few errors).

[2] For Chinese immigration statistics, see Coolidge, *op. cit.*, pp. 498–500.

[3] In 1865, 80 per cent of all the labor in the woolen mills of California was Mongolian.—J. S. Hittell, *Commerce and Industries of the Pacific Coast* (San Francisco, 1882), p. 118. In 1866, about 2,000 Chinese were employed at cigarmaking, while only 200 whites were employed. One-half of the cigarmaking firms were owned by the Chinese.—*Times*, November 7, 1866. "In ten years the cunning of the Chinese has made them workers in cloth, in leather, in cotton and wool, and they monopolize the various manufactures of tobacco; they have usurped the places which in the Eastern States are filled by women."—*Chronicle*, May 20, 1870. "At the end of 1872 nearly one-half of the working-men employed in the factories of the city were Chinese."—*Morning Call*, April 27, 1873. There were none in the foundries, boiler shops, or machine shops of the city, and there were only a few in one of the file factories. The *Morning Call* of April 27, 1873, gave the following statistics concerning the numbers of Chinese employed in certain industries in San Francisco: in cigar factories, 3,000; boot and shoe factories, 2,000; the canned goods industry, 500; woolen mills, 500; making tinware, 100; furniture factories, 20; sash and door factories, 30; match factories, 50; making woodenware, 40; cigar box factory, 60; shirtmaking, 100; the making of syrups, cordials, etc., 20; the making of artificial champagne, 30; glass factories, 28; hair factories, 30; the making of artificial stone, 30; broom factories, 30; the making of block pavement, 19.

[4] New York *Tribune*, May 1, 1869.

[5] Bancroft, *Essays and Miscellany*, pp. 345–346.

[6] See Coolidge, *op. cit.*, chap. 22, for a pro-Chinese discussion of the question of assimilation. While much has been made of the argument that the Americans would not permit the Chinese to assimilate, it is doubtful if assimilation could have taken place even under the most favorable economic and social conditions.

[7] "The Chinese Six Companies were really contractors and importers, although they attempted to pass themselves off as benevolent organizations. They governed and controlled with an iron hand, all the Chinese in the country."—Bancroft, *History of California*, VII:344, n.

[8] A perusal of the list of trades at which the Chinese worked, and a comparison of the respective scales of wages paid to them and to white laborers, leads to the conclusion that this latter argument is not valid. In reply to the argument that they developed the State's resources, it was suggested that it is not advisable to develop natural resources in a manner detrimental to the welfare of the community or to that of future generations.

[9] Introduced into the Assembly, March 6, 1852.

[10] *Assembly Journal*, 3 Sess., p. 353; *Senate Journal*, 3 Sess., pp. 306–307; *Alta California*, March 10, 21, May 4, 1852.

11 "In place of the general indifference with which we anticipated it [the bill] would be regarded, it has received the most ardent and determined opposition."—*Alta California*, March 21, 1852. "At the largest mass meeting ever assembled in Tuolumne County, held in Columbia, April 3 . . . the contract labor bill was characterized as 'unjust in principle, ruinous in its tendency, and that we pledge ourselves, should it become the law of the State, TO RESIST ITS EXECUTION to the utmost of our power until such time as we shall be enabled to effect its repeal.' "—*Ibid.*, April 12, 1852.

12 The *Alta California* of May 4, 1852, said: "The feeling is strong against permitting the thousands [of Asiatics] flocking to our shores to share the wealth of our mines untaxed, or without contribution to the support of the government and the property of the State." Soulé, Gihon, and Nisbet, *op. cit.*, p. 379, under date of April, 1852, wrote: "In short, there is a strong feeling—prejudice it may be—existing in California against all Chinese, and they are nicknamed, cuffed about, and treated very unceremoniously by every other class."

13 *Cal. Stats.*, 1860, p. 307.

14 *Ibid.*, 1863–1864, p. 492.

15 *Ibid.*, 1854, p. 230.

16 *Ibid*, 1855, p. 194.

17 *People v. Downer*, 7 Cal. 170.

18 *Cal. Stats.*, 1858, p. 295.

19 *Ibid.*, 1862, p. 462.

20 *Ling Sing v. Washburn*, 20 Cal. 534.

21 *Cal. Stats.*, 1850, pp. 230, 455.

22 *People v. Hall*, 4 Cal. 399.

23 *Cal. Stats.*, 1863, pp. 60, 69.

24 *Cal. Code of Civil Procedure*, pp. 493–494.

25 The *Alta California* of September 14, 1859, contained the following notice:

" . . . At a Special Meeting of the Cigar Makers' Association of San Francisco held at their rooms this 12th day of September, 1859, for the purpose of investigating the charges preferred against Mr. Chas. Weber, a member of said association, . . . the following resolutions were unanimously adopted:

"Resolved, that Mr. Charles Weber of the firm of Messrs. Zadig and Co. . . . and a member of this association, after having been impartially tried, has been found guilty of employing China or cooly apprentices with intent to learn them the cigar trade in violation of our constitution, and to the great injury of the objects of our organization, notwithstanding our conciliatory course and offers of assistance to him to discontinue the same.

"Resolved, that the said Charles Weber be and is hereby expelled from our association for having broken his solemn pledge: one, who to promote his private ends, has commenced a system that will be destructive to the general interest of his fellow tradesmen.

"Resolved that we deem it our imperative duty to abolish this system and to confine the cooly class within limits that will insure the American white industrial classes immunity from dangers so surely destructive to their interests and independence, and for the accomplishment of these ends we ask the co-operation of all industrial classes.

"Resolved, that we, as an Association, shall continue our most active and determined efforts until the ultimate end shall be attained,—the protection of American industry in all its honorable and useful branches. . . .

"Thos. Alovan, Secy.   Wm. M. Zanker, Pres."

26 *Alta California*, November 2, 1859.

27 *Ibid.*, November 18, 1859.

28 *Times*, November 7, 1866.

29 White laborers had previously been employed at $1.75 per day, but they were replaced by the Chinese, who received $1.12½ per day.

30 See *supra*, p. 45.

31 See Eaves, *op. cit.*, chap. 6, and Coolidge, *op. cit.*, chap. 9, for discussions of Congressional action in connection with efforts to modify the terms of the Burlingame treaty.

32 *Cal. Stats.*, 1870, p. 330.

33 *Chy Lung v. Freeman et al.*, 92 U. S. 275.

34 *Cal. Stats.*, 1875–1876, p. 747. *Ibid.*, 1877–1878, p. 529.

35 *Ibid.*, 1875–1876, p. 906.

36 *Chinese Immigration: Its Social, Moral, and Political Effect* (Sacramento, 1878).

37 Passed December 12, 1870.

38 *People v. Ex parte Ashbury.* Reported in *Alta California*, February 5, 1871.

39 See trial of Lou Ci Tat, as reported in the *Evening Bulletin*, September 9, 1873.

40 *Cal. Stats.*, 1875–1876, p. 759.

41 A somewhat similar ordinance applied to the vegetable peddlers, who were required to pay a license of $2 per quarter if they used a horse, or horses and wagon, but if they did not, they were required to pay $10 per quarter.—*Opening Argument of F. A. Bee before the Joint Committee of the Two Houses of Congress on Chinese Investigation* (a pamphlet; San Francisco, 1876), p. 2.

42 *Ho Ah Kow v. Matthew Nunan.* 5 Sawyer 552.

43 It was stated at the time that about 10,000 Chinese had been so employed.

44 The following associations were represented in the convention: Carpenters' Eight-Hour League, Pacific Shop of the United Mechanics, Operative Stone Masons, Mechanics' State Council, Machinists' Association, Eureka Typographical Society, Boot Fitters' Association, Stone Cutters' Association, Knights of St. Crispin, Workingmen's Protective Association, Plumbers' and Gas Fitters' Union, Riggers' Union, Blacksmiths' Protective Union, Locksmiths' Union, Trunk Workers' Society, Carpenters' and Joiners' Union, anti-coolie clubs from the fourth, eighth, ninth, tenth, and eleventh wards of San Francisco, Caulkers' Union, Gilders' Association, Bakers' Association, Lathers' Union, and Sacramento Typographical Union.

45 Eaves, *op. cit.*, p. 23, incorrectly states that it was formed as the result of a split in the state anti-Chinese convention, held in August, 1870.

46 "It is a significant fact that the Industrial Reformers, an association of trade unions and labor leagues of this city who already number some thousands of voters and are a power in the land, have declared themselves in favor of the Subsidy side of the Railroad question."—*People's Journal*, San Francisco, February 18, 1871.

47 The "Declaration of Principles" of the organization, quoted in the *Chronicle* of September 14, 1870, says in part:

"We exact a firm attachment to our Republic and its form of government. We advocate a free elective franchise, honesty, capacity, and fidelity in public office, equal taxation, just and equal laws, economy in all branches of government, proper reservation of public lands for actual settlers, encouragement of all industrial pursuits, to the end that white labor may be properly rewarded and its true dignity maintained. We also declare hostility to the corrupt and unprincipled who seek to place us on a common level with the Asiatics and other inferior races swarming to our shores." Other articles of faith follow, strongly deprecating any violence to the Chinese or to their employers, and recommending only legal means as a remedy for the evil. The concluding article of the Declaration says: "We solemnly declare that we will not support any men for office, or vote for any candidate for office, who will not subscribe to them [the principles of the association], and pledge himself to use his influence to abrogate that portion of our treaty with China which accords to her subjects all the rights, privileges, and immunities which are accorded to the most favored nations."

48 *Morning Call,* April 27, 1873. The *Evening Bulletin* of March 27, 1876, said: "They keep the field in washing, notwithstanding that they have to contend with machinery, division of labor, and some legislation discriminating against them. . . . Chinese cigar shops are one of the features of the city. . . . They have driven out not only the laborer, but the capitalist. . . . The white employer is disappearing as fast as the white laborer."

49 This huge immigration followed the drought in China and the very severe winter that came after.

50 *Senate Report No. 689,* 44 Cong., February 27, 1877.

51 See San Francisco newspapers of February 28, 1879, for detailed reports of a mass meeting which adopted resolutions urging President Hayes to sign the bill. The gathering was addressed by Governor Irwin and many other prominent citizens.

52 *Treaties, Conventions, International Acts, Protocols, and Agreements between the United States and Other Powers, 1776–1909* (2 vols.; compiled by W. M. Malloy, Washington, D. C., 1910), I:237, 239.

53 *U. S. Stats. at Large,* 1881–1883, pp. 58–61.

54 *Ibid.,* 1891–1893, pp. 25–26.

55 *Treaties, Conventions, etc., op. cit.,* p. 241.

56 *U. S. Stats. at Large,* 1901–1903, pp. 176–177.

NOTES FOR CHAPTER VII

1 Cf. Bancroft, *History of California*, VII:352–362; idem, *Popular Tribunals*, II:696–748; T. H. Hittell, *op. cit.*, IV:594–615; W. J. Davis, *History of Political Conventions in California, etc., 1849–1892* (Sacramento, 1893), pp. 365–389, 396–402, 420–421, 424; James Bryce, *The American Commonwealth* (2 vols.; New York, 1891), II, chap. 89; Coolidge, *op. cit.*, chap 8; Eaves, *op. cit.*, pp. 27–39; Henry George, *Popular Science Monthly*, XVII:433 ff.; I. B. Cross, ed., *Frank Roney, Irish Rebel and California Labor Leader* (Berkeley, 1931), pp. 261–313. In subsequent pages the last-mentioned volume will be referred to as *Frank Roney, Autobiography.*

2 The great railroad strike of 1877 began on the Baltimore and Ohio railroad, following a 10 per cent wage reduction. The strike soon spread to other railroads. In order to quell the disturbance, the militia was called out in several states. Cars and buildings were burned, trains were wrecked, strikers were shot down, and an exceedingly hostile feeling was engendered on both sides of the controversy. Cf. G. E. McNeill, *op. cit.*, pp. 154 ff.; J. R. Commons and associates, *History of Labor in the United States*, II:185–191.

3 For a history of the International Workingmen's Association and the Workingmen's Party of the United States, see Morris Hillquit, *History of Socialism in the United States* (New York, 1910), pp. 156–192.

4 The sand-lots were the vacant plot of ground in front of the City Hall where for years speakers, street fakirs, phrenologists, politicians, and others had held forth during the day and evening before easily gathered crowds of idlers, who were ever willing to listen to their harangues or to buy their nostrums and novelties.

5 Eaves, *op. cit.*, pp. 25 and 28, says incorrectly that the meeting was called by the local branch of the National Labor Union.

6 Virtually all the Chinese immigrants had been brought to California in the vessels of the Pacific Mail Steamship Company.

7 *Evening Bulletin*, July 23, 1877.

8 The offender, John Griffin, was later sentenced to two years' imprisonment.

9 Variously estimated at from 4,000 to 6,000.

10 Mayor Bryant, in his proclamation to the people of San Francisco, declared: "The city has a force of ten thousand men ready for any emergency." —*Morning Call*, July 26, 1877.

11 *Evening Bulletin*, July 26, 1877.

12 A total of $58,296.60 had been collected to finance the Committee of Safety; $17,402.95 was returned to the subscribers.—*Morning Call*, February 18, 1878.

13 Bancroft, *History of California*, VII:358, n.

14 *The Evening Bulletin* of May 20, 1878, prints a part of the report of a committee appointed to investigate charges brought against Kearney by members of the Workingmen's Party of California. In that report it was declared that Kearney had organized "the Workingmen's Trade and Labor Union for the purpose of getting 'Bill' Buckley nominated for the Superintendent of Streets."

15 *Morning Call*, August 23, 1877.

16 Eaves, *op. cit.*, p. 26, says mistakenly that "they [the Workingmen's Party of California] effected their organization in August, and in the September municipal elections polled nearly six thousand votes." The Workingmen's Party of California was organized on October 5, 1877. In the election of September 5, 1877, the Workingmen's Trade and Labor Union printed no tickets, hence could have cast no votes.

17 In describing the activity of "piece clubs" in the election, the *Evening Bulletin* of August 29, 1877, said: "The Piece Conventions are numerous, the strikers almost numberless, as candidates have found out to their cost. It is noticeable that out of the dozen or more so-called Nominating Conventions, only two comparatively distinct tickets have been put before the people, and there are but four tickets advertised in the daily journals. Aside from the newspaper reports of endorsements, nothing is generally known of mushroom conventions, but candidates are honored with more than a passing notice of their endorsement by way of polite words to the effect that 'You are hereby notified that you have been endorsed by the Whang Doodle Convention, and your assessment is now due, amounting to $——.' Or, 'You have been nominated for the position of —————— by the Twaddle Association, and money is necessary to accomplish our work. Your assessment amounts to $——. Please, etc.' And again, 'We have placed your name upon our ticket for the office of ——————, and assess you $——. We shall print 3,000,000 tickets, etc., etc. Please arrange to pay before next Tuesday.' Other communications of similar import suggest the prompt payment of an assessment in view of a grand ratification of their ticket. A candidate for a prominent office has received notices of five assessments from that number of conventions, for the amounts of $500, $300, $200, $375, $200, respectively, and several notices that his assessments are due, the amount not being given." Cf. also *Evening Bulletin*, September 19, 1877. The Workingmen's Trade and Labor Union of San Francisco was such an organization. "Piece clubs" were prohibited by a law enacted in 1878.— *Cal. Stats.*, 1877–1878, p. 236. The *Evening Bulletin* of May 20, 1878, quoted the following part of the report of the committee appointed to investigate certain charges preferred against Kearney by members of the Workingmen's Party of California: "At the last meeting of this piece club, he [Kearney] was guarded by police so that the men he had defrauded could not wreak their vengeance upon him."

18 Data obtained through interviews.

19 Day was a Canadian carpenter of Irish extraction, "six feet in height, with a reddish beard. He was industrious and temperate, with a common school education. His language was good and his ideas thoughtful, and the opposite of incendiary." Knight was an Englishman, "short, squat, with a round face, twinkling gray eyes, and a small gray moustache. He had a strong proclivity for reforms, any kind being better than none. In 1842 he immigrated to the United States and settled himself in Missouri, where he was admitted to the bar. He served through the Mexican War, coming to California in 1852, where he engaged in mining for three years, gave some attention to law, finally becoming a social parasite."—Bancroft, *History of California*, VII:358, n.

20 *Evening Bulletin*, September 22, 1877.

21 Eaves, *op. cit.*, p. 30, says mistakenly that "at the meeting of September 12, the first platform of the California Workingmen's Party was adopted." The party had not at that time been organized. On page 25 of her volume, Eaves also declares that "at first Dennis Kearney and his friends organized as a branch of the Workingmen's Party of the United States." That this was not so has been shown by the data presented earlier in the present volume (pp. 93–95), and also by the fact that at the sand-lot meetings of September 30 and October 7, 1877, Kearney and his lieutenants clashed violently with the leaders of the Workingmen's Party of the United States, who were holding a meeting at the same time. Eaves, *op. cit.*, p. 25, says that "in California this [presumably the Workingmen's Party of the United States] seems to have been regarded as the successor to, or identical with, the National Labor Party." This was not so, for the two organizations remained separate and distinct, not only in the newspapers of the time, but also in the minds of the people. Both organizations continued to hold their meetings separately.

22 Davis, *op. cit.*, pp. 366–367.

23 Dr. C. C. O'Donnell was born in Baltimore, Maryland, May 3, 1834. He arrived in San Francisco in 1850. He served only one term as coroner of San Francisco, although he was frequently a candidate for that position; he was also a candidate for the office of mayor of San Francisco on three different occasions, but failed to be elected. He died in San Francisco, May 27, 1912.

24 Interviews with members of the party at one time prominent in the movement; *Morning Call*, November 24, 1877; J. P. Young, *San Francisco* (2 vols.; Chicago, 1912), II:534.

25 *Frank Roney, Autobiography*, p. 271; Bryce, *op. cit.*, II:392, 748.

26 Davis, *op. cit.*, pp. 368–369.

27 *Evening Bulletin*, November 5, 1877.

28 *Evening Bulletin*, November 1, 1877.

29 *Ibid.*

30 *Ibid.*, November 3, 1877.

31 *Ibid.*, November 5, 1877.

32 *Morning Call*, November 4, 1877.

33 *Ibid.*

34 Wellock was an English shoemaker, and had served in the Crimean War. He had come to the United States in 1873 and to California in 1877. "He was tall, with a long, narrow head, high forehead, full, short beard, and nervous temperament.... His phraseology was not devoid of culture... but its chief ingredients were the frequent gospel quotations of which his training as an evangelist had given him a ready command." From the time of his introduction before the mass meeting in Horticultural Hall until his expulsion from the party several years later, he was accustomed "to appear upon the sandlots, Bible in hand, read a text, and discourse thereon, interpolating arguments of a political nature."—Bancroft, *Popular Tribunals*, II:718.

35 *Morning Call*, November 6, 1877.

36 *Morning Call*, November 6, 1877. Captain Lees of the San Francisco police force, in testifying before the legislative committee on February 3, 1878, characterized Kearney as a coward in the following words: "Now I believe Mr. Kearney is perfectly capable of moving that great mass of people and doing just what he says he would do. I am not such an idiot as to believe that Kearney cannot do it. It is simply subject to his will. Whenever he takes it into his head, the thing will be done.... The Chinese steamer was due on Sunday, and before the steamer arrived, the agitation had got to such a pitch that authorities were compelled to arrest Kearney. In my judgment, there never was a time when he was required to remain in jail, and could not have got out on bail. He had got the mass of people so worked up, and had promised to carry out his purpose; the steamer was due, and Mr. Kearney wanted to remain where he was—in jail—until after the steamer had got in, for, among other things, I think he lacks moral courage individually; but there are a class of people with him that do not. There are very few men that want to lead on to certain death. ... He will never lead them, if he can find any hole to get out of."—*Evening Bulletin*, February 4, 1878.

37 *Morning Call*, November 24, 25, 1877.

38 The following organizations of San Francisco participated in the demonstration: Plasterers' Union, Boot- and Shoemakers' Union, Scandinavian Association, Tailors' Union, Coopers' Union, Printers' Union, Carpenters' Union, Young Americans, Order of Caucasians, Pile Drivers' Union, Iron Workers' Union, Cigarmakers' Union, Austrian Benevolent Association, and the twelve ward-clubs of the Workingmen's Party of California. A delegation from the Oakland branch of the Workingmen's Party of California was also in line.

39 During the fall and winter of 1877, J. E. Redstone, of Oakland, published a small paper called *Legal Tender*, as the organ of the workers of that city.

During the spring of 1879, William Wellock and others published *The Sand Lot*, in the interests of the Workingmen's Party of California.

40 They had undoubtedly been patterned after the military companies which had been organized by the Knights of St. Crispin in 1869.

41 *Evening Bulletin*, December 12, 1877.

42 *Ibid.*, January 10, 1878.

43 *Morning Call*, December 24, 1877.

44 *Evening Bulletin*, January 16, 1878.

45 *Ibid.*

46 *Assembly Journal*, 22 Sess., pp. 230–231; *Senate Journal*, 22 Sess., pp. 122, 134; *Amendments to Cal. Codes, 1877–1878*, pp. 117, 118.

47 *Assembly Journal*, 22 Sess., pp. 789, 790, 802; *Senate Journal*, 22 Sess., pp. 122, 175, 454; *Cal. Stats., 1877–1878*, p. 879.

48 *Cal. Stats., 1877–1878*, p. 879.

49 *Morning Call*, January 19, 1878.

50 Frank Roney was born in Belfast, Ireland, in 1841. Although he was the son of a wealthy contractor, he early joined the Fenians, a revolutionary organization which plotted to overthrow English rule in Ireland. Possessed of great organizing ability and of magnetic personality, he soon rose to a position of responsibility in the revolutionary movement. He was arrested, formally charged with treason, and given the choice of standing trial or of becoming a voluntary exile. He chose the latter course and emigrated to the United States. After living in New York and Chicago, he went to Omaha, where he joined the local molder's union, later becoming its president. He arrived in San Francisco in April, 1875, but did not affiliate with any of the Labor or radical associations until the time of Kearney's first arrest (December, 1877), when with thousands of others he joined the Workingmen's Party of California because he felt that the city authorities were persecuting its leaders. His commanding figure, experience, personality, education, and eloquence made him a valuable acquisition to the radical movement. He was elected chairman of the Eighth Ward Club of the party, and was subsequently made a member of the executive committee of the parent body. As a delegate to the state convention he drafted the first constitution and platform of the party. For some months after the adjournment of the convention he took a leading part in the councils of the organization, always urging upon its members the necessity of conservative and constructive action. His long connection with the San Francisco labor movement is told in subsequent pages. He died at Long Beach, California, January 24, 1925. For his life-story, see *Frank Roney, Autobiography.*

51 About one hundred forty delegates were in attendance, representing the numerous branches of the party in San Francisco, Oakland, Alameda, Petaluma, San Jose, Vallejo, Brooklyn, Mono County, and Siskiyou County. The following associations of San Francisco were also represented by delegates: Printers' Union, Cabinetmakers' Union, Carpenters' Union, Coopers' Union, Tailors' Union, Stonecutters' Union, Cooks' and Waiters' Union, Boot- and Shoemakers' Union, Order of Caucasians, Scandinavian Club, French Club, and several others.

52 The other charges were formally dismissed on October 22, 1879.

53 The district had always given a Republican majority, ranging from 400 to 1,200 votes. In the preceding election the vote had stood: Republicans, 3,713; Democrats, 3,255; Workingmen, 118; but in this contest the vote stood: Republicans, 2,038; Democrats, 572; Workingmen, 2,730; showing conclusively that it was from the Democrats that the new party had drawn the greater number of its adherents.

54 *Morning Call*, January 19, 1878.

55 *Evening Bulletin*, February 15, 1878.

56 In Sacramento the party split into Kearney and anti-Kearney factions. The candidates of the party were badly defeated in the Santa Rosa municipal elections. In Salinas, it elected but one supervisor, and in San Jose only the chief of police.

57 *Evening Bulletin*, March 16, 1878.

58 See the *Morning Call*, May 20, 1878, for a summary of the report of a committee appointed by the opposition to investigate these charges. It concluded by summing up the damaging evidence which had been obtained, and by accusing Kearney of too intimate relations with the officials of the Southern Pacific railroad and with Flood and O'Brien, two prominent San Francisco bankers. *Truth*, a San Francisco labor journal, in its issue of July 21, 1883, contained the following statement concerning Kearney:

"During the incumbency of Thos. Desmond, Kearney's sheriff, an assessment of $6,500 was taken up for him [Kearney] among the deputies. He received $65,000 for placing White on the W. P. C. ticket. He also received a gift of a lot of land out on California Street, and some $18,000 with which to build a mansion. But at the time, not desiring to have the property appear in his name, he had it entrusted to the good care of a certain well known politician and contractor, in whose name it was put. This man now holds it as his own, and dares Kearney to sue for it in court.

"Some time after Kearney's sell-out to monopoly and capital, collections were taken up even among the capitalistic Supreme Court Judges for him, to the amount of over $600. He received for his Butler campaign in Massachusetts some $3,000, and yet during all this time, he was taking up collections among the deluded workingmen for his 'support.' "

Kearney, in a letter to James Bryce (*The American Commonwealth*, II: 750), denied having "received a dollar from public office or private parties" as a result of his activity on behalf of the Workingmen's Party of California.

59 *Evening Bulletin*, May 7, 1878.

60 Strange to say, the state convention of the Workingmen's Party of California on May 18, 1878, adopted a resolution recognizing the Workingmen's Party of the United States as a kindred organization.—*Morning Call*, May 19, 1878.

61 The delegates elected on the ticket of the Workingmen's Party of California were of the following numbers with respect to profession or occupation: lawyers, 8; farmers, 7; merchants, 5; carpenters, 3; miners, 2; physicians, 2; cooper, telegraph operator, bootmaker, lithographer, tailor, tinner, printer, school teacher, painter, gardener, gas fitter, cabinetmaker, turner, rigger, grocer, sign painter, furniture dealer, clerk, plumber, justice of the peace, bookkeeper, restaurant keeper, and cook, 1 each.—Davis, *op. cit.*, 390–392.

62 The *Evening Bulletin* of November 4, 1878, published the following telegram:

"N. Y. Nov. 3. The *World's* Boston special says: ... After the close of the meeting, Kearney said to the *World* correspondent that he meant business, and that if Butler were not elected, Beacon Street and Back Bay would run with blood, as the resolutions which had been adopted proposed. He said that all the military power in the United States could not put down the workingmen, and that Massachusetts would never be safe until the 'Blue Bloods' were hanged to lamp posts, two on every post."

63 This was Knight's last appearance in connection with the Workingmen's Party movement. Thereafter he engaged in newspaper work in San Francisco.

64 Bancroft, *History of California*, VII:399–400.

65 *Op. cit.*, IV:639.

66 *Ibid.*, VII:404–406.

67 W. R. Andrus was a carpenter who had been elected mayor of Oakland in 1878 on the Workingmen's Party ticket, and reëlected a year later. He had served acceptably in that capacity.

68 The Workingmen's Party elected C. J. Beerstecher to membership on the State Railroad Commission. German by birth, he had come to the United States in 1851 and to California in 1877. He had never been a man of wealth, but during his term as Railroad Commissioner he acquired property valued at $27,000. He announced that his parents had died and had willed him a fortune. A few years later, however, they appeared and took up their residence with him. In 1883 the Assembly Committee on Corporations was ordered to investigate, among other things, "whether said [State Railroad] Commissioners or either of them, during their term of office may have made any extraordinary acquisitions of property, over and above the income of their salary diminished by expenses of individual and family support." It reported that one of the commissioners had not increased his wealth so as to attract attention, that one had done so, and in a rather questionable manner, and with respect to Commissioner Beerstecher, it found "that by general report, and in the opinion of his associates, he was without means at the time of his election, and his sudden acquisition of wealth while Commissioner was without adequate explanation."— *Assembly Journal*, 25 Sess., pp. 33, 449–450.

Stuart Daggett, *Some Chapters on the History of the Southern Pacific Railway* (New York, 1922), p. 194, says: "The charge is made that the Central Pacific bought and paid for Beerstecher's services while a member of the Railroad Commission. . . . The evidence in the case is purely circumstantial, but seems convincing."

69 Had it not been for the murderous attack upon Kalloch, his election would have been doubtful. The feud between the two families continued. On April 23, 1880, I. M. Kalloch (the mayor's son) shot Charles deYoung fatally while the latter was seated at his office desk. Young Kalloch was subsequently tried on a charge of murder and acquitted.

70 William Steinman was the leader of the movement.

71 *Morning Call*, February 8, 1880.

72 *Acts Amendatory of the Codes of California*, 1880, pp. 1, 2.

73 *In re Tiburcio Parrott*, 1 Fed. Rept. 481, March, 1880.

74 *Evening Bulletin*, March 9, 1880.

75 Claus Spreckels was one of the wealthiest men in San Francisco.

76 *Ex parte Kearney*, 55 Cal. 212. In the general election of 1879 all but one of the Supreme Court justices who later sat in this case had been supported by the Workingmen's Party of California.

77 *Evening Bulletin*, March 24, 1880.

78 Kearney went East in February and March, 1888, to speak in favor of an anti-Chinese measure then before Congress, which, however, was not adopted.

NOTES FOR CHAPTER VIII

1 For data concerning labor conditions and wages in 1881, see J. S. Hittell, *The Commerce and Industries of the Pacific Coast*, chap. 5.

2 The unions of the cooks and waiters, the boot- and shoemakers, and the cigarmakers were about the only organizations actively connected with the Kearney movement.

3 Eaves, *op. cit.*, p. 40, incorrectly speaks of efforts of the Workingmen's Party of California "to form a central representative assembly of the trade-unions of San Francisco."

4 At that time it was estimated that there were about 25 trade unions in San Francisco, with a membership of approximately 3,500.—Bancroft, *History of California*, VII:351.

5 Forty-four delegates were in attendance, representing the following trades: carpenters and joiners, ironmolders, tailors, cabinetmakers, stair-builders, bookbinders, woodcarvers, printers, riggers, cigarmakers, carriage-makers, stonecutters, shipwrights, pavers, custom shoemakers, coopers, and advertising agents and solicitors.

6 *Chronicle*, April 1, 1878.

7 *Morning Call*, July 7, 1879.

8 At that time the Trades Assembly represented approximately 1,200 organized workingmen, although in October, 1878, it had a membership of 14 unions, representing about 4,000 men.

9 Wilson, in his early days, had been a school teacher in Ireland, but upon arriving in San Francisco he had opened a small stationery store. He was broad-minded, well educated, and kind-hearted. It is said that he could have become wealthy had he given more attention to his business and less to the emancipation of his fellow-men. Hagerty was a mechanical genius, an inventor of rare ability, but first and foremost a Socialist. Starkweather was an enthusiast. Handicapped by poor health, he could labor only at odd jobs, but no one ever asked him to aid in carrying forward the working-class agitation without finding him ready and willing to serve. His is the distinction of being the first person in California arrested for boycotting. His arrest grew out of his participation in the anti-Chinese agitation of 1882. So incessantly did he labor for the cause of the masses and so deeply was he beloved by those with whom he came in contact, that, at his death on November 29, 1884, a crowd packed the hall in which memorial services were held by those for whom he had made sacrifices in his lifetime.

10 For a more detailed history of the Seamen's Protective Union see I. B. Cross, "First Coast Seamen's Unions," *Coast Seamen's Journal*, July 8, 1908; Paul S. Taylor, *op. cit.*, pp. 41–45. Roney's own story appears in his autobiography, *Frank Roney, Autobiography*, pp. 328–345.

11 Roney was succeeded as president of the Trades Assembly by Henry Marsden, in February, 1882; Thomas Watson followed in August, 1882, and J. K. Phillips in February, 1883.

12 Through its efforts, the following trades were organized in 1882–1883: hodcarriers, patternmakers, boilermakers, foundry laborers, machinists, beer bottlers, custom cutters, metal roofers and cornice-makers, cartmen and coal haulers, blacksmiths, bag- and satchel-makers, house-movers, coopers, brass molders and finishers, ship painters, plumbers and gas fitters, marble cutters, varnishers, marble polishers and rubbers, stair-builders, wharf-builders, watchmakers, painters, and expressmen. At that time unions were also in existence among the bakers, barbers, carpenters and joiners, locomotive engineers, cigarmakers, draymen and teamsters, fishermen, German butchers, hat finishers, hotel bakers, pastry cooks, ironmolders, bookbinders, shipwrights, longshore

lumbermen, plasterers, riggers, seamen, ship and steamboat joiners, printers, tailors, waiters, harness-, collar-, and whip-makers, marine engineers, and ship caulkers. Only the unions of the printers, ironmolders, and carpenters were affiliated with their national organizations.

13 See *supra*, pp. 27–31.

14 The *Chronicle* of January 15, 1874, from which these last-mentioned data are taken, also said that there were 150 convicts employed in the harness shop, 115 in the shoe shop, and 200 in the furniture shop.

15 *Cal. Stats.*, 1880, pp. 67–75.

16 Cf. Eaves, *op. cit.*, chap. 18; J. G. Brooks, *Bulletin of the United States Bureau of Labor Statistics*, No. 15, pp. 197 ff.; E. R. Spedden, "The Trade Union Label," Johns Hopkins University *Studies*, Ser. XXVIII, No. 2. The first union stamp or label was adopted in San Francisco in 1869. In August of that year the House Carpenters' Eight-Hour League resolved, "That this league will furnish a stamp to all eight-hour mills that they may stamp their work, so that we may know what materials to put up and avoid using the work got out by ten-hour mills."—*Evening Bulletin*, August 3, 1869. The League was meeting with considerable opposition and it was suggested that the plan as outlined would prove beneficial to the eight-hour movement. I have found no data that would lead me to believe that the stamp or label was subsequently used by the league.

17 After the introduction of the union label by the cigarmakers, it became the common practice of cigar dealers to fill an empty cigar box bearing the label with Chinese-made cigars, thus defeating the object of the union. It was proposed by Frank Roney that the label be made in the form of a narrow band and placed around each cigar. This would have prevented effectually the deception which the use of the box label permitted; but the proposal was never adopted.

18 *Evening Bulletin*, March 11, 1878.

19 *Truth*, October 4, 1882, makes this statement, but I have been unable to find any trace of the measure in the records of the legislature of 1876. Attempts were frequently made to counterfeit the labels and also to use them on Chinese-made goods. When cases involving counterfeiting or the wrong use of the union labels were brought before the local courts, the decisions were uniformly in favor of the unions.—Cf. *Evening Bulletin*, August 22, 1878; *Morning Call*, June 14, July 8, 1882; *Truth*, July 12, 1882. *Burns et al. v. Matthias & Co.*, Case No. 39,578, Superior Court, City and County of San Francisco.

20 *Evening Bulletin*, February 19, 1878.

21 *Assembly Journal*, 22 Sess., p. 362.

22 *Ibid.*, 23 Sess., p. 78.

23 *Cal. Stats.*, 1887, pp. 17, 167–168. Many years later the first of these two measures was declared to be unconstitutional because of a defect in the enacting clause. With the necessary modification it was reënacted in 1905.—*Cal. Stats.*, 1905, p. 669.

24 *Morning Call*, December 28, 1878.

25 Spedden, *op. cit.*, p. 89, n. 1.

26 Delegates from associations in the following trades were present: bakers, barbers, blacksmiths, carpenters and joiners, cigarmakers, can-makers, expressmen, coopers, foundry laborers, grocers, ironmolders, jewelers, painters, patternmakers, pressmen, retail butchers, seamen, shipwrights, spring-makers, stationary engineers, tailors, printers, tool workers, varnishers, shoemakers, woodcarvers, and harness-, saddle-, and whip-makers, all of San Francisco; also from the Cherry Creek Miners' Union, Gold Hill Miners' Union, Moore's Flat Miners' Union, North Bloomfield Miners' Union, Ruby Hill Miners' Union, Virginia City Miners' Union, the Mechanics' Union of Storey, Nevada, the Tailors' Union of San Jose, and the Temescal Grange.

27 Cf. *Frank Roney, Autobiography,* pp. 359–380, for a detailed story of the League of Deliverance.

28 *Morning Call,* May 26, 1882.

29 *Cal. Stats.,* 1883, p. 6.

30 *Senate Journal,* 22 Sess., pp. 138, 285, 459, 521; *Assembly Journal,* 22 Sess., pp. 740–741.

31 In Sacramento the bricklayers organized in May, 1880, and the printers revived their union in June of that year.—*Third Biennial Report, California Bureau of Labor Statistics, 1887–1888,* pp. 128, 131.

32 *Cal. Stats.,* 1880, p. 80.

33 *Ex parte Westerfield,* 55 Cal. 550.

34 The five Oakland unions listed were those of the iron and steel workers, carpenters, bricklayers, plasterers, and the Laborers' Protective and Benevolent Association.

35 James K. Phillips was for many years the oldest member of the San Francisco Typographical Union. He was born in Augusta, Maine. In 1853 he came to San Francisco, and at once began his participation in the local labor movement. In 1854 he founded the *California Farmer and Journal of Useful Science,* but later disposed of his interest to his partner. With the exception of the period 1864–1866, during which he was prospecting in the Catalina Islands, he lived in San Francisco and was active in the interests of Labor. At one time or another he was an officer in every printers' organization; he belonged to various central labor bodies and was an officer in all of them. His participation in the San Francisco labor movement was terminated by his death in August, 1914.

NOTES FOR CHAPTER IX

[1] The following statement concerning the form of organization and the policies of the Knights of Labor is taken from a circular prepared and issued by the officers of San Francisco District Assembly, No. 53, in the days when the order was engaging the attention of the workers of California:

"Assemblies may be formed of any particular trade or calling, or they may be composed of all trades. The latter are termed 'mixed' assemblies.

"Assemblies can only be instituted by regularly commissioned organizers.

"The Order has a Mutual Benefit Insurance Association, on the co-operative plan, just going into operation, which, in the event of securing five thousand members, will give one thousand dollars upon the death of a member, on an assessment of only twenty-five cents upon each death.

"After a Local Assembly is formed, a candidate for membership must be proposed by a member of an Assembly in good standing, who has had acquaintance with the applicant.

"The Order of the Knights of Labor is not a mere Trades Union or benefit society; neither is it a political party. Some of the specific aims and objects of the Order are set forth in the preamble and declaration of principles, but any and every measure calculated to advance the interest of the wage-worker morally, socially, or financially, comes within the scope of the Order. To abolish as rapidly as possible the wage system, substituting co-operation therefor; the settlement of all difficulties between employer and employee by arbitration; to educate its members to an intelligent use of the ballot for their own benefit and protection, free from the restraint of party, or the undue influence of employers or monopolies; opposition to land, transportation, currency, and all other monopolies that affect the interests of the masses, and the protection of all its members in the exercise of all their rights as citizens, are some of the principal objects of the Order."

[2] In the newspapers of the period I have also found occasional reference to the following assemblies: No. 2405 (mixed), Los Angeles; No. 3167 (painters), Los Angeles; No. 3337 (mixed), Eureka; No. 3424 (mixed), Arcata; No. 3425 (mixed), Blue Lake; No. 3555 (lumbermen), Eureka; No. 4122 (mixed), Pomona; and No. 4350 (tailors), Los Angeles.

[3] Volney Hoffmeyer was a native of Denmark. An accomplished musician, he tired of teaching music to the sons and daughters of the "new rich" and became one of the prominent labor leaders of San Francisco in the eighties. He was a member of the Musicians' Mutual Protective Association of San Francisco, serving for a time as its president, and of the Knights of Labor. He was president of the San Francisco Federated Trades Council from August, 1888, to August, 1889.

NOTES FOR CHAPTER X

1 Morris Hillquit, *op. cit.*, p. 178, states that a German section of the International Workingmen's Association was organized in San Francisco in 1868.

2 Cf. Hillquit, *op. cit.*, pp. 156–188, for an excellent sketch of both International groups.

3 The land was filed on by Haskell and associates on October 5, 1885, but the colony did not get under way until somewhat later.

4 Sigmund Danielewicz.

5 From the *Minutes of the Central Committee of the International Workingmen's Association for the City and County of San Francisco,* February 24, 1885.

6 The *Morning Call* of March 13, 1885, said that at that date the Association had a total membership of sixty-three groups.

7 Pp. 230–232.

8 Cf. *Frank Roney, Autobiography,* pp. 471–474. T. V. Powderly, in *Thirty Years of Labor* (Columbus, Ohio, 1889), pp. 533–542, says that "during the telegraphers' strike in 1883, the leader of the International Workingmen's Association of the Pacific Coast submitted to the group of which he was a member a proposition to destroy the property of the Western Union Company."

NOTES FOR CHAPTER XI

¹ J. B. Johnson, a patternmaker, was born in Jefferson County, Kentucky, in 1822. He worked for a time as a carpenter in Louisville, and was driven out of his trade in 1842 because of activity in connection with a ten-hour day movement. He arrived in San Francisco in 1850, and took up patternmaking, becoming associated with the local labor movement in 1876. He was the first president of the San Francisco patternmakers' union, and for some years was active in the local labor movement.

² Joseph F. Valentine was born in Baltimore in 1857, and while yet a boy went to San Francisco with his parents. He joined the molders' union in 1880, and soon became its president, a position which he held until 1890 when he was elected first vice-president of the international organization. He became president of the latter in 1903, and so remained until 1924 when he resigned because of ill health. He served as vice-president of the American Federation of Labor for nineteen years and as first vice-president of the Metal Trades Department of that body for fourteen years. He died in San Francisco in February, 1930. He was a trade unionist of the old school, a conservative, capable leader of his fellow-craftsmen.

³ This association had been organized among the steamship cooks and waiters in 1884. Haskell had taken an important part in the proceedings of the meeting at which the union had been formed.

⁴ The proposal to publish a sailors' journal came from Alfred Fuhrman. The first editor of the *Coast Seamen's Journal* was Xavier Leder. He was succeeded by W. J. B. MacKay, who held the place until 1895. Walter Macarthur, the third editor, was for many years a prominent leader in the local labor movement. He was born at Glasgow, Scotland, March 9, 1862, and arrived at San Diego, California, in 1887, on a sailing vessel. He joined the Coast Seamen's Union in 1889, became manager of the *Journal* in 1891, and editor in 1895. In 1913 he was appointed United States Shipping Commissioner of the Port of San Francisco, and held the position until 1932. He was president of the San Francisco Federated Trades Council in 1892, secretary of the Pacific Coast Council of Trades and Labor Federations in 1893, and chairman of the committee which organized the State Federation of Labor in 1901. The present editor, Paul Scharrenberg, has been secretary-treasurer of the State Federation of Labor since 1909. For some years he was a member of the State Housing and Immigration Commission. The *Coast Seamen's Journal* became the *Seamen's Journal* in 1918. In 1922 it changed from a weekly to a monthly. It is the official organ of the International Seamen's Union of America as well as of the Sailors' Union of the Pacific.

⁵ It is not possible in this limited general survey to do justice to the history of the Sailors' Union of the Pacific, its leaders, and its accomplishments. The story is told, with ability and sympathy, in a small volume by Paul S. Taylor, entitled *The Sailors' Union of the Pacific* (New York, 1923). A detailed discussion of the three predecessors of the present organization will be found in an article by I. B. Cross, "First Coast Seamen's Unions," in the *Coast Seamen's Journal* of July 8, 1908.

⁶ Andrew Furuseth was born in Norway in 1854. After following the seas for some years, he arrived in San Francisco in 1880. Joining the Coast Seamen's Union shortly after it had been organized in 1885, he became its secretary in 1887, and has held the position almost continuously since then. He rose rapidly to prominence, not only in the local labor movement, but also in the national and international sailors' federations. He has fought steadfastly for the liberation of sea-faring men from their economic bondage, for the abolition of ancient abuses, both physical and legal, from which they suffered for

centuries, and for the establishment of sailors' rights and privileges on a basis of equality with the rights and privileges of other groups of workers. He has been especially interested and active in the campaign for the abolition of the injunction in labor disputes. No man in the California labor movement has been so constant in his loyalty to the ideals of the working class. His life is a distinguished example of one man's devotion to the cause of the workers without hope or expectation of reward other than that of the satisfaction to be derived from having assisted in improving the lot of his fellow-men.

7 *Evening Bulletin,* June 1, 1876.

8 About this time the cigarmakers of Los Angeles also affiliated with the International Cigar Makers' Union.—*Daily Report,* November 5, 1885. In 1886, branches of the latter organization were established in San Jose and Oakland.—*Ibid.,* February 27, 1886.

9 The *Daily Report* of August 21, 1885, said that about 10,000 men were unemployed in San Francisco at that time. On February 10, 1886, it declared: "Within the past few months, more men have committed suicide or attempted it in this city on account of inability to obtain work, than during any similar period in four years."

10 "There is hardly a considerable town or village in the State that has not taken action by the organization of anti-Chinese clubs."—*Morning Call,* February 14, 1886.

11 The petition sent to Congress by the Knights of Labor was 2,000 feet long, and contained 50,000 signatures.—*Daily Report,* May 11, 1886.

12 The *Daily Report,* March 17, 1885, said that 250 delegates, representing 49 labor unions, were present at the first meeting of the conference. The list given above, however, is taken from the report of the credentials committee of the conference, which I have in my possession. According to that committee's report only 135 delegates were in attendance.

13 At this time the National Brotherhood of Carpenters and Joiners had branches in Alameda, Benicia, Los Angeles, San Bernardino, San Rafael, Santa Rosa, and San Francisco. The plasterers of San Diego organized on December 13, 1885.

14 Unions were organized in various crafts in the six months from January to June, 1886, as follows: the horseshoers' on January 30, the brass workers' on February 4, the colored cooks' and waiters' on February 17, the furniture workers' on February 24, the Musicians' Reciprocal Protective Union (a rival of the Musicians' Mutual Protective Association) on February 26, the harness-, saddle-, and collar-makers' on March 19, the wool graders' and sorters' on April 12, the glove-makers' on April 15, the Officers and Stewards' Union, the steamship sailors', and the coopers' in the latter part of April and the early days of May, the Barbers' Progressive League on May 6, the water-front bootblacks' on May 21, the willow- and cane-makers' on May 22, the waitresses' on May 25, the galvanized cornice-makers' on May 27, the newsboys' on June 1, the cracker bakers' and the candy-makers' on June 5, the freight handlers' on June 14, the trunk-makers' on June 16, and the coremakers' about June 25.

The reason for the organization of a second musicians' union in San Francisco was the high initiation fee charged by the Musicians' Mutual Protective Association. After the Musicians' Reciprocal Protective Union was formed, its members agreed to dissolve their society and become affiliated with the older body, if the latter would reduce its fee. This it refused to do. The older union was not a member of the Federated Trades Council, but the Musicians' Reciprocal Protective Union joined the federation on April 2, 1886. Intense rivalry existed between the two musicians' unions for some time thereafter.

15 *Second Biennial Report, California Bureau of Labor Statistics, 1885–1886,* pp. 419–438.

16 *Ibid.,* pp. 438–442.

17 The boilermakers had received a charter as Local No. 32 of the national boilermakers' union.—*Morning Call*, September 7, 8, 1886.

18 The cooks' and waiters' union organized branches in Stockton, Sacramento, Los Angeles, and Oakland. In the latter part of 1886 it had a total membership in California of about 1,200.

19 At that time the following unions were in existence among the waterfront workers: Coast Seamen's Union, Steamshipmen's Protective Union, Steamship Sailors' Union, Marine Firemen's Union, Shipwrights' Union, Ship Joiners' and Carpenters' Union, Lumbermen's Protective Association, Stevedores' Protective Association, Steamship Stevedores' Union, Riggers' Association, and Wharf-builders' Union.

20 The Ship Owners' Protective Association had remained active for about two years.—*Fifth Biennial Report, California Bureau of Labor Statistics, 1891–1892*, p. 168.

21 In 1886 unions were also formed among the cigarmakers of Oakland in March, and of San Jose in July; among the carpenters of San Diego in June, of Pasadena in July, and of Santa Barbara in December; and among the printers of San Bernardino in September.—*Third Biennial Report, California Bureau of Labor Statistics, 1887–1888*, pp. 128, 129, 131.

22 *Assembly Journal*, 20 Sess., pp. 368, 523, 900, 1115–1117; *Senate Journal*, 20 Sess., p. 642.

23 The *Daily Report* of March 10, 1887, asserted that the two street-car strikes of 1886 had been engineered at the suggestion of and with the connivance of certain interests which wished to purchase the lines against which the strikes had been declared. The confidence of the stockholders being shaken by the strike, the "negotiations for the purchase of the roads went on simultaneously with the operations of the strikers." There have been other occasions in later years when the local unions of the street-car employees have been used by outsiders for ulterior purposes, political and otherwise.

24 *The Political Code of the State of California*, Sec. 3246.

25 *Cal. Stats.*, 1887, p. 17.

NOTES FOR CHAPTER XII

[1] A change of city officials forced Roney out of his position at the City Hall; the foundries of San Francisco were closed to him because of his activities on behalf of Labor; and he found employment for a while with the United States Immigration Service and at odd jobs in San Francisco, finally getting steady work in the foundry at the Mare Island Navy Yard at Vallejo in 1898, where he remained until 1909. He assisted in the organization of the Trades and Labor Council in Vallejo in 1899, and served a term as its president. In 1909 he moved to the southern part of the State, but took no active interest in its labor movement until 1915–1916, when he became secretary-treasurer of the Iron Trades Council of Los Angeles. He died at Long Beach on January 24, 1925, at the age of 84 years.

[2] W. A. Bushnell was born in Ohio in 1851, and was brought to California by his parents in 1855. He served an apprenticeship as a printer, and in 1877 established the Rio Vista *Enterprise*. In 1879 he obtained employment in San Francisco, and became a member of the local typographical union, subsequently serving as its financial and corresponding secretary. He was three times elected president of the Federated Trades Council. In July, 1890, in association with E. W. Thurman, he began the publication of the *Pacific Coast Trades and Labor Journal,* which did not long survive. He died in San Francisco on January 20, 1930.

The subsequent presidents of the Federated Trades Council were E. W. Thurman, Volney Hoffmeyer, Charles Grambarth, Alfred Fuhrman, W. J. B. MacKay, and Walter Macarthur.

[3] Alfred Fuhrman was born in Solingen, Germany, on October 12, 1863. His parents were well-to-do. As a boy of fifteen years he went to sea, and first arrived in San Francisco in 1880. He returned to Germany and entered the University of Bonn, but did not receive a degree. The call of the West and of San Francisco induced him again to make his way to the Pacific Coast as a sailor. He became a member of the Coast Seamen's Union shortly after its organization in March, 1885, and from that time until 1893, when he entered the practice of law, he was one of the most prominent leaders of Organized Labor on the Pacific Coast. He was serving as a delegate in the Federated Trades Council from the sailors' union when the representatives from the brewery workers asked for assistance. He gladly undertook the task, and succeeded not only in establishing a union in the brewery trades, but also in winning the first struggle against the brewery employers. He once more left San Francisco for the sea, and on his return some months later found only six members of the union still loyal to its cause. He reorganized the craft, and was secretary of the union until 1893. He became a prominent figure in the national brewery workers' union, as well as in the organized labor movement on the Pacific Coast. He was president of the Federated Trades Council in 1890–1891, and president of the Pacific Coast Council of Trades and Labor Federations, which he founded, from 1891 to 1893. In 1893 he was admitted to the bar, and severed all connections with the labor movement.

[4] *Fifth Biennial Report, California Bureau of Labor Statistics, 1891–1892,* p. 135.

[5] *Seventh Biennial Report, California Bureau of Labor Statistics, 1895–1896,* p. 132.

[6] In 1887 the San Francisco union also established branches in Los Angeles, San Diego, San Jose, Sacramento, and Portland.

[7] *Third Biennial Report, California Bureau of Labor Statistics, 1887–1888,* p. 154. The cooks' and waiters' union began the publication of a labor journal, *Our Union,* in the fall of 1887, but it survived for only a few issues.

[8] *Third Biennial Report, California Bureau of Labor Statistics, 1887–1888*, p. 157.

[9] *Ibid.*, pp. 160–166.

[10] *Ibid.*, pp. 128–131.

[11] The first national association among the brewers had been formed sometime in the decade 1860–1870. The Brewers' Protective Association of San Francisco had been organized in 1874. In 1880 it had a membership of 37 breweries.

[12] *Fifth Biennial Report, California Bureau of Labor Statistics, 1891–1892*, p. 136.

[13] Herman Schlüter, *The Brewery Industry and the Brewery Workers' Movement in America* (Cincinnati, 1910), p. 174.

[14] Cf. *Fifth Biennial Report, California Bureau of Labor Statistics, 1891–1892*, pp. 101–166, for the report of the investigation made by the State Labor Commissioner of the labor controversies in the brewery trades of San Francisco in the years 1887–1892.

[15] It had been chartered by the American Federation of Labor in 1888.

[16] Schlüter, *op. cit.*, pp. 174–177.

[17] E. W. Thurman, a member of the Typographical Union, was for many years active as a local labor leader. Thurman was born at Pleasant Hill, Illinois, February 21, 1849, and was brought overland by his parents, who arrived in Portland, Oregon, September 13, 1850. He came to San Francisco on March 17, 1875. In the eighties he allied himself with Haskell and the radical group, and served as a delegate to the Trades Assembly and the Federated Trades Council from the typographical unions. He was elected president of the latter organization in 1888. At present (1933) he lives in San Francisco.

[18] In January, 1888, the members of the printers' union employed by the San Bernardino *Times* struck against the employment of non-union printers. In March, 1888, the San Francisco typographical union levied a boycott against the non-union shop of Bacon & Company, and this was continued for several years. In November, 1888, the book and job office proprietors of San Francisco signed a closed-shop agreement with that union. The ironmolders of Sacramento organized on April 10, 1888. The shoemakers employed by Porter, Slessinger & Company of San Francisco struck successfully against a reduction in wages in July, 1888. The harness-makers' union of that city also struck against a reduction in wages in September.

[19] *Third Biennial Report, California Bureau of Labor Statistics, 1887–1888*, p. 115. The total number of unions here given should be reduced to 76, because the list in the Labor Commissioner's report includes the San Francisco Building Trades Council, as well as the branches of the Coast Seamen's Union in Eureka, Port Townsend, San Pedro, and San Diego, all the members of the latter being affiliated with San Francisco unions. The total membership of the unions should be reduced by approximately 1,000, because at that time the White Cooks' and Waiters' Union had a membership of only about 200, instead of 1,260 as listed by the State Labor Commissioner.

[20] The typographical union of San Diego struck against and boycotted the San Diego *Sun* in the summer of 1889. In May, 1889, the tailors' union of San Francisco struck successfully against the employment of non-union men by Cavanaugh Brothers.

[21] Eaves, *op. cit.*, p. 52.

[22] *Coast Seamen's Journal*, May 2, 1894.

[23] On February 15, 1890, the California branches of the United Brewery Workmen's Union of the Pacific Coast met and demanded a nine-hour day and an increase in wages on and after May 1. Their demands were granted.

24 *Fifth Biennial Report, California Bureau of Labor Statistics, 1891–1892*, p. 40. California was the twenty-first state in the Union to enact an Australian ballot law.

25 *Fifth Biennial Report, California Bureau of Labor Statistics, 1891–1892*, pp. 92–93.

26 *Ibid.*, p. 51.

27 *Ibid.*, pp. 124–125, 143–144.

28 *Ibid.*, p. 144.

29 The local beer bottlers organized as a separate branch of the United Brewery Workmen's Union in April, 1899 (reorganized in March, 1902) ; the beer wagon drivers did likewise in December, 1900.

30 For data relative to the struggle of the sailors' union against the Ship Owners' Association in the nineties, see especially P. S. Taylor, *op. cit.*, pp. 64–74; Eaves, *op. cit.*, pp. 54–57.

31 The coal miners of Alexander Dunsmuir & Company, of British Columbia, went on strike for shorter hours and improved working conditions. As an appreciable amount of the coal which they mined was marketed in San Francisco, in the spring of 1890 they appealed to the Federated Trades Council for aid. The boycott against the Wellington coal was prosecuted vigorously, and although the strike was declared off in January, 1892, the council continued its boycott with effective results.

32 *Fifth Biennial Report, California Bureau of Labor Statistics, 1891–1892*, pp. 52–53.

33 In March, 1892, fourteen unions were affiliated with the Building Trades Council of San Francisco.

34 Fuhrman severed his connection with the Federated Trades Council, and in January, 1893, also resigned as secretary of the brewery workers' union. He studied law, was admitted to the bar, and is still (1934) a successful practicing attorney in San Francisco.

NOTES FOR CHAPTER XIII

[1] The number of unions affiliated with the San Francisco Labor Council in the month of July from 1896 to 1901, respectively, was as follows: 1896, 16; 1897, 15; 1898, 18; 1899, 21; 1900, 34; 1901, 90. Cf. Eaves, *op. cit.*, pp. 59–60.

[2] 1893. In March the shoe turners of Jones & Glanville, of San Francisco, struck against the introduction of machinery. The strikes of the sailors and the brewery workers have been mentioned. In May, the bakers' union of San Francisco struck for a reduction of hours.

1894. The Marine Cooks' and Stewards' Union of the Pacific was organized in October.

1895. The actors of San Francisco organized a union in January. In January fifty employees of Cowell's lime kiln at Santa Cruz struck against a reduction in wages. The street-car employees of San Francisco and the electrical workers organized in January. In May the bricklayers and stone masons at Folsom struck against the employment of non-unionists. In July the grain handlers on the San Francisco docks struck for a reduction in pay. The waiters of San Francisco organized as "The White Waiters' Protective Association" in October. On September 13, the pressmen of the Schmidt Label and Lithograph Company of San Francisco struck for higher wages, and on October 2 the women press-feeders of that firm struck for the same purpose. In the spring of 1895 the brewery workers' union again struck for the recognition of the union and the closed shop.

[3] T. R. Bacon, "The Railroad Strike in California," *Yale Review*, III:238.

[4] *Seventh Biennial Report, California Bureau of Labor Statistics, 1895–1896*, p. 149.

[5] *Ibid.*, pp. 149–152.

[6] *Cal. Stats.*, 1895, p. 246.

[7] *Ex parte Jentzsch*, 112 Cal. 468.

[8] M. McGlynn was born in Litchfield, Illinois, August 18, 1864. He became a member of the St. Louis Typographical Union in 1881, was active in the labor movement of Chicago and of Colorado, and arrived in San Francisco in August, 1887. He was a capable, farsighted, and conservative labor leader, who sacrificed his health to the cause of the workers. In 1890 he was sent to Los Angeles by the International Typographical Union to direct a boycott against the Los Angeles *Times*. In 1894 he was a candidate for Secretary of State of California on the Populist Party ticket. He died shortly thereafter.

[9] On July 30, 1896, one Collins was elected president of the newly organized council. He was followed by H. C. Hinchen, of the paperhangers' union, who served for the greater part of 1897–1898. F. Cranford, of Carpenters' Union No. 22, succeeded Hinchen. P. H. McCarthy was chosen for the office in July, 1898, and served continuously until January 12, 1922. No one man exerted greater influence over the policies and destinies of the San Francisco Building Trades Council and its affiliated unions than P. H. McCarthy. Born in Ireland, March 17, 1863, he learned the carpenter's trade, and came to the United States in 1880. He assisted in organizing the National Brotherhood of Carpenters and Joiners, and in 1886 arrived in San Francisco. He joined Carpenters' Union No. 22, and later was elected its president, and president of the local District Council of Carpenters. He was active in the formation of the State Building Trades Council in 1901 and was its president until 1922. He served as a member of the Board of Freeholders of San Francisco in 1900 in drafting a new city charter, and was appointed a member of the City Civil Service Commission. A Democrat by political faith, he opposed the formation of the Union Labor Party in San Francisco, but in 1905 he joined forces with it and supported its mayoralty candidate. In 1909 he was elected mayor of

San Francisco as the Union Labor Party's candidate, but was defeated in 1911 and 1915. After his retirement as a labor leader in 1922, he became a building contractor in the San Francisco Bay region. He died in 1933. McCarthy was a capable organizer, domineering, and able to build up in the ranks of the building trades unions a powerful machine through which he retained his power over the local and state movements in that field for twenty-four years, albeit he was continually clashing with the other branches of Organized Labor.

10 *Organized Labor*, January 28, 1905.

11 *Morning Call*, March 11, June 7, 1896.

12 1896. In San Francisco, in January, the coopers employed by the Pacific Woodenware and Cooperage Company struck successfully against a reduction in wages; in March the hodcarriers and bricklayers of San Jose notified their employers that on May 1 they would demand a wage increase of 50 cents per day; in San Francisco the hack drivers of the Pacific Carriage Company were partly successful in June in opposing a reduction in wages; in December the employees of the Pacific Rolling Mills struck against a 15–20 per cent reduction in wages, but were compelled to accept a 10 per cent reduction.

1897. In January the riveters employed on the Claus Spreckels building in San Francisco struck successfully for an increased wage; in February the pressmen employed in the State Printing Office at Sacramento struck for higher wages; in October the upholsterers, and in November the mattress-makers, of San Francisco, obtained higher wages through strikes.

1898. The plasterers of San Francisco struck in October for increased wages, and these were granted after the men had been out for ten days.

13 In January, 1896, the barbers of San Francisco revived their union and later obtained a charter from the International Barbers' Union. The tailors of that city met on January 28, 1896, to form a union, and later received a charter from the United Garment Workers of America. Some dissatisfaction was expressed over the fact that small employers were included in the tailors' union, and in January, 1898, another organization was formed, composed of journeymen tailors only. In March, 1896, the cooks and waiters of San Francisco revived their organization. The press-feeders and helpers of San Francisco were reorganized in October, 1896, the painters and decorators in the latter part of 1897, and the Alameda County musicians in October, 1898.

14 *Barto v. Supervisors of the City and County of San Francisco*, 135 Cal. 494; *Stanley-Taylor Company v. Supervisors of the City and County of San Francisco*, 135 Cal. 488; *French (Typographical Union) v. Citizens' Alliance*, Case No. 90,847, Superior Court, City and County of San Francisco.

15 *Twelfth Biennial Report, California Bureau of Labor Statistics, 1905–1906*, pp. 88–160.

16 The central labor federations were the following: the Allied Printing Trades Council of San Francisco; the Bay District Council of Carpenters and Joiners, with headquarters in San Francisco, organized in 1894, and having six unions affiliated with it; the San Francisco Building Trades Council, organized in 1896, with 26 affiliated unions; the San Francisco Labor Council, organized in 1892, with 35 members; the San Diego Federated Trades Council, organized in 1891, with 5 members; the Trades and Labor Council of Vallejo, organized in 1899, with 8 members; the Los Angeles County Council of Labor, organized in 1896, with 17 component organizations; the Alameda County Federated Trades Council of Oakland, organized in 1900, and having 6 members, and the Federated Trades Council of Sacramento.—*Ninth Biennial Report, California Bureau of Labor Statistics, 1899–1900*, pp. 92, 96, 108.

17 The total number of union members in 1902 was given as 67,500. Of these, 45,000 were in San Francisco.

18 *Tenth Biennial Report, California Bureau of Labor Statistics, 1901–1902*, pp. 76–78.

19 The Hackmen's Union of San Francisco was formed in the latter part of 1900. In order to obtain complete control over persons so employed, the union members refused to drive in funeral processions unless all drivers of cabs and hearses were union men. In a two weeks' period, twenty-two funerals were delayed and one funeral was held up for more than an hour while the union was attempting to compel the hackmen to join the organization. At times one part of a funeral procession, manned by union members, would go one way and the other part, manned by non-union men, would go another, meeting finally at the cemetery, where there was always the possibility of a clash occurring between the two groups. The union openly declared that "a non-union corpse is practically as bad as a living scab."—*Organized Labor*, January 19, 1901.

20 The cement workers of San Francisco were organized in June, 1899. Within three months the union had more than 200 members and had succeeded in increasing wages from $2.50 to $4 per day, and in reducing hours from ten and twelve to eight per day. It was subsequently active in bringing about the organization of a Bay District Council of Cement Workers and in forming, in 1913, a State Council of Cement Workers.

21 May 2, 1901.

22 *Organized Labor*, June 22, 1901.

23 In July, 1900, the San Francisco laundry workers began a campaign for shorter hours. In September, 1900, they induced the Board of Supervisors to pass an ordinance fixing 6 A.M.–7 P.M. as the hours of laundry work, but about a month later the ordinance was held unconstitutional by a local court.

24 All the planing mills in Stockton and San Rafael and several in Oakland granted the eight-hour day in September, 1900.

25 Art. II, Sec. 3, of the *Constitution and By-Laws of the Building Trades Council of San Francisco* provided: "No union which holds membership in any central body or Council foreign to the building industry shall be eligible to membership in the Council; and any union which holds membership in the Building Trades Council and which affiliates with any central body or Council not an integral part of the Building Trades Council shall by such affiliation or action forfeit its membership in this Council, and shall stand suspended without further trial."

26 Olaf A. Tveitmoe was born in Norway and received a good education. He emigrated to the United States as a young man, taught school in Minnesota, and went to San Francisco in 1897, where he became a cement worker's helper. He served as secretary and then as president of the cement workers' union, and attracted the attention of P. H. McCarthy. At McCarthy's suggestion he was elected recording and corresponding secretary of the San Francisco Building Trades Council in July, 1900, and general secretary of the State Building Trades Council in 1901. In 1911 he was national vice-president of the Cement Workers' Union, and third vice-president of the Building Trades Department of the American Federation of Labor. He was active in the anti-Japanese movement in the early years of the twentieth century, and served for several years as president of the Asiatic Exclusion League. In 1906 Mayor E. E. Schmitz appointed him to the Board of Supervisors of San Francisco. After indictment and conviction (the conviction later being reversed and the indictment *nolle prossed*) because of implication in the dynamiting of the Los Angeles *Times* (the McNamara episode, 1910), Tveitmoe lost much of his influence among the working class. Nevertheless he remained editor of *Organized Labor* until 1920. In 1922, because of ill health, he severed all connection with the building trades movement. He died on March 19, 1923.

27 J. J. O'Neill was born in Benicia, California, March 19, 1865, and died in San Francisco, June 3, 1908. In 1907 he was appointed one of the supervisors of San Francisco, and held the position until January, 1908.

Will J. French was born in Auckland, New Zealand, August 13, 1871, and went to San Francisco in 1892. Since that time he has been an active participant in all movements concerned with the welfare of the workers of California. He held at one time or another the various offices in the local typographical union, was editor of the *Pacific Union Printer* from August, 1898, to December, 1899, served as president of the San Francisco Labor Council and of the Allied Printing Trades Council, and in 1911 was appointed a member of the State Industrial Accident Board. In 1913 he was placed on the State Industrial Accident Commission, with which he has since been associated, the period 1924–1928 excepted. In 1925 he was called to Australia, where he assisted in drafting a new workmen's compensation act for New South Wales. From 1928 to 1933 he was also Director of the State Department of Industrial Relations. From 1927 to 1932 he was a lecturer in economics in the University of California. From 1931 to 1933 he was a member of the State Unemployment Commission, in addition to his other duties as a state officer. He has given freely of his time to civic duties, and is well known as a speaker and writer on a wide range of subjects.

James W. Mullen was born in Iowa in 1875, and arrived in San Francisco in 1902. He was active in the local typographical union before becoming editor of the *Labor Clarion* in 1911. He served in the latter capacity until his death on July 25, 1931. At one time he was a member of the San Francisco Board of Health. In January, 1931, he was appointed State Labor Commissioner. The fourth and present editor of the *Labor Clarion* is Charles A. Derry.

28 In July the journeymen bakers started a coöperative bakery, hoping by that means to supply union products to the restaurants that were cut off from supplies by the Employers' Association.

29 During the later nineties the iron trades unions of San Francisco were in a demoralized condition. In order to put them in better shape for the impending struggle, the national machinists' union sent one of its most successful organizers, Russel I. Wisler, into the San Francisco Bay district. For a number of years thereafter he played an extremely important rôle, not only in the iron trades, but also in the general labor movement of the community.

30 T. W. Page, *Political Science Quarterly*, XVII:675.

31 *Organized Labor*, July 27, 1901.

32 The Draymen's Association had been organized in 1899. The teamsters' union had been organized on August 5, 1900, with thirty-five charter members. Teamsters had worked from twelve to eighteen hours a day, seven days a week, and for an average wage of $14. The union struck in September, 1900, for increased wages and shorter hours, which the Draymen's Association granted. In February, 1901, they were again successful in striking for a shortening of the workday and for the abolition of the requirement that teamsters must board at the employer's boarding house.

33 The members of the City Front Federation were the unions of the sailors, marine firemen, ship and steamboat joiners, packers and warehousemen, porters, ship clerks, pile drivers and bridge builders, hoisting engineers, steam and hot water fitters, and coal teamsters, the Brotherhood of Teamsters, and the three longshoremen's unions.

34 *Coast Seamen's Journal*, July 31, 1901.

35 *Ibid.*, August 4, 1901.

36 Franklin Hichborn, *The System, as Uncovered by the San Francisco Graft Prosecution* (San Francisco, 1915), pp. 12–13.

37 The Citizens' Alliance of San Francisco was formally organized in 1904 with Herbert George, of Denver, Colorado, as president. The organization, it is said, was able to enlist several thousand members in the Bay region. By 1908 it had disappeared from the field, but in 1910 it was revived and was

active for a few years in a local open-shop campaign, ineffective in San Francisco, but fairly successful in Oakland, especially in the building trades.

³⁸ The City Front Federation lay dormant until 1916, when it was revived as the Waterfront Federation.

³⁹ In this contest more than 1,000 men were thrown out of work. The strike, which had been declared for the eight-hour day and an increased wage, lasted for six months (May 5 to September 5, 1907) and was lost by the union. Thirty-nine persons were killed, 701 strike breakers were so badly injured as to require hospital treatment, and scores of others suffered wounds less serious.

⁴⁰ Cf. *infra.*, p. 278, for the story of the Merchants' and Manufacturers' Association of Los Angeles.

⁴¹ The Manufacturers' and Employers' Association of Stockton waged a bitter fight against the unions of that city in 1914–1915.

⁴² This paragraph is based on statements made in an unpublished manuscript, "Industrial Relations in the Building Trades of San Francisco," by Dr. F. L. Ryan, and in communications received from the secretary of the Industrial Association.

⁴³ Many excellent discussions of the Japanese problem in the United States are available. Some of the more important contributions are: Yamato Ichihashi, *The Japanese Question* (Stanford University, 1932) ; K. K. Kawakami, *The Real Japanese Question* (New York, 1921) ; Kiichi Kanzaki, *California and the Japanese* (San Francisco, 1921) ; E. G. Mears, *Resident Orientals on the American Pacific Coast* (Chicago, 1928) ; H. A. Millis, *The Japanese Problem in the United States* (New York, 1915) ; T. Iyenaga and K. Sato, *Japan and the California Problem* (New York, 1921) ; James A. B. Scherer, *The Japanese Crisis* (New York, 1916) ; *Reports of the United States Immigration Commission* (Washington, D. C.), vols. 24–26.

⁴⁴ *Seventh Biennial Report, California Bureau of Labor Statistics, 1895–1896*, pp. 101–126.

⁴⁵ *U. S. Stats. at Large*, 1907, p. 898.

⁴⁶ *U. S. Stats. at Large*, 1924, p. 153.

⁴⁷ *Cal. Stats.*, 1913, p. 206.

⁴⁸ *Cal. Stats.*, 1921, p. lxxxiii.

⁴⁹ *Cal. Stats.*, 1923, p. 1020.

NOTES FOR CHAPTER XIV

[1] For much interesting data on the open shop fight in Los Angeles, see the *Reports of the United States Industrial Relations Commission*, VI:5,485–5,999.

[2] H. K. Norton, *The Story of California* (Chicago, 1913), p. 294.

[3] *Third Biennial Report, California Bureau of Labor Statistics, 1887–1888*, p. 131.

[4] In October, 1884, a labor convention was held to nominate candidates for local offices. It was reported that delegates were present from the painters', carpenters', plasterers', tailors', bricklayers', and printers' unions.

[5] *Third Biennial Report, California Bureau of Labor Statistics, 1887–1888*, p. 128.

[6] P. 113.

[7] Arthur Vinette was born in Montreal, of French Canadian parentage. He learned his trade in Troy, New York, mined in Colorado, and arrived in Los Angeles in 1883. He was active in the formation of the local carpenters' union and of the Trades Council, participated in the Nationalist (Henry George) movement, joined Coxey's Army, and took a prominent part in all matters affecting Labor's interest in Los Angeles, until, in 1905, ill health forced his retirement. He died in July, 1906. He was one of many who sacrificed self and family for the cause of the workers of southern California.

[8] Lemuel D. Biddle was born in Philadelphia, Pennsylvania, April 27, 1846. He first learned the machinist's trade and then the shoemaking trade. He became a member of the Knights of St. Crispin in 1868, of the Sovereigns of Industry in 1872, and of the Knights of Labor in 1877. In 1879 he was nominated for the governorship by the Socialist Labor Party of Ohio. He arrived in Los Angeles in 1888. In 1890 he organized Machinists' Union No. 311; in 1894 he was blacklisted for participating in the Pullman strike; and in 1901 he was appointed district organizer for the American Federation of Labor, a position which he held for seven years.

[9] There is an abundance of data on this epochal struggle. The union's argument has been briefly summarized in a pamphlet issued by it in 1915 entitled *Mr. Otis and the Los Angeles "Times."* The best statement by the *Times* is embodied in a series of daily articles which it published, beginning on October 1, 1929, under the general heading, "The Forty-Year War for a Free City: A History of the Open Shop in Los Angeles." This statement was later issued in pamphlet form.

[10] It was reorganized in 1909 under a charter from the State Building Trades Council as the Los Angeles County Building Trades Council.

[11] The charter members of the Allied Printing Trades Council were the printers, pressmen, bookbinders, and press-feeders.

[12] *Ninth Biennial Report, California Bureau of Labor Statistics, 1899–1900*, pp. 92, 97.

[13] *Tenth Biennial Report, California Bureau of Labor Statistics, 1901–1902*, p. 78.

[14] The Los Angeles County Metal Trades Council was organized in June, 1908. In June, 1910, at the time it presented the demands here mentioned, it was composed of the following crafts: machinists, molders, patternmakers, blacksmiths, boilermakers, brass workers, and sheet metal workers.—*Reports of the United States Industrial Relations Commission*, VI:5,551.

[15] *Reports of the United States Industrial Relations Commission*, VI:5,797–5,800.

[16] The *Industrial Age* began publication on April 2, 1892. Its editors were Joseph Phillis, for many years a prominent leader in the Los Angeles labor movement, and S. A. Collins. It was discontinued after a few months.

[17] F. B. Colver was born at Hudson, New York, in October, 1833. He learned the printer's trade in Cleveland, Ohio, and joined the local typographical union. After serving as a lieutenant of volunteers in the Civil War, he published a newspaper at Sandusky, Ohio, and worked as a printer in Kansas City, Missouri. He arrived in Los Angeles in 1883, but did not affiliate with the local labor movement until 1885, when he joined the typographical union. From that time until 1898 he was active in the ranks of Organized Labor, serving as a delegate to the various central bodies with which his union was affiliated, and as the treasurer and president of the union. In 1898 he was appointed Inspector of the Port of San Francisco.

[18] The unions of Los Angeles are housed in their own seven-story reënforced concrete Labor Temple, the construction of which was begun on Labor Day, 1906, and completed on February 22, 1910.

INDEX

INDEX